In Search of the Warrior Spirit

Also by Richard Strozzi-Heckler

*The Anatomy of Change: A Way to Move
   Through Life's Transitions*

Holding the Center: Sanctuary in a Time of Confusion

*The Leadership Dojo: Build Your Foundation
   as an Exemplary Leader*

Anthologies edited by Richard Strozzi-Heckler

Aikido and the New Warrior

*Being Human at Work: Bringing Somatic Intelligence
   into Your Professional Life*

In Search of the Warrior Spirit

Teaching Awareness Disciplines to the Military

4th Edition

Richard Strozzi-Heckler

BLUE SNAKE BOOKS
Berkeley, California

Published by Blue Snake Books

Blue Snake Books
are distributed by
North Atlantic Books   Cover photo © istockphoto.com/photog Clay Cartwright
P.O. Box 12327   Cover design by Brad Greene
Berkeley, California 94712   Printed in the United States of America

In Search of the Warrior Spirit is sponsored by the Society for the Study of Native Arts and Sciences, a nonprofit educational corporation whose goals are to develop an educational and crosscultural perspective linking various scientific, social, and artistic fields; to nurture a holistic view of arts, sciences, humanities, and healing; and to publish and distribute literature on the relationship of mind, body, and nature.

Author's Note: The names of the soldiers, the team designation, as well as the Army Post have been changed.

Blue Snake Books' publications are available through most bookstores. For further information, call 800-337-2665 or visit our websites at www.northatlanticbooks.com or www.bluesnakebooks.com.

Substantial discounts on bulk quantities are available to corporations, professional associations, and other organizations. For details and discount information, contact our special sales department.

Library of Congress Cataloging-in-Publication Data

Strozzi-Heckler, Richard.
  In search of the warrior spirit / by Richard Strozzi-Heckler. — 4th ed.
    p. cm.
  Includes bibliographical references and index.
  ISBN 978-1-58394-202-4 (alk. paper)
  1. War—Psychological aspects. 2. War—Moral and ethical aspects. 3. Soldiers—Psychology. 4. Soldiers—United States—Psychology. 5. Military education—United States—History—20th century. 6. United States. Army. Special Forces—History. 7. Aikido. 8. Strozzi-Heckler, Richard. I. Title.
  U22.3.S77 2007
  355.001'9—dc22
                                                          2007035525
                                                          CIP

4 5 6 7 8 9 UNITED 12 11 10 09 08 07

To D.J. and Tiphani
and the new generation of warriors

ACKNOWLEDGMENTS

I would particularly like to acknowledge Richard Grossinger, who made a major contribution to the anthropological text, and whose support, encouragement, and vast editorial skills helped make this book what it is. Many thanks also go to Lindy Hough for her editing skills; George and Annie Leonard for fresh eyes and fine tuning; Robert Hall for his encouragement; General Jim Jones for his vision, courage, and support in MCMAP and the Afghan project; Sergeant Royce Coffee for his friend-ship, wisdom, and humor; Lieutenant Colonel Fred Krawchuk for his visionary thinking and support around counterinsurgency work; and Al Santoli for his big-hearted effort in establishing an alternative to armed conflict in the Philippines.

CONTENTS

Preface to the New Edition   ix

Introduction by George Leonard   xi

The Invitation   1

Preparations   9

In the Belly   43

War   73

The Encampment   85

The Original Warrior   119

Bodymind   143

Camaraderie   171

The Western   187

Maritime Operations   213

Integrity   235

In Search of the Warrior Spirit   257

Shadow and Light   295

Epilogue   307

Five Years Later   315

Fifteen Years Later   343

Twenty Years Later   373

About the Author   423

PREFACE TO THE NEW EDITION

I could never have imagined twenty-two years ago that the Trojan Warrior Project and its influences would reverberate within the ranks of the Marines and the Army and, in turn, inspire countless projects throughout the military, as well as in government and business. An innovative, classified experiment funded by the Army to improve the physical, mental, and team capabilities of its elite Special Forces, the Trojan Warrior Project today has exceeded my most ambitious expectations for it—that traditional warrior disciplines would someday be widely integrated into the training of America's military.

The Marine Martial Arts Program now begins for Marines as they enter Recruit Training or Officer Candidate School and continues throughout their career—whether it's four years or thirty. This concept was discussed many times in the offices of the Commandant of the Marine Corps, the Secretary of Defense, and the Secretary of the Navy. Other branches of the military, and local and federal law enforcement agencies, have since become interested as well. I believe that the values and skills of the traditional warrior are especially relevant in today's "war against terror" and Operations Other Than War.

As we enter into a new era of warfare, it is clear that the lessons learned from the Trojan Warrior Project, and the two decades of work spent developing and supporting its applications in the field, deeply inform and influence our current concerns of counterinsurgency and antiterrorism—now more than ever.

George Leonard's original introduction to *In Search of the Warrior Spirit* remains a firm foundation to introduce the ways in which awareness disciplines can positively influence the modern U.S. military. In addition, my work researching a combatives/leadership program for the Afghanistan National Army, through NATO, shows that reinventing the concept of the warrior in the twenty-first century is a viable alternative to cold-war strategies and thinking. The reader will find that the work with Israelis and Palestinians in Cyprus demonstrates that aikido and somatics can make a significant impact in helping diverse people in centuries-old conflict find a meaningful common ground.

It remains my conclusion that the ancient warrior archetype—one who embodies compassion and wisdom, as well as the ability to take effective action when necessary—is the model to bring sustainable peace and balance to humans and an endangered planet. I believe it is possible to train these strengths in our military and citizens. Embodying this sensibility and implementing this training both continue to be my mission. I invite the reader to share in the mission with me in this new edition.

—Richard Strozzi-Heckler, Ph.D.
Strozzi Institute
Petaluma, California
October 2007

INTRODUCTION by George Leonard

In the spring of 1972, a new student appeared at the aikido school where I was training. He was in his late twenties. He moved with unusual grace. He was distressingly good-looking. Who is this guy, I thought?

Aikido is probably the most difficult of the martial arts to learn. The very idea on which it's based—the release of power through harmonizing with, perhaps even loving the attacker—isn't easy to understand. Then there are the intricate moves and the strenuous, scary rolls and falls that are a central part of the training. It's no wonder that relatively few people come to this art, and that most of those who do come drop out during the first month or two. Thus, the arrival of a newcomer who shows promise of persevering is a significant event.

I had been practicing aikido for a year and a half and wore a blue belt, only a step up from the fresh, innocent white of the beginner. But ours was a very new school and I was the senior student. So I watched the newcomer with the proprietary interest of an older boy sizing up the new boy on the block. He wore a white belt, but it was obvious he had practiced aikido before coming to our school—probably some other martial art as well, from the way he moved. He kept himself mainly on the far edge of the mat and watched our teacher gravely during the demonstrations. He practiced the assigned technique with a focused, contained intensity, a *presence* that set him apart from all the other students.

On the second day after his arrival, I made it a point to sit next to the newcomer while the teacher was demonstrating, then bow to him as an invitation to train with me. We stood, I extended my right arm, he took my wrist with his right hand, and I performed a technique known as *ikkyo,* which, through torque on his arm and shoulder, caused him to bend over. We took turns practicing *ikkyo* for perhaps ten minutes. We never spoke because there was no need to. It was through the eloquent language of bodies joined in movement—impossible to describe in words not because it's less precise but because it's more precise than words— that I met Richard Strozzi-Heckler. We didn't know it then, but there were already threads that connected our lives. Now there are so many that no one could count them. It was one of those threads that in 1985 was to lead Richard Strozzi-Heckler to play a key role in what must be classed as one of the boldest and most imaginative experiments ever attempted in the training of the military forces. Back in 1972 that experiment, the subject of this extraordinary book, was still far in the future and, to say the least, entirely unforeseeable. Richard and I continued training together on the aikido mat and gradually came to know each other off the mat. I discovered that he was working on a doctorate in psychology and that he had studied aikido for six months on the island of Kauai, where he had co-founded a school of mind-body psychology with a medical doctor who some time earlier had given me ten sessions of a deep massage known as rolfing.

The years passed. Other students came and went and faded from memory, and we kept on training, experiencing the quiet, enduring joys of a strong, beautiful discipline and suffering the inevitable bumps and bruises that accompanied those joys. Sometimes, the injuries were more serious. At brown-belt level, Richard had his arm broken in two places during a particularly powerful throw by our teacher; everyone there heard the bone snapping. A couple of weeks later, he was back on the mat wearing a cast up to his elbow, still training. Nothing special.

Our teacher made Richard and me and a gifted student named Wendy Palmer assistant teachers even before we became black belts. It was our job to run a special class for beginners. In February of 1976, at age fifty-two, I passed my black belt exam. Wendy and Richard went up three months later. I served as Wendy's designated attacker during her exam, and sat at the edge of the mat while Richard was being tested. That test still shines in my memory as the most dramatic moment of all my nineteen years in aikido.

The circumstances were harrowing. During the three months' period of intensified training that led up to the exam, our teacher had subjected Richard to the kind of reduction of ego that you normally read about only in the legends of Eastern masters. For the final three weeks, he had never looked Richard in the eyes and had referred to him only as "what's-his-name." Up to a few moments before the test, in fact, he had not even let him know for sure that he would be tested. Only when Richard saw his name on the schedule did he assume his test was on. Our teacher, in his curious wisdom, still wouldn't speak to him.

The test began and, as I was to write in *The Silent Pulse*, "it was apparent that something extraordinary was occurring. It was like one of those sporting events that are later memorialized, perhaps a World Series game or a bullfight, during which every last spectator realizes at some level that what is happening out on the field is more than a game, but rather something achingly beautiful and inevitable, an enactment in space and time of how the universe works, how things are." Richard's exam was so beautiful that there seemed to be—I hesitate to bring up such matters—distinct changes in the illumination of the room, noticed not only by me but by many other aikidoists and spectators as well. The event reached its climax in the final *randori*, a simultaneous, all-out attack by three black belt aikidoists.

To a first-time spectator, the rushing, swirling, tumbling, crashing motion of *randori* is simply overwhelming; the senses can't handle it. An expert aikidoist observes techniques and moves, watches for breaks in the energy field that subsume both defender and attackers. But on this day spectators and experts alike saw

Richard's *randori* as harmony, the promise of reconciliation. No matter how hard or swift the blow, he was not there to receive it, but always at the moving center that holds all opposites in perfect tension. As for Richard, he experienced no effort or strain whatever; only a voice in his head, repeating, *"This isn't Richard."* There, in the eye of the storm, stripped of the certainty he had always deemed necessary for survival, denied the support of his teacher, divested even of his name, Richard found the deliverance he had not known he was searching for. He had no question that he would be hit or trapped. If need be, he could go on forever, realizing all the while that "he" was not doing it. The voice in his head was clear: *"This isn't Richard. This isn't Richard."*

Four months after Richard's test, in October of 1976, the three of us opened our own aikido school in Mill Valley, California, a move that caused more than a few raised eyebrows in the aikido community; first-degree black belts don't usually start their own schools. But Aikido of Tamalpais was successful from the beginning. The three of us have continued training and developing our skills, and our school is now a respected and a happy one, a constant and unqualified joy in our lives.

The phone call that was to take Richard away from us for six months came in the spring of 1985. Chris Majer was the president of a Seattle firm called SportsMind which, among other things, had conducted a successful conditioning program for Army basic trainees. Now, Majer told me, SportsMind had the opportunity to train a group of twenty-five Special Forces troops—Green Berets—in the new human technologies. That meant meditation, biofeedback, aikido, and mind-body psychology—not quite so far-out as it might sound, since the soldiers' mission could involve remaining still for long periods and being acutely aware of their surroundings. Did I have any ideas, Majer asked, as to who might run the project?

I hesitated for maybe a half-second before answering. Jack Cirie was unquestionably the man for the job. A year earlier he had completed a rigorous two-month training program in a discipline I had developed by blending aikido with Western psychology. He had come to the program directly upon retiring as a lieutenant colonel from the Marines, with two combat tours in Vietnam and a chest full of medals. Those military credentials alone would command the respect of the Special Forces troops. But Cirie wasn't just a war hero. His proven leadership ability was tempered by playfulness and poetry and a large measure of *soul,* which I defined for Majer as being the faculty of having ready access to deep and authentic feelings.

A man named Joel Levy was already aboard as a teacher of biofeedback and meditation. When the subject later arose of who might join the team of Cirie and Levy as an aikido teacher, I immediately recommended Richard Strozzi-Heckler, hesitant to do so only because I knew we would miss him at the aikido school. Thus were drawn together the three leaders of an experiment the likes of which had never been seen or even imagined in the military.

The program got underway at the beginning of August 1985. In mid-October I flew in for a three-day stint as one of eleven guest teachers who participated in what was listed under the Army code name, The Trojan Warrior Project. I stayed in a spare room of the big old house the leaders had rented off-base for their quarters, and it was easy to see that all three of them were already pressed to their limit. The days were long, the training rigorous, and sleep was in short supply. Still, I noticed that even at the end of a 16-hour day, Richard would take the time to make entries in his journal. How did he plan to use the journal? He really didn't know; the project was classified at that time. He was just doing it because he felt it should be done.

We are fortunate that he felt that way, for Richard Strozzi-Heckler has expanded those journal entries into a book that is as original, unexpected, and startling as was the program itself. *In Search of the Warrior Spirit* serves first of all—though this is by no means its only or even its most important function—as a white paper on the subject of the military in today's world. I can't imagine anyone from here on out writing a book about the warrior in a technological age, in a nuclear age, in a terrorist age, without referring to Strozzi-Heckler on the subject.

This book deals with some very tough questions indeed. Even before the program got started, Richard was excoriated by people he respected for even considering teaching aikido and other awareness disciplines to Green Berets, to "trained killers." Does this imply that those of us who love peace would have no soldiers at all? And if we do have soldiers, do we really want them to be deprived of the best possible training? Do we want low-grade soldiers with no awareness or empathy? And if we do teach awareness and empathy to our soldiers, will they be able to perform the brutal tasks sometimes assigned them? Surely we don't want a horde of Rambos loosed upon the world. But if not Rambo, then who?

There are no simple answers. Once, during a meditation retreat, Richard opened his eyes and noticed that the man next to him seemed to be in a deep meditative state. He was sitting very straight. His breath was moving rhythmically from the very center of his belly. "My eye is caught," Richard writes, "by something on the black T-shirt that hugs his huge biceps and barrel chest. Printed in bone white on the front is a large skull and crossbones. The words over the skull read '82nd AIRBORNE DIVI-SION:' and the broad letters below the skull scream, '**DEATH FROM ABOVE.**'" Richard was momentarily disoriented. People don't wear T-shirts like that at meditation retreats, yet the person inside the T-shirt looked exactly like someone at a meditation retreat. "I have absolutely no mental file for what I see," Richard writes. "Killing and meditation simply do not go together."

It is precisely through the acknowledgement of such seeming con-tradictions that this book proceeds, arriving at unexpected truths through the illumination of paradoxes. We ultimately learn that the young men who wear Green Berets are nothing at all like Rambo, but rather like the rest of us: idealistic and cynical, thoughtful and thoughtless, brave and fearful, vulnerable and touching in their strategies for concealing their vulnerability.

More than anything else, *In Search of the Warrior Spirit* is an adventure story, a personal odyssey of one man's search for his own manhood, for a way to get it right in an age that offers few absolutes. And what an adventure it is! From the first chapter to the last, Richard is under attack—from civilian friends, who insist on seeing the military from an "us vs. them" perspective; from the Green Berets themselves, who are equipped with sensitive shit detectors and let nothing in this strange new program pass unchallenged; from his own internal doubts and fears, and from the anger and competitiveness that sometimes break loose despite years of aikido training. I am reminded here of *randori,* the sort of rushing, swirling, crashing multiple attack that Richard faced during his black belt exam—except that this *randori* is multilevel and never-ending. And when Richard finally accepts one of the soldiers' numerous challenges "to see if this stuff really works," there's yet another question, another level to explore: Will he be able to handle a physical confrontation in the loving spirit of aikido?

It would be unfair to tell more, only that you should be prepared for a marvelous story that will take you down through level after level of insight and understanding and vivid writing. On the very deepest level, you might discover that "us vs. them" really doesn't exist, that peoples and nations, civilians and military, Green Berets and their trainers, and even you and I all share a common humanity. As the founder of aikido, Morihei Ueshiba, said many years ago, the only opponent is within.

—George Leonard

When the samurai Kikushi put down his sword and was initiated into Zen, his master said to him, "You must concentrate and consecrate yourself wholly to each day, as though a fire were raging in your hair."

The Invitation

On a hot day in early June of 1985 I was interrupted at my desk by a phone call. I was completing the final draft of a book on aikido, so I welcomed a relief from the tedium of editing.

"Hello, Richard; this is Jack Cirie. How would you like to teach aikido to the Green Berets?"

Bewildered by what I suspected was a not-so-funny joke I made a stab at a comeback.

"Yeah, sure. And how would you like to teach bowling to the Hell's Angels?"

Jack laughed: "I'm serious. We start in six weeks. Twenty-five Green Berets. You'll train them every day for six months." I was stunned. This was a challenge I had both longed for and feared. He continued: "We'll also do all of their activities with them—running, hiking, swimming, meditating, even some of their military exercises."

I suddenly felt like I was being served up a meal I had ordered a long time ago. But first some background:

In the early 1980s, SportsMind, a Seattle-based organization with a successful track record among business executives, as well as with athletes (Olympic, college, and professional), was approached by the Army's Special Operations division to design an experimental program for Green Beret A-Teams. As unlikely as it seems, the Army pictured a holistic approach for enhancing the skills of individual soldiers. After three years of developing such a radical concept, designing a six-month plan of instruction, and then guiding it through the fabled bureaucratic maze,

SportsMind had its brainstorm approved and funded by the Department of Defense. A senior officer who had supported the venture baptized it with the code name *The Trojan Warrior Project.* He was onto something—that soldiers initiated this way, perhaps like the Greek warriors hidden in the belly of a wooden horse, would be an elite cadre converted to the leading edge of inner technologies, in the belly of the U.S. Army. They took the logo of a flying horse above two crossed light sabers; underneath was the inscription, *Vi Cit Tecum,* Latin for "May The Force Be With You."

Based on my experience as an aikidoist and psychologist, I was being asked to become part of the three-man core team within this program. I would also be partly responsible for organizing a one-month meditation retreat and a section called "psychological values." My two colleagues would be entrusted with a variety of tasks, including the administration of the program, biofeedback, and mental training, physical fitness, diet, and also some of the so-called psychological values.

The offer was basic and unambiguous because the required involvement would be nothing less than total. Our life would become the life of the Special Forces soldiers, attending every activity, including their military exercises, with sixteen-hour days the rule.

When Jack gave me the chance to become part of this project, I immediately felt a resounding "Yes!" emerge from the core of my belly. There was no way I could turn down such an invitation. My life would be interrupted and I would have to rearrange the next eight months with my children and former wife (as well as explain to clients why I would be gone, choose teachers to take my aikido classes, and find someone to live in my house and take care of my animals); yet I felt grateful for the opportunity. This would be the first school in the Army with a curriculum based on the holistic model—optimal performance of all human aspects: mind, body, and spirit. I would be able to teach an advanced martial art to a group of highly trained soldiers, thus get to study firsthand a subject that had fascinated me as long as I could remember: warriorhood and the modern warrior. It *was* the meal that I had ordered. After I accepted, I was overwhelmed by what I had to do to get ready, though sustained initially by a mild state of euphoria. It took only a day for me to be jolted into the other reality.

"How do you feel about teaching meditation to trained killers?" Andrea's pale blue eyes were filled with contempt and accusation. Her tone read like a plague warning: 'This man is ill for what he's about to do.'

"Wait a minute," I responded, "this is an opportunity and challenge to teach the aikido version of warriorship to the military."

"It's a male ego trip," she snapped back. "What are you trying to prove to yourself anyway? To think that you would even *consider* teaching aikido to the military shocks me."

I was taken aback, but it was a paradox I would eventually have to confront, both in myself and from others. Andrea is an old and dear friend who is a Berlin psychotherapist. She accused me of being immoral for taking part in this training, and after an evening of heated discussion I found myself countering that she was one of the most hostile people that I knew, hiding behind a passive/aggressive facade of spirituality.

Staying up most of that night we launched a dialogue that continued for me with friends and colleagues over weeks. Their images of what I was doing emerged like *National Enquirer* headlines: "Rambo Learns Mind Control!" "I Meditated With 25 Green Berets and Lived To Tell About It!" "Special Forces Killers Trained In Human Potential Techniques!" Those that were most openly critical assumed that it would be a disaster to transmit awareness techniques to the Army. They argued that the military would use them for destruction, that I would merely refine their methods of aggression and make them more sinister. They reminded me that my students, after all, would be the Army's elite, "Be All That You Can Be" to the tenth power, already trained to be the instrument of force for our political process. In the eyes of some of my friends I had become a demon of their most horrible nightmare, Public Enemy Number One: "How could you pass these sacred teachings to *Them*?"

Us and Them. Here was a caste system of which I hadn't been consciously aware. In my mind the soldiers were not *them*. Teaching the disciplines that have most positively affected me, to a population that seemed most obviously in need of them, was an obvious outgrowth of my work. Obvious to me if not to others. Although I knew I would get a reaction from being part of this project, I thought it would be entirely different from the Us/Them scenario.

The issue I first struggled with revolved around the interventionist policies of our government and its hostile use of the military in places I thought it shouldn't be. Coming of age during the Vietnam War, I felt forever cautioned against our country's intrusion in foreign wars. By teaching the Special Forces would I be in effect supporting an imperialistic policy that we are now extending to Central America? Would I simply be a piece of fuel on the fires of our nation's aggressive and paranoid posturing? Would involving myself in this program make me a representative of the part of our government that I most oppose? Or would I be able to express my ideals of warriorship within the military context? Could the principles of aikido add a needed dimension to our limited concept of national defense?

Almost everyone who was opposed to my teaching in this program voiced very different considerations from my own. It wasn't our foreign policy; it was Us and Them. They are bad people. If We associate with Them, We'll be tainted. We're better human beings than Them. We're different from Them, therefore They cannot be trusted. I could see that in some way my friends felt hurt or betrayed by my choice. Meditation and therapy had taught us the timeless message that compassion is right and harming others is wrong; aikido, as opposed to the martial arts that stress competition and fighting, emphasizes the loving protection of life. How, asked my friends, could I teach this power form to Them, men who might use it for harmful means?

I was shocked. What did they mean *Them?* Are these men different in kind from myself? Won't they be the same men that I played basketball with, marched with in the Marines, knew in martial arts dojos, double-dated with? Was it only because I was raised in a military family and wore the uniform myself that I think this? Was it because I have known many men in many different situations, some good, some bad, some I liked, some I would never want to see again, that I understood that these men would be different in degree, but never in kind?

Wasn't it important that these men—*especially these men*—be exposed to the contemplative and martial arts that teach the power of harmony and wakefulness? They were the buddies, the guys I had known from childhood growing up in San Diego. I wanted to encounter them again and bring them what I had learned. I even wanted to find out why they were in the Special Forces and what they thought about warriorship.

I wasn't afraid of them. I was more afraid of those who continue to make the same terrible choices in our foreign and military policy. The men in the military, after all, are the chess pieces who carry out policy. They aren't subhuman, or even different from me. I had long wanted to begin a discussion of these issues with them. This was my opportunity.

For instance, if I were asked to teach aikido to those in the White House I would do it without question. Likewise, if I were asked to teach aikido to the Soviet Politburo . . . I would teach it to senior citizens. I would—and have—taught it to urban gangs, chronic juvenile offenders, police officers, corporate executives, and emotionally disturbed children. Did that make me an "aikido mercenary"? Was I hero or fool?

Both sides of this issue were certainly real, and even as I tried to bolster my position by arguing that Master Morihei Ueshiba, the founder of aikido, taught the Japanese military and police, I felt a residual hollowness in my argument. More and more I began to see that I had fewer answers and more questions. I only knew that I had been given a choice to act.

When I would voice these hopes and aspirations I would often be met by either outright opposition and slander, or a stony silence. I was told I was too idealistic, naive, or downright traitorous. I was accused of crossing over a line many of my friends felt I shouldn't have even been close to. On the eve of my departure the students at my aikido school honored me with a farewell party and presented me with a traveling bag as a gift. George Leonard, my longtime colleague and friend, gave a speech declaring that I "was taking the work from the Tamalpais Aikido dojo into the dragon's mouth." He voiced his clear support for introducing the values of aikido into the code of warriors known as the Green Berets.

Then the people I was closest to, those who had shared my highest and most difficult moments in aikido and life, shook my hand, slapped me on the back, and wished me well. It was a warm and supportive occasion, but inside I felt empty and alone. I thought of Joseph Conrad's hero in the *Heart of Darkness* who was inexorably drawn "to face the abomination."

There is certainly a legacy that distinguishes the warrior from war. The sacred path of the warrior is part of an ancient moral tradition. It includes the Indian warriors Krishna and Arjuna in the *Bhagavad-Gita;* Homer's hero Odysseus who outwitted his opponents rather than slaying them; the post-sixteenth-century Japanese Samurai who, in his finest hour, administered a peaceful government while still maintaining a personal discipline and integrity through not only the martial arts but the fine arts of calligraphy, flower arranging, and poetry. It includes the American Indians who lived in harmony with the land and whose ritual wars were exercises in bravery rather than slaughter; the Shambhala Warrior of ancient Tibet who applied power virtues to spiritual development; and Carlos Castaneda's celebrated warrior shaman, Don Juan Matus. These historical and mythical warriors found their strength and integrity by defeating their own inner demons, living in harmony with nature, and serving their fellow man. I believed—and still believe—that if we embody the virtues of these archetypal warriors we are acting in support of the whole planet instead of constantly fighting external enemies for petty ends.

The tasks of packing, renting my house, completing my current work with clients from my psychotherapy practice, and finishing my aikido book were all relatively easy compared to saying good-bye to my children. I explained to Django, who now calls himself D.J., and Tiphani what I was going to do and I invited them to come with me. At fourteen Tiphani didn't want to leave her friends, and D.J., age six, preferred to stay with his sister and mother. I felt remorseful about leaving them and imagined myself walking in my own father's footsteps. It was a tearful farewell, and with a lump in my throat I promised to write and call. Looking out of the airplane window at the parched brown hills of the San Francisco Bay Area, I wondered who I would be when I returned.

Preparations

August 4

Spent the weekend moving into the rambling two-story, four-bedroom Victorian that will be home for the next six months. We're a few blocks off the main street of a small, tidy, western Massachusetts town that's about twenty minutes from Thoreau's Walden Pond. I'm in the upstairs middle bedroom between Jack and his wife Anne Bartley, and Joel and Michelle Levey. Joel and Jack have worked together the past six months in Seattle. In one sense I'm the odd one out, since I'm the only single person, but above and beyond that we're an instant family. Jack is a former Lieutenant Colonel in the Marine Corps. After logging twenty years and two tours in Vietnam with the Marines, he decided to retire upon completing a two-month training in energy awareness with George Leonard. A Yale graduate, Jack was captain of both the football and boxing teams. He also has a Master's degree from Wharton in Business Management. A hard charger and natural leader, he was last stationed at the Pentagon itself. The word is that he would have eventually landed in the Marine Corps Commandant's chair if he had reenlisted. I like Jack immediately. He's a serious man who has done well to combine keen intellect with physical prowess. The perfect liaison between our team and the military. I instinctively trust him. My main consideration is that, after working for myself for so long, will I be able to follow orders?

Joel is about ten years younger than Jack and myself and heads the meditation and biofeedback section. He is tall, thin, and bearded, with shining eyes. We call him The Wiz, Mr. Science of the New Age. His primary interests are meditation and altered states of consciousness. He's studied with Kalu Rinpoche and Zong Rinpoche, two highly respected Tibetan meditation masters, and is completing a Ph.D. in transpersonal studies. He'll coordinate the complex and highly sophisticated Brain Wave Training and will be responsible for the meditation retreat. At this point, it's difficult to imagine him with hardcore military types. He's too off the ground and intellectual.

Along with Jack, Joel, and myself, Michelle Levey is the only woman who participated in the design and will be in some of the teaching elements. Michelle has been involved with the project since the beginning, primarily in the development of the "biocybernautic training." This includes the biofeedback and neurofeedback training and the complementary arsenal of inner-technologies that complement the highly technical biofeedback section. Along with Joel she also plays a key role in the overall research, design, and development of the month-long meditation encampment. Joel and Michelle carry with them the insights from nearly four years of preparation, research, and interviews with many neuroscientists, peak-performance experts, and inner-science masters as they helped shape the original proposal for the program.

August 5

Today we're at the Post to conduct preliminary interviews with the men. Moving through the guard station I'm immediately struck by how familiar it all seems. My father was a career Naval officer and I spent many years living on bases. The sight of the uniformed men walking among the well-ordered grounds and numbered buildings puts me in a strange nostalgia, a mixture of familiarity and suffocation. The last time I was on a military base was in the mid-sixties as a twenty-year-old Marine. It's almost as if time is standing still. I remember being in uniform myself, but I also remember a ten-year-old boy walking proudly next to his father the times he would take me to his base. He and I have been stubbornly isolated from each other for over twenty years and I wonder if this work will be a healing or simply an opening of old wounds?

Joel and I head for the Special Forces buildings to interview our team. A friendly top sergeant with a southern drawl let us into a small room and says he will "send up one of the men so y'all can get started." The first man comes in wearing cut-off jeans, a sweat-stained T-shirt, rubber sandals, and carries a Coca Cola can. I'm a bit surprised. Did I expect Rambo? John Wayne? He introduces himself last name first, rank and serial number, shakes our hands, and sits looking at us with an expressionless gaze. He isn't sullen, but he's not friendly either. His thin, sticklike legs seem barely able to support his well-developed arms and massive chest. The classic American male body. Big on top, not much on the bottom. Chest out belly in. From the wad of chewing tobacco under his lip he spits a thick brown liquid into the Coke can. He looks so young; twenty-two it turns out, one of the youngest in the group. We start with basic questions about military specialty, marital status, health, time in the service, career goals, etc., and then more specific questions about the program.

"What do you expect to get from the program?"

"I don't know." Long silence.

"What are you looking for personally?"

"I heard we might get stronger and have more endurance. I'd like that." Long silence.

"Why did you sign up for the program?"

"Well, most of my team thought it was a good idea and I want us to stay together." Long silence.

"Do you have any considerations about the program?"

"I'm not sure what it's about, but I guess I'll find out."

"Do you have any questions you want to ask us?"

"No." Spit in the can.

When he leaves Joel and I look at each other and shrug. But then most of the interviews go like this. Some are more animated, some less. Some want to know if their families will be included (They would), others want to know if they will get extrasensory powers (If you apply yourself to the program all your capabilities will increase). Will there be a lot of time spent in the field? (Yes, a number of exercises will take us away from garrison for as much as a month at a time). Will I have to quit smoking? (We're encouraging everyone to give up smoking and chewing tobacco). What is aikido? (A Japanese martial art that emphasizes centering and blending). Will I have more control? (You'll learn that control follows awareness). Some men answer solely with "yes, sir" or "no, sir." Only two say they have been waiting for an opportunity like this for a long time. Others merely comment that they have been to many Army schools and they will judge this one when the six months are over.

Some ask if there will be other teachers. We tell them we have invited fourteen experts to present their diverse disciplines. They will stay anywhere from a morning to ten days and their ranks include a Tibetan monk; a Master of Capoeira (a Brazilian martial art); a bodyworker who will give every soldier a complete session; a medical psychologist whose expertise is Brain Wave Training; a well-known philosopher, author, and aikidoist who is in his sixties; the Stanford karate coach; a Benedictine monk; and a world-class triathlete.

They are guarded and probing—psychic radar. I feel them take in every detail. They're sharp and accustomed to camouflaging themselves. Jack and Chris feel the same way about the other team.

First impressions: We have our work cut out for us. Nothing will be swallowed at face value. These are practical men and everything we put before them will have to be backed by our own personal experience and relevance to their job. They're interested in results, not theory.

My original suspicion is also true. I know these guys. They're the college athletes I played sports with, the philosophy students with whom I discussed literature and politics. Some remind me of men I knew in the Marine Corps and the martial arts world, others I know because of the way they speak of the joys and struggles of fatherhood. Some are courteous and friendly, others are reserved and suspicious. No one looks like Sylvester Stallone or Sergeant Bilko.

At the same time there's a distance. The Us and Them thing again, now I'm the outsider looking in, wanting credibility. Will they let me enter into their world? How do I develop trust without being seduced by their mentality of eliteness: "We're special because we wear the Green Beret." Is this also a consideration of *theirs?* Them not wanting to be too easily seduced by my world of the new inner technologies? Am I looking into a mirror?

August 6

When we leave for the Post at six A.M. it's already hot and muggy. An hour later sweat darkens our T-shirts. By the time we finish our morning run I feel I have no water left in my system. Jack, Chris, and I run together while Joel rides his bike because of a knee injury. Besides conditioning ourselves we use the time to talk about the soldiers, the program, ourselves. I went to college on a track scholarship and it feels familiar to be running; I welcome the opportunity to get in good physical condition. I'm usually sore the next day, but I expect this and actually enjoy the feeling of working myself in new ways.

Today's interviews have a slightly different tone. The way they anticipate the questions and make comments about the program tells me word's traveled; they've been briefed by those we saw yesterday. I make a mental note that they stay in good communication with one another, at least on this level, and that they are probably putting us in somewhat of an adversarial position. Us and Them from the other side too. Today we see the older, higher-ranked men: they are more present and willing to engage. They have things better thought-out, a stronger sense of what they want and don't want. They're not just on board for the ride. These men have clearly chosen to take part in this program. They reflect that if there's something here that will be helpful for them they want it; if not, can it. These guys are also somewhat familiar with ideas of awareness and energy training. Not so much from specific practices but from reading and discussion with others.

When I ask him how he would define a warrior, Top Sergeant Mattelli's New York street fighter face softens into Florentine dignity. "A warrior," he says confidently, "is someone who is always striving for self-mastery, to improve himself and to better serve his goals."

The twenty-five soldiers in this project are white, middle-class men who come mostly from the South and Midwest, though this is not true for all Special Forces A-Teams. Over half are family men. They range in age from twenty-two to forty-one and come in all shapes, sizes, and weights. Their average time in the Army is ten years; the longest is twenty-two years and the shortest five. Only four of them are college graduates (two from West Point), but they all have passed tests that place them at college level.

We're astonished to find out how little they have been briefed about the project. Most of them have just a vague notion about what will be taught and what will be expected of them. While most of them have a general sense that they will improve themselves physically and mentally, a few of them have an inflated view of graduating six months later with superhuman powers. SportsMind had made it clear that all the participants should know exactly what the program consisted of and then be able to choose freely whether to join. As it turns out only half of them are true volunteers. The other half are "military volunteers"; that is, if you don't sign up you can look forward to a desk job for the next year.

There are four Special Forces Groups billeted in the U.S., Latin America, and Europe. Each group has basically three battalions, with approximately three companies in a battalion. There may be anywhere from four to six twelve-man teams in a company. We have two A-Teams of twelve men each. Team 560 is an established team that is highly regarded within this Special Forces Group. They're older, more experienced, SCUBA-trained, and tightly knit. Team 260 is newly formed, with an inexperienced Team Leader and very little group cohesion; some of the men have been on the team for only a month. Captain Thorne, their company commander and West Point graduate, will also be part of the project.

Jack, Joel, and I are getting to know one another through getting to know the soldiers. We agree that unity and clarity among ourselves is vital to the success of the program. I make a personal commitment to frankness and openness in communicating with them. If we're not allies for each other it's going to be a long, cold season.

After lunch we visit our classrooms and dojo. An old movie theatre is being turned into the aikido dojo, with one end being closed off for the classroom. An entirely separate building will serve as offices, library, and biofeedback center. Today the buildings are alive with activity; old walls being torn down, new ones being framed and wired, floors swept and mopped. There are a number of recognizable faces from my interviews but also new faces from the other team. A few nod in my direction, but most act as if we're not there.

One barrel-chested soldier with the rank of Warrant Officer swaggers up next to me, sets himself in a wide stance, crosses his arms over his chest, and gazes out over the activity. After a bit he says to the space in front of him, "So you're the martial arts sensei?" I look at him; his jaw muscle ripples rhythmically, he continues to look straight ahead. He has a Teflon face; nothing would stick to it.

"I'm the aikido teacher," I reply. He turns slowly and looks at me, sizing me up. His eyes are gray green and hard.

"Are we going to be training every day?"

I extend my hand and tell him my name. He has a firm grip and the stern line of his mouth breaks into a wide grin. Suddenly he's warm and animated. He's a fourth dan in a Korean form of karate and ranked in a few other arts, he's heard of aikido and he looks forward to the opportunity to learn it. He's also a sensei and has taught his form of karate to some of the men on his team as well as his children, which I gather are many and of whom he's quite proud. Soon we're swapping martial arts stories and talking philosophy.

He's the Warrant Officer on Team 260. Been in the military for almost eighteen years. His first six in the Marine Corps included a tour in Vietnam. After getting out he found he was restless and unhappy, until one day "my mother said, 'I know what's wrong with you. You're a soldier and you miss being in the military.' So I joined the Army this time and got in the Special Forces pretty quickly. You can be an individual here. I don't like having to spend a lot of time on the spit and shine of a line unit. That's crap. I guess I'm a warrior at heart. Now I have just a few years to go and when I get out I want to open my own dojo." When I'm leaving he gets my attention again: "Call me chief; that's what everybody else does." Then he folds his arms across his chest, takes a wide stance, and resumes a hard-guy position.

August 7

On the way to the Post this morning Jack and I resume our recurrent discussion about the warrior. We both agree that the Army's goals for this project do not necessarily have to depart from ours. The question is, can we deliver both? I do know that a primary motivation for my being here is to see if the warrior—or what I envision as the warrior—has a place in today's Army.

The sentry at the gate today is a woman. First, the obvious question, "Does 'warrior' include both men and women?" Jack and I both agree yes. For the warrior power arises from a source that does not rely on a sexual hierarchy or, for that matter, any hierarchy. It's a power of self-knowing, self-educating, and self-accepting free from trends or tyrannies, including gender. The warrior is connected with him- or herself. And only from that connection does he or she connect to others and the environment.

Just inside the gate, a "Be All That You Can Be" billboard shouts encouragement as we pass in front of a World War II tank. There is a very comfortable, safe, country-club feeling in the air; well-kept grounds, golf course, tree-lined streets, an orderly attitude prevailing. Safe harbor. "Be All That You Can Be." That certainly fits the modern concept of the warrior. A brilliant marketing ploy, or a genuine need from the military unconscious?

And the question remains: What does the Army really want from this? The official contract mandates a program to make "full use of Emergent Human Technologies to enhance physiological and psychological awareness and control in Special Forces Detachment members." But what does this *really* mean? Of course they must have concrete objective goals, but what about the deeper psychological motivations? What is the military's present paradigm for the warrior? What are his or her values? In other words what do meditation, or a Japanese martial art, or visualizations, or brain synchrony training have to do with the men of the Army's Special Forces? (Rambo didn't take on any of that; he also didn't, as these soldiers mockingly testify, carry a ninety-pound pack.)

If our military is to survive and grow stronger I believe that the warrior ideal has to be brought into the bigger discussion. More than that I have the audacity to believe that the military can still be a formative ground for the training of the modern warrior. The military man I'm imagining would also be trained in the discipline of harmony.

So the answer to the question of why the military is open to a program such as this may be twofold. First, a growing number of middle-level officers—Captains, Majors, and Colonels—recognize that the bloated defense budget is not making a stronger military. For instance, as Amitai Etzioni argues on the op-ed page of the April 6th, 1984, issue of *The New York Times,* the decline of combat readiness in the years 1981–1984 coincides with the most costly peacetime build-up in America's history. Military planners themselves are recognizing that a tremendous expansion in arms and technology does not necessarily make a military more prepared for its job. It appears, in fact, as if it's doing the exact opposite. Since 1980 we have spent more than one trillion dollars on defense. This is an average of $9,440 per second during the Reagan administration. In the past six years the defense budget has increased by thirty-three percent, with inflation discounted, without our military being anything like a third stronger. Not a single unfavorable element of the U.S.-Soviet military balance has been reversed by all this spending. NATO ground forces are still inferior in Europe. We're similarly at a disadvantage in Korea; in Southwest Asia we are underequipped with respect to submarines and fighter aircraft. Spending one trillion dollars on technology has not magically transformed our inferiority to superiority.

The second point is that our military record over the past thirty-five years has been anything but successful. Our bitter stalemate in Korea was followed by an even more painful failure in Vietnam. In taking the *Mayaguez* from Cambodian hijackers, forty-one Marines were killed rescuing forty seamen. The irony is that they were killed as the crew and ship were being released from their captors. The raid to liberate the American prisoners in Teheran was botched and eight servicemen were killed when their operation was aborted at the Desert 1 site. In 1983, 241 Marines were killed when a single terrorist drove a truck bomb past guards with unloaded weapons and inadequate barriers into the Marines billet. Even our commuter war with Grenada, which we "won," is not a model for inspiration. The discipline in a number of the Eighty-Second Airborne units broke down, and a combat-experienced officer who monitored the Division's communications said that it sounded as if the whole division was on the verge of panic. In three days it advanced approximately five kilometers. At the end of the campaign the Army awarded 9,800 medals when there were only about 7,000 soldiers on the island. We're spending more money on technology and winning less.

Many of the officers who recognize the need for a reformed military are Vietnam veterans who saw our complex technology and weaponry beaten by an enemy who relied on small-unit tactics, simplicity, and heart. These career officers are committed to improving the individual skills and capabilities of our soldiers, while focusing on maneuver instead of attrition warfare; they see through the fallacy of high technology and complexity. During conversations with both active duty and retired career officers, I often hear their concern about the loss of warrior virtues in an increasingly technology-oriented military. While millions of dollars are spent developing robots to fight wars, the role of the soldier is quickly being reduced to that of technocrat and computer operator. It gradually became clear that the officers and men who supported our program with the Special Forces were the ones hoping to reconnect the military with the traditional warrior virtues of service, courage, selflessness, loyalty, and commitment.

By reinstating the dignity of the warrior spirit in our Armed Forces I believe it would be possible for us to develop a military that would make America secure without making other countries insecure. Audacious? Yes. But we have to begin someplace.

August 8

A General is coming to town and that means an inspection; pressure on everyone. It also means that work on the offices and dojo are behind schedule; we may not be able to start on time. Spent part of the morning in Battalion headquarters taking care of administrative details. It's the first day of the inspection and everyone is looking smart in their full-dress uniforms complete with campaign ribbons and green berets rakishly pulled to the side. I'm warned that the Battalion Sergeant-Major as well as a few of the other senior NCOs are skeptical about the program ("a bunch of mumbo jumbo as far as I'm concerned") and I expect to field some flak while I'm there. No such thing happened; the worst is some hard glances and cold shoulders. I'm introduced to Major Wilson, a beaming-faced giant who is a cross between Jon Voight and Conan the Barbarian. He nearly pulverizes my hand, and without a trace of irony he says he hopes to get over and take some of my aikido classes. I make a note to get a jump on him next time we shake. At one point he tells a story to a group of officers that goes something like, "After we G-2'ed the op we packed M16s, 104s, 98s, humped our rucks with 031 and 027, passed the grunts in the APCs like it was PT, stopped for some MREs, 86ed hill 19 . . ." The string of acronyms continues for about five minutes and ends with him letting out an ear-splitting war whoop and everyone, except me, laughing their heads off. I feel like the new kid on the block who is turning out to be a nerd.

Major Wilson has just been selected to try out for Delta Force, the elite anti-terrorist cadre, and it's in question whether he will be at Battalion during the length of our stay. As it turns out, he was accepted and after the first six weeks I never saw him again.

The SportsMind team has its own "uniform" of khaki pants, rose purple shirt and sweater, and purple belt with brass buckle. In addition we have a workout uniform of black shorts with a gray T-shirt with the Trojan Warrior logo printed on the left breast: two crossed light sabers over a Trojan horse. Underneath is written the Green Beret motto, "*De Oppresso Liber*" and beneath that the project motto, "*Vi Cit Tecum.*" The Green Beret motto means "Free the Oppressed." We thought ours would be a great secret from the soldiers, but the first day we wore the shirts Sergeant Martin immediately commented, "That's cute, 'May The Force Be With You.'" He is fluent in a number of languages and Latin, it seems, is one of them.

I don't like the idea of having our own uniforms. My idea of warrior-ship is individuality, not homogeneity. I'm concerned that we will be pulled into the military game and thus lose our perspective and effectiveness.

"It defines us as a team and it makes us easier for the soldiers to relate to," Jack argues.

Joel radiates his beaming smile, "I don't really mind," he says evenly. "I understand the need for us to be presented this way for the soldiers." Chris is ever the administrator, saying it doesn't matter what anyone thinks because this is the way it will be. More and more I appreciate Jack's evenness and continual effort to look at the big picture. More often than not, he puts himself aside for the larger good. But since he's so recently out of the Marine Corps, I feel the need to keep an eye on him so we don't become swept away with too many military-isms.

It looks as if we will be working the weekend in order to complete the dojo and offices. Although the Army promised the buildings would be completed by the 12th we can't seem to find out who "the Army" is. The soldiers have been hindered by preparations for the inspection and difficulty in procuring building materials. The officers seem burdened by protocol and bureaucracy. Some of the men have also been temporarily assigned to other duties. They complain, but the flatness in their voices borders on resignation. These interruptions are frustrating; we were promised that they would be free of any other duties while they were in the Trojan Warrior Project. When I mention my annoyance with the bureaucracy Griggs laughs and says, "That's nothing; the reason a Delta Force team wasn't able to reach the hijacked Pan Am plane in Athens two years ago was because they weren't able to procure a military plane fast enough to get them there."

We have just completed our pre-program interviews. Joel goes into the office to pick up his briefcase before we drive home and I walk to one of our two rented cars to wait for him. Jack and Chris are walking up the street after completing their interviews; Jack is shaking his head and raises his hands in a gesture of futility.

"Why is it that they haven't been briefed about the program?" he demands. His voice is insistent and drops lower than his usual deep baritone, as though he's talking from the inside of an oil drum. "We knew from the beginning it was essential that these men be able to choose freely to be in this program and not be railroaded into it . . . " He pauses and looks up at Chris who is a good half a foot taller than he is. "Half of them," he continues, "have no idea what they've signed up for and the other half are in it because they were told to be in it." He shrugs. "What happened? You were supposed to handle that end of it."

Chris waves him off like shooing a fly away, but his face is taut and serious, "Settle down, Jack, you're exaggerating. One man told us they signed on because they didn't want to leave their team and somebody else said he was pressured to join. That's not half the men by a long shot. I told Colonel Flynn what we needed and he said it would be handled."

Joel walks up and I add, "My sense is that at least half of the guys in our interviews somehow just drifted into the program."

Joel nods in agreement. Chris frowns and his lips tighten against his teeth.

"I don't have a good feeling about it," Jack says morosely.

"Well, we've got to work with it now," Chris says. On the drive home his talking increases, as though Jack's moody silence is a hole he's trying to fill with words.

Outside the car window the evergreens sag under the late afternoon heat. The smell of sweat from our workout gear cuts through the vinyl newness of the car. Somewhere down the line it could be a serious problem that a significant number of the men signed up because of external pressures rather than free will. A half-hearted approach will result eventually in frustration and bitterness.

The urge to confront personal ghosts and uncover our full potential is ignited only by an inner need. This arises from a discontent about who we have become. When the need becomes strong enough to challenge the status quo we summon the commitment and courage to attempt the unknown. In order to face the demons that arise when we move past the boundaries of our small self, we need precisely the courage of our commitment to move us forward. If we do not have this commitment, it's altogether too easy to say it hurts or is uncomfortable, and then return to our smaller self. If many of these men don't feel this inner need and commitment to change, we may be headed for rough seas.

On the other hand, the Special Forces soldier, as a member of the military elite, is well suited to be in a program like the Trojan Warrior Project. He is already distinguished by his individuality, intelligence, self-discipline, and ability to adapt to new situations. If there's anything approaching a living warrior archetype in the U.S. Army it most likely will be found in the Green Berets. And a warrior is committed, by nature and training, to face the demons that come.

The notion of a Special Forces Unit trained in unconventional warfare arose in the early 1950s in the Pentagon office of General Robert McClure's Psychological Operations Staff Section. When General William J. ("Wild Bill") Donovan's Office of Strategic Services (OSS) was terminated in 1945, the U.S. had nothing resembling an unconventional warfare unit until the Korean War broke out in 1950. Special operations then were largely ineffective; accounts are filled with terms like "amateurish," "ineffectual," "poor planning," and "lack of coordination." Most of the units that took part in engagements were hastily assembled and lacking in both planning and training. It became apparent that a successful special operations detachment had to be selected, trained, and fully prepared before the outbreak of another war. General McClure first gathered a group of men who had had guerrilla experience in World War II with the OSS; he was developing guerrilla warfare plans for World War III, which in the immediate postwar years seemed inevitable.

There was considerable opposition within the Army to a new Special Operations branch, particularly from the two existing sections, Intelligence and Plans, and Operations. Only after a number of bitterly fought contests at the Pentagon was the concept finally accepted, and in early 1952 the Army reluctantly allotted 2,500 personnel spaces to the program. Colonel Aaron Bank who had served in the OSS during World War II became the first Group Commander of the 10th Special Forces Group in April 1952. The basic missions of the Special Forces were twofold:

1) To seek out, train, and support men capable of becoming effective guerrillas.
2) To seek out, engage, and neutralize guerrillas.

There was, additionally, even more serious opposition outside the Army from the newly formed C.I.A. and the Air Force which had just recently broken away from the Army as a separate branch. But in the climate of international fear, Soviet build-up in Europe, and the disappointing experience in Korea, the Army Special Forces survived its various detractors. However, opposition to a military elite continues from both inside and outside the Army to this day and it provokes ongoing battles over finances and equipment allocations.

In 1961, at the beginning of a golden era of counterinsurgency, President John Kennedy reviewed the Special Forces Group at the Special Warfare Center at Fort Bragg, North Carolina. The commander of the center, Colonel William P. Yarborough, wore the controversial yet unofficial green beret for the presidential visit. Impressed by the elite troops, the President sent a message back from Washington proclaiming the green beret as a symbol of excellence, a mark of distinction and badge of courage. Shortly thereafter the Army officially authorized the wearing of the beret. Kennedy's approval also had the effect of further promoting, and perhaps permanently establishing, the mystique of elitism and romanticism that still pervades the Special Forces soldier.

Within the Army the code specifies that a complete A-Team (a Special Forces Operational Detachment A) have a team leader (often a captain), a warrant officer, team sergeant (often a top sergeant), and nine non-commissioned officers (NCOs). Each man trains in a specialty, in which he becomes somewhat of an expert, as well as cross-trains in other specialties that ideally interlock the skills and talents of all the men into a self-contained unit. I say "somewhat of an expert" because a few men are absolutely brilliant in their fields and others are still working for mastership. It's often the difference of those who have studied their specialties for fifteen years and those who have for only two. These specialties include operations and intelligence, light and heavy weapons, demolitions, communications, and medical care (each team has two medics). Since the role of instructor is a specific goal of a Special Forces soldier, each man learns how to impart his skills to others. In the Trojan Warrior Project we have operational command of two complete A-Teams of twelve men each plus their company commander, twenty-five men in all.

Besides their specialties and cross-training, most of these men have graduated from such schools as Urban Operations, Sniper's School, Mountaineering, Ski Training, Escape and Evasion, and HALO (as in High Altitude Low Opening: they jump from over thirty-thousand feet and free-fall until one-thousand feet before opening their parachutes). They're all airborne-trained and the greater majority have been in Ranger Battalions. A number are bilingual and have field experience in intelligence gathering. Team 560 is a SCUBA team, which can carry out underwater operations. Many of them have been instructors in other schools, including some in foreign militaries. Sergeant Dudley put it rather succinctly, "We're million-dollar men."

This is certainly one version of "Be All That You Can Be."

August 9

Abrupt weather change today. A soft rain and cooler temperatures mercifully replace the heat and humidity of the previous week. The men go through a modified A.P.R.T. (Army Physical Readiness Test) this morning. During the six months of the program they will take the test four times to quantify any changes. In addition to push-ups, sit-ups, and a two-mile run, we have added pull-ups and a stretch test for flexibility. Everyone is approaching the first test with an air of seriousness and camaraderie reminiscent of high school and college sporting events. They cheer one another on in the different events, muttering about having improved or falling below their personal best. They have also dropped hints that they will make an especially strong effort to score high so that it will be hard to improve. They want to make sure this training works. The scores at the end of the test demonstrate they did make a committed effort; most of them exceeded the Army maximums by considerable margins.

The afternoon is the famous Special Forces ruck march—a macho event that, as one soldier says, "tests the size of your balls." A one-hundred-pound pack plus an M16 rifle (approximately eight pounds)—and if you're a small arms specialist, an M9 grenade launcher (approximately three pounds)—full camos (camouflage uniform), and boots are to be humped fifteen miles in this steaming weather as fast as you can. The race is against the clock and not one another, therefore it's an individual effort, not a team event. When you finish you get three shots to find a bulls-eye the size of a silver dollar at fifty meters. The same yardstick will be used here as in the physical fitness test: They do it now and then later and we see if the program has affected their performance.

With their rucks, weapons, and uniforms they no longer look like jocks on college intramural teams. There is an ease and knowing in the way they shift the weight of their packs and hold their rifles. This is home.

This is what the animal is trained for. All the conditioning is not just to look good in the tight sleeveless T-shirt, but to hump this unforgiving load over long distances at the highest speed possible. A gut check of this type, but much longer (three days), over cross-country terrain is one of the tests required to pass Special Forces qualifying school. We will also administer a three-day gut check midway through the program.

These soldiers in camouflage uniforms, boots, and automatic weapons immediately evoke media images of their equivalents in Honduras, El Salvador, Beirut, the Philippines, South Africa, Ireland, and South Korea. A camouflage virus spreading over the planet. A culture of violence infecting the bloodstream of every race and creed. A global uniform designed to appear indistinguishable from the earth, so you can shelter yourself on the earth, then blow holes in the earth and in each other in the name of right and justice. I experience a moment of doubt about why I'm part of this. "Am I training them to be better killers?" "Don't be naive, this isn't the Boy Scouts." "What exactly does aikido have to do with these men?" The inner dialogue accelerates from a dead start to one hundred miles per hour in a micro-second.

As they come across the finish line about two and a half hours later their uniforms are dark with sweat and they're complaining about the "no running rule" (because of a rash of injuries the command has prohibited running with the heavy rucks). These men scoff at the idea and complain that their times would be much better if they could run. Sounds half macho and half true. Most of them look pretty wasted and dehydrated, although almost all of them put their three rounds dead in the center of that black circle.

I feel out of it in my clean SportsMind uniform observing the activity while not really involved. Some part of me would like to be out there seeing if I could do it. Jack asks the officer at the firing range if there are any weapons we can use. In a moment's time a staff sergeant is reviewing the M16 for us and telling us how to use it. Pushing an indicator switch he drawls, "This is single shot, this is semi-automatic, and this is Roock and Rolllllll my friends!" as he switches it to full automatic. Now I'm lying in the dirt chambering a round and slowly taking a bead on the target. Weapons are going off on either side of me and fire spits out the muzzles. I have a memory of the time I shot my first .22, and then my father's 30.06. I think of my grandmother shooting prairie dogs out the kitchen window, and later myself firing the M14 in the Marines.

Wham! The weapon next to me explodes in fire. A young buck sergeant from our group brings his target over and hands it to me. The bullseye is shot almost completely out. He flashes a crooked grin and tramps off in his drenched uniform. Spending the entire day in full-out physical effort and then finishing with this kind of steadiness is impressive.

My first shot is upper left. I group my next three and the sergeant looks at the target appreciatively but with no outward acknowledgement. He suggests that I squeeze the trigger more slowly and relax as my breath exhales. This sounds like my message: Relax, breathe properly, work with one's energy. They know this, yet how can I deepen it? I need to discover their point of weakness, bring it to awareness, and then let it become their strength.

August 11

It's two-forty-five A.M. We've just spent the entire evening preparing for our opening day tomorrow, or I guess it's now today. Jack is at the other desk making some final notes, the others have been in bed since midnight. At the last minute we discover an incomplete section in our presentation and even though everyone else is asleep I can tell Jack is going to see it through. He wants to go in tomorrow fully prepared, so I decide to stay up and finish it with him. Although I can barely see the keys in front of me and dread the thought of getting up in three hours, I have the satisfying feeling of closure. I probably wouldn't have decided on my own to do a marathon, but Jack's commitment and thoroughness inspire me to see it through with him. This sense of commitment is one of the hallmarks of a warrior; and in Jack's case, probably one of the things that helped him survive two tours in Vietnam.

August 12

OPENING DAY. The classroom presentation is attended by all the men, the Battalion Commander, Colonel Flynn, and Colonel Barnes, the commander of this particular Special Forces Group. Horst Abraham, who will teach classes in exercise physiology, is also present and will be with us for the next ten days to lay the ground for a physical training regimen. Chris Majer introduces all the instructors and then delivers some fairly dramatic words about the historical significance of this program and how the word "warrior," in its truest sense, will be enhanced by this work.

"Those that put themselves in harm's way," he booms out, "deserve the leading edge of human technology; and this is what the program will deliver." This is a big carrot to dangle in front of them and I swallow uneasily. He finishes by invoking the warrior traditions of the past, including the African Zulus, the Roman Centurions, and the Japanese Samurai. He then presents Colonel Barnes with a samurai sword from our team, and Barnes responds with a dagger from the Special Forces. Colonel Barnes gives a short talk about the uniqueness of this program and the special opportunity each and every man has to make themselves better soldiers. He says that even though much of the material will be new and perhaps even strange, he wants everyone—and he gives a meaningful pause here—to make a one-hundred-percent effort. I have an uneasy feeling about his emphasis. Does he know something about the attitude of the men that we don't? There must be backroom talk about not all of these men being true volunteers. I also sense the unease and skepticism the men have with the ritual and speech making. They have already let me know that one of the reasons they are in S.F. is so their training and soldiering will be free of unnecessary ritual and salesmanship.

For the aikido section I'm to wear my *hakama* and *gi* and speak about the history and tradition of the art. Jack and I have briefly rehearsed a scenario whereby in the middle of my talk he will rush at me from the back of the room with an eight-inch butcher knife. The plan is for me to disarm him and then demonstrate additional techniques while he's on the mat. What we don't rehearse, because we're unable to get the weapon until the day of the tour, is for Jack to charge me with a pre-hidden M16 automatic rifle with a fixed bayonet. Never having practiced before, I know there's plenty of room for surprises, but we decide that if we pay attention no one will get hurt and there will be the added benefit of having the soldiers see the effectiveness of aikido in response to a weapon familiar to them.

As planned I'm standing in front of the men speaking about the role of aikido in the Trojan Warrior Project. They're sitting attentively, like kids on the first day of school, wearing their new white *gis* with Army name patches sewn on their left breasts. Sitting in chairs off the mat are a small group of officers and senior NCOs from Battalion headquarters. Midway through my talk a loud scream from the back of the room shatters the air and Jack explodes from behind the men waving the knife above his head. There is a stiffening in the room as he races toward me, the knife poised to strike. As Jack lunges with the flashing blade I step to the side, grab his knife hand and turn his wrist in a *kote gaeshi* technique that makes him flip head over heels. I twist the knife from his hand and place it out of reach. Jack springs to his feet and aims a front kick at my groin. I trap his kicking leg and up-end him. He then attacks with a variety of strikes, kicks, and grabs. Blending with his movements, I demonstrate the numerous possibilities that aikido has to offer in dealing with an unarmed attack. In response Jack rolls forward, backward, sometimes flipping through the air in a dramatic breakfall, or is held immobile in a painful joint lock.

This is called *jiyu-waza*, or free form, and it's one of the sweetest pleasures of aikido. There is no set sequence and each partner is constantly adjusting to the other's rhythm, speed, and force. If his attack is hard and fast I yield and let him move by; at other times I enter into his attack so I end up behind him; or I move in such a way as to initiate and lead his attack. He varies his force and adjusts his intensity in relationship to my energetic presence. If I'm not energetically full he lets me know by moving into my weak spot, upsetting my balance, or striking me where I'm open. His attack is a wholehearted expression of intent; my response is listening to his message and embracing it, allowing it to resolve into an earthbound spiral. It's a call and response, a speaker and a chorus, an invocation to the martial god to inspire our movements. We're separate and we're one.

Jack rides the momentum of one long throw ending up at the hidden M16. Without a pause he handles it knowingly and charges me in his best gung-ho Marine. His brow knits determinedly and his flat hard gaze reminds me that the man behind the pig sticker is a two-combat-tour survivor of Vietnam. The sucking in-breath of the spectators is drowned out in Jack's battle cry; he looks like a runaway train barreling down my track. I sidestep his lunge, grab the rifle, and guide his ferociousness in a tight circle. Jack takes a hard quick fall, but I'm holding the rifle, the collateral for his aggressiveness. "How did this happen?" their bewildered faces ask.

I put the weapon a few paces away. This is where our mental rehearsal has ended. But Jack is pumped up and attacks again. There is a giddy exhilaration from working with the bayonet and we're onto a fresh conversation, not knowing what will happen next. He grabs for my throat and I turn his attack to the side. I take him to the mat and pin his shoulder, waiting for the tap that signifies "enough" so I can let him up. But

Jack doesn't give up. His free hand is reaching toward the M16; thirty pairs of eyes crowd into those few inches between his fingers and the trigger guard. I have him tightly pinned but he continues to struggle, trusting that I won't seriously hurt him, but also telling me that if I don't take command he will have the weapon again. It's an exquisite edge that we're riding. The only sound in the large room is Jack's hand clawing against the mat as he struggles forward. A drop of sweat falls from my forehead to the mat. Even though his shoulder could be torn loose he's requesting a very definite statement from me, and I finally give him the clarity that he demands. I tighten my grip and his margin of choice evaporates as his shoulder, my center of gravity, and an energetic plumb line into the depths of the earth become one coherent statement: Relax and be still or your own struggle will cause you pain. He wrenches back to free himself from the pain and taps. I release my hold and the room sucks in a collective in-breath. Afterwards, one of the officers, his eyes still wide with excitement, says, "It was like watching a movie, I had no idea what was going to happen."

Later Jack and I talk about what transpired and our animated reliving of it is epic in description. For the people listening it seems bewildering that there's little mention of the technical aspects of the moves, or how hard a throw may have been, or even the reaction of the audience. Instead we talk about our interaction on the mat as a highly sophisticated and complex conversation—a communication with layered meanings, brimming with moral questions and answers. Those that hold me in contempt for working with these soldiers would probably consider our philosophical discussion about a martial art that can maim, and kill, also dangerous and immoral. Even aikidoists who are only concerned with physicality and technique would scoff at our descriptions of command and respect, intention, and guiding. But it's in this relationship between the *uke,* the attacker, and *nage,* the one who will perform the technique, that we find a philosophy of language, plus the deepest truths that aikido has to offer.

August 13

Fort Davis is a wooded sprawling Army Post with lakes, golf courses, shooting ranges, running courses, pools, gyms, schools, and hundreds of soldiers traipsing around in green uniforms. But after only a week I'm repelled by the uniformity. Rows of buildings painted the same color, same uniforms, same vehicles, same mentalities. Fortunately these Green Berets are rugged individuals. They're tough physically, very conditioned, with a honed disregard for officers, a vast cynicism that spares nothing, and a genuine curiosity for those things that they think will make them better soldiers and people. I really don't think I could do this if I had to work with the regular Army. It would be too stiff and even more oppressive than it is.

The aikido dojo with its bright blue mat, freshly painted walls, and ceiling-to-floor banners depicting samurai in battle is an oasis of color in this sea of homogeneity. Because they have never seen aikido before and because there are no senior students to assist me we go slowly, laying a strong foundation in the basics. While some teachers consider certain elementary techniques like *ikkyo* or *nikkyo* the basics, I emphasize the principles of centering, blending, grounding, and how we use our *ki*, or energy, as the foundation. If these principles are learned the techniques easily follow.

Today I'm teaching *ukemi*, the art of attacking and falling. As I expected these men have little fear about hurling their bodies over the mat; my challenge is to slow them down so they will feel their movements and not simply perform them. While they are enthusiastic about what they are learning they seem equally bewildered by the movements. They pepper me with questions about what they saw in the opening presentation. "How long will it take me," a young soldier asks, "before I can throw someone across the room?" While they enjoy the techniques and physical interaction they are more deeply drawn to the notions of *ki* and blending—power without domination and force.

"In *ukemi*," I point out, "you learn how to give up your ground without giving up your center."

"What's the difference between the two?" Farley asks.

"Center is the connection with your own sense of personal power. Ground is extending that power into the environment."

Farley narrows his eyes, "Give me an example."

"Imagine yourself standing on a well-polished marble floor and you have wool sweat socks on. You can be centered, but not too well grounded. Take the sweat socks off and you can ground yourself."

I call Jack over and have him throw me. I demonstrate that while I give up my ground, as I turn upside down in the roll, I can still keep my center, my own sense of personal power and choice.

"Learning how to do this on the mat we can learn how to roll with any incoming energy, or difficult situation, without giving up who we are."

A faint smile breaks through Farley's bulletproof face, "I think this is exactly what I need with my wife."

Preparing for the start of the project Joel, Jack, and I have been going sixteen hours a day for almost two weeks and I'm bone tired. I rise at five A.M. for a short meditation and then leave the house at around six A.M. so we can be at muster at six-thirty. Morning physical training includes a five-mile run, industrial strength calisthenics, and an hour and a half of aikido. Afternoon classes in nutrition, exercise physiology, and learning theory are followed by a mile-and-a-half run, a half-mile swim, and a three-quarter-mile run back to our lockers. Evenings are spent in our team meetings and with administrative work. Heavy bags are forming under Jack's eyes, but he seems tireless. He is often the last one to bed and the first one out the door. Sometimes I think he's simply a workaholic, but I've made a personal commitment to go the full distance with him, however hard he pushes.

August 15

Hot and sticky. The barometer still rising at ninety-five degrees and eighty-seven percent humidity. By midday the asphalt on the company street is spongy and the heat fixes a stale, bloodless taste in my mouth. Sergeant Tom James, the medic in Team 560, catches up with me on the way out of the classroom. "Do you mind if I put something personal to you?" I'm pleased and ask him what's on his mind.

"Are you a Christian?"

"I was raised Lutheran, but I'm not a practicing Christian," I reply.

His eyes blink away my answer and I can tell that he hasn't really asked the question he wants to.

"Do you believe in a Supreme Being?" His jaw inches forward. I know that we're into something serious but not yet to the point.

"I'm not exactly sure what you mean, but I do believe in a power that is greater than my individual ego. The best way to describe my feelings is to say that I'm spiritual but not religious. My relationship with God, or a Universal Being, or whatever you call it, is a personal one."

He pauses for a minute, takes a deep breath and says, "No offense, but I'm not comfortable bowing to the picture of Master Ueshiba in aikido class. It just doesn't feel right to me."

James was raised in a small east Texas town and his parents raised him with strict Christian ideals. The idea of bowing to an Asian martial arts teacher, much less any person, is repugnant to him.

"One of the main reasons I wanted to be in this program is that I thought it would make me a better person. But I don't know if bowing to this photo will make me a better person."

I explain that we aren't deifying Ueshiba but rather bowing in respect to the long and honorable tradition from which aikido came. He frowns and shakes his head. "I don't know," he says, "I'm just saying that it's not right for me. It may be okay for you and some of the other guys, even for some of the other Christians. I'm not saying you're wrong, but with my belief in Jesus as my Savior it doesn't feel right." He looks at me earnestly, firm in his belief while at the same time looking for some kind of solution.

"Tom," I say, "part of this program has to do with accepting values from other cultures." Even though this is technically true it sounds like bullshit the moment I say it, some kind of academic leverage that has nothing to do with the struggle he's really going through. He looks at me coldly without saying anything and we let the comment go. I feel awkward and embarrassed.

Suddenly a light goes on in my weary head. "Why don't you think of it as a kind of salute? When you salute an officer you're respecting the rank and tradition, right? It doesn't mean you're putting them on a pedestal or comparing them to God, you're simply respecting the rank. Think of it as a new kind of salute."

His soft eyes gaze imploringly into mine. Slowly and almost imperceptibly his head begins nodding up and down. In the judicial corner of his mind that weighs right and wrong he's straining to see if the scales will come to some balance between the heavy moral hand of linear Christian fundamentalism and the Asian philosophy of many spokes leading to the hub. Being raised in a backwater town of the Bible Belt where everything is as clearcut as the endless plains meeting the endless sky did not make James a less complex man. Behind the firm patriotic jaw and resolute good looks he whirs with the complexity of an advanced turbo jet. He married a Catholic Panamanian girl while on tour in Central America, has ambitions to play the piano, takes a massage course at the local University, despises communists, has a love-hate relationship with his radical feminist sister who lives in Berkeley, and is a top-rate medic, father, and understanding ear for the rest of his teammates.

He continues to search my eyes, his jaw muscles rippling, 'Can I trust this guy? Is this liberal psychologist hipster type (he must be liberal, he's from San Francisco) trying to pull something over on me?' The part of him that is fascinated by the program and likes to hang out with the humanities students over coffee is trying to cut a deal with the part that has a Bible in one hand and apple pie in the other. It's not as simple as yes or no.

"I'll try it," he finally says. The head nodding increases and his blue eyes relax their knifelike edge. "I'll try it and see how it is. I'll just try it," he repeats. He stands up abruptly, puts out his hand and in his best east Texas drawl says, "Thank yew. Ah appreciate your time."

This was the most personal contact I had made with any of them, although I wasn't quite sure what had happened. James has that strange mix of traditionalism and openness that is common to these men, and perhaps to America. On the one hand there's a rootedness in the traditional American values of God, country, and family, a single standard that declares apple pie and the flag are right and anything different is wrong, a deep river of conservatism that reacts against anything that is even close to the outside edge. On the other hand they also identify with the maverick, the lone hero who lives outside the law, unaffected by the demands of society. The factors of individualism, non-conformity, the ability to make decisions on their own, and the desire to be more than just the rank and file are the very qualities necessary to be part of the Special Forces. Is this two-sided coin a strength or weakness? If the military Special Forces represent, as Roger Beaumont claims in his book *Military Elites*, a cross-section of the society it serves, then I'm looking into the soul of the American male. A soul that I also happen to share.

August 18

We finish the first week with family night. A drenching thundershower lasts into the early morning; after the previous days and nights of heat, it's a cooling relief. It's also beautiful. The heavy moist sky lights up with distant lightning, creating a spectacular show of light and sound. Then the rains come. It's as if the heavens simply turned a bucket upside-down and released the tears of a lifetime. It feels purifying, and everything instantly cools off.

Scheduling time with the families is our way of including the spouses and children in the work we're doing. We all meet in the dojo, so it resembles a PTA meeting in some small town. Everybody shows up (it must have been an order) including a few grandparents, nursing babies, teenagers ogling each other, a pack of kids (Chief Harner has six himself), and the single men standing in pairs looking slightly forlorn and out of place. Without their uniforms, stripes, and insignias these men look more like contestants on the Dating Game than the notorious Green Berets. I laugh when I think of my friends back home spying on this gathering. If they were dropped unknowingly into this scene they would probably think they were at their ten-year high school reunion instead of a gathering of their imagined bloodthirsty killers. In the middle of an attentive crowd is the star halfback, the serious one with glasses was the former Student Body president, the intense talkative one a member of the debating team, the lanky awkward boy the MVP on the baseball team, the charmer with the wide smile was voted most likely to succeed, the two slouching together in the corner spent all their time under hoods in auto shop, there's the nerd who loved electronics, and the disheveled one with the bright, inquisitive eyes the editor of the school newspaper. The older men, who could actually be their fathers, look like the basketball coach, the principal, the woodshop teacher, and the school counselor.

Captain Parker and his girlfriend are one of the surprises of the evening. She is French and strikingly beautiful with long auburn hair falling wildly to her waist. Not that the other wives and girlfriends aren't beautiful, but her attractiveness is contemporary and she has all the earmarkings of the counterculture. What is Parker into I wonder? Psychedelics, politics, feminism, alternative lifestyles? He is tall, blonde, blue-eyed, intellectually bright with a boyish face. In another life I could see him as Viking-in-training, sailing from the cold North to plunder Europe. One of the last Great White Hopes.

The five SportsMind team members who taught this week—myself, Joel, Jack, Chris Majer, and Horst Abraham—give short presentations. Horst is our exercise physiologist who was a member of the Austrian Olympic skiing and sailing team; he's presently a world-class marathoner. He is also a gentleman in the best of the European tradition.

The most popular event is Joel's computer-based biofeedback game. One end of an EMG biofeedback unit is attached to a person's fingers while the other end is fed into the computer. The EMG unit monitors muscle tension and relaxation. The computer screen displays colorful hot-air balloons rising into a blue sky. The more tension the player has the faster they will rise, the more relaxed the quicker they descend. The goal is to move the balloons skyward while avoiding the rockets that the computer shoots toward the balloons. You dodge the rockets by consciously adjusting your muscle tone between relaxation and tension. Cheers and shouts arise from around the table as players try to move their balloons to freedom.

This is a difficult game to master and it's interesting to watch the men play. Most of them have a frustrating time because their primary strategy in dealing with obstacles is to exert massive amounts of force and effort. This produces an inability to control the balloons. The more effort and force they apply the less control they have and the more the rockets shoot their balloons down.

"Damn!" Sanders shouts. He tightens in frustration, tries harder, and becomes more vulnerable to the rockets. He is caught in this loop, the balloons pop like firecrackers.

"Damn!" The little "blip" sound that happens when a balloon is shot down becomes a duet with the player. "Blip" "Damn!" "Blip" "Damn!" "Blip" "Damn!" "Blip" "Damn!"

The way they respond to this simple computer game speaks of something, not only in the military culture, but in the culture as a whole. We're taught that in order to succeed we simply need to push harder, louder, or longer. If there's an obstacle, overpower it. If there's resistance break it down. The military's wet dream is conjured by the culture as a whole: If something is in your way just bowl it over. In a single sentence General Curtis LeMay embodied the national attitude during the Vietnam War when he declared, "Bomb them back to the Stone Age."

"Americans try so violently to be non-violent," the Tibetan meditation master Chögyam Trungpa Rinpoche has observed.

As we leave, Chief Kirby of Team 560 stops me at the door and says, "You have won all our respect. We're all on board together now." Hearing this while still feeling the warmth of the family gathering is satisfying and important to me. I know that this first week has been very powerful for both soldiers and trainers. There has been a collective sharing which has moved us toward a deeper and more intimate look at ourselves. And yet . . . I wonder about the shadow side. Somehow it all seems too hunky-dory. But knowing the rhythm of these kinds of things I'm sure that the dark side will claim its throne soon enough.

At home Jack, Joel, and I talk about the evening and evaluate one another's presentations. I voice my concerns about going deeper with the men—they've been thinking the same thing. We remind ourselves that while the element of trust is important, our goal is not to be friends with them, although that may happen over the course of time.

"What is important is that we deliver those things that will increase their potential as soldiers and individuals," Joel says.

"Why do we say soldiers *and* individuals?" I ask. "In some ways it's a false distinction, but . . . can a soldier ever be an individual? In the classical sense a warrior is an individual, but can the modern-day soldier be a warrior?"

"If there's such a thing as a warrior, with individual initiative, in today's military it's these men; they are the crème de la crème," Jack says. "We need to find their strengths as well as their limitations. But their being so good at what they do, and knowing that they're good, isn't going to make this an easy task. This morning Rader said to me, 'What can you teach us? What could you possibly know that would make me better at what I do?'"

Jack's eyes brighten. "They need to know that what they don't know *will* hurt them."

In The Belly

August 19

I dreamt last night of hiding a blonde woman dressed in black. I wore a pistol and there were rooms of black snakes through which we had to navigate. She was very frightened but said that she trusted me. We moved seamlessly from room to room with a quiet vigilance, always alert to the presence of the snakes. It was as if we were in a maze and the purpose was simply to survive the constant threat of the ubiquitous snakes. I woke repeatedly during the night; my shadow side was on the move.

As we begin morning P.T., Johnson, a young sergeant from 560, yells out, "I know you guys don't want to be here. I know you want to be home. You can't fool me." His tone is mocking. "Come on admit it!" he continues, his voice slicing through the humid air. "You would rather be back in bed, be back in your own home in San Francisco and Seattle with your wives, right?" Only a few of the other men join in his laughter, but everyone watches our reactions. He is testing us, but he's also right; there is an unspoken feeling of fatigue, and maybe even homesickness among our team today. I think of my dream, of protecting a woman and the threat of snakes.

"Maybe that's where you'd like to be, Dan," I say.

He laughs; his reply is quick and biting, "No psychology, Ricky; I can tell you guys don't want to be here. I've got to be here; this is my job." I'm both pissed and transparent. Embarrassment presses on my face like the sun. These men are sharp and they know how to find the jugular. This is only the beginning.

Doing interminable repetitions of brutal abdominal exercises during morning P.T. I notice that they're watching us with these shit-eating grins. Soon there's an endless stream of comments: "How you doin', coach? You're getting behind, don't lose count. Getting tired, SportsMind? Keep your legs straight now, no cheating." On and on. I'm thinking, 'Hey, most of these guys are half my age and don't do anything but train for this.' But I smile back and act as if I'm breezing through it. I refuse to let them get to me. A raging fire spreads across my stomach as I finish the last twenty sit-ups. When we culminate with a long stretching session, I tell myself that it's a good challenge; I'm building trust with them, I'm getting in decent shape. But this nagging thought from the night before keeps popping up, "What really challenges them?" It surely isn't sit-ups. These guys jump out of planes at thirty thousand feet, hike for three days with ninety-pound packs, and then hit the center of a bulls-eye at fifty meters with their M16s. Sergeant Thayer of 560, for example, is an acrophobic; he's scared to death on a step ladder—and I mean deathly afraid; yet he makes a couple of parachute jumps a month! No, I can't believe that all this emphasis on fitness really challenges them. It's good that they learn new ways to train physically, but it's not their edge. So where is it?

During the morning lecture Joel is explaining the biocybernetic axiom of: Control follows Awareness. As he explains what this means he launches into the description of certain states of consciousness and their corresponding powers. He uses the case of certain Tibetan yogis who can raise their body heat so high they are able to withstand the Himalayan cold with nothing on. Partway through his description all the men begin to hum loudly the theme song from "The Twilight Zone." I'm stunned. Joel's mouth falls open. Jack begins to laugh. We're all laughing. The joke is on us, but it's more than a joke. They don't want tales of the supernatural, they want applications. This is another confrontation. We're being given notice that the first week is over and they're going to start talking back. They're letting us know that they are not just empty shells waiting to be fed. They're challenging us because they want to be challenged, they want to be tested. They want teachers who can take them to their edge.

August 21

I skip lunch today and borrow Joel's bike for a ride around the post. The military aesthetic is about as attractive as an elbow, but the physical layout and feeling of community is very inviting. The post is in many ways a model of communal living. By some strange paradoxical twist a military base is as close to socialism as you can get in America. It's a mini-society; along with the hierarchy of command, there are free dental and medical services, child care, recreational services, tremendous discounts on entertainment, housing, clothes, food, appliances, and furniture, not to mention a well-run security system.

Riding the bike through the enlisted men's housing I'm swept into dark waves of memory. It all seems familiar; distant and fresh at the same time, like a déjà vu that won't stop. My father enlisted as an eighteen-year-old out of high school and worked his way through the ranks, retiring as a Warrant Officer twenty-seven years later. He served in combat in World War II, Korea, and the early stages of Vietnam.

I knew my father first through a photo that held a prominent position in our living room. He was in his khaki uniform, ribbons decorating his chest, a rakish grin spreading across his handsome face. My mother told me that I used to go up to every man in a uniform—mailmen, policemen, firemen, even deliverymen—and ask if they were my father.

One of my earliest memories of him is returning from a year-long cruise loaded with exotic presents and stories from around the world. We gathered at the docks with the other children and mothers to welcome home the victorious warriors, waving our flags and pennants as the Navy band played "Anchors Aweigh." It was a heady time as the women laughed through their tears and the men shouted and threw their caps high into the blue sky. I felt small and intimidated trying to find my place in this vast uniformed family.

My father seemed every bit the hero with ribbons and medals colorfully decorating his white uniform. My mother rushed into his arms as he stepped off the gangplank while my sister and I stood anxiously to the side. I felt proud of him, proud that he was my father, proud that after not seeing him for a year and not even sure what he looked like, I still had a father. He came up to me and extended his hand in his stiff, formal way, "Hello son. Have you been taking care of your mother and sister while I was away?" I was nine years old and I wanted him to hold me and have him tell me that he loved me. But he didn't, then or ever, so I swallowed hard and felt glad that at least the hero remembered me, and I shook my head yes, pretending that I knew what he meant about my sister and mother.

When the excitement of the homecoming became the routine of everyday life, the hero was replaced by an angry man, restless at home with his wife and children. I wanted to enter into his world, but I felt as though I was bothering him. He treated me like the men he commanded. Soon he and my mother would argue and I felt a confusion in loyalties. I wanted desperately to get to know him, to learn from the hero, but he acted as if he were allergic to me. I couldn't understand how he could fight wars but not talk to his son. Maybe he was mad that I hadn't taken good enough care of my mother and sister, I would think. It never occurred to me that he didn't know how to be intimate with his son, or perhaps anybody, and was too afraid to find out.

We would be home together for a while and then he would be reassigned to a new ship. We would pack everything up and drive cross-country to a new base, a new school, new friends, and another duplex in a Navy housing project. The hero would sail off to some new adventure, the Navy band playing the same "Anchors Aweigh," the wives and children waving the same flags and pennants, as the men walked *up* the gangplank. It was the same movie as a few months earlier but now in reverse. While the men were away, which was most of the time, it was the women who ran the neighborhood.

Many of the men had taken wives from some cruise and it was common to see women from Korea, Japan, Puerto Rico, Panama, and the Mediterranean countries. It was a rich melting pot of race, color, religion, and often violence. More than once I remember a friend's father returning unexpectedly to surprise an "uncle" staying with the wife. There were fights and shouting matches, there were also the occasional stabbings. All the kids in the neighborhood saw John Hernandez's "uncle" bleeding from an upholstery knife in his chest.

Continually moving from one military project to another, I soon learned that being the new kid on the block meant an initiatory trial of harassment. Street logic is based on intimidation and one is constantly being evaluated in terms of how much you can give and how much you can take. It becomes necessary to learn a bodily language that is neither too threatening nor too submissive; the former inviting challenge, the later domination. Survival means transmitting a muscular message of "I don't want to fuck with you, but if you fuck with me I will be ready." Not fully understanding that this had as much to do with posturing as it did with genuine skill, I thought I might be better prepared to meet the resident bullies if I knew how to defend myself. So I found my way to the drafty hangars and Quonset huts where Navy seamen, fresh from studying judo or karate while stationed in the Far East, would teach these Asian martial arts. With a dozen other kids I would learn choke-holds, how to block a punch, how to throw someone over my hip. The young sailors who taught us smelled like sweat, cigarette smoke, and something else that has no word, but belongs to the world of men. After class they laughed and joked with each other as they changed clothes in the locker room, while we turned to the wall and hurriedly put our pants on. Perhaps I learned something about self-defense, but mostly I enjoyed testing my skills against someone else; and as corny as it sounds, learning self-defense does build self-confidence.

Now I'm back full circle, teaching martial arts to the Special Forces in an abandoned Army theatre, and life on the base looks much the same as I remember: women hanging out the wash, kids playing, the worn buildings, an off-duty soldier washing his car, people's heroic efforts to individualize their homes by planting flowers or putting out a doormat with their name on it. Suddenly I feel a lump in my throat and my eyes begin to mist. A surge of emotion sweeps over me. Two women talking over a fence wave as if they know me. I wave back half-heartedly and then unexpectedly I'm crying. I'm overwhelmed by a tremendous sense of relief and I start to laugh, first quietly and then more loudly and suddenly I'm almost doubled over with laughter. Great peals of sound come out of me and I'm happy, very happy. I understand why I'm back on this military base, working with these soldiers, teaching them aikido, mingling with their families. I'm completing a cycle, finishing something that was left incomplete many years before. Something very deep in me is being released and something else is taking its place and making me whole. I wobble happily off on the bicycle feeling very grateful to be here.

August 22

I'm sitting in the traditional Japanese kneeling posture, *seiza,* at one end of the sixteen hundred square feet of a bright blue judo mat that covers the floor of what was once an old movie theatre. A framed photo of Master Morihei Ueshiba, the founder of aikido, gazes benevolently from the head of the large hall; large banners depicting Japanese Samurai in battle hang from the ceiling; and weapons racks hold *bokken* and *jo* (Japanese wooden sword and staff) and Filipino *escrima* sticks. At the back of the hall is a large calligraphied sign we pinned up that reads, **WARRIORS**; underneath this sign are paintings, drawings, and photographs of various warrior traditions that we and the soldiers have posted. The most poignant of these is an old *Life* magazine photo that shows a group of mothers mourning the deaths of their sons in Vietnam.

The air in the dojo is heavy with heat. A single line of sweat runs down my back. Facing me on the other side of this wide blue expanse is a single line of men also sitting in *seiza*. They're each wearing the white cotton practice uniform called a *gi*, and tied around their waist is the white belt signifying that they are novices. Standing between myself and this line are two men, dressed like the others, facing each other in charged expectation. They bow and the *uke*, the one to my right, suddenly breaks toward the other man, reaching out to grab his lapel. The defender, or *nage*, slips to his attacker's side, deftly evading his grasp, and begins to lead his attacker into a circle. For a moment they are one, a single body blended into a tight, power-collecting spiral. The attacker loses his balance and is hurled from the spiral into a graceful fall.

They exchange roles, as is customary in aikido, but this *nage* leans forward impatiently as he defends against his partner's attack. The result is a clash and they begin to labor clumsily against each other; like two bulls locking horns they finally stalemate in a frustrating contest of wills.

"David," I say to the *nage*, "you are too focused on throwing your partner down. Make more of a blend, guide his energy and intent instead of trying to muscle him down."

David tries again and there's more ease and natural power in the throw. They bow to each other and return to the row of men. Two others stand and repeat the sequence until everyone has engaged.

At the end of the session we sit together quietly for a few minutes. Much could be said about the various strategies that were enlisted to deal with the stress of handling an attack while being watched by everyone else—strategies that ranged from primitive male aggression, to spaced-out disassociation, to a graceful daring; but in the stillness of the large hall there's already a volume being said without words. To comment on the strengths and limitations that were just revealed would somehow take away from the directness and simplicity of the seeing itself. For instance, after struggling painfully and unsuccessfully to execute the movement properly, Thayer abruptly turned to me and said, "What I want to do is break his neck . . . but I know it's not what you're looking for." Every presentation reveals entire histories of a life's triumphs and failures, but always with a rugged determination. Aikido, in its simplicity of reflection, is becoming a mirror by which these soldiers can experience how they deal with pressure.

Of the twenty-five men in the program, only three have had any experience with a martial discipline. All of them, however, have completed the Army's hand-to-hand combat course. Some of them boxed or wrestled in high school or college, and then there are the two or three street fighters and bar brawlers that are invariably part of any cross-section of young American males. But all of them are sufficiently tough, mean, or conditioned enough for me to want them on my side in a dark alley. Although only two of them had even vaguely heard of aikido, they are all interested in learning a martial art that represents a warrior tradition and will benefit them professionally and personally. In many ways I can't ask for better students—they are superb learners, disciplined, physically pragmatic, and very willing to take physical risks.

They're also surprised by what they are finding in aikido. To their soldierly minds a Japanese martial art evokes images of occult pressure points that could kill a man with a single touch, the power to break bricks with their forehead, bodies of steel. Invincibility is what they crave. What they get instead is this white boy who comes in wearing a dress (the Japanese *hakama* is the traditional samurai wide-legged pants properly worn by all aikido black belts) who tells them that their big muscles and sucked-in bellies are useless for this form. Then they are told that aikido is not based on fighting and hurting an opponent but blending with and neutralizing his aggression. When I further inform them that aikido will be taught primarily as a discipline for mind/body synchronization and secondly as self-defense, their faces subtly betray the rejoinders racing through their shocked minds, "This guy has got to be kidding. The first time I get my hands on this wimp I'm going to make him a new asshole." But their daily challenges, though hard-bitten and driving to the marrow, honor me. They value the fact that what they learn may make the difference between living and dying. If they didn't respect me there wouldn't be these challenges, they simply wouldn't bother.

August 23

Johnson is the small-arms specialist in Team 560. He's a boxer and he walks with that swaggering gait of youthful confidence. He's big and well-built in a lean way, but it's the combination of his boyish good looks and biting sarcasm that throws you off balance. He's on everyone's list for Most Likely to Succeed, until you get to his cynicism. Johnson has a tongue like a cane-cutter's machete. His father retired as a Sergeant-Major with over thirty years in the Army during which Johnson moved from one Post to another. After drifting from job to job out of high school he decided to join. He was too much of a rebel to be in the regular Army, and his physical prowess, intelligence, and ability to act independently made him an obvious candidate for the Special Forces. Johnson needs to be challenged. A regular line unit would be too much like being a clerk in civilian life. The feeling of being a member of an elite team, plus the powerful bonding between the men in a Green Beret A-Team, gives him some of the intensity and meaning that he's seeking.

Johnson approached the Trojan Warrior Project with both enthusiasm and uncensored cynicism. He is clearly looking for something more in his life, but he has had enough disappointments to make him wary of being wholehearted about anything until it has passed his "being for real" test.

I like him, but I give him a wide berth. I think that he likes me too, although he would never say it that way; it would be much too intimate and make him too vulnerable. In our own ways we see ourselves in each other. He calls me "Ricky," which is what I was called as a child, so his sarcasm is rooted in an unconscious intuition. He is continually trying to bait me into some verbal or physical contact. I'm responsive to him because he has so much potential; I know that the more contact we have the more learning will take place.

He is rough-housing with a few of the other men after P.T. and when he sees me watching, he motions me over, yelling out, "Hey Ricky, let's see what you can do." They're playing a Ranger battalion wrestling game and he quickly demonstrates the rules. As he wraps his large hand around mine his jaw juts forward, the jaw that invariably holds a bulge of tobacco under the bottom lip; he looks at me mischievously. With full knowledge of his strength, weight, youth, and height advantage he says mockingly, "No fair using your aikido, Ricky." We grapple for a bit, I feel out the game, his balance, and any openings. He makes a quick turning movement, there's a large popping sound and a stab of pain shoots through my wrist. We stop in astonishment as my wrist begins to swell before our eyes. A feeling of embarrassment and awkwardness replaces our competitiveness, and we stand awkwardly together like two boys who were caught knocking over a lamp.

"Jeez, I'm sorry man!" he blurts out. "Are you okay?"

My wrist is swelling and throbbing and I'm not sure if I'm okay and I'm not sure what to do next. There we are, the younger and older version of each other, vulnerable, open, not knowing quite what has happened and not knowing what to do. It's a priceless moment; our vulnerability and care is suddenly on display.

Janowski, the senior medic on Team 560, takes charge and begins to examine my wrist. He is a huge man with broad thick fingers and sad eyes. His family is originally from Eastern Europe and he carries a quiet depth about him. It's touching to feel the care and warmth emanate from this hulking man. He examines my wrist with great tenderness. Training hundreds of people myself in body work, I know Janowski has as sensitive a touch as anyone who has ever worked with me. I feel an instant trust in what he's doing. He doesn't think it's broken but suggests that I have it x-rayed.

My trip to the base hospital is, among other things, a lesson in the Special Forces way of doing things: Do what it takes to get the job done. Be inventive. Take risks. Drive ahead but slide through the tight corners. As a civilian I can't technically use the hospital privileges but Sergeant Scott, the medic from Team 260, leads me through the hospital in our sweaty P.T. gear, acting as if we belong there, pulling every string he can and getting favors back where he gave them out some time in the past. The x-ray says the wrist is not broken and I'm led to physical therapy where they apply an ultra-sound treatment. All the while Scott is carrying on in an uninterrupted monologue about everybody we see—who screws who, who is with who, who is dog meat, who we can trust, and reasons why I should call Lieutenant Kincaid, the officer in charge of physical therapy, and ask her out.

It's an interesting contrast to be suddenly out of the Special Forces domain and into the regular Army. Not the same animal at all. It makes me appreciate our group of men even more. There just seems to be less integrity, care, brightness, and commitment than I'm getting at the Trojan Warrior Project. I also see that the genuine concern I feel from the Special Forces medics is not because they are medics, men doing their job, but because they are in fact caring individuals. I feel this same care from most all of the men we're working with; some of them are more explicit than others, but even those that are more recalcitrant still have a genuine concern for our well-being. Once you are accepted into their fold they watch over you.

At this point I would define the main intention in my work to be the forming of them as more complete and integrated human beings. Indeed I feel this to be their interest as well. Yet how do I do this successfully in view of their mission and in the context of the U.S. Army? In order for a man to perform optimally in war, it's now believed, he must see the enemy as an abstraction. The enemy must be viewed as a mechanical obstacle to be overcome; not as a human being with feelings, with a family and identity, the ability to experience pain and pleasure. This is so because the soldier must also see himself as an instrument, a means to an end. If one is viewed this way how can he possibly become, or allow himself to become, a complete human being? When I look at my work in this context I feel as though I'm working in a double-bind situation. While I accept the fact one can be tender and caring and also have the instincts and training to kill and hurt, it's difficult to reconcile how the work of becoming more complete can develop in a context that treats humans as mechanical and abstract. Yet throughout the entire military it's probably these Special Forces soldiers, more than any other, who maintain their human qualities. Today, through the medics, I felt the healer's heart; and through Johnson I felt the warrior's power. Life and Death. Love and Violence. Can these men be the warrior prototype for the twenty-first century? Am I kidding myself?

August 26

This morning we introduced our first guest presenter. The visitor is a friend of Joel's, an American who has taken the vows and robes of a Tibetan Buddhist monk. He has spent years in India and Nepal studying and practicing with the great Tibetan meditation masters. Part of his training included months of icy solitude meditating in a Himalayan cave.

He also graduated *summa cum laude* from Amherst College for his research into the foundations of modern physics in light of Buddhist ontology. With the retreat coming up shortly we feel he might be helpful in preparing the soldiers for meditation practice. And by exposing the men to the beliefs of a non-Western philosophy we hope to expand their understanding and acceptance of other people, religions, and cultures. Our agenda is to have him discuss his mind/body training and then lead us in his form of walking meditation. "Perhaps the commitment and discipline of this Western monk," Joel says, "will strike a resonant chord in the heart of the men."

When I first come upon this man I'm stopped dead in my tracks. He looks like an extra from a Gandhi film who has mistakenly wandered into a John Wayne set. He is standing outside our classroom in ocher robes and sandals while thick, powerful men in green berets, boots, and camouflage uniforms walk by him. He's extremely thin and his close-cropped hair accents a very lean, angular face. He moves like a bird with short, quick gestures and there's an extraordinary intensity about him. As the men pass by they aren't disrespectful but they don't hide their curiosity either. They stare, nod; some say hello.

At first glance the soldiers and this monk appear to be opposites. While the monk is thin to the point of emaciation, his robes barely clinging to his terribly white shoulders, the soldiers are fit and robust in their proud rolling gait. Yet I'm struck by something very much the same about them. Despite the difference in uniforms and posturing both are on the fringe of society, both are outlaws in their own ways; and in this there's a common pride and tenacity. There is a powerful inner fire that burns in both of them, a heat that can be self-consuming if it isn't checked with compassion and understanding.

As the soldiers sit quietly listening to the monk I can feel their attention probing him. He is obviously nervous, constantly arranging his robes and fidgeting in his chair. He is talking about the clarity of mind that comes from intensive sitting practice when suddenly the arm of the chair gives way and he loses his balance. Two of the soldiers immediately rush forward to help fix the chair, but he brushes them aside. Red-faced and out of sorts he clumsily puts himself and his robes back together as if erasing the incident, but what has happened is not lost on the men. It isn't so much that he has fallen off his chair or even that his words aren't connecting with his actions: it's more that he isn't acknowledging his present anxiety of being out of balance with himself. Inauthenticity is a cardinal transgression in the eyes of these men and it has the effect of unleashing the predator in them.

It starts during the question/answer period. The first questions are polite: "What was it like to live in Asia for so long?" "Did you get sick while you were there?" "What was it about Buddhism that made you choose it as a religion?" Then James says in his Texas drawl, "It seems a little strange to me to hide away in a cave in a country as poor as India when you might be able to go out and do something to get rid of the poverty and suffering." The monk replies with a disjointed argument about the need to help yourself first before you can help someone else.

James presses on, "But you're healthy; you could probably do a lot to teach people how to live more healthy."

"In Buddhism," the monk replies, "it's more important to deal with the core of suffering, our mind states, than to only deal with the symptoms."

The sergeant medic leans forward a bit, "Excuse me if this sounds rude, but I think that's a selfish attitude that you have."

There is a moment of everyone-holding-their-breath silence, and the monk, a bit flustered, says condescendingly, "There are different levels of understanding." James fastens his gaze on him. There is a weight in the room.

"You seem kind of nervous, do we make you nervous?" Dunham finally asks.

Before he can answer Grigg asks dismissively, "What good is sitting in a cave if you lose your composure in a simple situation like this?"

"It seems selfish to be paying so much attention to yourself when people around you are suffering," someone hollers from the back. We finally intercede and return order to the situation, but by this time the men have found the vulnerable point, gone in for the kill, and removed themselves. Their bodies are in the room, but they are no longer interested.

Later the same day James takes me aside, "I hope I wasn't too rude; I didn't really mean to hurt this monk, but I just had to speak my mind." He wasn't excusing what he had said, but he was sincerely concerned that he had hurt someone's feelings. In the two weeks that we have been together I've seen this pattern repeated with our training team: First probe for any inconsistency, find the vital point, unleash the predator, measure the response to the attack, accept or reject the person in relationship to their response to the confrontation, and finally express a genuine concern if the person has been hurt or if they, the soldiers, have been too brutal. They're tough, but they are equally tough on themselves—sensitive to weakness (their own and others), and sensitive about hurting someone's feelings.

August 27

Our morning P.T. begins and ends near a small military cemetery. Surrounded by elms and maples it's an oasis of tranquility, and I'm in a routine of taking a few moments, either before or after the training, to walk among the gravestones. I feel that it's somewhat ironic that we do our physical training next to a graveyard. Here we are, sweating and stretching and exercising to be all that we can be, and next door is the constant reminder of where we're all headed. Depending on my mood it's either a very depressing thought or a good reminder to live every moment as fully as possible.

Some of the inhabitants of this cemetery are children, some obviously died of old age. But the greater majority are those who died in combat. The wars they fought begin in the nineteenth century and stretch to Vietnam. Their birth and death dates tell me that most of them were young—teenagers—or in their early twenties.

The history of civilization is partly the history of war and of its combatants, and this small graveyard chronicles a small but dark piece of that history. Historians estimate that there have been approximately fifteen thousand wars in the past five thousand years, an average of two or three wars a year. The great turning points in history emerge from battles such as Marathon, Caana, Waterloo, and Stalingrad. Many of our parks, streets, statues, events, and buildings celebrate the results of war and war makers. But it makes no difference that there were hundreds of battles where nothing at all was decided and where thousands of men died unheralded. It makes no difference that this cemetery is lined with those who gave their lives for some forgotten hill or beach. As Phil Caputo lamented in an account of his experiences in Vietnam, "Those who had lost the struggle had not changed anything by dying. The deaths of Levy, Simpson, Sullivan, and the others had not made any difference. The war went on without them, and as it went on without them, so would it go on without me. My death would not alter a thing."

If these dead men could talk I wonder how they would respond to John Adams' statement that "My generation of Americans have to be soldiers so our sons can be farmers and merchants so that their sons can be artists." I wonder if any of them had aspirations to be artists or if they hoped to live as peaceful merchants. I wonder what they would say about our sophisticated training regime and latest research on fitness. I wonder if what we're doing is going to save lives or at least cause soldiers to consider what they're fighting for.

But stretching from well before Adams exclaimed those words in 1775 right up to the moment that I walk among these tombs, America has been and is a warring nation. In the years 1689–1697 the so-called King William's War ran its course, to be followed less than five years later by Queen Anne's War. The battle against the Spanish then raged from 1739 to 1743. After the colonies fought the Revolutionary War for their independence from England, the new nation of America went to battle in the War of 1812, and then brothers shed the blood of brothers in the tortuous Civil War, 1861–1865. Following World War I came World War II. In the 1950s we fought a "police action" in Korea, and the sixties and seventies were consumed by Vietnam, a war that twisted America apart. During and between the early wars were the constant battles against the Indians, and lately the covert of wars of the C.I.A. have filled the gaps. A war for every generation.

Of the sixty million people who lost their lives in the destructive wheel of violence between 1820 and 1945 a fraction ended up in this graveyard. In the last two years of World War II a million people were killed a month, more civilians than military combatants, something that America has not yet had to face. Despite this staggering blood-letting, our leaders have persistently reinforced the call to arms. In his book *Soldiers and Civilians* the military historian Marcus Cunliffe notes that combat or military life is "an important claim to America's chief office." The President is called the Commander-in-Chief of all the armed forces, a position which originates from George Washington, victorious general, father of our country, and our first President.

Theodore Roosevelt, who led the charge up San Juan Hill, said, "The nation that has trained itself to a cancer of unwarlike and isolate ease is bound, in the end, to go down before other nations, which have not lost the manly and adventurous virtues." When in his *Journey to America*, Alexis de Tocqueville commented on America's romance with military honor, he asked himself "What determines the people's choice in favor of General Jackson, who . . . is a very mediocre man?" His answer was simple and direct, "The battle of New Orleans."

With this habit of war and military it's easy to see how each generation, either consciously or unconsciously, prepares its young males for manhood by preparing them for war. The myth of the soldier warrior has generated society's ritual for introducing men into maturity. Except, of course, those buried at my feet and those who were so dismembered they couldn't even be found.

Now our warlike attitude has positioned us on the very edge of extinction. Clausewitz's nineteenth-century view of war as "politics by other means" is ridiculously dated by the possibility of a nuclear exchange. We have finally created The Weapon. Who needs a warrior when all it takes is a finger on a button? Now we can stare point-blank into the barrel of our collective shadow. We're so stunned by the horror that we make up answers. But those that say they know, don't know. In our think tanks (I have the image of a philosophy shaped like a tank with a large barrel) we slide around the obvious by talking about deterrent capability, missile size, and foreign policy as if they are the moves on a gleaming high-tech board game. And how many ways can the liberals and religious leaders say "swords into plowshares"? We don't have any answers because we're still not asking the right questions. The human activity of war is far too ancient to pass off as abnormal. We have so confused ourselves that on the streets we call it murder, yet sanctify it as duty when enacted on the battlefield. From our first pre-verbal moments of conscious awareness we teach "Thou shalt not kill," then we create weapons for killing. This too is part of our shadow, and we have no answer. We need to disarm, but we don't know how to, and in any case an edict or a demonstration won't stop the mayhem.

How do we help our young men become men and warriors without the violence and brutality of war? How do we cultivate and shape the place within ourselves that yearns for peace? How can we enact our unavoidable aggression without blowing the planet apart? What can I teach these men so they won't become a name on one of these granite slabs? What do I teach them so they won't be responsible for putting some man, woman, or child in a distant land in a tomb like this? Walking through the graveyard I can see men exercising through the trees. With a certain sadness I think of the words of W.H. Auden, "We must love one another or die."

August 28

Clear sunny days with a light wind blowing from the west and northwest. A few trees showing the first hints of color and the sun starting, just starting, to travel a lower arc on the horizon. As the light thickens in the late afternoon the shadows deepen toward autumn. This is a refreshing and uplifting change from last week's rain, dampness, and gray skies, when we ran in the rain and did our sit-ups, push-ups, and stretches on wet steaming ground. It was ecstatic to "never mind" about the mud and get down with the elements; it was also, as the troops say, "a motherfucker."

Today is jump day and we do everything we can to go up in the plane with the men, but to no avail. We have clearance all the way, but at the last moment it's somehow discovered that all the seats are taken. I'm upset and go through the chain of command to argue our point. After being shuffled up and down the ladder of Army bureaucracy, I finally realize that the tack is useless. It's our fate to watch them land instead of being in the plane.

It scares the spit out of me thinking about being in the plane and it turns me inside out even to consider doing the jump. A month earlier when we mentioned the possibility of getting jump training Sergeant Galt said, "We can give you the training," and then laughed as he mimicked kicking us out of a plane. But when we are turned away at the last minute today I am surprised to feel disappointment rather than reprieve. I feel let down not because of being shortchanged the possibility of a personal challenge, or because of a teacher's professional interest in his students, but because I suddenly feel severed from a process that has been deepening and growing between myself and these men. The bond that is forming is suddenly interrupted and I become the odd man out. We spend twelve to fifteen hours a day going through very intense processes together and the effect of that shared time is beginning to express itself. It's not all easy time, in fact much of it is struggle, but it's bringing light to the struggle. The contact is becoming more genuine.

As they board the plane I watch Thayer, who despite being a true acrophobic, finds the courage to make at least one jump a month, and James, who gets motion sickness and has to throw up in a bag just before he jumps. Then there's Oreson, the strange but likeable young sergeant of 260 whose parachute didn't open on a previous jump; with eyes like headlamps he retells the story of wondering if his reserve chute would open as he fell like car keys from one thousand feet. I thought of the fear and vulnerability they showed during the pre-jump briefing and I was touched by how they called me over and included me while they were mingling with men from other companies and battalions.

I've come to believe that they suffer the miseries of Army life not out of patriotism, duty, or even to prove their courage, but because of the camaraderie and fellowship they share with their teammates. This is why I wanted to be up in the plane with them and it's the same feeling I had with men I played sports with, those I marched with in the Marine Corps, those who sing and dance with me, the men with whom I practice aikido and other martial arts. It's the hunt, the silent trance by the fire, trembling together under the night sky, dreaming greatness for our children. It's the call from our genetic ocean to embrace and engage and test one another. It's a cry to stand on the edge, together, in fear and joy, to move from our knowing to the deep blackness of unknowing. It's the impulse not of Cain, but of Apollo. Before our jealousy and competitiveness we shared the love of poetry, healing, and the urge to protect.

It's not surprising that the first armies supposedly were organized from the gangs of men who maintained the irrigation systems in Mesopotamia. Those male forebears must have become very close as they spent their days together digging trenches, designing waterways, building roads, and inventing machines that would irrigate the newly domesticated grains. Thus when a security force was needed to protect the surplus crops these men, constantly together, sharing strengths and weaknesses, organizing themselves along the most efficient lines, were already the first army.

I wonder how these ancients felt being conscripted into a new military class. Did they feel honored to defend the harvest of their society? Were they moved by the warrior virtues of heroism, courage, and service in risking their lives for a greater good? Or did they resent being uprooted from their pastoral life to be trained in organized killing? Would they have wished the same for their sons?

When I later tell Jack that I feel myself getting closer to these men he agrees; he feels the same way. We speak about the fear and vulnerability that comes with this closeness. We understand that real closeness will mean an inevitable breakdown in roles. But how far can this breakdown surely go? Do we actually have the time to let everything be reduced to its natural common denominator? Can we allow ourselves to be simply a band of men, our roles emerging naturally from who we are on the most essential level, as people, and as men, aside from military rank and our assignments as teachers? These thoughts excite and terrify. I know that some of the men would be willing to risk everything and let this breakdown happen as much as they are willing to risk their lives jumping out of planes; and to others it would be their worst possible nightmare.

Jack reminds me it would mean a breakdown in the chain of command, which is the necessary glue that makes the military work. I counter that possibly a more true and natural chain of command would emerge. What would happen, I wonder out loud, if there were a sudden post-apocalyptic back-somersault of history that would reverse the film of time to the beginnings of civilization. This vision is of a twenty-first-century neo-Mesopotamia where the military would reorganize into a labor force maintaining extensive irrigation, housing, and road projects instead of a military force. Without the infrastructure of the military mind would the chain of command of this work force be the same? If there were no external enemy what would constitute leadership and authority? I imagine a culture of warriors, warriors embodying a tradition of honor and skillful means, who would also cultivate the land while being a peacekeeping force. Jack agrees but that glint in his eyes says, "What a dreamer."

(Later I read that Masaki Nakajima, the eighty-three-year-old head of the prestigious Japanese think tank Mitsubishi Research Institute, proposes the need for the future is to build roads and irrigation canals instead of bombs. He projects a series of highways and bridges connecting Europe to China and Moscow to Anchorage; irrigation canals to cultivate the deserts of the Middle East; a tunnel to join Africa to Europe at the Straits of Gibraltar. He also proposes a giant thermal energy plant somewhere near the Equator, or a fifty-trillion-dollar collection station for solar heat. He points to the great economic success of Japan spending only one percent of its GNP for defense, in contrast to America and the Soviet Union which are both faltering economically and spend over eight percent. His critics compare him to Don Quixote, but Nakajima quickly points out that skeptics said that both the Panama and the Suez Canals could never be built.)

What makes this situation in the Trojan Warrior Project both unique and problematic is that it's an all-male environment, with trainers and the soldiers being from two totally different mind sets. We're "experts" in our fields and they're "experts" in theirs, and these two fields are 180 degrees apart. Fertile ground for male competitiveness. But at this point a closeness is emerging out of our differences. Through our constant interaction and testing of one another, we're seeing the underlying ground of our sameness. "Contact," said Fritz Perls, the father of Gestalt therapy, "is the appreciation of differences."

Sometimes I think I will be successful in this program if these men can look each other in the eye and say, "I Love You." I imagine them cringing if they heard this, believing I was a homosexual and calling me a "psycho-queer" before punching me in the nose or fleeing screaming through the door. Already, whenever we introduce material that is threatening or act in an unconventional way, they express their disapproval (which is really fear) by calling us "psycho-queers"—". . . and especially you Strozzi, psycho-queer from San Francisco." I would probably be less threatening if I came from Mars.

But the truth is that they do love each other, and deeply. I see it in the way they listen to one another's problems, the way they are attentive to each other's needs, and especially how they kid each other and get physically close by wrestling and poking at each other. It's really only a matter of letting them own this affection and learn avenues of expressing it without feeling so threatened. Like most American men they are extremely homophobic, which means missing out on intimacy by not allowing their affection to find expression and flow freely. When this love is not expressed it turns into frustration, competitiveness, and a constant need to affirm one's own manliness.

In his fascinating book *Acts of War,* Richard Holmes, the military historian, documents how love and fellowship are common themes among combat veterans as they face the hardships of war. One soldier he interviewed during the Falklands War eloquently reenacts this when he says, "Facing the same enemies, fear, death and other horrors, you are absolutely one, and one gets momentary glimpses of that truer and greater democracy which gradually opens out to solve all human problems." A World War II platoon commander mentions "how wonderful the human spirit can be and how privations, fear, hunger, cold, wet and all the horrors of war serve to bring out the very best in people." In the same book,

Donald Featherstone, a World War I veteran, remembers the pleasant memories, ". . . the comradeship and togetherness . . . the awareness of being in it together." A soldier dwells "in an ordered class beyond the haphazard scope of civilians." Guy Chapman, a World War II veteran, writes that his relationship with his comrades was "so much a part of me that its disintegration would tear away something I cared for more dearly than I could have believed." The combat veterans that S.L.A. Marshall interviewed in World War II for his controversial book *Men Under Fire* clearly expresses that their performance was not inspired by patriotism, duty, or even coercion from officers, but a feeling of loyalty to the man next to them. It's a horrifying thought that men need the brutality of war and the hierarchy and tight constraints of military life to allow themselves to feel love and tenderness toward each other.

August 29

I was born on an Army base in Spokane, Washington, forty-one years ago and today I celebrate my birthday on another Army base. A full circle. There is an eerie feeling of completion. I don't understand it in any rational sense, but being involved in the military feels as if it's fulfilling some part of my personal destiny. I'm completing unfinished business from the past to be more fully alive in my present life. It's the bringing together of two worlds: the world of growing up in a military family with its elements of aggression, competitiveness, and machismo, and my present world of meditation, martial arts, and understanding how to be a warrior without being warful.

At the end of today's aikido class the troops, much to my surprise, sang "Happy Birthday." I sat in the front of the dojo as their deep, rich voices filled the entire room. My eyes misted over and I felt somewhat self-conscious about the men seeing me this way. My hesitation to share these kinds of feelings is that I still don't trust that they will take care with my feelings of vulnerability. When things begin to get real on an emotional level—that is, issues of tenderness, intimacy, or vulnerability—they respond with, "It's not the manly thing to do." "The manly thing to do" means to tough it out, be courageous, be in control. We all learned how to cry with our mothers and to tough it out with our fathers. The irony is that it takes true courage to break such a pattern.

After they finished singing Jack and Joel gave me big warm hugs while the men either shook my hand or slapped me on the back. The difference in gesture was conspicuous and not lost on anyone. It's not that the soldiers feel any less warm toward me, but it had to do with a sense of sanction and boundary. It's acceptable to touch another man if it's in sports, or something like aikido, or simply rough-housing with each other. It's acceptable for athletes to pat each other encouragingly on the butt or hug in celebration or whisper in an ear as long as it's sanctioned within the boundary of the playing field. But without the official cover of the sport it looks too much like a heart-to-heart caring between two men, being a psycho-queer, and that's . . . not the manly way to do things.

August 30

Daryl Sheffield told me something important about himself today that we need to pay close attention to.

Our morning routine is to meet at six-thirty A.M. for muster and then rendezvous at the large grass field next to the cemetery for physical training. We begin with stretches and flexibility exercises, run three to seven miles (sometimes a swim is also included), and then finish with sit-ups, push-ups, more stretching, and a guided relaxation session.

In the stretching and guided relaxation segments we emphasize going slow, paying attention, and using minimal effort. This is the opposite method from the normal "tough-it-out grit your teeth and try harder" approach to learning and physical conditioning which dominates and determines all their other training. The type of relaxation sessions we're teaching lowers blood pressure and heart rate, improves circulation, and relieves chronic muscle tension; but the real value is that it asks these men to direct their attention internally, to what they feel, sense, and image. This is a radical change from their normal pattern of being outwardly directed toward an external goal. Through these exercises we're asking them to experience the power that comes from relaxation and focusing one's attention internally. For men trained to perform feats of bravado and to succeed through sheer will power this is like asking The Hulk to try knitting. Although some have read books on the use of visualizations for high performance, for most of them this is their first experience in exploring their inner landscape. The morning we introduced the guided visualizations they coughed loudly and snickered behind their hands; later they once again hummed the theme from "The Twilight Zone."

As the soldiers lie quietly on their backs with eyes closed, they are instructed to stay present by actively guiding their attention through different parts of their bodies. They're given techniques to strengthen concentration and to cultivate awareness of mind, body, and spirit. We do this together, in a circle, our heads pointing toward the center, with one of the training team members leading the exercise. These are ecstatic moments lying on the grass, steam rising off our bodies, the satisfying feeling of having completely spent ourselves. A brilliant blue sky is overhead; the earth receives our tired forms and weighty thoughts, and our breath moves as one wave in, one wave out. I experience a deep still point within myself. I chuckle imagining that in the cemetery next to us some steely-eyed, square-jawed drill sergeant is turning over in his grave as we go through these exercises.

After this morning's session I notice that Sheffield looks somewhat bewildered. Nothing really extreme, but I know him well enough by now to recognize that something is off. Sheffield is in his mid-twenties and he's from rural Georgia. He's your dream son-in-law—bright, well-groomed, cheerful to a fault, a smile the size of a Pontiac grill. An Eagle Scout with merit badges to spare, he's also a patriot and a rebel Southerner. When I asked him why he always runs by himself and not in a group he drawls, "Ah'm just workin' on my own pace, mah' own rhythm. The rest of the guys are always racin' with each other, like horses tryin' to get back to the barn. Hell, ah'm not doin' this to race, but to understand mah own rhythm and be in the best condition I can." He won my heart with that one. But this morning there's a shadow across his usual sunny disposition.

"How're you doing, Daryl?" I ask as casually as possible.

He glances away, uncomfortable with my unsolicited attention. He looks back and mumbles, "Ah'm okay." Before the program began he might have said something like, "What the fuck do you care?" or "Who wants to know?" Like most men these soldiers have developed deft strategies, usually macho ones, to mask their sensitivity. But at this point enough trust has developed between Daryl and me for him to remain emotionally present.

"What's bothering you?"

He watches the rest of his team members walk away before he speaks. "You know ah'm really getting to like this relaxation thing. I even do it at home before I go to bed and I taught mah wife how to do it. But ah'm not so sure that it's really good for me."

"How can relaxation be bad for you?" I wondered out loud.

"I just don't feel like my normal self after I go through the visualizations. Like now when we finished. I get rested and feel comfortable inside myself and the knot in my stomach is gone, but when I stand up I feel . . . well . . . I feel too weak."

"What do you mean by too weak?"

"Mah chest feels sunken, like I can't protect mahself." He looks dismayed.

Standing in front of me is a strong, powerfully built man who is telling me he feels too weak to protect himself. It would have been hilarious if he wasn't so serious about it.

"Who do you need to protect yourself from?"

"When you're in the S.F.," he replies quickly, "you're supposed to look a certain way, you know, strong and proud," and he pounds his fist against his chest. He then sets his jaw, narrows his eyes, and pushes his thick chest out. The relaxed, open Daryl is replaced by the "official" image of the Green Beret: armored, high center of gravity, hard eyes, withdrawn and suspicious.

I'm startled by his instant transformation. We walk back to our building in silence. "I think what's important is that you have a choice about how you want to be," I finally say. "You can let your guard down around your wife and kids, right? And if you're as close as you say you are with your teammates, you can let down there too."

He looks at me out of the corner of his eye. A council of chickadees swarm noisily over the English oak at the corner of the cemetery.

"I think you're also seeing in aikido that when you're up in your chest you're much less effective. You're stronger and more balanced when you're relaxed and in your center, you know that."

"Well, that's true," he says reluctantly.

What I heard behind Daryl's words is that he's beginning to change and he's uncomfortable with it. His self-image is beginning to shift and it's threatening to him. At a deeper level I also heard that he doesn't know how to make the transition from a smaller identity to a larger one. Learning to relax in a way that can heal the knot in his stomach and rejuvenate his energy is contradicting the official Army line, which in this case is the image of the tough Special Forces soldier with the armored body who always needs to be on guard. To learn the processes whereby they can become self-healing, self-educating, and self-knowing, we're asking these soldiers to feel themselves more deeply. In this deepening other things are beginning to surface, like emotional issues, and whether or not it's okay for a Special Forces soldier to be open and relaxed. What we don't know now is that it won't be until the middle of the second month, during the encampment, that we will begin to realize how central this issue is to our work. It will haunt us for the rest of the program, a festering boil on the back of an angry warthog.

War

August 31

The blanket of heat is oppressive and our *gis* are soon damp with sweat. I open the side doors of the dojo but instead of a cross breeze we get two plump chickadees watching curiously from the doorstep. The familiar acrid musk smell of men mixes with the dull sound of bodies falling to the mat. Because they have never seen aikido before it's been slow going shaping them into the proper *uke/nage* relationship. It's also educational and challenging for me. Instead of the clear grabs and disciplined strikes that I'm accustomed to from "normal" aikido students, they present an array of combinations that range from hard-charging football tackles to wild beer-hall right hooks.

I walk them along that line between fierceness and harmony. While there's a directness in aikido attacks and a follow-through in the throws, there is also an on-going bodily conversation that absolutely requires cooperation. Aikido is a strikingly beautiful art, but to think of it only in terms of flowing and blending would be to slander it. The practice of aikido demands that we live in contradiction and paradox; answers and solutions are guided by what is presented in the moment, not by fixed predispositions. This spontaneity of spirit makes it threatening for institutions and rigid minds.

Even though the moves may be soft at times, they are always done with a wholeheartedness of spirit. Aikido is rooted in the Japanese martial tradition of sword and jujitsu, arts that teach that the first move is a killing move. This lesson was conveyed to me by a teacher in Japan. During a practice session I had been irritated by an insistent and bothersome mosquito. Finally in exasperation I slapped it down to the mat. The instructor immediately came over to me and started shaking his head as if I had done something very wrong. He carefully picked the mosquito off the mat, cupped it in his hand, and began to blow on it gently. After a few moments the mosquito began to quiver and seemingly regained strength. The instructor solemnly opened his hand to show me the mosquito which was now very much alive. I was about to feel guilty for trying to kill this small insect when the instructor brought his hands together in a powerful and commanding crash. He opened his hand a second time to show the dark stain that remained of the mosquito. With a gleam in his eye he said, "Like this, fully!"

This intention toward total commitment, whether it's for creating or destroying, is a major lesson to be learned in aikido. But it's also balanced by a natural flow and order of things which Xenophon, even in the fifth century, commented on: "There is no beauty when something is forced or misunderstood."

Today we're focusing on joint locks and pins. Applied correctly these techniques, taken originally from jujitsu, can easily break a wrist or tear a shoulder from its joint. This is appealing to the men, but in their vigor they forget to center and ground. The tendency to lose ourselves in our work, relationship, or desires is a clear metaphor here. The bottom line is that we're only as effective as we are balanced within ourselves. This is a lifelong lesson—it's one that aikido throws in your face every day. If they bunch up in their shoulders, for example, or lean into me while doing one of these techniques, it's easy for me to stop them.

These men have initially seen aikido as something outside their masculine, patriotic, middle-class values, and the attempt to do it brings out the ways they've handled aggression. The larger ones try physically to intimidate me, others tell me their suspicions in their own ways, "Let me have a baseball bat and I'll show you an American martial art," Karter says. "Give me my .44 magnum—and then you try your technique," Farley challenges.

A primary strength of these men—the ability to quickly learn new skills and excel in every undertaking—has become somewhat of a liability during aikido. Their typical military record depicts a high-achieving risk-taker who consistently graduates at the top of his military classes. He's met and overcome obstacles where thousands of other soldiers have failed. Studying aikido challenges this history of certain achievement and success.

"It looks easy, so why can't I do it?" When Andrews asks me this question he's reflecting the idealism and certainly of post-Second World War America, that any obstacle can be overcome by the step-by-step application of will, reason, sweat, and if necessary, massed force. As they struggle to learn this powerful but subtle martial art they're having to face a fundamental tenet of the warrior's path. They're learning that the path of the warrior is lifelong, and that mastery is often simply staying on the path.

To compensate for their difficulties they do what almost everybody does in this art: They force when they should flow, hurry when they should wait, and tighten instead of relaxing. With frightful grimaces they hold their breath, flex their well-cultivated muscles, and try to push me around with mass and brawn. They're puzzled why they, with their superior strength, weight, and youth can't physically dominate me—I'm older, smaller, and less conditioned. The American recipe of a powerful will ordering around obedient muscles is ultimately an obstacle to experiencing the non-resistance of aikido. To their bewilderment, they are finding that aikido is not something one succeeds in by being stronger, and it's not just one more sport you can simply figure out and then do. It's a complete reprogramming in mind, body, and spirit.

September 1

I'm lying on my back in a hammock that is strung between a weathered elm and a Jonathan apple tree. The way the green leaves of the Jonathan rest against the blue sky is comforting; it reminds me of my early childhood when I would lie for hours dreaming into the sky. A few minutes earlier I had been unexpectedly provoked and I've come outside to be with myself.

This weekend I drove one hundred and fifty miles to Amherst to spend some time with old friends. This is a university town in a liberal state—the bulletin boards are brimming with posters advertising classes in meditation, radical politics, punk poetry, lesbian and gay rights, ecological action, and self-help groups. The psychological distance between this free-speaking society of intellectualism and the disciplined life of the Special Forces is considerably greater than the obvious political and cultural gulfs between them.

I go to a party at the home of friends of my friends. It's a restored handsome Victorian with spacious gardens. Most of the people at this gathering are professionals who are politically to the left and are actively engaged in their personal and spiritual development. They're similar in their beliefs and interests to my friends in the San Francisco Bay Area. People ask me what I'm doing in Massachusetts, and I tell them. The reaction is the same as it was in the Bay Area a month ago—they recoil at the mention of the Army. One woman, friendly until I spoke of my work with the Special Forces, summarily dismisses me with a hard glare, wheels abruptly on her heels, and stomps away as if to imply I have given no thought to what I am doing. But most become silent and act as if I had suddenly evaporated. They naively disregard me as a visitor from the wrong planet. I'm no longer the psycho-queer from San Francisco, but a conspirator with the Evil Empire.

At one point in the afternoon I wander into a large study and find myself part of a group discussing politics and foreign policy. A bearded fellow sitting quietly in the corner suddenly comes alive: "I've worked for the peace movement since 1970 and I believe that the military should be abolished because it's impossible to change the military mind." He's a faculty member at one of the local colleges and he speaks to the group as if he's in the lecture hall.

"I'm not so sure if I agree with that," a young man in a plaid shirt and tie offers. "It seems impractical and improbable that we could be without a military."

"There can be no peace as long as there's the military mind. **No Peace Whatsoever!!!**" the professor shouts threateningly. His jaw thrusts forward and his voice becomes shrill and demanding. Soon he's red in the face, jabbing his finger at the throat of his detractor. The room becomes still. People begin studying their shoes. His victim looks crushed, his eyes are glazed with humiliation. The peace advocate calmly sits back and resumes his composed professorial airs.

I'm offended and angry, but I say nothing. The peaceman reminds me that you don't have to be in the military to have a military mind; and it recalls the aggressive rhetoric of the peace movement: *Fight for peace, Stamp violence out, Throw out the bad elements, Eliminate the military.* When I watched this man erupt in violence and rage in the name of peace I thought of Krishnamurti's words, "War is but a spectacular expression of our everyday life."

I, too, am faced with my aggression. During this brief confrontation a surge of white heat pumps into my chest and arms. My urge is to stuff the professor's insulated righteousness, along with my fist, down his pompous throat. Here in the mannered living rooms of liberal, progressive thinking prowls the endless cycle of violence, polite and muted, but violence nonetheless. If feelings could kill it would have been a blood bath. I see the anger not only of the supercilious professor and myself, but in the pained expressions of the others, in the white knuckles gripping the chairs, the tightly held breath that so easily kills feeling. We're a violent people, at war with ourselves, and we carelessly spill this conflict into the lives of others. I leave the room for the back yard and I'm happy to find the multi-colored hammock empty.

Now lying in its easy rhythm I find the mosque blue sky forgives and absorbs my anger. I'm moved to draw meaning from this episode. What is most obvious is that the pent-up anger and undisciplined aggression of the peaceman is greater, by light years, than anything remotely similar to the men I've worked with for the past month. But to conclude anything from this comparison would not only be simplistic, but beside the point. I'm not interested in making one side right. But I do find myself searching to understand the complex relationship between our warrior heritage, aggression, and our addiction to war.

Almost anyone you ask—the professor, the liberals at this gathering, conservatives, the Special Forces—will decry war. Their reasons may differ—economic, religious, moral, historical—but their arguments all make sense. Yet with all our reasons not to fight, the human species has not lived in peace since its beginning. Instead of moving toward peace we're headed in the contrary direction, total annihilation, the destruction of life itself. Instead of lamenting, "Why is this?" we need to ask, "What is it in war that attracts us? How do we free the warrior spirit without destroying ourselves? How do we separate the warrior from war?"

We need to focus on these questions in a way that includes the deepest yearnings of our psyche. Historical, anthropological, philosophical, ethological, and ethical studies of war, and men in battle, are customarily posited from an other-than-me distance. Survey the countless world and military histories, or philosophical inquiries including Clausewitz's *On War,* and Sun Tzu's *The Art of War,* and the resistance to the idea that our martial heritage is a need originating in our psyche is quickly apparent. Even excellent works like S.L.A. Marshall's *Men Against Fire,* John Keegan's *The Face of Battle,* and Richard Holmes's *Acts of War,* reflect on men and war from a sociological and statistical perspective, keeping a good arm's length from the passion of their souls. Is war in man (and violence part of human nature)? Does war create men (do we use war to initiate young males into manhood)? Is war the result of our social organization? All these questions seem to have ended up in the laps of social scientists, while the rest of us act out policies national leaders determine. Animal psychologists report on caged rats eating their babies and male baboons punching it out on the savanna. We accept nature objectively, even stoically, but there is, it seems, a deep-seated complicity to repress the dark shadow of our warrior urges. Social scientists ignore their own professional aggression and symbolic homicides.

It occurs to me that part of being human is the longing, or perhaps even need, for the experiences of courage, selflessness, heroism, service, and transcendence. Young men have traditionally been led to believe that war will provide the sole context for these experiences. We're heir to that first human whose wholehearted commitment to bravery, selflessness, and service provided security for his family and tribe. The connection between the young boy of 500,000 years ago who learned to throw a spear from his father, and his twentieth-century incarnation who is taught marksmanship from his father, endures in the long muscles of our back, the sensitive grip of our hands, and our ability to stand upright and to look forward, with vision, across the plains, and then abstractly back into the lives of our ancestors. The urge that moved our warrior ancestor to pit his hunting skills against an opponent is replicated by us not only in war, but through the martial arts, sports, and even our recent paint-pellet war games. In our oral and written traditions the Greeks' Mars, Ares from the Romans, Christianity's St. James and St. George, the Africans' Ogu, Hinduism's Krishna and Arjuna, Islam's Mohammed, and the sword-bearing Manjusuri of the Buddhists are warrior spirits awakening our consciousness to the trumpet call of battle.

There is a connection, as crucial as an umbilical cord, that ties our aggression and war-making to the repressed urges of our warrior legacy. We need to own, celebrate, claim, release, and above all, de-literalize, in body and soul, the warrior within us. Let's liberate King David, Alexander the Great, Miyamoto Musashi, and Geronimo from our psychic closets before we falsely promise young soldiers their manhood by dying fighting communists in Nicaragua.

Instead of categorically disclaiming war as an evolutionary backfall into animal territoriality, or blaming industrialization, technology, geographical boundaries, ideologies, or the modern state, or burying our combative urges under exotic New Age rituals, we urgently need to embrace our warrior impulse. Wars are the work of man, and we must discover how they feed a hunger, even a love, that we as a people otherwise refuse to nourish. By discovering what needs war answers, perhaps we can design activities that fulfill them, activities that don't endanger the life of the planet.

People stroll by leaving the party, the professor stops at the gate to talk to someone. I feel more open to him now and I see that he's tired, probably under stress at home or work. He wants to do what is right, but he looks unhappy, bent over with his efforts to make a peaceful world. I imagine the men from the Post at this gathering, maybe even talking to the professor at the gate, and it makes me smile. I then imagine him in a green beret and camouflage uniform and I burst out laughing. Like them, he wants to have peace in the world, and like them he will fight for it.

September 3

Watching these men take their first steps on the aikido path, I recall when I started—the Hawaiian Islands, 1972. My five partners and I had just recently moved the Lomi School to Hawaii to teach our first training in a body-oriented psychotherapy. We had given up our homes and private practices in California for a communal living/work experiment. People were arriving from the mainland to join us and we were excited about our future.

I had heard about aikido the previous year, but it wasn't until a friend on the island of Kauai encouraged me to take it up that I made an effort to find a class. I can't really say why I was so curious about it; maybe it was the insistence of my friend, maybe it was my lifelong interest in the martial arts. Driving halfway across the island alone to my first class I kept thinking about my friends at their picnic on the beach. Why was I going, anyway? But the moment I walked through the door of the rusted Quonset hut that served as the dojo, I knew I was in the right place. Stepping into that building, I was immediately struck by an ancient feeling that remains poignant to this day. There were perhaps a dozen people, moving with such a natural beauty, grace, dignity, and fierceness I thought, "They're *living* the Tao." I marveled as the men and women before me actually embodied, and not simply contemplated, the timeless Taoist virtues of non-resistance, effortless effort, and the triumph of yielding. I quickly bought a *gi* and much to the bewilderment of my friends drove forty miles round-trip three times a week to practice. If there were classes seven days a week I would have been there. I was in love. My zeal was not fully shared and I was cajoled, criticized, and finally given up on by my friends, who were, after all, mellowed-out mainlanders newly moved to the islands.

"I'm not sure about you," they would say as if they were dealing with a lunatic, "driving halfway across the island at sunset. You might as well have stayed on the mainland if you like driving that much."

After a year in Kauai, our dream folded (interpersonal disputes) and I moved back to San Francisco. In the Bay Area I had the great fortune to study with three rather remarkable teachers, Mitsugi Saotome, Robert Nadeau, and Frank Doran. In 1975 I spent a season in Tokyo studying with Japanese masters. But I returned because the best instruction, or at least the best suited for me, was in my own back yard. Frank Doran taught me the fine detailing and sweeping-clean cuts of aikido; Mitsugi Saotome, who spent sixteen years at the side of Master Ueshiba as his *uchideshi,* startled me with the power and depth of his art; Robert Nadeau offered what is perhaps the most far-reaching and indispensable gift of all, a living map of how aikido can illuminate and enhance daily life. These men transmitted the knowledge of aikido to me, not only as a fierce and complete martial art, but also as a path for human understanding and communion. Pursuing technique one can become a competent martial artist and even excellent aikidoist, but without the guidance of an inspired teacher it's difficult to inhabit that dimension where one can become a healer, visionary, or diviner.

From the first moment I began studying aikido it has done nothing less than inform every aspect of my life, creating changes of earthquake proportion. While I could talk about its transformative effects on, say, my relationships, work, communication, ability for self-defense, or health, beyond language it has altered who I am in the bedrock of the spirit. I use this word spirit to signify an internal state of being that emerges into life as an embodied attitude. This state expresses a coherence between who we are internally and how we are in the world, as opposed to merely what we think about the world. The daily practice of aikido can teach us how to enact the virtues that we most value. Through this art I have learned that it's possible to bring my energy, or *ki,* into the world to touch others and be touched by them.

The sacredness of aikido is not limited to the dojo. As I've said before, I've also taught aikido and its principles to law enforcement officers, senior citizens, urban gang youth, the physically disabled, corporate executives, convicts, emotionally disturbed children, dancers, Olympic athletes, and professional football players. Aikido helps them perform and work better, and it's also a transformative physiological and psychological tool. It teaches those who must change how to change.

When Master Morihei Ueshiba, or "O-Sensei" (Great Teacher), as his students fondly called him, first began calling his art aikido (in 1942) he had already accumulated years of experience in other Japanese martial arts. By studying and mastering Daito-ryu jujitsu, sword, staff, and spear, Master Ueshiba rooted aikido in the ancient Bushido tradition. Testing his ideas in actual combat and armed confrontations he established aikido as a potent self-defense form. At the same time he spoke of aikido—The Way of Harmony—in a revolutionary way, a way previously unheard of among the martial traditions. He taught that aikido is a *budo* of love and that its purpose is to unite the people of the world. He repeatedly told his students that aikido was not to be used to hurt someone, but to provide loving protection for all people. It was as if the Secretary of Defense suddenly announced that the role of the Armed Forces was to provide a safe, loving environment for the entire world. There were, of course, guffaws when the word got out about a "budo of love" and many came to challenge Ueshiba and his new art. His adversaries included Sumo wrestlers, Western boxers and wrestlers, and the vast legion of trained warriors that are Japan's samurai legacy. Most of Ueshiba's detractors and challengers, however, were so moved by his personal power, calling him a man of "immovable spirit," that they remained as students and have since spread the teachings of aikido throughout the world.

As he developed aikido as a superior martial form he also concluded that the emphasis on winning at any cost and domination of others through force were anachronistic to the spiritual needs of contemporary society. Searching for a martial art that would meet the needs of the modern age, the Founder stayed true to the original vision of Budo: The cultivation and perfection of the spirit. Stressing that aikido was not a competitive sport, Master Ueshiba developed a martial form that empowered human beings from the inside out, without competition to decide winners and losers. He said that the "opponent is within" and that we must first work with our own minds and bodies before trying to correct and change others. He established dignity, compassion, and integrity as values more important than greed, domination, and the acquisition of power. Through the techniques developed in aikido he brought to the world an alternative to our current polarity of heavy-handed militarism or turn-the-other cheek pacifism.

But ultimately the aikido of Master Ueshiba is a spiritual path, one that teaches people to bring their spirit into harmony with a larger or Universal Spirit. Encouraging the physical practice of unifying our spirit with a Universal Spirit he envisioned the possibility of people participating in shaping a world of harmony, right action, and compassion. Through this ideal and his own ceaseless training, exploration, and struggle, Master Ueshiba created a prototype for a new warrior, able in self-defense, but dedicated to working with others without violence.

The Encampment

September 4

I'm in the downstairs office at home; the glow of the computer splashes into the darkened room, Anne's dog Shaba lies at my feet. I'm lonely and tired. It's almost midnight and I have been up since five-thirty A.M.; I'll be back up in another five and a half hours. I hear Jack rustling around upstairs, but everyone else is asleep. I feel I've been running on this schedule for years, even though it has been only six weeks. Up at five-thirty A.M., meditation, two workouts a day that include running, swimming, stretching, calisthenics, an hour and a half of aikido, classes in fitness, nutrition, and learning theory, the demanding and seemingly unending contact with the soldiers and my own team, in bed between eleven and twelve P.M. It's both exhilarating and fatiguing. At best it's a prototype for a warrior's training in the development of mind, body, and spirit; in the moment it feels like an exercise in endurance.

The one-month meditation retreat begins in less than a week. We're putting in extra hours planning logistics and scheduling. We have decided to call it an encampment instead of a meditation retreat. The word "meditation" creates too much of a reaction among the men. Mental training is acceptable, but to them meditation is mumbo-jumbo. In addition to two Army cooks, Joel's wife Michelle and her friend Barbara, who has experience cooking at large meditation retreats, will head the kitchen staff. A remote and rustic facility on a lake approximately two hours north will serve as the site. It's an old Boy Scout camp that is used only in the summers.

We've told only the company commander what will happen this month; at this point the troops know very little about the structure of the encampment. They do know it will be a field exercise spent in isolation, with most of the hours devoted to contemplation and mental training. We've told them the diet will primarily be vegetarian and we've asked them to abstain from tobacco and alcohol. This will be an *extreme* change from the first month's schedule. It will, in fact, be an extreme change from almost anything they have ever experienced. A one-month meditation retreat is cold turkey for anyone, but for these men—having little or no experience in a meditative discipline (or even sitting still for long periods of time), and who are accustomed to a schedule of rigorous physicality and to constantly interacting with each other verbally—this will be like fitting a Bengal tiger into a pair of spandex jeans. I hope we all survive it.

The type of retreat after which the encampment will be modeled is a sitting/walking silent practice that eventually builds to sixteen hours of meditation a day. While these retreats are built on the tenets of Buddhism, our will be strictly non-denominational.

Since nothing like this has ever been done in the American military before, much less in the Special Operations branch, we are following a point about an inch in front of our nose. Joel will be in charge of the encampment with me as his co-leader. This is pressing some of Jack's control buttons. He has reservations about asking the men to give up too much—tobacco, socializing, meat, alcohol (though this is no real problem)—too soon.

"Perhaps we could ease them into it," he suggests.

"I think we should go for it from the beginning," Joel counters thoughtfully. "Over the years I've seen many beginners enter a retreat with no experience at all and do very well with both the meditation practice and abstaining from their vices."

"I've even seen individuals use the retreat setting to begin taking themselves off a drug habit," I add. "It hasn't been easy, but with the proper support it's possible."

"This is a very supportive environment for the men to challenge these habits and give them up, or at least to look at the effects they have on them." Joel sits relaxed but ramrod straight in the cross-legged position, as though he were born for the posture. I'm beginning to feel him line up to the retreat. I like the way he's taking more responsibility.

Jack shakes his head and rolls his eyes, although I know behind his irony is a great deal of concern. "Okay, I'll go with it," he says slowly. "I don't feel totally comfortable with it, but I'll just have to trust your experience in this area. I also plan to get some meditation time in for myself. I could use it."

My meditation experience goes back almost twenty years. Every year for the past fifteen I have participated in a ten-day intensive meditation retreat. When I first began meditating I was motivated by vague, billowy notions of enlightenment. I longed for an antidote to the discontent in my life; the spiritual teachings of the East seemed to offer answers. In retrospect I realize that I was looking for a way to skip over the rough edges in life. Toward the end of the sixties I met my spiritual and meditation teacher, Maharaj Charan Singh, and through his instruction it quickly became apparent that meditation wasn't about flying over the barnyard, but very much about getting your feet down in the shit and walking through it. I fought it, fell in love with it, cursed it, ran away from it, and always returned to it.

I half-jokingly say that I meditate for my mental health. Meditation has numerous benefits: it sharpens concentration, reduces stress, and increases awareness. It also touches something much deeper than that, but deeper in a very immediate and direct sense. In a culture built on competition, instant gratification, and materialism, meditation cultivates our spiritual nature. And when I'm in contact with my spiritual side I'm more compassionate, more loving, and more forgiving. To the men, all this is foreign. We've barely introduced them to the rudiments and next week they'll begin their first retreat.

Joel is also a longtime meditator, having studied in depth with the Tibetan masters Kalu Rinpoche and Zong Rinpoche. Before the program began Joel and Michelle asked these and many other of their respected teachers what advice they had for them: did they even think he should be involved with a project like this? Both Tibetan masters supported the concept and emphasized the great opportunity for teaching soldiers alternative uses of power. Zong Rinpoche said cryptically, "Teach them courage." The Dalai Lama, spiritual leader of Tibet, also gave his complete approval and encouragement to Joel and Michelle and the program.

Joel has skillfully and creatively bridged the notorious distance between Eastern mysticism and Western science. The work he will present in the biofeedback lab and the brain synchrony training demonstrates and quantifies the effects of meditation on the performance of these men (again we frame it as mental training or inner technologies for the soldiers). Although he doesn't have an extensive background in leading or managing groups, his experience in meditation and mental techniques for stress reduction makes him the appropriate leader for the encampment. Joel's a large-hearted man. He doesn't want power, only for the encampment—our entire project—to succeed.

"I'm only the point man," Joel says. There is a distinct melody in his voice that sounds almost like a Canadian accent. "I want you two to continually give me suggestions and feedback. I know that the encampment may be the pivotal point for the success or failure of the project and that a great deal of responsibility is in my lap. So I'm open to all of the help I can get." There is silence, he looks Jack and me squarely in the eye. "Then let's go do it, guys." He gestures with his fist as if we're going into the Super Bowl in a few minutes.

Unexpectedly, I realize that I've no idea what kind of clothes Joel wears outside of the project. I've seen him only in our SportsMind uniform—khaki pants and lavender shirt. I have an overwhelming urge to ask him how he *really* dresses. I look closely at him. He has the spiritually rich countenance one sees in the paintings of the early Christian mystics—thin and bony, with his curly hair and bright eyes standing out in a sharp, angular face. He responds to my studied gaze with a bright smile, eyes shining like headlights.

I suddenly have a wave of appreciation for him. "I'm glad you're in aikido class," I tell him. "I know it's tough on your knee. I guess I just want you to know that I like having you in class. I know the men like it, too."

"I get a lot out of your classes," he responds. "I also feel like the men take good care of me in aikido. They could easily break me in two, but they're actually quite sensitive. I had a great time in yesterday's class fooling around with Dunham."

His rapport with the men is different from the physicality and male camaraderie that Jack and I have with them. Because of his chronic knee ailment he's unable to attend the physical training or aikido portions of the program regularly and this puts him in even less contact with the soldiers in areas on which they place a great deal of importance. While they admire his scientific knowledge and dedication to meditation, he's also a bit exotic to them. The other day Oreson said to him, "Joel, I'm surprised how much I like you. I guess old hippies aren't all bad."

In an affectionate way they half-jokingly half-seriously talk about the shine in his eyes as being either pure madness or the beneficent gaze of a saint. He has a sign above the passage to the biofeedback lab that reads DANGER: MIND FIELD. This amuses them and—as much as they openly allow—endears him to them. Sergeant Martin, the brilliant communication specialist of Team 260, paid their ultimate compliment: "Joel makes the grade in our book because he's genuine. He doesn't try to be something he's not. He is who he is."

Outside I hear the faint hoot of an owl. The words on the page are starting to blur into each other. Even now I dread thinking about getting up in five hours.

September 5

The results from the second Army Physical Readiness Test (A.P.R.T.) came in today. I feel both encouraged and concerned. In terms of the physical fitness project they demonstrate an enormously successful first month. We've stated our goals as: 1) to maintain the men at their already-high level of fitness, 2) to improve their areas of weakness, 3) to improve overall team fitness rather than focus on the highest individual performance attainable. To meet these goals we've been emphasizing a synergistic approach to performance that includes mind, body, and spirit. We didn't train specifically for the test or customize individual training regimes to produce extraordinary scores.

The improvement from the first test is dramatized by the fact that most of the men entered the program with scores that already surpassed Army *maximum* standards. Team 260, for example, averaged 21% above the Army's maximum scale by age groups for push-ups, 12% above maximum on the sit-ups, and 2% above on the two-mile run. Team 560 averaged 12% above for push-ups, 1% above for sit-ups, and 3% below for the two-mile run. Many of the individual scores were considerably higher than these high averages.

Even with these high entering marks, every area was improved in the second test. In Team 260, push-ups increased by 6.2%, sit-ups by 4.9%, pull-ups by 29.7%, stretch by 7.8%, and an average 32 seconds was dropped from the two-mile run. In Team 560, push-ups increased by 6.2%, sit-ups by 4.8%, pull-ups by 29.7%, stretch by 7%, and again an average of 32 seconds was dropped from the two-mile run. Some of the individual scores began to border on the supernormal: five soldiers performed over 90 push-ups within the allotted two minutes, one individual pumping out almost 120.

To our minds this dramatic increase in strength, endurance, and flexibility has as much to do with the mental training in concentration, visualization, relaxation, and mind/body integration as it does with the physical training itself. A great deal of credit goes to exercise physiologist Horst Abraham, who headed the physical training section for this first month. His inspirational lectures on fitness and nutrition were made all the more credible by his ability to stay with and often surpass the men in their physical training. These men see running as an area in which the mettle of an individual can be tested. Horst, in his late forties, became the embodiment of his message by outrunning many of the youngest and strongest of them. His being able to "walk his talk" transformed them into a rapt audience for his lectures on the importance of the mind/body/spirit triad for successful performance.

While I should be celebrating these test scores, I feel troubled instead. Being in such tremendous physical shape has a quality of seductiveness about it that I don't trust. If we interpret these scores to mean that we're successful at our job we might as well be coaching trained monkeys. For the men to reach their full potential, it's necessary for each one to know his Achilles' heel. I say, illuminate their blind spot. Knowing themselves internally, rather than perfecting a skill, is the crux of what we have to offer.

The reputation of these men as rough-and-tumble fellows preceded them for each of us, and we were somewhat wide-eyed about teaching Green Berets—but basically we were just unfamiliar with who they really are. To a certain degree we had bought into the Hollywood version—we thought the cornerstone of our work would be to teach them how to do things in a more subtle and effortless fashion. But since they're fast learners, able to integrate new skills quickly, the goal of emphasizing new ways of learning became a foundation stone, certainly not the cornerstone. Providing new skills or correcting an imbalance is far different from discovering and illuminating their limitations and deepest fears.

Unless we provide a strong emotional and energetic base the techniques and skills we're teaching will not be totally integrated. If we don't touch a certain depth of their being, the information we're passing on will be one-dimensional and superficial. Simply said: To tap the full potential of these men, or of any practitioner or student, it's necessary to touch the whole person, not just the physical athlete. It is simply not possible to pluck a potential or capacity out of someone, train it, and then re-insert it as an integrated part of the person's identity. In order for this potential to be fully embodied and woven into their moral fiber, the whole person—physical, mental, emotional, and spiritual—must be taken into account. "We need," as Jack so aptly put it, "to uncover and work with what these men fear most because what we don't know does hurt us."

The question is: Does the institution of the Army want their Special Forces soldiers to experience themselves as whole persons? Do they want them to feel at all? If they feel themselves they will feel others, including their enemies. If they experience others as living, sentient beings they will no longer become abstractions. If they are not abstractions they will think and consider more for themselves. Will the Army tolerate this? Will any institution tolerate this? Is this the Achilles heel?

September 6

Joel is sitting cross-legged on the floor of his room sorting through stacks of books, papers, and odd-sized piles of clothes. The calming sound of an Indian flute floats from a tape cassette buried somewhere in his chaos. His back is toward me and his hair spirals out wildly from his head. He sits very straight and is absorbed in a slightly rumpled and soiled manuscript.

After a moment he turns in my direction: "Oh, Stroz. Look at this. I thought this might be interesting reading for the troops during the encampment." He hands me an article titled "The Perfection of Concentration" by Geshe Rabten, a Tibetan lama; he then picks up another paper and is immediately absorbed in it. The first line of the manuscript states, "Concentration is important in both Dharma practice and ordinary life." Further down a paragraph begins, "Primary consciousness itself is pure and stainless, but gathered around it are the fifty-one secondary mental elements." On the next page there's a line drawing of a Buddha with a halo around his head; on the facing page is a picture of a monk guiding an elephant along an ascending path. At the bottom of the page the elephant begins on the path completely black with the monk herding him from behind. As the monk and elephant move up the page a transformation takes place. At the top of the page, which is the end of the path, the elephant is completely white and the monk is sitting serenely on his back.

Joel's bright blue eyes appear in front of me: "I thought I might take some of this, too. A friend just back from India sent it to me." He lights a long stick of brown incense and conducts the smoldering wand in front of my nose. He flashes his crazy-wisdom smile as the flute sound reaches a high octave and buzzes around our heads.

"Let me read this, Wiz," I say, "and I'll tell you what I think." He hands me the incense as I walk away.

Down the hall I peek into Jack and Anne's room. Anne is lying in bed wrapped in a down comforter reading a book while Jack sits on the floor tying a piece of leather into the O ring of a Swiss Army knife. Shaba lifts his head in my direction and wags his tail lazily.

"Oh, hi Richard," Anne says, noticing Shaba notice me. It looks as though everything from the drawers and closets has been emptied onto the floor here, too. There's two of everything: rucksacks, clothes, books, sleeping bags, papers, blankets; a horde of small nylon bags produces a rumpled landscape on the floor.

"Stroz, you might need an extra pair of these." Jack tosses me a pair of thick polypropylene socks, barely glancing in my direction. "Do you have any of this? It will probably come in handy, too." He passes me a small plastic container of Cutter's mosquito repellent.

The encampment is beginning to take on the feeling of a long voyage. The things that I unpacked a month ago I'm packing up again. Heading into fall up north I pack more cold-weather clothes—sweaters, jackets, polypropylene long underwear, boots, rucksack, sleeping bag, extra *gis* for aikido. As well as preparing for sitting meditation we will be taking long rucks in order to maintain the physical conditioning program, albeit with less intensity. In addition to this I'm in charge of moving the entire dojo—eighteen hundred square feet of mats—to the encampment site. Have dojo, will travel.

September 8

The first leg of our journey to the encampment actually takes me back to the Post to pick up some files. I have an unexpected urge to see the dojo so I walk alone up the deserted company street and go in through the classroom. With the mats gone, weapons removed, and O-Sensei's photo taken down it again looks like the empty shell we started with; it's an abandoned nest, all the birds having migrated away.

Darwin wrote in *The Descent of Man* that this impulse is so strong some mothers will abandon their chicks in the nest to make the long journey south. He wrote that a certain goose, when deprived of its flying feathers, began to walk the migratory route on foot. Another species of bird, penned up during the migratory season, bloodied itself beating against its cage for release. Ours is a migration of the soul.

Jack and I are in one car, Joel and Michelle are ahead of us in the other. We'll be in the camp a day before the men to scout it out and set up. We travel east and northeast for about an hour and then head almost directly north toward the Canadian border. The trees blush gold, yellow, red in the clear autumn light. We pass roughly framed roadside stands selling the harvest of apples, pears, corn, squash, juices, beans, jams, and honey. While we are stopping for some fresh-squeezed apple juice the red-cheeked woman who takes our money looks at our packed car and says, "Nice day to go camping."

By the time we reach the site, threatening clouds have rolled in from the north and a thick mist turns things cold. Changing to wool sweaters we begin to explore the cabins and meeting rooms that will be our home for the next month. Boy Scout emblems and totems decorate the rustic buildings. A large pond stretches to the north; the wood cabins, dining area, and shower rooms cluster on the small hills edging the southern portion. We choose a cabin that is located just off the dirt road that enters the camp. We decide to house each team in their own set of cabins behind the dining hall. The dining/meeting hall has an enormous stone fireplace with large rough timbers framing the walls and ceiling. We move the tables and chairs to the side and lay the aikido mats in the remaining space.

I like the feeling here: it'll be a fine place for aikido. I've practiced the form in almost every conceivable situation—from the classic dark-wood, *tatami*-matted dojos in Japan, to training on dusty straw mattresses in a two-centuries-old courtyard in Greece. This rustic, sturdy building fits somewhere in the middle.

Our cabin has one bedroom, a small sitting room, and an enclosed porch with windows on three sides. Joel takes the bedroom and Jack and I bunk on the porch. We unpack our gear in silence and use our sleeping bags as blankets. There is a view through the foliage of the lake. With the trees shedding their leaves I know this vista will look entirely different in a month. I drop quickly off to sleep.

Sometime later I'm startled awake by a deep rumbling sound. At first I think an animal has broken into our cabin and I reach for the wooden sword I keep by the side of my bed. I sit up on one elbow to see where the sound is coming from and then realize it's Jack snoring. And I mean SNORING. Nobel Prize Snoring. Suddenly I'm filled with dread realizing that this is the end of my sleep for a month. I'm also impressed by how loud and resonant the sound is. "How does Anne do it?" I wonder.

"Jack," I whisper. No answer. "Jack!" I say a little louder. Nothing. "JACK!" I shout.

"Huh? What is it?" he mumbles.

"Jack, you're snoring," I whisper.

"Oh," he says and drops back on his pillow asleep. In a few moments he resumes his large bellowing roars. I walk over to his bunk and look down on him. War hero, father of three, boxing champ—but here with the moonlight softening his face he looks young and innocent, sleeping peacefully like a small boy. He must sense me and he shifts position. For a moment he stops snoring. Outside the forest is thick and close; far off in the distance the dry leaves rattle under the movement of some animal. I feel a great love and appreciation for this man. The intensity of the six weeks we have been together make it seem like a lifetime. In this moment I know Jack and I are brothers. We'll be friends for life.

His snoring starts again and rumbles like thunder through the room. "Jack," I whisper, "turn on your side." I nudge him with my hands. He turns over and stops snoring.

September 9

The small convoy of vehicles can be heard first grumbling in the distance as it moves through the dense forest. As the men disembark they are joking, whistling, making snide remarks. Farley unbuttons his trousers and pees on one of the tires of the truck. What is he saying? "I'm marking out my territory," or "Don't try to domesticate me."

"These men," Jack says to no one in particular, "are in a profession that requires an almost mythical capacity and at the same time they often act like children."

"Maybe the skill is to address them as soldiers and men while remembering that young boys lurk in those hulking bodies."

Joel joins us, "A couple of days ago Farley told me how afraid he was of the encampment. He said, 'Except for being in a hide site, I don't think I've ever sat still in one place for any period of time. I'm afraid I might go crazy sitting in one place for so long.'"

"Him and twenty-four other guys."

Because directly after the encampment we will go on a three-day forced march, they're wearing their cammies, full rucksacks, and everyone is carrying his M16, some with attached grenade launchers. I'm surprised that I don't find it out of place to see a strong military presence in such an idyllic setting. It seems that we, the teachers, are being trained as much as the soldiers. Trained in what? Acceptance. Breaking down stereotypes. Seeing the person through the uniform.

A few of the men are gathered around Wilson as he points to something in a nearby maple. I go over and they're looking at a small bird the size of a swallow with a dark head.

"Blackpoll warbler," he says quietly. The mood is almost reverent. "We're on his migratory path," he continues. "He flies south from Canada every fall to the Northeast U.S. and spends about two to three weeks feeding and filling up before he flies twenty-five hundred miles, *nonstop!*, to South America."

Somebody whistles softly, "That's stamina. Can meditation do that for us?" We're intently absorbed in this remarkable little creature as a stream of information pours from Wilson about feeding habits, mating rituals, and migratory paths. I imagine Mr. Blackpoll relating to his kin about us:

"They migrate in every direction regardless of the season. All the males stay together and most of the time they wear the camouflage plumage to hid themselves in the woods. They can be boisterous and noisy but also very quiet and attentive. Watch out for the fire sticks they carry. They think of themselves as being spontaneous and free, but they are really very predictable. Their behavior has more range than any of the other animals. Their greatest attribute is their ability to love. Their greatest fault is that they think they know something."

A quick flick of his wings and he's gone. We stay for a moment looking into the reaches of the forest—the deciduous trees are whimsical and sad in their turning colors, the conifers majestic and graceful with their long swooping branches and straight trunks.

I look at Wilson: "Thanks, that was nice." He looks back and nods.

September 10

When Jack started snoring again last night I shouted very loudly, **"Jack! Roll on your side!"** which he did and instantly stopped snoring. He doesn't really remember what happens and Joel doesn't hear either the snoring or my shouting. I suspect that this nocturnal drama is going to be mostly mine.

At six A.M. muster the mist rising off the pond casts everything in an otherworldly light. Figures seem to emerge out of nothing, then are swallowed up again. The men stand at attention in formation while the flag is raised; Joel, Jack, and I stand a bit to the side in our own formation. The barking of a large crow dominates the stillness, a grey heron lumbers through an opening in the mist and glides toward the western shore. Top Sergeant Dudley barks a command, the men snap off their salute and we quickly break into our running groups—the Wolves, Poodles, and Stallions. We do a light stretch, run for forty to forty-five minutes, and then end with abdominal work, push-ups, and stretching. The Wolves are mostly the younger men, the fastest and the most fit. The Poodles are the middle group, and the Stallions are mainly the older men. Back at the Post I tried running with the Wolves, men sometimes half my age, but in trying to keep up with them I was running out of my fitness range and it was taking me too long to recover. Seeing me after a run doubled over, out of breath, and on the verge of heaving my guts up, Johnson said, "You're getting your ass kicked." Jack runs with the Stallions; and because of his knee injury Joel does a workout on his own, either cycling, swimming, or fast walking.

This morning the Poodles run like a single animal through the colorful fall forest. Steam rises off our bodies. There are moments when our breath becomes one breath and we fall into a collective rhythm absorbing all effort. This sense of togetherness is a sacred democracy.

Except for an hour and a half of aikido the day focuses on the sitting and walking meditation. Today we sit for only fifteen minutes at a time, with a thirty to forty-five minute walking meditation; as the month progresses we will hopefully increase the sitting time to two hours at a time. At the height of the encampment we will ideally be doing a sitting/walking meditation from sixteen to eighteen hours a day. I personally savor the time to sit and focus my mind, but I feel an underlying restlessness among the troops. The older men seem more settled in, but there's a resistance among the younger men that is being manifested as an aloofness, even a cold, smoldering anger. They're also talking freely among themselves as if they never agreed to silence during this time. I feel a bit like a teacher riding herd on a bunch of first-graders. I'd like to be free of this role as soon as possible. I keep reminding myself how novel this is for them and that it will take some time for them to adjust to the newness of this kind of mental training. The quiet, contemplative time will surface many issues. The psychic landscape will change as much as the colors of the trees.

We just found out that the Army has failed to deliver meat for the encampment meals. Somewhere along the supply line someone forgot to order it. Do we have saboteurs in the ranks? The menu was not planned to be totally vegetarian and with the many carnivores in this group this is not good news. We're unsure if we can get the meat now and it's clear that the men aren't happy with the news. This adds an unwanted twist into an already tense situation.

September 11

After a day and a night of a damp, weeping sky a brisk wind from the north uncovers a brilliant morning. The pond has small whitecaps on it, foam crystals collecting the sun. Staggered Vs of migrating geese punctuate the freshly scrubbed sky.

I'm sitting on our back porch overlooking the small glade that borders this part of the pond. I'm balancing my notebook on my right knee and holding an icepack to my left hamstring. Running wind sprints this morning I felt strong and fluid. On the tenth and last sprint I was neck and neck with Captain Parker, as I had been all morning. I could feel I had another gear so I pushed ahead. As I started to accelerate, a searing pain seized my left leg. It was as if someone with a hot iron glove grabbed the back of my leg and wrenched it as hard as they could. The pain shot me in the air and I immediately pulled up; the medics were instantly by my side. Scott had me lie on his sweatshirt and he carefully probed the leg and joints. I was my usual horrendous patient trying to push him away, but he gently and firmly kept me in place.

"Just settle down and wait a few moments, sensei. Let's get an icepack on that bugger first thing," he chided.

He sat with me and Karter, the other junior medic, ran for the medical bag. Soon they had an icepack taped to my hamstring. I used them as supports as they both walked me back to my cabin. As he left, Scott looked over his shoulder and chuckled through his toothy grin, "Hey, now you can practice that healing stuff on yourself. Let me know how it works."

So again I find myself injured because of competing with one of them. The leg is painful enough that I have to be mindful of it, but if I pay close attention I can still teach aikido. It's the feeling of vulnerability and helplessness that is the hardest for me. I want to be vital, in charge, and one hundred percent able to respond to any situation. When I'm vulnerable like this I feel helpless and when I feel helpless I get angry. When I struggle with pain like this, I'm also less capable of healing myself. And yes, it's in this way that I'm also impatient with the pain of others. I have long realized that I become angry and impatient when my children are sick because it's so difficult for me to tolerate the feeling of helplessness. I have a strong urge to do something, when what is really needed is simply to be with them in their suffering. I also believe that my competitiveness is linked to this sense of vulnerability. That is, if I win and am better than others, then I won't be so vulnerable. In truth I'm actually stronger when I'm feeling my vulnerability, because I'm not expending so much energy defending myself.

Through the thick limbs of a black spruce I can see Joel walking down the path to our cabin. His head is forward in thought. He doesn't see me on the steps with my icepack. With his notebook, papers, and books in hand, he looks like a college professor mulling over some deep philosophical question. The last twenty-four hours have been something of a minor mutiny and he has a lot on his mind. The men have expressed angry complaints about the food, the silence, the sitting, and the walking meditation.

"What's the point? I just don't get what the point of it is!" Martin kept repeating, as though he were the keeper of the mantra for their collective frustration. For most of the men a deep-seated rage is beginning to boil under their surface irritation. I speak personally to Oreson, Braddock, and James and tell them that the first few days always invoke these kinds of responses; it's important and valuable to examine their resistances. Later in the day Oreson approaches me and says he is beginning to settle in more and making the blend. But most of the men are withdrawn and not dealing with the feelings that are rising in them.

I call Joel over: "I think we need some kind of group meeting where the men can have some opportunity to ventilate their feelings." He's chewing on something in his mind and he's distracted by my suggestion.

"Yes, we should think about it," he says vaguely.

"Probably before it reaches much more of a head," I persist.

"Let's you and I and Jack talk later," he offers. "I have to go through some notes for my talk tonight." He walks in the cabin and the screen door slams itself after him.

As I shift my weight a stab of pain shoots up my leg. I don't know if I reached Joel or not. I'm suddenly concerned that we're veering off course, a runaway train with no one at the wheel. A group of soldiers walk along the road talking among themselves. They glance briefly at me. Rollins nods and then quickly looks away. There's a conspiratorial feeling in the air that I'm uncomfortable with. This is like no other meditation retreat I have ever been to and I'm not so sure I like it.

September 12

The sitting period after lunch is usually the hardest. Full stomachs and the afternoon heat make it more difficult to concentrate. Someone in the back of the room is snoring and when someone farts a few men laugh much harder than is called for. Reardon stares absent-mindedly out the window; Thayer looks like he's picking his toenails; Rader is staring hard at me with an expression of contempt on his face. Something rises in me and takes form as thought and emotion.

'We should have never done this in the first place,' I think angrily. Then fear wells up in me: 'Who knows what these guys might do. One of them could explode under the pressure. We're asking too much of them too soon.' I can feel my center lift to the top of my head. I'm lost in thought. I close my eyes, let my breath completely out, and refocus my attention. There is a dull ache in my leg where I pulled the muscle. I relax into it; the ache gives way to a throbbing sensation about the size of a golf ball. I imagine my attention as a laser beam of white light mending the torn muscle. My breath deepens; somewhere in the distance a plane buzzes lazily in the sky. I wonder what Tiphani, then D.J., are doing now.

I collect my attention again and focus it on the rising and falling of the breath. It's a tide that sweeps in and then flows out in an endless circle, a relief from the tension in the room, a cistern from which I can drink the cool waters of the soul. A surge of paranoia pierces me like a splinter of light, 'What about Rader? Maybe I should keep my eyes on him; he looks like he's ready to pop.' I again pull my attention back to my breath and settle under the rush of energy that is streaming through my body. Someone to my left goes into a coughing fit. 'Is it because they're quitting smoking or because they haven't quit?' I wonder. I bring my attention back. The quiet soothing waters are still there, always there, always waiting. It's me that leaves.

Joel rings the small brass bowl that we use to signal the beginnings and endings of the sitting sessions. The sound seems to spread both out into the room and inward filling my bones. In his soft, cooing voice Joel begins to speak, "As you begin the walking meditation try to maintain an on-going awareness of . . ." Before he's finished Braddock and Rollins are on their feet walking out the door. The screen door slams; they stamp loudly down the steps. Some of the other men begin to get off their sitting cushions; others sit quietly.

Joel clears his throat: "It's important that there's a continuity between your sitting practice and the other activities of the day. In a relaxed way apply the same presence of mind that you have in your sitting practice to your walking, eating, aikido, and P.T." Someone farts; there's laughter;

Thayer dramatically holds his nose and groans. There's a tightening in my stomach. I can't distinguish whether it's fear or anger.

Two jays squabble in the eaves outside a window, but for a moment it's quiet in the cabin. Harner, Mattelli, Dunham, Rader, and Thorne continue to sit; despite the rough edges they have an anchoring effect in the room.

"You can now begin the forty-five-minute walking period," Joel says, his voice barely carrying above the quarreling jays.

September 13

A dark thunderhead of tension arrives with the men as they file into the meditation hall. They're sullen and withdrawn, hiding behind masks of indifference. The usual horsing around is replaced by an explosive silence; my chest tightens in response. I inhale deeply, straightening myself on the sitting cushion. The men take their seats and stare blankly at nothing.

Freeze-out.

This is the "I will give you nothing" game. It's near the end of the first week of the retreat and all the pressures of the previous two weeks, or perhaps since the program began, have been compressed into this small space. It feels as if a sudden noise or movement will combust the room.

No sooner do I wonder who will light the fuse when Jack breaks the silence. "In the weeks before the retreat," he starts, "we briefed you about what would be required in terms of the silence, no-smoking rule, diet, and intensive meditation practice. You gave your word to follow the procedures, but now that the idea has become a reality most of you, as far as we can tell, have continued to talk among yourselves, the smokers have continued to smoke, and there's a minimum, if any, effort toward the meditation practice. We need to talk about this and we need to know what you're going to do to make it right."

They sit like tombstones. Jack's comments fall flat against their stony exteriors. There's a strained silence before he continues, "We expected more from Special Forces soldiers." A ripple surges through the group: jaws tighten, eyes come into focus, there's the forced sound of expelling breath. "If you are the best the Army has to offer . . . " he shrugs, holding his hands up in a gesture of loss. This pulls the plug.

Dunham jumps to his feet, face beet-red, barely controlling his anger. "What right do you have to question who we are? You don't know what we're about! We'll be here long after you leave!" he shouts.

Rollins joins in, spitting out the words as though they're a bad taste in his mouth. "You're civilians!! What the fuck do you know about the Special Forces anyway!?"

Suddenly a barrage of accusations pour from the group; everybody seems to be shouting at once. They're angry at authority, angry at having to be silent, angry about the food, angry that we would judge them, Special Forces soldiers. They're contemptuous of the emphasis on Eastern thought and at the idea of a Special Forces soldier sitting in one place and meditating. The cacophony of shouts and insults is suddenly broken by Rader, who stands up, his six-foot-plus frame filling the room. He takes a few menacing steps forward and in turn gives each of us the finger as he bellows, **"Fuck you and fuck you and fuck you!!!"**

There is so much rage in the room I feel as if it will burst open at the hinges. I have visions of us desperately fighting our way to safety; then I think we should go back to the meditation practice. Paranoia and denial. I've been practicing meditation for almost twenty years and nothing has prepared me for what is happening now. At the height of the uproar a small group of men raise clenched fists and chant, **"Attica! Attica! Attica!"** This is not the contemplation and insight of monastic life, it's the bedlam and anarchy of the jungle. The terrifying breakdown of order. The thought that comes to mind in the middle of this chaos is, "So this is meditation in everyday life."

The shouting discharges the surface layer of tension. Then one at a time their grievances pour out, creating a dark river of discontent. Joel takes a tremendous amount of flak and I feel like his big brother, wanting to rush to his defense. Many of the men are careful with him, prefacing their comments with, "Don't take this in the wrong way, but I'm not really sure you know what you're doing."

Rader, in his usual point-blank fashion, sums up their feelings: "Joel, you're just too airy and up in the clouds. You're not grounded. I don't think you know how to reach us and what we need. Maybe you can meditate but I don't know if you can teach it. It's your voice, Joel, that drives me crazy. It's too . . . I don't know, it just drives me crazy! I feel like you're telling us a bedtime story, like you're soothing me to sleep. I don't want to go to sleep! I don't want to be told stories about the Buddha. I want to know how this will help me. Quit cooing at me in that tone of yours!"

The complaints toward me are centered around teaching aikido while in the meditation retreat: "Are we sitting in silence or are we doing aikido? We should do one or the other. It's too confusing otherwise." Their issues with Jack are control and trust. For ambiguous reasons they don't trust him and they feel he holds the reins too tight. Listening to them lodge their complaints I sense a huge chasm between us.

"Look, guys," I begin, "you're simply sitting quietly with yourselves and then this rage pours out of you and you blame us. What's that about? Take responsibility for your anger and quit laying it on us." I'm starting to heat up myself. "I'm tired of your resistance. Making us your problem is beside the point. I think this anger is in you all the time, it's just coming out now because you're not distracted by the rest of your life."

Rollins snaps back, "No, it's not natural to sit like this. Anyone would get upset over it. I hardly ever feel like this. The situation is making me angry."

"The anger is yours," I point out. "Maybe if you're more aware of it, it won't interfere with your mission, or family life."

"I'm not angry," he testily responds. "Ask any of these guys. I just don't want to do this." I'm frustrated that they're so irresponsible about their emotional lives, especially when this is such an incredible opportunity to work with them. It's staring them point-blank in the face, but it's obvious they're missing it.

"You do all these dangerous things," I continue, "but you're afraid of your own feelings. This is the emotional equivalent of jumping out of a plane for you guys. Take a risk! Jump!"

Jack tries a different tack, "You broke your word and now your honor and integrity are at stake. I want to know how you're going to account for that?" His disappointment in them turns him resolute. Joel, for the most part, sits quietly and takes everything in. Either he's the embodiment of the Buddha nature—patient, open, compassionate, understanding—or he's in a state of shock.

A number of the older men—and the few that are serious about the meditation practice (though it's also true that some of those who were angry are also serious about the encampment)—keep quiet during the tirade and speak when things settle down. They remind me of parents watching their children act out, who are wise enough not to react. At one point Mattelli, combat veteran, keen-minded intellectual, warrior, a professional through and through, leans over and whispers, "They have to do this. Don't take it personal; just let them go through it."

"I'm concerned that all this stuff is going to get in the way of those of us who want to take advantage of this time," Harner says. "Hell, you all knew what was expected; it's not going to kill you. Let's get on with it!"

James captures everyone's attention when he speaks in his soft measured voice: "What about if those of us who are serious stay in tents or hooches away from the others. That way we won't be bothered or be tempted to join in on the socializing. Maybe we'll affect the others in a positive way, too." This raises eyebrows, and some eyes roll. There's a long silence. He's suggesting the unspeakable—break up the teams, let go of the chain of command.

"No, I don't like it," Dudley gnashes his teeth and shakes his head. "I'm responsible for these men and if we're sleeping all over the damn place I won't have any control at all." He glances at Captain Harwood for support.

"Yeah, yeah, why not try it?" someone in the back of the room says.

Rader, who has settled down after getting his rocks off giving us the finger, says, "I think Tom has a great idea. We could report in once a day and the team sergeant would know where our sleeping area is. It's not like we're going to be running off somewhere."

"I'm not so sure some of you might not try and leave," Jack retorts.

"I'm not so sure either," the company commander says. There's something about this idea that sticks. We finally decide to have the teams go back to their quarters and talk it over.

The entire program, and the meditation retreat in particular, asks these men to look within themselves for authority and responsibility. This challenges the most sacred of all military institutions, the chain of command. Like most of us, they seek autonomy and the freedom of choice; and at the same time they're afraid of it, wanting an external authority to tell them what to do. In his essay "Ego and Group Psychology" Freud warns us over and over never to underestimate our need to follow, to give our will to an outside authority. In the context of the Armed Forces this struggle is even more intense for the Special Forces soldier. While they are chosen for their qualities of independence, self-reliance, and resourcefulness, they are also expected to follow orders and fit into the code of the U.S. Army. While they *are* the elite, they are also part of the institution. This puts them perilously close to a double-bind situation. The modern warrior may ultimately be asked to pay tribute to valid institutions such as the chain of command when necessary, and also to have the freedom to make personal choices from a set of inner values and morality. Now these men are experiencing the fear that arises in the transition from an external authority to an internal authority.

Tonight we're learning how important it is to work with and give expression to that fear.

Jack, Joel, and I talk about the frustrations and anger long into the night, and a great deal of emotions and feelings are cleared. It's apparent that on one level we are asking too much of them too soon. We designed the meditation retreat so there would be minimum time spent on physical activity and maximum time for sitting quietly developing concentration, attention, and awareness skills. We also asked them to give up tobacco and alcohol, to limit their conversation to matters of operational necessity, to live in isolation from their families and society, and except for a few meals of fish or chicken to eat a vegetarian diet. We asked them, in other words, to give up much of their usual routine and habit, in order to sit and pay attention to what they feel, think, and sense. This is a tall order for anyone, especially for men who shudder at the mere mention of the word "meditation." If you're a strong, young man accustomed to a life of physical activity and constant interaction this change of pace might be enough to drive you crazy.

The radical shift in diet, physical activity, and daily routine has created pressures that have revealed the Achilles' heel of these soldiers. At this point their vulnerability *is the denial of their vulnerability*. For a warrior this denial is very dangerous. When I mentioned this to Jack and Joel, Jack said, "Believing you can be perfect is the fatal imperfection. Believing you're invulnerable is the ultimate vulnerability. Being a warrior doesn't mean winning or even succeeding. It means risking and failing and risking again, as long as you live."

Without question these men are good, very good, at dealing with pressure and dealing with it on a daily basis. They jump out of planes with ninety-pound packs, SCUBA dive under frozen lakes, infiltrate hostile areas, swim four miles under adverse conditions in the open sea, march long distances with heavy loads, and on and on. But the combination of the retreat elements asks that they take a different type of risk. Our entire program, in fact, asks them to take emotional and spiritual risks that are entirely new territory for them. Instead of having them leap out of planes we're asking them to leap into new psychological parts of themselves. This is novel ground and it makes them feel vulnerable and out of control. They aren't supposed to feel vulnerable and out of control so they try to hide it and blame others and the environment for their anxiety. They become rowdy and loud, as they did tonight, and attempt to overwhelm us with sheer force and volume. They tell us that as outsiders we can never understand a Special Forces soldier or the loyalty he feels for his team. They shout that we will never be able to "smoke them" (present them with something they are unable to do). They blame us and abdicate responsibility when things aren't going right. "If you were doing your job right," they tell us, "things wouldn't be so crazy now." They do everything they possibly can to smokescreen and defend, from themselves and us, any likelihood of being vulnerable or out of control. As the program progresses the litany "It's not manly to be weak. It's not the way of the S.F. man" is becoming a frontline defense against what we're teaching.

It's late when we return to our cabin. There is no moon and we stumble along the dark trail. My body aches. We shuffle inside the cabin, drop our gear on the floor; Joel and I collapse on the worn couch while Jack goes into the kitchen and heats up water for tea. We're quiet for a long time.

I turn to Joel, "You took a lot of shit tonight and I'm impressed the way you handled it. You were present and non-reactive. I know it was hard, you did a good job with it." He stares into the floor, barely acknowledging my comments. Jack comes in with the tea; he has monstrous bags under his eyes. He rolls his head from side to side, relieving the tension in his neck.

"We need to rethink our game plan for the retreat," he says. "The question is, how much do we change? It's clear that the issue of them breaking their word must also be confronted."

"I think we also have to acknowledge we asked too much of them too soon," I add. "You had some foresight on this, Jack; I think you saw it coming." Jack shakes his head silently. I wonder if he's thinking, 'I told you so'?

We agree with the radical suggestion of letting those men who wish to meditate and live alone do so; that way they won't be distracted by the restlessness of the others.

"The worst possible scenario would be that they'll take advantage of the freedom," Jack surmises.

"The best is that they will hunker down and get some good inner work done," Joel responds. "I think a lot of these guys are real serious about the practice. We should give them every opportunity to take advantage of it. And, who knows, maybe they'll affect the other guys positively." We compromise and schedule sitting periods the men can do on their own, away from the others, outside or in their quarters. If the teams decide so, the men can also live on their own.

Before we go to bed I take Joel aside: "I think you should tone down your talks." I watch him carefully. It's been a long night; I don't want him to feel criticized or put down. "It's like you're trying to teach graduate work to third-graders," I continue, "You're going over their heads. You need to explain meditation in more elementary terms." He's taking in what I'm saying without reacting. "Talk to them in their language. More common sense and practical terms will reach them where they are. You have to remember that while so much of this meditation business is second nature to you, it's absolutely new and foreign territory to most of these men."

"Thanks," he says wearily. "I feel your support. I just need to reassess a lot of things for myself. Goodnight."

Falling into my bunk I realize that as tired as my body is, my mind is alert and racing. Out the window I stare into layers of darkness as I go over the events of the evening. Jack begins his snore and turns restlessly in his sleep. I light a candle and my reflection appears on the dark windowpane.

In their own way the soldiers have been telling us that their established forms are starting to break down and their reactions are simply the reflexes of a predator when it feels in danger. The predator fights back, it doesn't tell you where its weakness is. Sun Tzu in *The Art of War* advises not to press an enemy at bay: "Wild beasts, when at bay, fight desperately. How much more is this true of men! If they know there's no alternative, they will fight to the death." As a team we didn't have the foresight to read this dynamic early on. While we're teaching relaxation and flexibility, we're actually being rigid and unyielding. When they claimed we didn't keep our word we became defensive and trivialized their complaints. Our inflexible adherence to the program schedule, and our need to be right, shield us from the insight that their anger and frustration are actually good news. The emotional energy that is now surfacing can be made the ground of our work with them. In our own way we're reflecting their behavior. We too do not want to be seen as vulnerable.

Instead of pressing the cornered beast we need to offer an alternative. We can begin with ourselves and try to blend with what they must be experiencing. In the past six weeks almost everything in their life, from the way they exercise, to their self-image, to what they eat, who they take orders from ("Damn civilians!"), to a reordering of the chain of command, to team unity has been cast into question. Whoever they thought they were is in a state of breakdown and reorganization after years of a rigid hierarchical structure. Tonight's mutinous upheaval is the beast's way of saying, "I AM" to the terrifying horizon of the unknown. It's the last response to the death of the ego.

They remind me of the metaphor of the cup and the quart. The cup represents who we are now. It's the amount of love, responsibility, power, what have you, that we have come to call our own. Across the table we see the quart. The quart represents what we can become, our potential. Realizing that the quart is within our reach and that the cup is no longer satisfying to us as we decide to go for more, to reach for the quart of our self. As we put down the cup in order to take the quart we realize in terror that we are empty-handed; we have left the known, yet we have not yet reached who we can become. Passing through this "empty-handed" state is terrifying and crucial, a passage in which our institutions have failed to educate us. Many of these soldiers are releasing the cup and they are entering into that boundless state of the unknown—a terrifying place for anyone who has let go of the old order to embrace the new. Their cry of "I AM," whether it's expressed through rage, brooding, silence, or the demand to be released from darkness to light, emerges as the failing voice of a dying ego. Their journey is also mine. How many of us will make it to the far shore? Do we have the strength and wisdom to support them across? Do we ourselves have the strength to move across?

Jack is snoring steadily now. I'm preparing to shout at him to roll on his side when he does so on his own. It's silent again. I blow out the candle and give myself willingly to the darkness.

September 14

Duck season begins today. Perfect Vs of mallards, pintails, and mergansers continue their southward migration undaunted by their new status. Everyone seems calmer and sobered by last night's episode. Harwood, Dudley, Riggs, and James, however, have shadows over their heads. Harwood can hardly look at me, but Dudley mutters under his breath that, "It's not just the Army to do things this way. We're soldiers, not damn yogis! Ah just don't like it. Hell, what ah'm I suppose' to do anyway if they're not going to follow my and the Captain's orders? Ah just don't like it." He glances at me as if he's expecting some kind of reply. I keep my mouth shut because I want to support keeping the idle chatter to a minimum and because I really don't know how to reply. Everything he says is true, and because we're involved in an experiment that has no previous precedent there's no way to answer except to get involved in the experiment and then draw your conclusions afterward.

A few days ago Harner pulled me aside as I was coming out of the meditation hall. In his Army-issue camouflage jacket, black watch cap, soiled running shoes, and very tired-looking pair of sweat pants he looked like a street person from the Tenderloin district of San Francisco. Hunched against a weathered Douglas fir he talked to me as though we were making some secret deal.

"I want to get as much out of this retreat as possible," he tells me, "but there's something bothering me. You know, my sister has psychic and clairvoyant abilities. So I'm familiar with some of this stuff. But for the past couple of days every time I start to get concentrated a door appears in front of my mind." He looks at me quizzically. "Have you ever heard of anything like that before?"

"Well, I know that it's not uncommon for images to appear spontaneously in meditation. They can even be memories from the past."

"It's always the same door. It never changes and I've never seen it before." His hazel green eyes are level with mine. Their inquiry is deep. He's like a man going into battle, serious, intent, aware of the myth that he's about to enact.

"Why don't you walk through it?" I suggest. He seems relieved by this and his gaze softens.

"Yeah," he says, "that's what I thought, too. Only problem is that the door hasn't opened."

"Maybe you should wait outside until the door opens."

He looks at me for a long moment and then nods his head. "Right. Thanks." He turns and ambles down the trail toward the main lodge.

After this morning's sitting he leans over to me and whispers in my ear, "Remember that door I told you about? Well, it opened and I went through it."

"And . . . ?"

"And . . . there was nothing there." A touch of resignation colors his voice. When we turn to look at each other our eyebrows raise simultaneously. He shrugs.

"Buddhism and most of the other sacred and mystical paths say this is the nature of being. Nothingness. The Great Void," I offer.

"I know."

"Maybe you had an insight into the true nature of things."

He gives me his hazel green level-eye look and smiles enigmatically: "Maybe."

I walk down to the main lodge and stand at the railing that looks out over the pond. The sky is freshly scrubbed blue and the forest is blazing with color. Maples red, poplars and sycamores yellow, elms and alders orange, ferns a buff color. A final surge of life before dying. Something catches my eyes at the far end of the pond and I shade my eyes to get a better look. On the northeast shore a moose emerges from the trees and walks into the water. I've never seen a moose before. A surge of excitement rises through my chest. It steps gingerly into the pond; soon only its head and massive antlers can be seen. I look around to see if anyone else has seen this. Behind me and just to my left Oreson and Farley are standing very still, absorbed in the scene. Farley has a smile of deep satisfaction on his face and the three of us are suddenly connected by the magic of the moment. This is the experience we strive for in the meditation hall: stillness, concentration, receptivity, a connectedness. We watch in silence as the moose swims across the pond, surges powerfully out of the water at the other end and quickly disappears into the tinted forest. We stand together in a reverent silence for a few moments before we continue our walking meditation. Farley catches my eye with that fraternal look of sharing something with someone that is beyond words. Oreson whispers to no one in particular, "I could have bagged him."

I walk past the lodge to circle around to the back of the meditation hall when Rader ambles toward me. He's wearing the usual running shoes, sweat pants, a soiled T-shirt, black watch cap pushed to the back of his head, a water bottle around his shoulder, and a blue bandanna tied around his neck. He's twirling his *jo*, the aikido staff, which has become his constant companion during the encampment. He looks very happy. His nose is running and he suggests a cross between a twelve-year-old boy who is playing hooky in the woods and Lao Tzu, the Chinese philosopher. "Hi, sensei!"

I immediately go through a change about the issue of silence. What am I going to do? Obviously he's intent on talking to me. Oh well, oh hell, as they would say.

"So it's Lao Tzu," I say. He dismisses the remark with a shrug, just more San Francisco psycho-babble that isn't worth trying to understand.

"Hey, sensei. When are you going to show me the rest of the *jo kata?*" No matter what he's saying, Rader's voice has a note of sarcasm in it, which is particularly noticeable when he addresses me as sensei. His buddy Johnson says that Rader was a mockingbird in his previous life.

As part of the aikido training I have been teaching them to use the Japanese sword and staff, which are called *bokken* and *jo.* The *jo kata* is an intricate and precise set of thirty-one moves that one practices without a partner. I've been teaching the men a segment at a time; the truth is Rader integrates the material as quickly as anyone I've ever taught. He's always chomping on the bit for more.

"There's time," I say. "Keep perfecting the moves you know and we'll move forward as a group. You're doing fine. Just keep practicing what you know."

He curls his lip in chagrin. "Oh come on, sensei, show me the next section. I can use the *kata* as part of my meditation here." As he's talking he twirls the *jo* perilously close to my face and makes an occasional strike in my direction, pulling up just short of my chin. I keep centered and discipline myself not to flinch, although I'm fully aware he could lose control and I could get a nasty bump. As usual, he's also testing me, wanting to see my reaction under pressure. "Does this guy walk his talk?" is the unspoken question.

Rader is an extremely bright man. He could have easily been a physicist or mathematician instead of a sergeant in the Special Forces, but he knew he wanted to be a soldier from the time he was a young boy. He's also a proud father and working hard to keep his marriage intact despite the demanding schedule of the Special Forces. During the initial interviews his primary question was how much time the program would take him away from his family. He's also captivated by aikido, which naturally endears me to him, and he continually wants more teaching. He's actually interested in the entire program and sees its possibilities for the Special Forces command. He's also critical, sharp, and very demanding, both of himself and his teachers.

"Be patient," I say. "Aikido is more than just learning a set of techniques. It's a way of life. It's a way of thinking about things."

He looks at me thoughtfully for a moment, then comments, "It's like that part in *The Empire Strikes Back* when Luke Skywalker says to Yoda, 'Yes, I'll be patient Master; just teach me now.'"

In the break after lunch Rader finds me again. "C'mon, let me show you something." Walking ahead of me he cheerily whistles a familiar melody, ("The Bridge Over The River Kwai"?) punctuated now and them by a fluid snort as he pulls the snot from his running nose back in. He punches the air with his *jo,* slaying invisible demons as he leads me through the trees to a small clearing hidden among a stand of conifers. Janowski is sitting on the ground hacking away at a small branch with an enormous Bowie knife.

"Howdy," he says in his soft intimate way, a big broad smile illuminating his lantern jaw. He's got a blue bandanna wrapped around his head and he hasn't shaven for a couple of days. He's building a sweat lodge, and the infrastructure, which is almost complete, looks as though it could easily accommodate four to six people. In his slowed-down Midwest rhythm he explains how he assembled the structure using everything from the local woods. Almost apologetically he adds, "But I'll have to use an Army poncho to cover it with." He takes me methodically step by step through the procedure of taking a sweat, finishing with, "And then we can come right down here, and jump in the lake to cool off. Pretty much like the Indians did."

All this time Rader is leaning against his *jo* with a big grin on his face. Janowski pauses for a moment and he jumps in like he's got a fire under him. "Yeah, sensei, if Larry finishes today we'll fire this thing up and you're welcome to come over and have a sweat tonight."

Janowski is already back to trimming his branch. He looks up and breaks into his wrap-around smile, "Yeah, please come back. You're always welcome, Richard."

I walk down the trail and stop for a moment, looking back at the two men in the small clearing. They're busy fitting branches to the lodge—I've never seen them so happy.

The Original Warrior

September 15

It's the seventh day of the retreat. I'm the first one at the large cabin we use for a meditation hall. The weathered porch offers the best view of the pond and neighboring forests, and I often come early to take in the spectacular view. The water is mirror-still this morning, reflecting the exuberant colors of autumn. I watch a hefty gray squirrel scramble up a large pine until it disappears into the thick green boughs. Inside the cabin I slowly exhale and lower myself to a sitting cushion. The room is cool and dark, a respite from the heat of Indian summer.

The sound of voices, as if distant bells, wakens me out of a reverie. The voices get closer and closer until heavy boots climb the steps. The voices quiet but don't cease. Soon the owners of the boots are in the room noisily taking off their coats and adjusting themselves on the sitting benches. With my eyes closed it sounds as if a huge elephant is trying to fit itself into the small room. Reluctantly the beast begins to settle down and a moderate silence slowly takes over. We're practicing the meditation technique of concentrating the attention on the movement of the breath. The practice is to anchor the attention on the breath, either at the nostrils or the abdomen, and then carefully note whatever comes to the foreground of awareness. When the attention wanders the practice is to return it directly to the breath. It's a simple but subtle mindfulness practice that both quiets and focuses the mind.

After twenty minutes of sitting, the atmosphere in the room becomes charged with a quiet intensity. I open my eyes and look out over the seated figures. The person to my immediate right seems especially still and I instinctively turn toward him. He's sitting very straight, motionless, alive with presence and concentration. His breath moves rhythmically from deep within his belly. My eye is caught by something on the black T-shirt that hugs his huge biceps and barrel chest. Printed in bone white on the front is a large skull and crossbones. The words over the skull read "82nd AIRBORNE DIVISION" and the broad letters below the skull scream, "**DEATH FROM ABOVE.**"

Something is wrong. 'People don't wear T-shirts like this at meditation retreats,' I tell myself.

'But the person inside the T-shirt looks like someone at a meditation retreat,' the voice responds.

I look back.

The skull and crossbones glare menacingly back at me. "82nd AIRBORNE DIVISION: **DEATH FROM ABOVE.**"

I have no mental file for what I see. Killing and meditation simply do not go together.

This contradiction recalls an event that happened to me many years earlier. When I was twelve years old my father called me aside and said there was something very important he wanted to tell me. His tone of voice was personal, almost secretive, and I felt that rare privilege of a son when a father includes him in his circle of intimacy. Once we were alone he stood solemnly before me, a Remington model 514 bolt-action .22 single-shot rifle cradled in his arms. With great seriousness he told me that I had reached the age where I was entitled to have my own gun. My heart raced with excitement as I gazed at the gleaming barrel and well-varnished walnut stock. Guns were not new or strange to me; I had frequently seen my father and uncles cleaning their rifles or packing them for a hunting trip. But this was to be my first rifle and I knew that I was about to take the first step toward becoming a man and a warrior.

Before my father handed me that rifle thirty years ago he spoke seriously about the responsibility that went with it. "This is not a toy," he said admonishingly. "This is a tool, a weapon, and you should always handle it with great care and safety. This can do great damage," he warned, "and you never, never point it at anyone *unless you plan to use it.*" The words thundered in my head, "*. . . unless you plan to use it.*"

Deep within my pre-adolescent mind something radically shifted. Not only was I being initiated into the first rites of novitiate warrior, I was being asked to rethink what had been, up to that point, the guiding tenet in my moral life—*Thou Shall Not Kill.* Now I was being offered the right to kill. In some distant and frightening way I knew I was being inducted into a power that was both sacred and profane, the power of taking another life. In a far corner of my mind a thought was planted that exempted a warrior from the first and most holy of laws.

Could this be?

As the rifle passed from my father's hands to mine I felt a surge of responsibility and awe. I had just been symbolically accepted into the first circle of warriorhood.

This simple initiation, enacted in a lower middle-class setting in 1950s America, has been ceaselessly repeated in the thousands of years of civilized and pre-civilized history. But as we move into the twenty-first century the contradiction of war becomes more and more evident. The warrior has likely been with us since the moment man and woman stood upright, not only protecting our hearths but expressing our highest values. Now, with the computer/nuclear battlefield, his legacy-drama, kindled perhaps millions of years ago on the savannas of Africa, has come to its final possible enactment before either a metamorphosis or annihilation. A law of the universe, certainly older that human history—a law of the Tao, of the turmoil of opposites in which nature itself began—has finally come into play on the battlefield. The killer half of the warrior sees not an enemy, not even himself alone in the mirror, but the whole planet.

Throughout human times weapons have been one of the major totems in the medicine kit that fathers and communities of men have passed on to their sons. We only have to imagine our origin as a distinct humanoid species to appreciate the significance of the bullet and missile. Those primal apes that were least skilled among the trees were the ones driven out onto the plains, or at least so anthropologists imagine the scenario whereby the dominant apes of the jungles exiled their mutant cousins from the ancestral domain. The event is called population pressure and adaptation rather than war, and it represents hundreds of thousands of years of accidents and free choices as well as skirmishes, but then the struggle of species for identity and survival is the prototype war at the heart of nature.

If, for a moment, we can imagine this event in a cartoon history, we see the great climbers and swingers dispatching their weakling relatives to apparent certain slaughter among the cat- and dog-like carnivores of the open wild. Then they sit around chuckling about it for a few million years, until the dispossessed return, carrying spears (and later guns) in those mutated forelimbs.

The ancestors of *Homo sapiens* in the open terrain were at a great disadvantage initially; they lacked the raw speed and agility of other animals, and now they lacked the protection of the forest. Anthropologists imagine they survived by gradually discovering an advantage of their lame, semi-upright posture—the freed limbs. They learned to make weapons and tools. They defended themselves with these artifacts, and they impeded and killed their prey. The commonly held theory is that tool-making reduced the biological importance of many simian organs and bodily functions, removing nature's selective bias toward bulk, speed, large jaws and teeth, and allowing the development of more brain tissue in the changing skull. The sudden importance of community, intelligence, and strategy would lead to a distinct favoring of the nascent "brain" and language genes. They were not pure killers; they were pack leaders of a new species, the chiefs of the original social bands.

It is impossible to know when murder originated as a cognitive deed, or when warriors first distinguished between Us and Them among their kind. While developing methods for killing animals, the early hunting/gathering societies presumably knew that the same techniques could kill people, and because confrontation is an inevitable aspect of human experience, the struggle to understand, symbolize, accept, and avenge homicide must have been one of the first trials out of which the primitive warrior was anointed. Between hunting and being hunted, there was no formal codification of rules and values; yet the warrior must have come inchoate out of their void, like some mythological demi-god, forging customs and conduct out of pain and conflict even as he came to stand for them and pass them on as if themselves already ancient from the dawn of time. The traditional warrior virtues of courage, loyalty, selflessness, service, and guardianship were probably first enacted by these hunter warriors as they stalked and killed game, protected their clans from predatory animals or looting bands, and even participated in ritual "war."

The Walbiri aborigines of Australia are a Stone-Age hunting and gathering society that has survived intact into this century, living their traditional way as recently as forty years ago. Through them we can see that the primitive notion of war in no way whatsoever resembled our modern equivalent. In their battles very few, if any, are killed. Walbiri warriors employ no tactics or formal strategy, nor do they have a military chain of command, and only the band that has been wronged takes part in the fighting. Their "war," when it does occur, is a community event that brings all the members of the tribe together. It provides the warriors with an opportunity to express their courage and skill in a sometimes dangerous ritual; but its purpose is not to kill, or acquire goods or territory; and it certainly isn't intended to destroy property. The attitude the Walbiri have toward war was most likely shared by almost all of the hunting/gathering bands of the Stone Age. Their approach casts serious doubts on theories that our martial leanings are built on an animal-inherited territorial imperative: "This is my bone, my woman, my turf. Leave or I'll kill you."

By studying the Australian Walbiris, the South African Bushman, and other societies that survived into the modern world, we can imagine their wars resembling something more like neighborhood rumbles than their modern counterparts of destruction and brutality. A peek back into pre-civilized history might show a few dozen hunter-warriors, cheered on by their fellow clansmen, gathered in an open field to wrestle, hurl stones against one another, spar with clubs, make intimidating gestures, and chase each other, but most importantly, calling it quits when someone was hurt. No doubt there were also some of the magical and mythological deeds of the shaman and priest. The story-teller and healer followed them on the early battlefield, and thus other aspects of the unconscious and human lore were brought into being.

Somewhere between ten and fifty thousand years ago these small hunting and gathering bands began to link together as tribal units, creating new and more complex forms of social organization. Some anthropologists surmise that strict sexual roles and sodalities (or guilds) arose during this time, culminating in the increased authority of the male warrior class and the depoliticization of women. Since women generally weren't hunter-warriors they were gradually excluded from circles of power. Although there were no doubt heroic and rebellious exceptions to every sanction over the millennia of tribal life leading to the early civilizations, it is clear that the male warrior was well institutionalized by the time we meet him as Gilgamesh and Diomedes in the tablets of Mesopotamia or the tales of Homer. Whether the first soldiers were pure warriors or hydraulic laborers in an unanswerable question that curiously reflects our contemporary dilemma. Does the modern Army exemplify the traditional warrior—the defender of society's values—or a guild of mercenary killers hired from the general labor force?

Even with the enfranchisement of a purely warrior class, there's no recorded example of a tribe fighting a war because of territory, material goods, or ideological differences. The early warriors may have performed as strong a ceremonial function *within* society (engaging and placating supernatural forces and challenging taboos in times of crisis) as they did a military one in confronting outsiders. These were warriors in the classical sense of power initiates and providers of security, but in no way were they the professional soldiers we know today.

Tribal warriors still regarded warfare as a sacred activity bounded by ritual, magic, and sanction. War was no doubt an arena in which the warrior could ventilate his tremendous physical energy, express his courage, establish his loyalty to the tribe, and demonstrate his martial and hunting prowess, but it was still not an institutionalized means of gaining political and economic advantages. Because there was no state, the tribal warrior acted mostly as an individual, free from the strategies and goals of a polity. War seemed part of the natural rhythm of the universe, like thunderstorms and phases of the moon. In more ritualized instances war was no more ferocious than a pick-up game of touch football or a paint-pellet war game—some injuries, few fatalities, a way for men to be together and act out their skills.

The clan-based warrior didn't deliberately organize the battle to make killing more efficient; he would have been horrified by such a notion and probably would have considered it blasphemy. Most tribal skirmishes ended after a single fatality or even a serious injury. A contemporary example of this is a tribe in New Guinea that uses a different arrow for war than it does for hunting. Fitted with feathers for accuracy, the hunting arrow is more lethal than the war one, which lacks feathers to direct its accuracy. Among the Plains Indians of North America it was considered much more courageous to "count coup"—touch the enemy with an ornamental ritual stick or open hand—than to kill him. To kill an opponent was in fact considered a display of weakness, a *lack* of courage. Despite having the weapons and skill to slay their opponents in close combat, the Shoshoni and Piegan Indians chose instead to ritualize their battles by standing just within reach of their opponents' arrows while protected by a three-foot shield. The Yanomamo tribe of South America even today holds ritual fights that are strictly supervised, lest they escalate into the use of bows and arrows. The Maring tribe who live in the mountains of New Guinea stage a war every twelve years. It begins with the distribution and feasting of pigs among allies, followed by ritual martial preparations, and then a period of battle. The final ritual is the planting of the sacred rumbin trees, which symbolizes a truce that lasts for another twelve years. The preparations and enactment of this self-styled war ritual seem to serve as an effective regulator for the human and animal population in relation to the available resources of the Maring's mountainous ecosystem.

Although these tribal battles produced their share of deaths, primitive warfare in no way threatened the societies that participated in them. The behavior of the Marings of New Guinea shows that tribal battles often play an essential and creative role in the actual survival and growth of the societies involved: redistributing goods, regulating domestic herds through feasts, and providing safe outlets for violent confrontations. Conquest, genocide, or brutality in the name of power and a nation-state were not part of the tribal warrior's code. Fighting for territory proved meaningless because land was associated with spirituality. To conquer and inhabit land apart from one's place of origin and ancestors meant to separate oneself from spiritual roots.

With the birth of civilization, somewhere between five and seven thousand years ago, the traditional role of the warrior changed. As a rapidly growing agricultural economy produced a surplus of goods, the need for an institutionalized protecting force developed. The professional soldier was born—the soldier-warrior trained and organized under the institutionalized leadership of a state-appointed commander. The arrival of the stratified city-state also heralded the original gestalt of elements that make war what it is today—impersonal killing, fighting for territory and goods, slavery, destruction, slaughter, finally a threat to humanity itself. The battlefield goals of mechanized and anonymous killing in the service of state policies also marked the end of the warrior as an individual.

The primary connection the soldiers of early civilization had to the tribal warriors of an earlier age was the vintage of weapons. The arrows, spears, knives, axes, and clubs wielded in civilization's first wars were pretty much the same ones that had armed their predecessors the previous thousands of years. But most similarities ended there. Where individual warriors once tested each other with the skills learned in hunting, now thousands of men moved against one another in crowded, well-practiced formations. When two men ultimately fought each other there was nothing personal or individualistic about their struggle. The men in the front of the formations were pushed forward by those in the back as they automatically responded to orders they had practiced over so many days and years. The tribal warrior's combat had involved other means of communicating with the opposition, similar to his hunting skills; the well-rehearsed drills of the civilized soldier had no connection to anything other than the systematic and impersonal killing of as many other humans as possible.

For centuries the basic pattern of warfare remained the same. The addition of horses, gunpowder, and conscription naturally changed the face of war in all countries, but it was ultimately the effects of industrialization, at the time of the Civil War, that forever altered the identity of the soldier-warrior. During this tumultuous period of history the might of technology finally overwhelmed the power of humans. The caplock-rifled musket increased the killing range to almost half a mile. Developments in artillery increased the ability to strike at the enemy's production centers. The soldier-warrior could kill his collective enemy, which now included women and children, without ever seeing them. The cries of the wounded and dying went unheard by those who inflicted the pain. A man might slay hundreds and never see their blood flow. Mechanization also exponentially increased the size of the battlefield. For the first time in history the infantryman didn't always make his way to the battlefield entirely by foot. Railways and riverways augmented the capacity for supply and reinforcements. The telegraph allowed troop movements to be coordinated over vast areas, including those primarily inhabited by civilian populations. As machines grew in importance the enemy became more abstract and the individual soldier-warrior less important.

Less than a century after the Civil War ended, a single bomb, delivered miles above its target, would take the lives of more than one hundred thousand people, almost all civilians. The moral distance between this event and the tribal warrior facing a single opponent is far greater than even the thousands of years and transformations of culture that separate them. Although the traditional warrior and the modern soldier have virtually nothing in common, government propagandists (in all countries) constantly evoke the warrior to seduce men to war. Young males can more easily be led into battle by the hero-warrior of their psyches than by the strategies and statistics of complex technologies and faceless automatons. Even without the substance of a warrior ritual the need for an initiatory circle remains.

Army recruiters continue to propagate a fiction about the modern-day soldier leading the life of a warrior, and our cultural images reinforce this fantasy. The mythmakers of Hollywood have set the pace for romanticizing this ideal. The prototype idealized warrior has been John Wayne. In *The Sands of Iwo Jima,* he plays the savvy, well-trained combat veteran who, despite great odds, almost single-handedly defeats the enemies of democracy and decency. In the setting-sun finale he dies valiantly, his heroic deeds to be remembered, but his need for such recognition sealed away in the brooding of his maudlin, masculine character. John Wayne fathers a tradition that empowers Chuck Norris in *Delta Force,* Sylvester Stallone as *Rambo,* and Tom Cruise in *Top Gun.* They are warriors of "might as right" and their motto is "I'll die for what's right." Never mind that these are one-dimensional figures unlike anyone we've ever met, or could meet; they satisfy the appetite of a culture for vicarious thrills and instant gratification. Though superficial, nationalistic, and abstract, these cinematic superstars are the primary models on which the young men of America project their fantasies of warriorhood.

In *Born on the Fourth of July,* Vietnam veteran Ron Kovic wrote that when he heard the Marine Corps hymn as a boy, ". . . I would think of John Wayne. I would think of him and cry. John Wayne in *The Sands of Iwo Jima. . . .*" When Kovic met the Marine Corps recruiters at his high school, he recalls that "As I shook their hands and stared into their eyes, I couldn't help but feel I was shaking hands with John Wayne and Audie Murphy." Jim Kelly, Vietnam combat vet and a San Francisco restaurant owner, gives another version of the same myth: "I believed in John Wayne when I was a kid. I believed I'd come back from the war and marry Patricia Neal. It turned out to be real costly to me. It was all garbage." Phil Caputo, who wrote *Rumors of War* after he survived Vietnam, confesses, "I saw myself charging up some distant beachhead, like John Wayne in *The Sands of Iwo Jima,* and then coming home a suntanned warrior with medals on my chest." From his college campus Caputo remembers "a poster of a trim lieutenant who had one of those athletic, slightly cruel-looking faces considered handsome in the military. Clear and resolute, his blue eyes seemed to stare at me in challenge. JOIN THE MARINES, read the slogan above his white cap. BE A LEADER OF MEN." What else?

Now we have Chuck Norris, Arnold Schwarzenegger, Bruce Willis, and the John Wayne of the eighties, Sylvester Stallone. These actors depict tough, unemotional men who violently defend peace by fighting the dreaded tide of communism, or terrorism. Heroically winning battle after battle without breaking a sweat, they are mysteriously provided with an endless supply of ammunition and lucky breaks. Returning victorious and unscathed, they are met by an adoring public and beautiful women. The mythical warriors are the entrée to the New Patriotism of the 1980s. This parade of celluloid images provides a nation with a myth that promises the young their manhood through the experience of the soldier-warrior in battle. But what we know from our engagement in Vietnam is that this myth is a hellish mirage. The Academy Award-winning film *Platoon*, and the more recent *Casualties of War*, jolt us to the fact that modern warfare, represented by Vietnam, has as much to do with creating psychotics as warriors.

We must face that war is no longer, and has not been for centuries, an accountable initiation for youth into manhood, or a trial ground for heroism, service, courage, and the transcendent. The product being sold is the mass slaughter of the modern battlefield; the image being used to sell it is the individual valor of the tribal chief. The contradiction lies not only in a moral double standard, but in our invoking the warrior archetype to sanctify and legitimize acts having nothing to do with warrior virtues.

The combatants in modern warfare pitch bombs from twenty thousand feet in the morning, causing untold suffering to a civilian population, and then eat hamburgers for dinner hundreds of miles away from their drop zone. The prehistoric warrior met his foe in a direct struggle of sinew, muscle, and spirit. If flesh was torn or bone broken he felt it give way under his hand. And though death was more rare than common (perhaps because he held the pulse of life and the nearness of death under his fingers), he also had to live his days remembering the man's eyes whose skull he had crushed.

When Joel rings the bell announcing the end of the sitting I glance at the skull and crossbones. What I notice now, and somehow missed before, is that it's Harner inside the T-shirt. He's carefully unfolding his legs and massaging his knees. When he sees me looking at him there's a twinkle in his eyes and he says with a satisfied smile, "That was a pretty good one."

It occurs to me that in a previous time, maybe when he was in Vietnam, or at a time when he's deployed on a mission, he could say the same thing about planting an explosive. But for now he's talking about a victory within himself. He won a battle where there were no casualties and success was simply a feeling of satisfaction and wholeness.

September 16

Karter is sitting next to me in the front seat, and Rollins is in the back with his left leg wrapped and propped up on the seat. Earlier in the day he hurt his ankle in a freak accident during P.T. He was on a wooden platform doing squat thrusts when one of his feet broke through the plywood floor. The medics huddled around him the moment he fell clutching his leg. He seems fine, but they decided he should go to the Post hospital for x-rays. Karter is along as one of the medics on Rollins' team. Somehow I feel like a parole officer with my two charges. Any question I have about us observing the silence or not is quickly dispelled as soon as we turn off the dirt road of the camp onto a paved highway.

"Okay, I guess it's time to light up," Karter says in his laugh that's always a half sneer. I give him a disapproving look and he sneer-laughs again. "Hey, I'm just kidding. I really want to quit, but boy, it's hard. I've been smoking since I've been fourteen." Since he can't smoke, he goes to work on his nails, which are already chewed to nubs.

Karter is what they call an "intense dude." Sitting next to me he feels like an oversized generator running at triple speed. He's one of those tough, wiry kids who feels like he has nothing to lose and pushes everything to its limit. He's made something like a zillion free falls; when he was stationed in Europe he couldn't get enough jumps in the Army so he joined an Italian sky diving club to jump on the weekends. He's also an expert skier, notorious for his breakneck runs down the most terrifying mountains.

Karter was raised in a middle-class family in suburban New Jersey. As an adolescent he began to run with a tough crowd that led him consistently into trouble. He was finally given an option by the courts: go to jail or join the Army. "That's the only reason I'm here," he says talking out of the side of his mouth. "I like it all right, but I would've never chosen it on my own." Once in the Army he began to excel; he joined an Airborne outfit, went to Grenada. "Naw, I didn't see much action, mostly mopping up. Jeez, it was goddamn hot down there! I don't like it so hot. I liked the people though, real friendly. They were real glad to see us." He joined the Special Forces and passed the demanding medic's training with colors: "I plan to do my twenty years, retire, become a vet, open my own office ...maybe somewhere up around here. My wife likes it here and I don't mind it. Maybe I can even get the Army to put me through school." He throws his tough sideways smile and goes back to work on his nails.

Driving southeast we pass through a succession of small towns, each more charming than the previous one. There's a consistency about them, like a series of Hollywood sets designed for Sinclair Lewis' *Main Street,* evolving steadily toward the twenty-first century as we approach urban sprawl: white steepled churches; the veterans' memorial with the names going back to World War I; the Town Hall with its well-tended lawn and proudly displayed flag; the new and awkward-looking Quik Stop with teenagers on bikes hanging out in front; well-dressed housewives stepping smartly in and out of variety stores. Framing every town is a stunning backdrop of trees, whole forests even, heavy with the weight and fever of autumn.

Rollins married his high-school sweetheart, joined the Army out of high school, had a child, and qualified for the Special Forces. He has that milk-fed, wholesome All-American look that will turn a certain kind of woman's head; and he's the first to know it. Just a few years ago he was an outstanding high-school athlete in a small town in Ohio, eating from his mother's table every night. If he doesn't shave for a week you can't tell the difference. In my rear-view mirror he's a happy man, not somebody who has just been injured; his face is bright and he's taking in the sights like an exile who has just had his freedom returned to him.

"I don't care about smoking," he joins in, "it's the food that get me, agghh!" He mimics someone throwing up. "Why do we have to eat that crap anyway? I hate tofu, and those fake hamburgers made out of soybeans make me sick. I want me a juicy rare steak. Why don't we have any meat, anyway?"

"You know why," I say. We've gone over this so many times I can't believe he's asking it. In the rear-view mirror I can see that he really doesn't really expect an answer; he's already on to the next thing—following the rear end of a blonde walking down the sidewalk. Karter sees the blonde too, but his eyes dart quickly to a customized '57 Chevrolet, then to a group of men working on the road, back to the blonde, and then to the car in front of us. He's cooking inside, taking everything in and probably planning his veterinarian office at the same time. Rollins, in the meantime, is still watching the blonde. It's going to be a close call between his head twisting one-hundred-and-eighty degrees and her disappearing from sight.

Listening to them talk I'm struck by how young they are, just a few years out of high school. Their conversation centers around sports, memorable drunken parties, women, cars, bitching about the Army, relationships with family members. Despite their age they shoulder tremendous responsibility; at any moment they could be called into a life-threatening situation.

"What do you think of aikido?" I ask them.

"I like it, I like it a lot." Karter is instantly there, as though he had been waiting for the question. "When the program is over I'm going to try and keep studying it. I don't know if you could really use it in a fight, and maybe you're not teaching it that way, but I think it'll help my skiing and I'd just as soon use a bat in a fight anyway." He sneers and laughs. "Pow!" he shouts and mimics swinging a bat.

Rollins is more lukewarm. "I really don't see what its purpose is. It's kind of fun to do, but truthfully—and I don't want to hurt your feelings or nothing—but I don't see that it has any value to me." He shrugs his shoulders and looks out the window.

"Has it made any difference in your personal or professional life?" I ask Karter. He's tapping his fingers rapidly against his knee, a safety valve for the overflow that's always building in him. His head begins to bob up and down quickly and the movement goes down his torso until he's moving forward and backward in a small but highly charged rocking motion.

"Yeah," he says evenly, "I don't hit my kids as much. I'm more centered so I don't react so quickly to them." He looks away for a moment. When he looks back his pale blue eyes, filled with such passion, longing, and fury, bore straight and true into me. "That's real nice," he says without a pause. "Everybody in the family likes it, too."

Something inside me relaxes. It no longer matters to me if we keep the silence, or if they quit smoking, or if they can do more push-ups, or go longer distances without sleep, or that they won't have to kill or be killed in war. Some connection has been made, some war has been won, we're talking and listening to each other. The inner warrior is alive.

September 17

Tight wedges of long-necked geese cut across the polished knife-blade of the sky. An owl hoots during the late-night sit. A gray heron flies out of the nothing of the early morning fog, settling on the western slope of the pond. Standing on one leg among the rushes he becomes a stoop-shouldered monk contemplating the folly of life. Witnessing these events I'm overtaken by a vague despair.

I've fallen into a downward spiral in the past day and a half. I don't understand the rapid swing between these steep peaks and low valleys. I tell myself to quit indulging. I have nothing to complain about; I'm in a beautiful setting, I have challenging work, I'm among friends. Don't be so weak, be the warrior that you talk about. This, of course, is a faintly disguised form of self-criticism which only makes my mood darker.

I'm unable to find the comfort I seek, neither in the beauty of nature nor the silence of my sittings. My concentration is scattered and fragmented; I struggle against everything, as if I'm allergic to my own skin. Every thought seems an accident. I fall into deep chasms of loneliness and then desperately try to fill the emptiness with plans and fantasies; anything but to be present with where I am, which is a sunless, grim darkness. I can hold my mind still for no more than ten or fifteen seconds and then I'm off and running, wanting to blame others for my misery. I'm mad at so and so for what he said a year ago. If so and so did this differently I wouldn't be so anxious about the situation. So and so is acting out against me and I have to watch myself around him.

Is this the first step toward war? Projecting our fears onto others? By not staying with and being responsible for our own feelings of emptiness and loneliness we blame others for our pain. Perhaps if we punish them, somebody outside ourselves, we can escape our discomfort and convince ourselves we will be vindicated.

Now anything seems better than sitting in this unrelenting darkness. I try to prop myself up with heroic warrior notions about the nobility of suffering on the path of self-realization and the integrity of facing our demons within. I try to justify this pain by manufacturing credentials about who I am or what I can be. I tell myself I'm learning simply how to be. This works for a moment, but mostly it sounds rhetorical, like something I read in a book someplace. The truth is that I'm just plain hurting and I don't know why.

I'm moping around by the small beach when James approaches: "There's something on my mind. I'd like to talk with you about it," he says. I know him well enough to read that pinched look between his eyebrows. He's a resolute, straightahead kind of guy; when he sets his teeth into something he'll run with it until it's played out. A pit bull with the heart of a saint. But in my dullness and irritability I feel absolutely inadequate to hear anyone else's struggles.

We sit silently in the early autumn sun. James soberly studies his hands. "I'm not exactly sure what I'm supposed to feel from doing this meditation, but I'm trying my hardest and I'm taking in what Joel and you all are saying. You know I take Jesus Christ to be my Savior. Some of what we're doing here goes along with my Christian beliefs, but some of it, well, I just don't understand. When Joel gave his talk on compassion it reminded me a lot of the teachings of Christ and how he talked about love." A bass breaks the mirror stillness of the pond and we watch the ripples fade before they reach the shore.

When he begins speaking again he's looking away, out over the pond, past the forests, to the rigorous blue dome of the sky. "Well, you know what our mission is. You know what we would have to do if we ran into someone, even if it was a civilian, maybe even a young peasant boy." He looks at me searchingly, "Well, what would I do now? With this meditation and my Christian beliefs, how could I kill someone?"

Although I'm not aware of any emotion, there's a sinking feeling in my stomach and I have an inexpressible urge to be somewhere else. I want to be free of the contradictions and paradoxes of this program, free of what James is now asking me, free of my wild swings between surrender and desperateness.

I have no answer. Suddenly I feel very tired and I just want to lie down in the warm sand and go to sleep. I want to be held in someone's arms until I fall into a deep slumber. James is scrutinizing me, waiting for an answer.

"What would you do?" he asks insistently. An obscure dread falls over me.

"I don't know." I feel like apologizing. Nothing seems simple. The stillness of the water and the openness of the sky offer no solace. "Maybe the best we can do is to perform our duty to the best of our ability and not be attached to the outcome." We settle quietly for a bit and I thankfully remember that my practice can be done here, now. We're simply sitting and breathing together. In a nearby pine two blue-black jays squabble noisily from branch to branch.

"I hope you never have to face that dilemma," I offer. He nods, thanks me, and walks back to the meditation hall.

Later that night I tell Jack and Joel about the conversation.

"That's a hard one," Joel says immediately. Jack looks into space, absorbed in thought. "It also says that they're getting something from the sitting, at least some of them," Joel continues. "I know that James is trying hard, very hard, even though this is all so foreign to him. I respect him for that." Joel goes on to talk about Krishna and Arjuna in the *Bhagavad-Gita* when they had to face the question of killing on the battlefield. Krishna takes the opportunity to sermonize on performing one's duty while detaching from the results. I add that of course many of the teachers in my lineage of meditation were professional military men who served in combat.

"We have to act for the greater good," Jack finally offers. This lures us into a brief and baffling excursion about what is "good" and what is the "greater good," and leads to a discussion of the Japanese Samurai who were trained in Zen meditation to be constantly prepared for death. The Samurai was inured to view life and death as the same; for them death had already occurred, it was their practice to live fearlessly and vividly in the moment.

Joel tells the story of the Zen monk who stayed in his village after everyone had fled the advancing Mongol warriors. When the astonished Mongol chieftain found the monk sitting peacefully he bellowed, "Don't you realize that I could run you through with my sword right here in this moment?" To which the monk replied, "Don't you realize that I'm ready to die right here in this very moment?" As the story goes, the Mongol leader was enlightened in that moment by the monk's simplicity, fearlessness, and wisdom.

Our conversation becomes a series of footnotes on killing and death. We range from euthanasia to serial killers to abortion to *My Lai* to the Bible's 'an eye for an eye,' to what would personally bring each of us to the point of taking another life. Jack and I are clear that we would kill to defend ourselves, our families, and our loved ones. Joel slowly shakes his head; he wonders about turning the other cheek, about ending the cycle of violence by not reacting with more violence.

The First Killing: Cain rose up and slew Abel.

The sons of Adam were to receive an equal share of the world. To Cain went the rightful ownership of property, to Abel the rightful inheritance of all living creatures. Cain was the tiller of the soil, the landowning farmer; Abel, the shepherd, the wandering keeper of the flock. One brother was destined to control and dominate nature, the other to follow the Way and live in harmony with nature and her creatures.

How did Cain in truth rise up and slay Abel? Was his 'rising' a coming up and out of his center? Did he separate from his natural link with nature in order to perform the most frightful of deeds? Or did he 'rise up' as an oppressed people against their tormentors? Or did he simply become jealous of the easier lifestyle of his brother?

Could it be that on the day of the First Murder, Cain was toiling patiently in the soil when Abel's sheep trampled his fields, destroying months of back-breaking labor. When Abel arrived to collect his flock Cain recognized the culprit and in his rage demanded that he make reparations for the ravaged crops. Abel, though sorry for what had happened, knew the importance of flowing with the unexpected ups and downs of nature and saw no reason for Cain to be so upset. Being a man of the Way he responded in a balanced and even manner to Cain's fury. Enraged by Abel's apparent lack of concern Cain, in a moment of murderous passion, raised his wooden hoe—the sharpened stone attached to it—and struck Abel a mortal blow.

Another rendition: the Bible tells us that the day of the First Murder was only a few days after the Lord had "accepted Abel's offering, but not Cain's." Cain asks himself why it is that he, who spends his days bent under the hot sun tilling the rocky soil, sweat stinging his eyes, his blistered hands aching, is rejected by the Lord; while Abel, who sits in the shade playing his flute to his animals, is rewarded and approved of by the Lord? Cain, a meticulous and hard-working man, found this difficult to accept and became "dejected and very angry, and his face grew dark with fury." Sullen and withdrawn, Cain suffers; his bitterness and envy grow until he suggests to his brother that they "go out into the fields." He lures him to a premeditated spot where he has hidden his roughly hewn hoe. In a frenzy of righteous violence, he strikes his brother down.

My aikido version begins at the point where Cain picks up his hoe to deliver his death blow. Instead of being the First Victim of the First Murder, Abel moves out of the way, blends with the force of Cain's strike, and uses his momentum to throw him to the ground, at the same time taking possession of the hoe. Abel then respectfully places the hoe to the side and walks calmly away. Over the next few weeks Cain tries unsuccessfully to catch Abel by surprise; the same scenario of Cain being thrown or pinned, without injury, is reenacted. Finally Cain understands—first, that he's unable to kill or injure Abel; second, that Abel isn't taking revenge on him even though he has the opportunity; third, that Abel continues to treat him with respect despite his attempts at murder. Cain and Abel begin to train together; they share their knowledge of the land, plants, and animals with each other; they decide to sit together in conversations with God. They become the founding members of the First Earth Battalion.

Even though it's late when we finish our discussion I'm charged with excitement and decide to walk over to the meditation hall. In the past day we have initiated a voluntary late-night sit for those who wish to deepen their meditation and I'm curious who will attend. Through the twisting branches of a box elder I detect a half moon darting in and out of dark clouds. It's a charcoal black night so I stay to the road walking the long way past the main lodge. Inside, a few men are sitting, quietly taking tea before they return to their meditation or to bed. I feel clear-headed, almost buoyant; the paranoia and despair that were my companions earlier in the day now seem to be part of another time. I'm elated to be out in the crisp air with the night sky so vivid and alive above me.

As I pick up the leafy trail that leads to the meditation hall the moon breaks free and I'm surprised by a dark figure a dozen steps ahead of me. His strides are precise and slow, almost pensive, as he patiently attends to his walking meditation. His deliberate manner, the hood of his jacket pulled over his head like a cowl, hands buried deep in his jacket pockets, could make him a monk on a contemplative stroll . . . except that there's an M16 automatic rifle slung over his shoulder.

I follow him up the trail into the meditation hall. Others are already there, arranging themselves on cushions or sitting benches, their M16s lying next to them. I have forgotten that after ten P.M. they are required to take their weapons from a storage locker, keep them all night, then return them to the locker before morning muster. It's only because of this additional late-night session that the weapons are brought to the sitting. The room is a quarter full, but I'm pleasantly surprised by the faces that I see. There are a number of the younger men who I had thought had given up on the encampment. I make a mental note to ask them later about their change of heart.

The weapons add a vividness and alertness to my sitting. It's as if they're deadly snakes sleeping at our feet and the slightest provocation could arouse them. Unaccountably, and unlike before, I'm easy with the paradox of the situation. For a moment I judge that as bad, that perhaps I'm deadening myself, or that I've compromised myself into a state of denial. But I don't feel numb; I feel a tremendous aliveness. Even the deeper, more unconscious mutterings of my mind are still. My breath is like a great and forgiving sigh that expands from the tiny openings of my nostrils to the far reaches of the galaxy, and then returns in a great rush charged with aliveness and vitality. I grow outward to a tiny still point and then fall back into a vast dark ocean. Behind the "I" who sees, hears, and seeks to control there's limitless space, a vast feeling of gratitude and love.

When the bell rings I continue to sit, reluctant to leave this warm, no-thinking place. I slowly unwind my crossed legs and wait until the surge of pain relents before I stand. I join the file of men walking slowly out of the room with their heads bowed, automatic rifles hanging intimately by their sides. The sky has cleared. I stand momentarily in a dish of moonlight just off the trail. Movement, stillness, movement; dark, light, dark; a meteor cuts an arc of light across the black. Above me the Pleiades glitter happily; under foot is the soft support of pine needles. The men break into different directions to go to their quarters. Soon the only sound is a great horned owl signaling from a distant place. For the moment I'm without choice, desire, or judgment. Men meditating with weapons is a part of the world. The faraway stars in their cold distance wink humorously at me.

Bodymind

September 18

Inexplicably it turned cold last night. The ground is left brittle and unyielding. By morning a clean, cutting wind races out of the north, throttling the trees and whipping up whitecaps on the pond. In the far upper reaches of sky are what look like the dark shapes of Arctic tern. I respectfully bow to them acknowledging the prodigious effort of their migrations.

In the morning sitting, I gather my concentration by becoming an image: a mountain lion, attentively scanning a forest valley for movement. The majestic head upright and proud in its gaze; the somber amber eye sweeping downwind, noting a change of color in the dawn sky, confident in the simple dignity of being.

An exquisite softness begins to radiate through me; soon I'm enveloped by a limitless space. The body frees itself of restless struggle, the mind ceases its chatter. Rising, falling, rising, the breath breathes through me, effortless, charging me with a deepening, vibrant calm. I join and become part of a great swelling into the far reaches of space. O-Sensei's "I am One with the Universe!" and the Buddha's "How wonderful! How miraculous! All things are enlightened!" echo in the space. I feel like a finely tuned instrument, vibrating delicately in harmony with the universe. Unexpectedly a loud and sonorous fart issues from the middle of the room and my self-conscious spiritualism collapses around me. There is scattered laughter. I bow as I would if struck by a Zen master with a *keisaku* (a sword-like stick) to remind me of my arrogance.

After lunch we meet to discuss the upcoming *gasshuku*. *Gasshuku* is a Japanese word that connotes an intensive practice situation where the aikidoist spends the entire time in the dojo eating, sleeping, and training. A *gasshuku* can be as short as a single day or as long as a week, or even a month. This *gasshuku* will be a single day and we will alternate periods of aikido training with meditation sessions—a format that is hard-won, as Joel is initially resistant to placing the aikido training and sitting meditation back to back. He argues that at this point in the retreat many of the men are deepening their practice, and excessive movement and contact will disrupt the inner stillness they are hopefully achieving. His point is understandable, but I counter that this is an ideal way for these men to combine the awareness and insight of silent meditation with the challenges of service and action in the world. I'm committed to having this blend of sitting and aikido, and I finally insist, reminding Joel that he will also be involved and can offer his feedback if he feels we go too far off track. In the end he acquiesces, urging me to stress slow movement and emphasize mindfulness.

My persuasiveness with Joel stems from my vision of the modern warrior: one who is grounded in a spiritual discipline and is at the same time committed to compassionate service in the world. This is, of course, a different path from retiring to a life as a cloistered monk, thinking only of one's spiritual redemption; and also different from turning attention outward to the world for fame and material success.

It seems to me that the key word here is embodiment. *To embody and live out our deepest values* is by definition an urge to call the spirit into the flesh; it's a yearning to experience our ideals as a living expression. This means, for example, that if we hold compassion as a virtue we will not only think compassionately, or think compassion is a good idea, but we will *be* compassionate. This is something quite different from a behavioral response to an ideological belief. It means to experience, within oneself, the cellular and muscular version of compassion.

To strive to be a living expression of our ideals is a desire to experience the heroic within ourself—heroic because to be embodied is to flesh out our weaknesses and limitations along with our strengths. To be fully open and vulnerable to ourselves in this way requires a warrior's courage. When we respond to this call we're challenging our self-image; we're asking to discover if the concept we hold of our self is the same as what we live out. In aikido we say, "put it on the mat"; which means let's see you do what you say you can do.

I suspect that my interest in this area was aroused when it became apparent that what people said and what they did had little or no relationship. At school, church, and home I learned that the world of ideals and the world of action often operated independently of each other. Growing up I was routinely advised to "do as I say and not as I do." I remember an "I almost made the major leagues" recreation leader wearily lecturing about "clean body, clean mind" while smoking a cigarette. In those rare moments when I met adults who lived their message they seemed to exist in an ambience apart from everyone else.

It was through sports and the martial arts that I was first introduced to the language of action and being. Sports added a vividness to my life while also investing me with self-esteem. When I moved into a new neighborhood my athletic prowess earned me credentials on the playing fields and in the dojo. After a baseball injury fractured my knee and put me in a cast for three months, I was encouraged to run to strengthen the injured leg, there being some concern I would be left with a permanent limp. Running led me to a college scholarship and honors as an All-American in Track and Field. Later I won the one-hundred-meter dash in the pre-Olympic meet and Central American Games in Mexico City.

Over time, I became disappointed with the lack of continuity between this language of the body—feeling, contact, breath, movement—and the rest of my life. The delight and empowerment that I engendered in pushing myself to a limit and being tested under pressure had no place outside the playing fields. Along with my fellow athletes I honored an unspoken agreement that the ecstasy and insight I experienced in sports were to be stored in our lockers, along with our sweaty workout gear. Except for a hearty "Way to go!" or "Great effort!" after a particularly good performance, we never spoke about the transcendent quality of our actions. Outside the gym, in the everyday world we were clumsy and awkward, as if our luminous bodies were rare animals that could not live apart from the hothouse of the training fields.

If I had remained solely in the world of athletics I might have found contentment and a room to call my own. But I shuttled in an uneasy commute between the gym and academia—the endorsed halls of learning. In the image-rich world of philosophy, psychology, and literature, I searched for language to satisfy a hunger in me that was not ever addressed among the jocks. And such a rich feast I found!—Keats, Shakespeare, Kierkegaard, Yeats, Wittgenstein, Rilke, Taoism, Buddhism, Jung, Hinduism, and Rumi offered a seemingly endless river of inspiration. But I learned that in the rarified world of the intellect it's enough just to know something; I discovered that, like the athletes, most intellectuals separated the life of the body from the life of the mind. Their hunched shoulders and disjointed movements told the story that the only life they trusted was mental. It was as if all their inspired ideals were to be left outside the body, deprived of life, just as the athletes left their luminous presences in the gym.

So with one group of companions I would share the language of breath, exertion toward a common goal, being outside in the sun and wind. But to share the resonance of that experience I would have to go to smoky coffeehouses where my intellectual and poet friends would be hunched over espresso gravely discussing the way to find meaning in life.

To forge a relationship between these two worlds, and therefore a language, it was necessary to find the right questions. On the philosophical-intellectual side these included, "What is the bodily experience of courage?"; "What is the relationship between emotional balance and your center of gravity?"; or "How do you muscularly organize your will?" The dancers, athletes, and martial artists, on the other hand, tended to ask, in action if not always in words: "How do I take the quality of relaxation I generate in physical activity into my life?"; "What is the process I use to learn something bodily, and can I apply that to situations outside my sport?"; and "Is the principle of centering, applicable when dealing with a fist to the face, relevant to the spiritual quest?" These kinds of questions do in fact initiate a dialogue between our thoughts and our musculature. They bring contemplation and action, mind and body, spirit and flesh, values and expression together. Participating in this dialogue thrusts us into a more direct experience with our lives; it means we can live with a greater sense of choice and meaning.

It's a disaster and a scandal that the mind/body disciplines, which investigate these questions, are not integrated within our educational institutions. Instead we're taught rational thought in the classroom, and performance in the gym and dance classes. As a result we have a culture built on competition and rote learning—people who understand their lives only as compartments: business, working out, family life. The schizoid resolution is to integrate these worlds vicariously by camping in front of the TV watching sports or other people's lives. The product is an anesthetized, muted nation of spectators. Such spectators then conduct passionless, disembodied wars. "Thou Shall Not Kill" is supposed to be their first commandment, but they send their military thousands of miles away to decimate civilian populations and their environment—a paradox exemplified in the grotesque parody of a Catholic Cardinal blessing F-14 jets before their bombing runs on North Vietnam.

September 19

Under a day moon Rader and I walk the rolling hills southeast of the camp. The fiery red-orange-yellow-gold palette of autumn matches my festering mood. I have little inclination to be on this walk, but Rader's lighthearted insistence finally overcame my angry brooding. Yesterday's *gasshuku* turned out to be a colossal failure in my eyes. I'm still seething with disappointment and anger.

The conflict arose when I proposed an exercise that asked the men to explore the difference between the verbal commands of the logical, cognitive mind and those impulses that arise from a deeper, more intuitive state. I wanted them to experience the difference between the thinking, "figuring out" self and the feeling, intuitive self. The exercise asked them to stand simply in the aikido *hanmi*, or ready stance, and to walk toward their opponent, but only when they received a "go" signal from a place deeper than the usual mental thought of "go now." After sorting out the basic confusions that normally occur in such an exercise, and presenting other preliminary exercises to support their intuitive capabilities, I let them work on their own.

When I brought them together as a group to talk about what they were discovering, the customary division soon became apparent: there were the one-third who were wholeheartedly engaged, even though they might have been skeptical; the one-third, consisting mostly of the younger men, who seemed to have difficulty grasping the point or had so little interest in it they were not resistant as much as lacking in maturity and experience; and the one-third who clearly had their heels dug in and, verbally or silently, were shouting *NO!* to whatever I presented. The hardcore resistors, led by Harwood, seemed much more entrenched than usual.

Speaking in his nasal voice and pointing to his head, he insisted, "The words or message or what-have-you that tells me to go always comes from here. I don't care what you say, it's always my mind that tells me to go." Through his thinly disguised words I heard, "Fuck you, Richard. No way am I playing along with your program."

"Try it," I'd say patiently. "Imagine that your brain is in your belly. What kind of information is it giving you?"

He would look at me blankly and shrug, "I don't get it. I have no idea what you're talking about." Pointing his finger stiffly to his head he'd say, "This is where my brain is; why would I want to think it's someplace else?"

In as many ways as I could think of I tried to bring him around to using his intuition or gut sense to guide his actions rather than his logical mind. Whichever way I approached the issue Harwood scoffed at my suggestions. Soon I found myself in a power struggle with him. Even though I knew that it was a mistake to meet him head on, my anger and frustration increased with his resistance. I could also see that the men were standing back watching, curious to see how I was going to react. I maintained a certain degree of evenness until he said, "I don't know what you want me to do and I have no idea what you're talking about." In that moment I blew up.

"Take a risk, Harwood!" I shouted. "What do you have to lose? Jesus man, use your imagination. It's not going to kill you!"

Jack tried to come to my rescue, but by that time I was so embroiled in my frustration I waved him off. Everything that I had hoped this *gasshuku* would be was falling apart before my eyes. Harwood and I had locked horns; our confrontation was becoming a focal point for the men, instead of their own work; worst of all I was doing the opposite of what I was teaching.

I was so infuriated by the end of the day that when Jack said, "Well, they sure got to you today, Strozzi," I literally snarled back at him.

As though reading my mind Rader now interrupts my obsessive thinking: "You shouldn't let us get to you. We have to be hard; that's part of who we are. Harwood doesn't really trust you guys in the first place. He's Team Captain; he feels like he's losing control. I personally don't even think an A-Team should have officers. Did you know that at one time there were no officers in an A-Team? I think we should go back to that. A Master Sergeant became Team Sergeant and the Team would work together without the enlisted man/officer hierarchy. First a Warrant Officer was added and that was okay because he's really an enlisted man. But we really don't need officers, I think they just confuse things."

"Do you trust me?" I ask.

He looks at me ruefully. "I'm beginning to, but you still don't understand us and I don't think you know how to present your material to us, especially now during the encampment. The meditation and mental training stuff is some of the most important information you can give us. Frankly, I'm not sure you're getting it across."

"I'm tired of always hearing that I don't understand you guys." I'm frustrated and feeling desperate.

He looks at me indifferently shrugging his shoulders.

I press my point: "Maybe this circle of specialness you draw around yourselves is a defense."

"For what?" he immediately fires back.

"For your vulnerability. You need to be aware of your limitations and I think you're running from them. If you cut off your feedback loop you'll shrivel up and die; that's true of any system."

"Listen," he replies after a few moments. "The team to us is everything. It's the main thing. We share everything together. It's family, it's closer than our own family. There's nothing I wouldn't do for any of my team members. Nothing at all. Our bonding has to do with life and death. I don't think you can understand that. We share everything, including our fears. There's a lot about us that you don't understand."

"I don't expect ever to be part of your team and in fact I don't want to be," I say wearily. "I respect the camaraderie and bonding that you have and I don't expect or even need to know everything about you. But I do know that I could fill in a few pieces that might make you even stronger as a team. But if I'm held out you won't be able to receive what I have to offer." We're silent for a moment. At our feet a column of red ants snakes through the leaves. "Let's keep walking," I say.

Circling around this issue we pass through a variety of moods; an emotional evolution begins to take shape between us. Momentarily free from our teams and the structure of the encampment there's a falling away of roles. A gradual intimacy is evolving, despite the rough posturing of our male egos. What he says cannot happen is happening: He's letting me in more and I'm beginning to understand him more. I also realize that I'm envious of the closeness and bonding these men have with one another. They have a genuineness in their closeness which shows a deep love and care. It's also true—terribly true—that even though they are in a peacetime Army their degree of intimacy and self-mastery could mean the difference between life and death, for them, their teammates, or even a good-sized part of an entire population. This perspective of life and death, of having everything count, is the view of the warrior, and, as narrow-minded as these men may be, it adds an element of responsibility and impeccability to their lives that seems sadly missing for most people.

They are the windbreak for civilization: their protective, tight-knit brotherhood is what society asks of them. We want their protection, but we don't want to know how they do it. At the same time we reserve the right to criticize and even condemn them for what we ask of them.

I've always prided myself on being a fast and strong walker, but Rader's omnivorous gait challenges me. Letting go of my restless thoughts I concentrate on my legs and soon my breath evens out. Rader is clearly at home out in the "bush" and as we move across the wooded fields, he talks easily. We emerge out of the woods into an area that has been recently cut to accommodate a seemingly endless series of power lines, and he tsks at the careless destruction. Pointing to a large clustering of ferns he says, "This buff color is my favorite." This launches him into an unaffected description of the local plant life. I'm impressed not only by what he knows but by his keen perception. While many of the men will see landscape purely in military terms, that is, as shelter or areas for ambushes or hide sites, Rader has the keen eye of the philosopher naturalist. He is a cross between Daniel Boone and Sören Kierkegaard.

"Ever since I can remember I wanted to be a soldier," he says unexpectedly.

"Does that mean you were fascinated with toy soldiers . . . or war?" I ask.

"No, I just knew that someday I'd be in the Army and it would be my life."

"Why not the Marines?"

He gives me a mildly condescending look. "Hard chargers, but no brains."

"Have you ever considered being an officer?"

"Yeah, I had an opportunity to go to Officer Candidate School. But I'm not interested. After a while officers start being moved into staff positions where they're just pushing papers. They start making decisions based on political considerations. Like how they will be promoted, for example, not what's best for the team or the Army or the individual soldier. I like being in the field, out in the bush, and if there's action somewhere I want to make sure I'm in a position to go. I don't want to get lost in some backwater office. If I wanted to be a desk jockey I would've joined the corporate world and made some money at it. It's not for me." He gazes over the rolling hills. The horizon deepens into a violet haze, a nuthatch chirps plaintively. "I really wanted to go to Grenada," he continues. "In fact I put in a special request to my C.O. at the time to be sent over, but I didn't make it." He's not regretful, but there's something left unsaid.

"Why'd you want to go so badly?"

He looks at me unbelievingly, that I wouldn't know. "To see if what I know how to do works."

This is what I call the Brown Belt Syndrome. In more than twenty years of various martial arts I've seen it over and over again. When the student reaches brown belt level, which is the rank before black belt—or sometimes even at black belt level—the student wants to know if "it really works." The internal question is, "Is what I'm doing in the training hall effective on the streets? Will this work in a real combat situation?" The prevailing joke at this level is "Oh boy! A mugger!" When I was a brown belt I used to walk in a nearby park alone at night to see if I might have the opportunity to test myself against one of the local thugs. Luckily for somebody, probably me, it never happened.

But it's not necessarily an adolescent urge. I believe that asking, "How good am I at what I'm doing?" is a natural question for anyone who is involved in a discipline that requires self-mastery and the use of a partner or an opponent. Athletes, boxers, equestrians can find their answers in their respective competitions. But can war games ever satisfy the dedicated professional soldier? Is it necessary to take or lose a life to find the answer? Does it mean that a peacetime army should be trained differently from a wartime army? Doesn't the nuclear age with its clinical technocracy force us to look anew at this question? We mustn't forget that when the Japanese Samurai enjoyed almost four hundred years of peace they complemented their martial training with poetry, flower arranging, and meditation. What is our alternative to using war as a testing ground?

We stop at a small knoll fringed with knots of dying grass and scan the valleys that open to the north and south. In the hazy sky a ragged flock of geese shifts abruptly into a single straight line, becoming a dark spear thrusting southward. Rader begins telling me about a favorite haunt of his in northern Europe. His voice is soft and melodious and he speaks reverently of the mountains, sky, and rivers where he has camped. I'm touched when he says, "I'd really like to share that place with you." When I turn to look at him I feel surprisingly shy. I awkwardly start pulling at an exposed root. We sit in a silence occasionally disturbed by the cawing of unseen crows. The expanse in front of us is vast; it seems to unburden the busyness of our minds. When it's time to go we rise at the same time and without a word walk north, thinking to circle back to the camp.

Partway back we begin talking about the night of the mutiny as a turning point for the encampment; neither of us can agree if it was positive or not. He tells me that the tension and paranoia were running so high that a few of the men had the fantasy that Jack had been captured by the North Vietnamese during the war and been brainwashed, a la *The Manchurian Candidate.* Their fantasy had him completely reprogrammed and then released, to infiltrate the U.S. Special Forces through Sports-Mind and to indoctrinate them.

"Indoctrinate them into what?" I ask.

"I don't know; communism, I guess," he replies.

As we enter the camp I feel happy and sad. The long walk with Rader has refreshed me, but being back I'm burdened with the memory of yesterday's *gasshuku.* Behind my disappointment is shame about how I handled myself with Harwood. While I ask these men to look at their limitations, mine are slapping me in the face. I can half-forgive myself, but in truth there's a heaviness in my heart.

"I feel real bad about how I was with Harwood yesterday," I say to get it off my chest.

Rader looks at me kindly, "Yeah, you were definitely off with him." He shrugs and twirls his *jo,* "Oh well, oh hell." As I walk back to the cabin I recall a line from Allen Ginsberg's poem "The Warrior":

". . . knows his own

sad & tender heart . . . "

Carrying these words over the footbridge to our cabin, I see Jack stepping smartly along the road. I chuckle out loud when I think of him as the brainwashed veteran clandestinely indoctrinating the Special Forces into communism. If Jack Cirie is Laurence Harvey I must be Frank Sinatra in *The Trojan Warrior Candidate.* "You seem better today than you were yesterday," he says warmly.

September 21

During the walking meditation I stay to a small path in the pine woods at the edge of the pond. Shrikes, redwings, starlings, and sparrows flit in and out of the sunlit lane while I take one slow, mindful step after another. When the mind twists restlessly against this bare focus on sensation, breath, and movement I coax it gently back to the present moment; generations of pine needles cushion the easy transfer of weight, the outbreath dissolves into an endless space. The world becomes simple; I'm filled with wonder. Graceful bristlecone pines become silent guardians for my contemplative walk. At the place where the path banks southwest and narrows darkly into the forest I stop for a moment to fill my lungs with the cool air and then return up the path. The pond is to my left now. Monet-like it subdues the raging colors of the trees.

As my path joins a larger trail, Farley and Karter appear to my right and walk quickly past me. The smell of cigarettes surrounds them. I'm disenchanted in an instant, back on the emotional rollercoaster that has been my companion this past week. I stop, close my eyes, and try to regain my state of tranquility. Like a ground-control officer talking to a disabled aircraft I talk myself back into the moment, back to the path by the pond, to my feet, to the pine boughs underneath, to the rich dark earth, to her immense forgiveness.

I fold my hands over my *hara* Zen-style and walk methodically back to camp. I'm clinging now to the walking meditation as a necessity for basic sanity, not a technique for achieving some ethereal spiritual state. My intellectual concepts and expectations are falling apart. One moment I'm ecstatic and filled with boundless energy, the next I'm unexpectedly swept away by a dark river of anger. I place each step with impeccable precision, careful not to lose balance and fall into either a heaven or hell world. By the time I reach the meditation cabin I'm engrossed in each step, in taking off my boots, in seating myself on my cushion, in attending solely to these small actions which need to be attended to.

There is no seam between my sitting and walking, between sensation and breath, between myself and that which is the object of my meditation. This seems not profound but gloriously direct and straightforward. The words of the Japanese Zen teacher Eihei Dogen come to mind, "So when you want spring or autumn to be different from what it is, notice that it can only be as it is."

September 22

A pewter-gray sky stretches over a kaleidoscope carpet of autumn leaves. From the north a dark and insistent wind tugs at my sweater and reddens ears and noses. The men go through a ropes/obstacle course in place of the usual P.T. routine and I'm happily surprised to find that I'm impervious to their boyish clowning. As they move from event to event all retreat protocol systematically dissolves, the prevailing mood not unlike a high-school gym class. Jack, Joel, and I exchange helpless looks but remain silent, simply recording the results of each team's effort. This detachment is a relief from a week of near-maddening reactions, yet I'm not resigned or aloof. In this clear-headed state I clarify and appreciate qualities about each team that I'm not able to see when I'm rigidly locked into my teacher position or reacting to their bull-headedness.

Although it was obvious from the beginning that each team had its own distinct personality, only now are these distinctions beginning to affect their evolution. Team 560, which has been together longer, began the program with a strong sense of team cohesion lacking in Team 260.

Team 560 also has a stable leadership to add to its strength and unity. Team 260, on the other hand, has a new and inexperienced team leader, new members on the team, and obvious discontentment with the team sergeant who has been referred to as the 'anti-Christ' by some of the malcontents. Next to 560, with its strong leaders, capable men, and reputation as the best team in the Battalion, and perhaps even in the Group, 260 often resembles a loose collection of rebellious individuals who require great harnessing to rein in their disparate moods and motivations. Team 260 could play *The Dirty Dozen* with Lee Marvin; Team 560 is the bright and shining knights of King Arthur's Round Table.

This contrast initially made 560 easier to work with, but the pattern is now beginning to reverse itself. The stress of the encampment is making every soldier have to confront himself and his team members on a more genuine level. Everyone's habituated patterns are breaking down, with the resulting confusion and struggle to reform into stronger and more integrated units. The deeper strengths and weaknesses of each team are beginning to surface. As the men of Team 260 begin to talk to each other in a no-nonsense sort of way, they are discovering their similarities and dealing with their differences. In their encampment interviews they speak of this as a time when their team is truly beginning to bond. Because they have little to lose in terms of cohesion—since there wasn't much to begin with—they're willing to take the risks that will strengthen themselves as individuals and as a team.

Team 560, on the other hand, with its fine record and exemplary reputation, is finding it difficult to deal with the experience of breaking apart in order to come together more strongly. Their reputation as the "best team" is now becoming a burden as they try to uphold the status quo of their past record instead of letting go into a new image of themselves. Despite their efforts to keep their best foot forward their image is beginning to tarnish. The stress of the encampment surfaces their deeper feelings, and it's becoming clear that the men of 560 have little tolerance for each others' differences. The Team leaders—Captain, Warrant Officer, and Team Sergeant—have been thrown into a panic as their control is challenged.

Unlike the members of 260, those in 560 are having difficulty letting go because they are so good, because they do have so much to lose. Their high performance level makes it difficult for them to accept the idea that they could even be better. This belief makes 560 more invested in keeping the status quo than 260, whose lack of a rigid structure makes them much more accessible to change and growth. How can I convince them that periods of growth are almost always preceded by times of "getting worse"; that there's a pattern of decline, or disorganization, before there is growth and expansion? As the Marxist philosopher Antonio Gramsci remarked during the Depression, "Crisis consists precisely in the fact that the old is dying and the new cannot be born."

As I watch them move through a particularly ingenious obstacle that requires all the men to pass through a small opening four feet above the ground without touching a wire boundary, I feel as though I'm witnessing two aspects of America. Team 260 takes a startling risk by hurtling their men quickly, but haphazardly, through the opening. If they fail it will either cost them dearly in time or push them into the lead. They're full of energy and sincerity as they mill about the opening, passing one man through one at a time. In their excitement Scott's elbow brushes the wire and they have to begin all over again. They rebound instantly from their failure and again choose the riskier, more creative path. Team 260, with its undisciplined, youthful vigor, is suddenly the reckless, freedom-loving, frontier force of our culture.

Team 560 with its stolid, in-place leadership and vast resources (experienced, fit, and intelligent men) represents the world leader, the established bastion of all that is proper and right. This is the America that's on top, unrepentantly committed to staying on top, even if it means keeping others down. This is the Chase Manhattan Bank America, unwilling to risk the status quo for originality, even in the face of economic and cultural crisis.

The leaders of 560 want to stay in control, but suggestions from the bright, ambitious younger members threaten their position. With strategy taking longer at the planning and organizational stage some of the men lose interest; their attention wanders while they wait for "the orders to be given." Team 560 isn't innovative or creative; they slowly feed each man through the opening, like fitting sardines into a can. Their methodical, safe plan has them complete the obstacle in about the same time as 260.

The strength of each team is also its weakness, which, if brought to light, can be transformed into strengths. America's traditional strengths have now put us into a position of having to defend a world stance of control and dominion, but in this defensive position we're stultifying the creative risk-taking and individual initiative that have made us a great nation.

As I stand watching the men move through the ropes/obstacle course I feel as if I'm passing through one doorway of perception to another. They represent two aspects of our culture, but they also represent our culturally contrived split between mind and body. Of course the mind and body are not separate; they are intimately linked together. As easily one could ask what is the real hand, the palm of the hand or the back? The mind and the body are simply two different aspects of the same living organism called "human being."

I see this split between each team, within each team, and within each man. There are endless ways to describe this division, but essentially it results in a feud, a conflict between that part of us which seeks to know and control and that part of us which seeks to become and join. We're engaged in a continual war with ourselves that we project into our lives, onto our teams, into our families, against ideological enemies who we believe are dedicated only to dominating and controlling our lives, just as one part of ourselves tries continually to dominate the other. Our self-hatred alienates us so that we build a technology of violence in a suicidal effort to be secure. We have outdone ourselves in this conflict by making the enemy not only the man in the other uniform who believes in a false God, but life itself.

Until we come into harmony with ourselves and relax the death grip on our own life, our dualistic thinking will separate and divide our every endeavor, no matter how many bulging arsenals of bombs we stockpile against an "other." The warrior must be savvy about his divided self, and not project his own shadow onto another. He must redefine his battlefield. Perhaps this is what William Butler Yeats was viewing through a glass darkly when he wondered, "Why should we honor those that die upon the field of battle? A man may show as reckless courage in entering into the abyss of himself."

September 23

Colonel Flynn leans against the wood railing above the pond and scans the landscape like a ship's captain at the bow of his ship. A yellow-breasted warbler lands on a post, gallantly cocking his head in his direction, as if trying to make sense out of this massive figure in green camouflage and beret. Flynn's eyes narrow against the thin autumn light as he stares intently into the distance. The warbler hops closer, angling his head to peer out of the other eye.

"It's so goddamn beautiful!" Flynn suddenly exclaims, sending the small bird into flight. He pushes himself back from the railing, crossing his burly arms on his chest. He rocks silently on his heels for a few moments and then nods his head. "Yes, it's beautiful," he says more softly.

Colonel Flynn is officially visiting the encampment to keep track of the program, and unofficially to check on the rumors that are circulating about our difficulties. When I tell him that the problems are not rumors he nods his head knowingly and twists his mouth into chagrin. "We'll do something about that," he answers decisively, spitting a generous brown stain of tobacco to the ground.

Flynn is a career Army officer commanding the Battalion to which these two teams belong. He's a tough, quintessential Green Beret reminiscent of the legendary Colonel Bull Simons: gruff, straightforward, laughingly referring to himself as "the mean kid from River City." He leads his men with a firm, but fair hand, never asking his troops to do anything that he wouldn't do.

Behind his thick neck and flinty gaze is a warmth generated by a sincere desire to serve others. It's primarily due to his bulldog insistence and visionary ideas that the Trojan Warrior came into being. Flynn's ideal of the modern soldier/warrior includes a heavy dose of mind/body work. He has a keen interest in biofeedback and Brain Wave Training. In his spare time, he hangs out at the project's biofeedback lab learning from Joel. It was Flynn's suggestion to use the term "holistic soldier" in the project's proposal, asserting his belief that today's Army is top-heavy in technology and armaments, but lacking in the development of the soldier's human potential. I once overheard him snarl that he had never read a book on Vietnam and wasn't ready to now. When I asked another officer about this I was told, "Flynn doesn't feel anybody really understands what happened in 'Nam; no one can represent it properly. He's also determined to do what he can to not let that kind of situation happen again. You know, get us in a war that we can't win because it isn't fully supported by the country."

As we turn to walk up the path we run into Farley and Oreson—who are almost on top of us before they realize it's Colonel Flynn before them. A moment of confusion arises before they blurt out, "Good morning, sir," their hands scrambling in a quick jig as if deciding whether to salute or not.

"Good morning, Jim; good morning, Larry. How's the encampment going for you?" he asks.

"Fine, sir," they reply in unison, stealing a quick look at me.

"Glad to hear it," he says and nods them on. They smile like school children complimented by the teacher. Walking toward our cabin we pass Janowski. Flynn says, "Hey, Jim! What's that you have on your face?"

Janowski spreads his broad lantern jaw into a smile and rubs the two-day growth on his face, "Well, sir, I was just exercising my beard."

"Just making sure you're not turning into a hippie," he says gruffly, but with a smile.

"No, sir," Janowski drawls.

As we move through the day I watch the intricate web of relationships between Flynn and his men. For many, mostly the younger ones, a father/son dynamic is being enacted here; while Flynn can fondly be referred to as the "old man," he is also the stern authoritarian who must be approached respectfully. The senior NCOs, on the other hand, who have served in the Army as long as he has, and sometimes longer, seem more like teammates with him, like members of a calf roping team.

Nowhere do I see the humorless, vindictive John Waynes, Sylvester Stallones, or Arnold Schwarzeneggers who portray these men in posters or the movies. In our romanticization of the Special Forces we have stripped them of their real character. If we characterize this kind of soldier as "hard" it's probably because most of his time is spent out in the elements and he has developed, like the Eskimos or Malaysian tribesmen, a thick coat to deal with the ravages of wind, cold, heat, and exhausting days. If he's thought of as having denied his personal needs it's because he's a professional and doesn't expect special acknowledgement. He's trained to kill but also has a genuine instinct to preserve and protect.

The Hollywood myth is that to be a hero, and therefore a real man, one must display physical courage. This fantasy thrusts all men into a narcissistic competition that is acted out from the earliest ages on the playground; in other words there's no context for the pursuit of danger other than the notion that this is the way to be a man. In the world of a Special Forces soldier, though, heroism is not a headlong rush into risk but a spontaneous responding to the needs of a situation.

The rabid, bloodthirsty robot that our culture perversely wants the Special Forces soldier to be is more likely to be generous, free-thinking, and eccentric. For these men being tough or heroic has nothing to do with the razzle-dazzle of domination and power. The macho icon that our culture has made out of the Green Beret soldier is in many cases true, it is also true that he may be an individual who has simply acquired the qualities of durability, selflessness, and resilience.

These straightforward qualities are also their shadow side. To a man they are your average American, through and through, the flaws and the virtues. In this ambiguity lies the potential for both the moral hero as well as the insensitive killer. Their tight-knit fraternity can seal off any constructive feedback from the outside, their down-to-earth directness lapsing into a narrow-minded, conservative backwater. If Joel, Jack, or I ever try to join in on their kidding about military life they quickly grow quiet. They can joke about the Special Forces fraternity, but it's *their* joke, excluding anyone from outside the brotherhood. Part of our job is to up-periscope their perceptions into a more panoramic view of the world; to allow the membrane of their community to stretch and trade breaths with the rest of society.

Flynn meets briefly with Jack, has a short powwow with the team leaders, and then rides off into the sunset.

"Why didn't he meet with all the men?" I ask Jack after he's gone. When he first arrived it was as if the sheriff had returned to Dodge City and law and order would once again prevail. Now that he's gone I wonder what the point of his visit was. I'd expected him to straighten things out, or at least to want to hear more openly about our experience here.

"He spoke to the team leaders about tightening up their attitude," Jack reassures me.

September 25

Alder, pine, maple, sycamore, elm, larch, fern; the wealth of autumn piles up at our feet. A slow-moving front pulls the sky a flat white in the promise of weather. A bushy-tailed gray squirrel scampers along a limb like a fullback with a nut tucked in its arm. Our male roughness is softened by the unrelenting weight of this slow undoing that flows from sky to plants to earth. I'm assaulted by melancholy and then inspired by a giggling joy. I stand in awe as the earth becomes a grave.

Lurching down the trail the twenty-seven men behind me sound like the snarling of a medieval dragon. Today's ruck is one of three or four we've planned to toughen our feet and coordinate the meditation with physical activity in preparation for the gut check next week. Today we'll march, meditate, march, meditate, until we've circumambulated the pond. I'll set the pace, Jack and the company commander will be in the rear, Joel will find himself a place somewhere in the middle of the beast. This is the square root of the foot-soldier's life; we march no differently from Alexander's battalions or the Roman legions. It's sweat, breath, pain, camaraderie, and exhilaration. This exercise in sinew and intent is a ritual that the crushing gears of time and technology have not dated.

Some of the younger men are right behind me. Their strides are effortless. Sheffield beams his big smile and urges me on in his Georgia drawl, "Come on Richard, let's let it go." His stocky frame seems no bigger than his huge rucksack, but he floats next to me. I've been given orders to keep the pace under a forced-march speed, but it's difficult to restrain the fire breathers at my heels. Once again I struggle equally hard with my own competitive urge to prove that I can match them stride for stride. After forty-five minutes company commander Thorne is at my side shouting uncharacteristically, "The pace is too fast! Everybody's going to be sitting in their own sweat. Which isn't going to do anybody any good." I'm embarrassed. When Jack arrives with a "what's going on here" look I feel even worse.

We stop in a fuselage-shaped ravine to meditate on the sandy banks next to our rucksacks and automatic weapons. We're street-fighting Buddhas irrigating the waters of the soul. Thayer stares dumbly off into the distance; Mattelli, Harner, and Rader sit quietly with what looks like great concentration; Farley, M16 cradled in his lap, scans the road; Oreson watches a helix of gnats above his head; Braddock, eyes closed, sits straight and still as a totem pole, his mouth busy with a wad of chewing tobacco. Joel rings the bell and after a few moments of stretching we again become the herd roaring down the trail.

I'm unceremoniously relieved of my position as leader. I choose to walk with Team 260. Mattelli strides up and tells me of his idea of an Army patch for soldiers who have attended meditation school: "Maybe it could be a halo made out of an olive wreath."

"It could include stripes showing how many retreats have been attended," I suggest.

He snickers, "We could have a signal calling the men to meditation." He circles his index finger above his head for the well-known gesture to gather and then puts his hands together in a prayer position. I laugh but the men around us remain silent, looking warily out of the corners of their eyes at their team sergeant, not sure if he's serious or not.

The next sitting we do in teams. I stay with 260. Galt, the stout, hard-driving point man, leads us to an idyllic spot on the northwestern edge of the pond among a group of Casarian pines. We drop our rucksacks, place the automatic weapons at our side, and sit cross-legged in our heavy combat boots. After fifteen minutes the distant thump of car doors slamming interrupts our concentration. The sounds of voices—a man and a woman—come toward us. With my eyes closed I hear:

Him: "Let's go this way."

Her: "Which way is the car? Do you think it's okay?"

Him: "Yeah."

Her: "Hmm, it's beautiful out here, so quiet and peaceful. Oh, there's the lake."

Him: "This looks like a good place. We can put the blanket down right over . . ."

Silence. Muffled whispering, the hurried sound of feet moving through the dried leaves, car doors slamming, an engine roaring off into the distance.

"That boy thought he was going to get some poontang. I guess we ruined his day!"

"Well, it's a dirty job, but I guess somebody's got to do it," Martin philosophizes. "It's not easy being the defenders of liberty and freedom."

On the last leg of the ruck through the forest I drop back and rejoin Team 560. The column of men spreads like a languorous centipede snaking through the filtered light. Rader comes to my side. He begins to talk about an earlier episode when Jack insisted everyone sit together by teams instead of alone. As usual he's full of his own opinions and, instead of reacting to him, I listen to his side of the story. Suddenly, without warning he lets out a cry of pain and stumbles to the ground clutching his ankle. He tries to regain his balance but it's obvious that his foot won't support his weight. The medics quickly huddle and examine his rapidly swelling foot. It's decided that the two teams will go ahead and send a car back to medevac him out. I volunteer to stay. We sit in silence watching the last of the men disappear into the forest.

Rader slumps with his head down, his jaw muscles showing utter frustration, as usual. Like me he's a nightmare of a patient, waving off all my efforts to make him more comfortable. Since I figure he doesn't want to be mothered I ask him how he accounts for injuring his ankle.

"I was wandering off in thought, not paying attention to what I was doing," he answers curtly. After a long silence he looks up: "I was thinking that Jack acted irresponsibly in his decision about our stop back on the trail. That's when I slipped and stumbled." His eyes began to fill with tears, his voice cracks: "Hell man, I was doing what I was critical of him about. I wasn't paying attention and I was irresponsible."

He begins to cry and at the same time tries to hide his crying. His frustrations about his ankle, about his struggle with the idea of self-responsibility, about the project and encampment, and about me seeing him vulnerable all come to the surface.

"What are you guys doing?" he suddenly yells at me. "Why am I crying? I'm not supposed to cry. The last time I cried was when my dog died. My wife is going to hate me for this."

Surprised, I ask him why his wife would be mad. "Because she always complains that I don't share my emotions with her and here I'm bawling my head off with you."

We sit together in the darkening forest. It's not in his code to cry, but I wish I could tell him that his emotions are the natural response to accepting this level of responsibility. While I know I only have to be present while he goes through his changes, I'm also afraid that I will be found wanting. To dispel my vulnerability I clumsily tell him it's okay that he feels this way, only to regret my words the moment I hear myself. In the awkward silence that follows we simply sit together in the transparency of the moment, without credentials, without the roles of being a this or a that. As the evening settles around us we slip uneventfully into an unspoken meditation, two warrior monks sitting quietly in the dirt, sharing the same tender heart.

Later I wonder about his words, "I'm not supposed to cry." As men we're raised to endure, to be strong, not to be carried away by our emotions. Crying is for girls; toughing it out is for boys. Though we laugh at this as a cliché, we're fed this garbage throughout our lives. The terrific fear of not being masculine enough, or being foppish—of being gay—teaches us to bottle up our emotional lives until we've forgotten *how* to express them. If we're not vigilant we'll pass down the same bullshit to our children. The work these men have been doing on themselves the past six weeks is beginning to release feelings strong enough to break through the image of the strong Special Forces man. They're feeling things that they're not "supposed" to feel. This is creating confusion, and ultimately the central paradox of this program. To develop the physical and mental qualities that the Army wants it's necessary also to develop the ability to express feelings; yet this seems to be outside the curriculum.

To continue this line of thought brings us face-to-face with the recent failures of our military in America's foreign policy. I believe that the reason we're seeing such success among indigenous Third World guerrilla groups is that they have a conscious, as well as an unconscious, permission to include their deepest feelings along with the deepest potentials. In fact, the willingness to own their feelings and passions empowers them to greater and greater performances. They fight for goals much more immediate than "ideal"—they fight for food, land, basic survival. For these people to experience their depth of awareness and feeling is not in contradiction to their goals. The contradictions for our soldiers begin with being on foreign soil, fighting for a cause, an ideal (democracy) that is physically and emotionally at a great distance from their family, community, and emotional loyalties. This is most recently confirmed by our performance in Vietnam where so many soldiers had so little spirit for what they were doing. Many of them reported that their primary goal was simply to survive. This is in contrast to the Viet Cong who were in their own country fighting for the land that their ancestors had been farming for generations.

As the martial historian John Gilbey put it: "In the end we lost our butt. We lost because the guerrilla theory of the Viet Cong rested on a stronger base than our massive injections of men and material. The Viet Cong out-suffered and out-fought us. Their dead left little debris on the trails and battlefields beyond their bodies and occasionally some poetry; ours strewed cigarettes and condoms. The only solace is that we were wrong and lost. It could have been worse—we could have been right and lost. But, mind you, if we had been right, we wouldn't have lost."

This scenario of a better armed and better trained foreign invader being slowly but surely beaten down by an ill-equipped and poorly trained, but higher spirited indigenous force, has since been reenacted in the Soviet invasion of Afghanistan. I also believe that it's the central reason why all the money that we pour into El Salvador and the money the Soviets invest in Angola have little effect on the outcome of their civil wars. The mercenary is never a true warrior—and pays the price in measure of heart.

Camaraderie

September 26

The turning toward fall is further along in New Hampshire. The long skirted valley at the foot of Mt. Monadnock spreads out in a soft quilt of bluffs, reds, and a fading ocher. We ruck up Monadnock, the largest mountain in this part of the country, in preparation for the three-day gut check and it proves to be surprisingly rigorous with its steep, rocky trails. As we ascend toward the sky, I feel uplifted, happy to be away from the encampment and the emotional rollercoaster it has come to represent. After the hothouse intensity of living side-by-side with these men two and a half weeks, twenty-four hours a day, I suddenly feel free, as if I've returned to my boyhood walks in the wet, damp forests of the Olympic Peninsula. I smile to myself, knowing that this lighthearted giddiness will also pass, but nonetheless enjoying the bounce in my step and the black-capped phoebe that keeps pace next to me in the tangled brush.

As I hoist myself over a large boulder, Braddock's bright, boyish face peers down at me and he offers a hand: "Good day for a walk, eh Richard?"

I have learned to suspect this kind of polite comment as a lead into a more provocative encounter, but there's no trace of irony in his voice. I see that he simply wants to share company for a while. At the next bend Reardon joins us. They quickly begin to pepper me with questions about my personal life. I've nicknamed them the Katzenjammer twins as they're always together, in aikido, in the gym lifting weights, or hanging out together in off hours. I also like them; there's a convivial directness about them that complements their youthful playfulness.

Braddock is from a close-knit, Midwestern, working-class family. His father's interest in souped-up cars was passed on to him. When I asked him about his family he first produced a photo of his mother and father, of whom he's obviously very fond, and then of a shiny red car for which he holds almost equal affection.

At twenty-two Reardon is the youngest member of either team. His bright red hair has earned him the obvious nickname. Braddock, his best friend, calls him "Big Red." Reardon was raised in a New England, upper-middle-class family and was sent to prep schools to prepare him for university and a professional career. Graduating as an average student and outstanding athlete he decided to skip college for enlistment in the Army.

"How'd your family take that?" I ask.

"I guess my Mom and Dad are a little disappointed that I didn't go to college, but they're getting used to it. I think they're proud of me, being a Green Beret and all that. They're very supportive. I feel fortunate about that. I'm not sure if I'm going to make the Army a career anyway. I still have time to go to college and get into another field."

When it comes up that I appeared on the cover of *Life* magazine in the summer of 1968 while I was living in a cave on the island of Crete, Reardon looks shocked. "I was six years old then," he says.

Shifting his chewing tobacco to the other side of his mouth Braddock wrinkles his brow, "Were you a hippie?"

I'm taken back, not only by his directness, but by the way he asks the question, as if he's suddenly stumbled across a rare historical document. "I grew my hair long and lived in Haight Ashbury, but I never felt I really adapted to the hippie lifestyle," I reply.

They continue to probe me with questions. Finally Reardon asks the clincher, "Was it true about all the free love stuff?"

I stop on the trail and look them in the eyes. "I'll tell you the truth, you guys," I say solemnly. "I had to lock my doors and turn it away just so I could have some peace of mind. Man, it was incredible. Any time of day you could get it if you wanted it." They're bug-eyed. When I laugh they look confused, wanting to believe in the lurid sixties.

At the summit a harsh wind from the north wraps us in a cold, wet fog. The sweat on my clothes turns icy. I huddle behind a small outcropping of rocks, digging in my rucksack for a dry fatigue jacket. As I struggle with a stubborn buckle on my pack big Jim Oreson appears from nowhere and quickly frees it.

"The trick," he says, "is to slide it through this end first." He repeats the maneuver a few times to make sure I get it. "You should also change into dry socks," he advises. "Anything else you need?"

"No, but thanks for . . . " Before I'm finished thanking him he strides away. He's the Lone Ranger, I'm the rescued settler—'I don't know who that masked man was but I'd sure like to thank him,' I think.

He's called Big Jim because he is big, but not in a flabby way. Six-foot-three and just under two hundred pounds, he sports an impressive rack of shoulders; a raw power resides in his lean frame. His head seems too small for his large body and his looks are often shadowed by a troubled brooding. I was disturbed once overhearing him comment that if he didn't kill something everyday he didn't feel right.

When I asked him what he meant he replied, "You know, shoot a chipmunk or a squirrel, go bird hunting. Hell, kill a bear." He noticed the shock in my face and he continued patiently, "I'm a hunter. Man is a born hunter; that's what we're supposed to do."

Like many of these men he's openly suspicious of authority, yet he secretly longs for a strong guiding hand. In his streaks of unabashed paranoia he's the one who complains bitterly that Mattelli, his team sergeant, is the anti-Christ and out to get him. When he's excited his right eye is young and innocent, like that of a child, eagerly seeking approval; the other eye becomes clouded and downcast, but with a wisdom surpassing his years. Beneath his quirkiness I suspect a river of unexpressed affection runs deep. In conversation he has said outright, "I just want to do something, to be of use. I want a chance to help someone and use my training." As I put on my dry fatigue jacket I want to tell him that in this small way he just did that.

Last night we held the Samurai Game. Team 560 won handily. This modern-day ritual was developed by my aikido partner George Leonard in 1977. Since that time it's been incorporated into the EST six-day training, and over four thousand executives of AT&T have participated in it—along with countless others in various programs, corporate and otherwise. It's a work of genius that reflects the original thinking of its creator. The context of the game is that of the medieval samurai: one is challenged to enact the disciplined living code of *bushido,* the way of the warrior. The game is an opportunity to participate for a brief period of time in a totally alien form of governance and consciousness. The idea is that once you cross the boundary into another reality you can then look back and see your own life with increased clarity. It's ultimately an anti-war game as it points out the senselessness of war; yet it gives one a chance to experience the intensity that is sadly so often associated with combat.

A group is divided into two armies (in our case it was the two teams). Each army elects a *daimyo,* or clan chieftain, who then appoints a second in command, a sentry, and a *ninja* (spy and assassin); the remaining participants become soldiers. There is also a War God (Jack and I were co-War Gods) whose role is to be capricious, unfair, and arbitrary. If a War God, for example, sees a soldier looking at him he can put him or her to instant death by simply saying, "You die." At that moment the soldier must instantly fall with eyes closed. He or she is then taken to a graveyard and "buried" with a formal ritual. If someone is killed early in a game they may lie in a graveyard for up to two hours.

An intricate protocol must be followed that cannot be reviewed once the "war" commences. To break protocol could mean one's death or the death or maiming of a comrade (soldiers are "blinded" or lose limbs). This necessitates a continuous and heightened awareness to everything that is occurring on the "battlefield." "Battles," fought by single contestants, require the skills of balance, endurance, energy awareness, and a certain degree of luck. One of our battles, between Janowski and Galt, required them to extend their arms straight in front of them, without moving or dropping their arms below the plane of the shoulder. Whoever moved or dropped their arms first would die. While other battles were taking place (Mattelli and Shell, for example, were vying for who could stay balanced the longest on one foot while clasping their hands together over their heads), Janowski and Galt stood motionless for over twenty-five minutes. Jack and I, as War Gods, finally rewarded their prodigious effort by calling it a tie.

As we finally broke apart into the starry evening I overheard one combat veteran sadly say, "It sure is a luxury to go to war, get killed, and then rejoin the living. There's a lot of men I know who didn't have that second chance."

September 28

The bell ending the final evening meditation chimes. The men slowly file out until there are just a few of us left. Some simply sit in quiet contemplation while others massage their legs before they stand up. With his usual nonchalant intensity Dudley is vigorously rubbing his neck.

"What's wrong?" I ask.

"Mah neck's been bothering me from sittin' in the same position for so long . . . but I'm okay."

"How long has it been bothering you?"

"At least fifteen years," he replies.

"You're kidding!" I say, shocked.

"Yep. Fifteen years is just about right. I had a bad parachute landing. It got so bad for a while that I had to be temporarily released from the Army. Doctors can't do nuthin' about it. I don't even think they know what's wrong with it."

"Have you ever been to a chiropractor?" I ask.

"A what?" He looks at me quizzically. "What exactly does a chiropractor do anyway?"

Dudley is a career soldier with over twenty years in the Army, most of them in the Special Forces. He is a Vietnam combat veteran and was a P.O.W. in Vietnam for a short period of time. He wears the dogged obstinance of his rural Southern heritage in the "try and punch me" dare of his jutting jaw and arrogant gait; he's seen his share of brawls, brothels, and combat zones. He acts as though he's carefree, but his body reveals an intractable, rigid man.

"I know something about fixing bad necks," I tell him. "If you'll lie down on the floor I'll see what I can do." He screws up his nose and cocks his head at me. I can tell he might be a little embarrassed by having me touch him, or perhaps by attention to his injury, but he makes it acceptable by denial, "Hell, I guess you can't make it much worse."

He lies on his back in the middle of the meditation hall. I begin to loosen the rigid muscles in his neck and shoulders by working deeply into the connective tissue.

"Yank it off, and save everybody some grief," Scott laughs.

"You sure you trust him, Sarge?" another man chides. "I don't know if I'd let him touch me."

I continue in the semi-dark room for about fifteen minutes. I feel him relax under my fingers. Without warning I quickly adjust his cervical vertebrae. They pop like a child's cork gun. His eyes widen in surprise. The men in the room give a lighthearted cheer, like celebrating a good jump shot. We fall silent for a moment, all eyes on Dudley.

He slowly sits up and rotates his neck back and forth. "Hey, that feels purtty good!" he drawls. "It don't hurt no more. Yeah, I like that. POP! I didn't even know it was comin'!" He stands up, still twirling and bobbing his neck. "Hey how 'bout that! How 'bout that!" The other men look at me with a mixture of admiration and misgiving, as if I've just performed some voodoo and might put it on them next. Dudley chatters on for a few minutes and then walks out happily into the night.

The moment I see him the next morning I know something is wrong, very wrong. He's standing alone in the corner of the lodge. The rest of the men are either eating or standing in the chow line. His face is the white-gray color of a dead fish, his eyes dart suspiciously from side to side. When he sees me he jerks his head in my direction, signaling me over. He glances furtively over both shoulders, leans into me and whispers. "I woke up this morning looking at the wall."

Confused, I shake my head quizzically.

"I woke up on my left side this morning," he repeats urgently, frustrated that I don't understand him.

"I don't understand, Sarge. What d'ya mean?"

"I haven't been able to sleep on my left side for fifteen years." He takes a deep breath, looks over his shoulder to see if we're alone. For the first time that morning, or maybe ever, he looks directly at me, his eyes squinting as if to block everything else out so he can see if I will tell him the truth or not: "Do you think I'm okay?"

I'm stunned. The poignancy of his question is too keen, too penetrating; I've been bitten to the quick. Never mind that he's a tough, experienced combat veteran, a leader among elite soldiers. His usual reference points are gone and he isn't quite sure what to replace them with. He wants to know who this guy is who sleeps on his left side and wakes up facing a wall he hasn't seen in fifteen years.

"Confusion and disorientation are common following a session of bodywork," I tell him carefully. "What we experience as real is intimately linked to the life of our body. So when our body changes, we change.

You're standing straighter now," I point out. "You probably have less pain and more flexibility in your neck now, right?"

"Yeah, it feels . . . good. Well, it feels different." He puts his hand to his neck and slowly rotates his head.

Standing in this new posture gives him an entirely new attitude toward himself and the world. And the increased range of motion in his neck also means an increased range of emotional expression. Dudley's new possibilities for a fresh perception, expanded choice, and creative response come at the expense of a well-known, well-cultivated identity. In his change from one identity to another he's saying, "I'm not who I used to be and I'm not sure if I know who I am now. Is it safe to be like this?"

Like most of us, he's terrified of change and will contort his body to prevent it.

Throughout my afternoon sittings this incident continues to nag me and I give myself over to thinking it through. There is a thread between the episodes with Dudley, Rader's sprained ankle, and Sheffield, who didn't feel like a S.F. man as he relaxed his chest and shoulders. This strand weaves back into the central dilemma of teaching mind/body awareness and self-responsibility in an institution that, consciously or unconsciously, does not support such a teaching. In this case the institution is the Army; but I believe that we would run up against the same obstacles in any traditional structure, such as IBM, the Senate, or our current educational system. If we look inward to take more responsibility for our lives we will become more self-educating, self-knowing, and self-healing. This is threatening to institutional life, for it gives control back to the individual.

The Army contracted for this program to increase the psychophysical performance of their Special Forces soldier. Their goal is to have these soldiers graduate from this training with enhanced skills that can be directly applied to their specific missions and professional military duties. This includes increased physical endurance, strength, and flexibility; enhanced mental concentration, focus, and awareness; and improved interpersonal communication between team members. All of these trainings would be beneficial to the Special Forces soldier's job of education and training, gathering intelligence, and finding and destroying guerrilla and terrorist operations.

Because potential and performance are increased in direct relationship to our ability to be aware it's essential that the soldiers be willing to deepen and expand their field of awareness. They're being asked to pay attention to and be responsible for their feelings, thoughts, and actions on increasingly more conscious and subtle levels. What is starting to happen is that the mind/body awareness work is birthing a new level of understanding, along with the newly acquired potential and skills. This understanding is grounded in the notion of an interconnectedness among all living things. It reveals certain principles, Universal Principles if you will, that govern life. These principles are infinitely more encompassing than the boundaries of race, religion, or politics.

In order for these soldiers to increase their ability to concentrate under pressure, for example, it's necessary for them to evoke the potential of their entire beings. The awareness that brings us closer to our own potential will also bring us closer to our humanity. Somewhere on the way to manifesting greater potential one realizes the truth of our common humanity and individual uniqueness, and in these discoveries are the seeds of compassion. The paradox that keeps coming back to me is that the institution of the U.S. Army (and, again, I believe that this is true of all institutions) prefers, even requires, its members to image themselves, and their enemies, as abstractions, not as unique, responsible, self-forming individuals.

J. Glenn Gray, in his book *The Warriors,* says it even more clearly: "The military man finds it almost a condition of his vocation that he regard men in terms of force, that is, as objects, and disregard all those subjective factors that distinguish every man from every other. The personality of each man becomes of interest to him, not for itself alone, but for its military effectiveness. Hence, the professional is caught in a world of means and instruments, himself one among others. The total human being has no chance to break through to consciousness because there's no official interest in the whole human being. So the professional image of the enemy is a consequence of the pattern of life imposed on those who serve as instruments and not ends. The abstraction of the image is more or less inevitable."

Asking these men to tap into their full human potential, without the Army's "official interest in the whole human being" means that whenever the going gets tough they can remove themselves by simply saying, "I won't go any further in being personally responsible for my choices, power, and influence, because the Army won't allow it." Over and out. Ever try to feed someone who won't open his mouth?

The institution of the Army wants these men to achieve deeper levels of power and control, but they don't want them necessarily to begin thinking and feeling too much on their own. The Army wants the mechanical application of the new performance skill without the soldier deepening into the experience of himself and the world. It's not possible.

Their slogan "Be All That You Can Be" should read "Be Only What We Want You To Be."

September 29

As if yesterday's insight was a virus too potent for my psyche to assimilate, I'm unexpectedly flattened by a devastating flu after aikido class. The moment I crawled into bed the western arm of Hurricane Gloria scythed through New England sending seventy-five-mile-per-hour winds raging through our camp. In my sorry condition the fierce storm could have pulled the roof off of our small cabin and I would've been helpless to do anything. After violently heaving up my stomach until only bile remained,

I burned with a fever while my bones chattered with cold. It was a great relief finally to lie down and give myself up to being sick.

One by one the anxieties around the men, the encampment, and the project drift away, until even yesterday's revelation of the paradox, which obsessed me through the night, succumbs, leaving only the dreamlike sound of the howling winds and a profound fatigue. At some point during the evening Jack arrives with hot tea and the mercy of cold towels. He lights candles in our cluttered bunk room and sits quietly next to the bed. He says nothing; in my fevered delirium the shadows on his face writhe like snakes. To me he looks like a man moving underwater as he towels my face, fills my cup with a bitter Chinese tea from Joel, then floats back to his chair. When he places a warm healing hand on my foot his touch feels a thousand miles away. Being too sick even to do my "difficult patient" routine I surrender to the comfort of Jack's nurturing presence.

Later, Janowski slips unannounced into the room, his medic's bag next to him as he gently sits on the bed. With the delicate touch of an acupuncturist or perhaps a safe-cracker, he takes my pulse with his bear-sized hands. His eyes are melancholic, filled with compassion and love. I'm reminded of a time in India when I was sick and visited by a white-bearded, turbaned physician who looked like an aged Balzac. He too sat holding my hand in a dusky room while a single tear fell from his eye and wet the back of my hand, as if all of his training and experience were finally reduced to a teardrop of compassion.

"I'll return later," Janowski says, measuring out small white pills into miniature envelopes. He strokes my forehead with a hand that could easily cover my face.

Drifting in and out of consciousness, always aware of Jack's steady presence, I recall the women who have nursed me through my sicknesses—my mother, Scout, Catherine, Wendy—and I sadly realize that until this moment I've never had, or allowed, a man to care for me. We're taught to shun physical closeness to another man. Except within the designated boundaries of sports or war, where we can hug, touch, or share with one another after we've beaten or killed other males, we rarely allow ourselves the intimacy of another male's healing contact. By only allowing women to nurture us we have abandoned the yin/feminine principle within us to atrophy. Its power is both our right and a natural healing force.

This homophobia not only strips us of the healing aspect of our male fellowship, it also promotes our separateness through competition and aggression. Yet we ache for an escape from our solitude. When we don't come to terms with this alienation it becomes a major factor in the ways we become sick and die. The ratio of male to female deaths from major causes tells a sobering story: lung cancer 6 to 1; other bronchopulmonic diseases 5 to 1; homicide 4 to 1; motor vehicle accident 2.5 to 1; suicide 2.7 to 1; other accidents 2.4 to 1; cirrhosis of liver 2 to 1; heart disease 2 to 1; AIDS 11 to 1. And while there are more women than men in America there are almost six times as many homeless men as there are women. We live in a vast desert in our male bodies.

Reaching across the tranquil, dark waters of my exhaustion Jack's baritone voice rumbles toward me, "I've never seen you so out of it, Stroz." In the pause that follows I try, but fail, to muster up the effort to reply.

"I remember a time in Vietnam when I was that out of it," he continues. "It was at the end of my first tour of duty and I'd just called in a napalm strike. I was standing bare-chested in the open without a helmet or flak jacket, shrapnel flying all around us, when my replacement said, 'You better find some cover.' I reached down and put my shirt on, not even bothering to button it up."

I grunt something to let Jack know I'm listening.

"Yes, I was at a real low ebb then . . . mentally and physically." His voice is distant, struggling out of him, wanting to find life after years of being locked away in some remote corner. There is a long silence. The wind rattles the windows.

For the next hour Jack tells story after story of his two years of combat duty in Vietnam. The room fills with the ghosts of the dead. In the time that I've known him he's rarely mentioned his war experiences. Now in a torrent of grief, frustration, insight, and humor, the memories layer and fold into one another like the tumultuous upheaval of an earthquake restructuring a landscape. Faces, bodies, and limbs float across my vision as Jack's voice mingles with the roar of the storm. In my helplessness I can only listen, without judgment or blame, and thus become the healer to *his* wound. An indistinct joy between us becomes this fragile trust. We have dropped the exertion of male competition, we have arrived at the effortless circle of friendship, knowing nothing, surrendering to the heart of the moment, healing each other by simply being together. I think of William Faulkner: "You don't love because: you love despite; not for the virtues, but despite the faults."

October 1

Broken limbs, bark, and felled trees lie scattered like corpses of a fierce battle; then capricious unseasonal winds lash the debris of Gloria into momentary whirlwinds. Cumulus formations the size of mountains migrate northwest across a chilling blue sky. Flakes of light flock on the leeward waves of the pond. The air is charged, detail leaps out of the landscape. If it's true that we use symbols to bridge the distance between the psyche and the world, then this day is the story of purification. Everyone seems transparent, without weight, like delicate quivering bubbles that could suddenly break and disappear into the vast stomach of space. I'm mysteriously euphoric, my thoughts purged to the skin and bone of things by my fever.

Unlike other animals we humans have not specialized into any prescribed biological niche. We eat most anything, live in all climates and locales, have sex at any time, create exotic new behaviors, struggle against instincts, and perpetrate genocide on our own species. The reason and the price for this is consciousness—a mixed bag of knowledge and choice. At one end of this spectrum is self-consciousness: Jack and I move shyly around each other, timid about the closeness we shared the other night; conversation is all business. We secretly tell ourselves that any reference to that intimate healing may pollute it, but we're also afraid of the contact. Balanced precariously in the middle of this knowing is compassion:

"How're you doing?"

"I'm glad you're feeling better!"

"Good to see you back, Stroz!" The men are genuinely concerned about my well-being. Rader is uncommonly gentle toward me as we paddle the canoe in the quiet inlets to watch the geese in their V-line south. In this attentiveness and compassion I also find myself questioning: Why all this attention on me? No doubt my very question is the symptom of a deeper illness. The healthy child never questions why he's loved, he simply accepts it.

Walking the trail back after a combat exercise I feel a faint bulls-eye-size sensation in the middle of my left shoulder blade. Turning to look back I hear a dull metal click. What I see sends a shiver through me. Seventy meters down the trail Johnson is in the military kneeling position with his M16 pointed directly at me. Catching up with me his ear-to-ear grin splits his smiling face, "Got you right in the middle of the back," he says happily, as though he had just won a kewpie doll at the fair.

"Not in the middle," I say still shaken, "it was to the left."

Walking together he explains how he would place land mines near a small footbridge. "I'd put them here in the soft dirt next to this small bridge," he instructs me, kicking a shallow hole in the ground. "You see most people would think the bridge would be mined, so they would walk around it. And that's where I'd get them."

"Oh, reverse psychology," I reply flatly. He looks at me confused, wondering about the edge in my voice. James joins us and tells us about the bodies of three European journalists he saw who were killed in an ambush in Central America. "They were twisted and misshapen where they were shot. One was a woman. This type of round expands, it distorts the flesh . . . it wasn't a very pretty sight." He tightens his brow as if he's trying to squeeze the memory out of himself.

Jack drew an imaginary line above his head the other night when he said, "One reason I went to war was to try and understand death—and I got it up to here." Other images and feelings flood through me:

The long-buried memory of the forgiving eyes of a dying rabbit and those eyes' unforgiving lesson about the terrible responsibility of taking a life.

The small neat bullet hole in the forehead of a man I saw shot in a drug quarrel.

Midwifing the birth of my son through a torrent of screams, joy, and scarlet blood.

"You want to carry this for a while?" I'm startled out of my musings by Johnson offering me his M16.

"I just thought you might want to see what it's like to pack the extra weight," he says almost apologetically, reading the perplexity on my face. These men have an extraordinary talent for going toward the soft underbelly, the jugular, that which is vulnerable in the present. Momentarily I consider whether holding the automatic weapon may be an antidote to aggression, like a homeopathic remedy. It's not unfamiliar in my hands. I imagine it as any other tool—a shovel, chain saw, post-hole digger. I shift the rifle into different positions, and when the trail breaks out of the woods into a clearing near the pond I stop and sight down the barrel. For a moment it's pure aikido—I'm grounded through the legs, centered in the *hara*, muscles relaxed and alive, extending my *ki* through my arms, down the barrel into the sights and beyond to the target. I'm filled with power and intention. Without knowing it I'm suddenly leading a teal-green mallard as it skims across the pond. Slowly exhaling I carefully increase the tension on the trigger, everything focuses in the sensation of my finger on the dense cold metal. It's a moment not unlike meditation, or aikido, brilliant in its clarity, an awareness of each fleeting sensation—touch, cold, outbreath, feeling, expansion, stillness, squeezing . . . I release the tension and drop the muzzle of the rifle. The mallard dances itself gracefully on the water, preens its pin feathers and looks perkily around. I remember having read someplace that the reason ducks continue to survive our environmental holocaust is because of the conservation efforts of duck hunters. Those that kill them are those that save them?

I'm suddenly chilled and tired. The rifle seems unbearably heavy, I long to take off my pack and lie down in the soft pine needles. I tell myself that I'm still recovering from the flu, that I should take it easy. The column of camouflaged men disappears solemnly into the woods ahead of me. I'm alone for a moment. A male, dark-crowned junco lands on an overhanging branch, turns his head to look at me, then releases a silver black dropping at my feet. I look up and see one of the men watching me from a bend in the trail. He's positioned himself so I cannot tell who it is; a shadowy figure half visible, half hidden. Is this the sacred warrior ready to serve me in case of need, or the dark god of war willing to destroy me if I fall unawares?

The Western

October 4

Jack, Horst, and the men have gone to Pennsylvania for the three-day gut check march. I'm flying back to California for a four-day visit with my children. In the first few days back home I'm happy and confused in turn. I'm at once ecstatic to see my children, then guilty about being away from them for so long. D.J. skateboards next to me as I continue my daily running routine. He's soaking up father energy. Tiphani has a mega-case of "boys," and though we have short bursts of affectionate contact she is running on a high-octane fuel of teenage hormones that makes it difficult to hold her attention for any length of time. She balances on that precarious threshold between adolescence and womanhood. Wendy, my former wife, is doing her best in a difficult situation and I openly acknowledge her strength and her struggle. While I want to spend as much time as possible with the children it's clear that they have their own priorities with their friends and activities. I find myself floundering in how to be with them. I also feel awkward trying to explain what I've been doing. Everyone seems to think working with the Army must be quite an experience, but no one seems really interested. The more I try and make sense of the last two months the less sense it makes.

On the plane back to the West Coast I fall into a deep sleep and dream: *I am a member of a team of four men whose mission is to capture a woman with dark black hair from a mountain-top estate. The plan is*

to put chloroform on a piece of gauze and to abduct her while she is uncon-
scious. We have a difficult time communicating with each other and the
mission is unsuccessful. I go home and there's a new dojo. The small
office/foyer is painted lavender and a woman's nylons are hanging from
the ceiling.

I tire myself turning this dream over and over for meaning. Whispering in my mind, however, I hear: I'm not communicating well enough
with my team members. There's a need to invoke the female archetype,
but it can't be done through force. The female energy is in my own dojo;
there's no need to look outside of myself to "capture" her.

This evening after dinner I can't sit still. I abruptly excuse myself
and walk out of the house into an unseasonably humid evening.
The dull orange glow of suburban streetlights swallows the thin phos-
phor of a crescent moon and I'm swept away by a deep loneliness. I wonder if I'm reliving the patterns of my father by being away from my family
for extended periods of time. Will I be a shadow figure to my children,
an absentee male who comes home after some adventure in the world
only to feel an outsider within his own family? For the first time I doubt
my choice about coming home instead of being with Jack, Horst, and the
men on the march in Pennsylvania.

I walk to the edge of the subdivision where Wendy and the children
live. A field of scotch broom slowly rises to a small hill dotted with scrub
oak and madrones. I make it halfway up the hill and sit beneath the moon,
my thoughts wandering to the men walking cross-country under this
same sky. While it's a relief to have some distance from the intensity and
ambiguity of the project, the distance also makes me appreciate the bonding and camaraderie that is taking place, both with my team members
and with the men. I'm beginning to recognize my constant drift between
appreciating and resenting these men as a ploy to conceal my own confusion about the modern warrior ideal. Why, in the first place, would an

independent, anti-authoritarian type of person join an authoritarian organization? So they can constantly rebel and bitch? So they can substantiate their outlaw nature?

Confused by trying to sort out my thoughts I'm suddenly saddened by the seeming lack of progress I've made in my meditation practice. Even this soon after the retreat I'm lost in the turmoils of my mind. I take a deep breath and return myself to what is at hand: the rocky ground underneath, the distant screech of a red-tail hawk, the rhythm of breath deepening into my belly. In this moment-by-moment awareness is the kernel of what all the great traditions teach, what the brilliant Tibetan lama, Chögyam Trungpa Rinpoche, refers to as "the precision and openness and intelligence of the present." The practice of a contemplative discipline is not for enlightenment, but to bring this living in the moment to bear into every situation of our lives. To be anywhere else but the vividness of the moment is to fracture our lives into a dull partiality. Regardless of our condition or situation we can embody the wholeheartedness of the warrior through the simple practice of paying attention to our moment-by-moment existence. And even while I try to capture this moment—it's gone!

October 7

I'm with my old friends Randy and Polly at their house on a ridge above San Anselmo. From my seat on the redwood deck I can follow the plunging slope of Mount Tamalpais as it curves gracefully into the valley floor and then slides into San Francisco Bay. In the middle of the Bay is the infamous Alcatraz island and past that the high-rises of San Francisco, which the poet Gary Snyder called "streambeds standing on end." In the east the late afternoon sun reflects shimmering gold disks off the windows of the more elegant homes in the Berkeley hills. With this view and the comforting warmth of a late summer breeze it's easy to understand why sociologists and economists report that the greater Bay Area, and especially Marin county, is the flower on the "quality of life" vine.

Earlier today I attended a large birthday celebration at one of the many fashionable homes that cluster along these hills. The elegant crowd danced to live music and mingled confidently on the garden paths. At one point a civil rights lawyer and Vietnam vet I know from aikido circles approached me and expressed interest about the Trojan Warrior Project. A few others joined our conversation. I found myself lamenting the close-mindedness of the soldiers and the struggle of working through their resistance. As the discussion focused on the difficulties of beginning a dialogue within the Special Forces about archetypal warrior virtues, a woman, who had earlier introduced herself as Starlight, suddenly blurted out, "Oh, you must need a hug!" She flung her arms around me and I barely escaped a puncture wound from the large crystal that dangled from her neck. Red-faced and mumbling I tried to get back on track when a shrill metallic voice interrupted, "It's not what you need. It's what *they* need!"

I turned and looked into the face of an expensively dressed man whose sniffling red nose and shifting eyes said: *Cocaine.* His flashy bleached-blonde companion was styled in mass hip—the cosmetically induced stressed-out look that has nothing to do with the wisdom of genuine struggle, but is worn as an accoutrement to an idealized life in the fast lane.

"Anybody who's in the Army is an idiot to begin with. They're robots who are the muscle for this administration's dirty politics," the man continued contemptuously. Starlight, her hands clasping the giant crystal, looked poised for another hug. My aikido friend hung limply somewhere between bemusement and embarrassment.

"They're not going to change," rednose went on. "They're macho idiots who have no principles. They're mercenaries who would do anything for money." He brushed something invisible from his nose and his eyes strafed the crowd.

"The men I work with," I began, "believe that the reason we can enjoy parties like this and can exercise the privilege of criticizing our government is because they are defending our constitutional rights. When they're in the field, which is often, and which means being on the job for twenty-four hours, they make about as much money as someone flipping hamburgers at McDonald's." The blonde, whose eyes look as though they're glued open, passed her tongue over an industrial-strength layer of lip gloss. She smiled slyly to somebody over my shoulder.

"Oh, come on!" rednose whined. "They don't have to be there if they don't want to."

"That's exactly my point," I replied. "They're doing something they believe in and it's not for the money."

"They like to kill, they're bloodthirsty idiots," he countered. I told myself to be calm and to speak as rationally as I can. I assured myself that there was no way he could understand what I was talking about. Like most of the people there he was seduced by materialism, and making money had become his major motivation—which he then put up his nose. When I told him that maybe we take for granted the rights these soldiers are paying interest on, he harrumphed, jerked his head to someone on the other side of the deck, and stomped off with his girlfriend in tow.

I'm left wondering why I'm suddenly in the position of defending the soldiers. Only a few minutes before rednose sounded off I was complaining about them, then in the next minute I'm running to their rescue. The truth is: the military elite are the windbreak for society; and while most people probably want them to take care of their dirty laundry they also don't want to hear about it.

Everyone else slowly drifted away until only Starlight and myself were left. With utter sincerity she said, "Breathe in the light and positive energy and breathe out the dark, negative energy." As I looked past the crowd of happy party-goers I could see the moon and the sun at the same time.

October 10

"You guys blew it!" Rader's mouth is twisted in disapproval and his eyes are full of reproach. "There's so much more we could have accomplished at the encampment if you guys would've had your shit together!"

"Maybe it's you guys who blew it!" I fire back defensively. Rader shakes his head as he turns and walks away.

I want to shake the insolence out of him and argue my position until I win, but the bottom line is that we both blew it. We asked too much of them too soon and then became rigid in our position as teachers. We didn't admit our mistake immediately on realizing it; we held it like a secret. They fell into their habituated mode of resisting anything new or strange. No way to recoup the loss.

We're all together again at Fort Davis. It's like pre-encampment days with two P.T. sessions a day, aikido class, and classwork, except there's a felt tension that crackles between us and the soldiers. The honeymoon is over. We lost our collective innocence at the encampment and now the hard work of mending wounds and moving forward lies ahead of us.

After aikido class a small group meanders toward lunch. We end up discussing Central American politics and the men express the full political range of opinions. Finally, as our group begins to break apart, I say, "Well, it pisses me off that we're involved militarily in Central America. It also pisses me off that some of you may be sent down there."

There's an awkward silence. They look at me as if I've just said something silly, or maybe I just feel silly for saying it. Finally Dent, a sergeant from a different company, stops, stares directly into my eyes and says emphatically, "Look, I don't especially want to go to war. I don't have anything to prove by being in combat, but I've made my choice to be a professional soldier and I'll go where I'm sent. The truth of it is that if I was from down there I'd probably be a soldier too. I might even be one of the guerrilla fighters, who knows? It's who I am. I'm a soldier."

"What about your children?" I ask. "You leave home to fight somebody else's war and get killed. What about your responsibility to your children? How do you think it'll be for them to grow up without a father?"

"I did," he says flatly. "My father was killed in Korea."

Somewhere in the distance I can hear Dent saying something about respecting his father's choice and how we all do the best we can, but I'm suddenly very far away. The force of the contradiction has spun me off, as if the axial spiraling of the earth has suddenly overpowered gravity, releasing me into a suspended free-fall. How do I comprehend the inconsistency of what I hear? Most of these men, especially the younger ones, never consider the politics of their service. They see themselves as serving the will of the people, through the policies of elected officials. Those that talk anti-communism seem to be reciting it from a book; I don't really believe them. Some feel they owe it to their country to serve in the military. Others, like Dent, link into the karmic chains of their fathers. But people die, children are left without fathers, homes are shattered, countries are torn apart. I feel angry and foolish for ever trying to suppose a world where a warrior can stand for fearlessness and service, instead of destruction.

As in a guerrilla war where there are no clear boundaries, the world can no longer be simply divided into easily identifiable camps of the good guys and bad guys: Christ-loving housewives are hawks; professional military men are doves. Battle chiefs speak sincerely and heartfully about morals and evolution; middle-class professors scold the government for not bombing Iran into a parking lot. Perhaps only threats to the Earth itself, such as the AIDS virus or the hole in the ozone layer, will create the battlelines for a new and more deeply spiritual warrior.

I begin to think of the precedent of limiting technology in war. In many ways it started when the armies of classical Greece, around 450

B.C., emphasized that valor in battle was the result of a strong moral character, not the latest weaponry. One who has the character of a hero, in other words, will act heroically, hence appropriately; hence, in a world subject to moral and divine law, victoriously. The Greeks so firmly believed in this development of moral character that they rejected any innovative military technology that would detract from the expression of heroism. Even after being introduced to the military effectiveness of the bow and arrow by Persian archers, the Greeks refused to implement these weapons on the grounds that it would make war too indiscriminate. They felt that by their eliminating hand-to-hand combat the measure of a man's prowess could no longer be judged. They reasoned that to shoot arrows up to distances of two hundred meters had little to do with mettle, and subsequently outlawed these "immoral" weapons for over four hundred years.

In his book *Giving Up The Gun,* Noel Perrin chronicles how Japanese society finally outlawed firearms after being introduced to them by the Portuguese in the sixteenth century. Recognizing that munitions threatened the social fabric of Japanese culture the clan leaders agreed to put the weapons aside. All firearms were collected, destroyed, and an edict was issued making the manufacturing of any new weapons punishable by death. When Admiral Perry arrived in Japan three hundred years later the knowledge of how to make firearms had been completely lost.

Even though the Chinese invented gunpowder, they chose not to use it in warfare because they felt their warriors were so morally superior they didn't need any inequitable technology. When the Swiss introduced the lethal triangulated bayonet blade in the seventeenth century the rest of Europe rejected it on moral grounds. The horrifying experience of poisonous gas in World War I prompted the rejection of its use in World War II. The ban on nuclear atmospheric testing has lasted for twenty-three years. In 1975 the Americans and the Soviets agreed to stop the deployment of anti-satellite weapons. In the last ten years, through the

Strategic Arms Limitation Talks, the superpowers have slowly reduced the quantity of nuclear weapons.

While the history of war is a gruesome tale, there has also been an almost unnoticed series of precedents for reducing military technology on moral grounds. We must continually remind ourselves that we have a choice about how we think about war, and we must find ways to exercise that choice and taboo alternatives so thoroughly even terrorists won't use them. Since that is presently impossible, we must take a first step by reenacting and revivifying the warrior—with his valor, courage, ability to wait, and moral principles.

October 12

Today is the last meeting of a six-hour workshop on The Psychology of the Body. During the course of the class I lectured on somatic theory, demonstrated bodywork, and introduced them to body "readings." As anticipated, the body readings drew initial stiff resistance. When I told them they would each stand in front of the group naked, or with their shorts on, and I would read their bodies—explain to them my percep-tions of their structural alignment, functional integration, and emotional expression—Wilson said, "No fucking way will I stand up there nude." Eventually Braddock agreed to be a model, with his shorts on. Waiting until they finished their homophobic comments—"What a pencil-necked geek"; "Take it off, take it off!"; "You gonna let him do some *body* work on you?"; "Oo la la, what a bod!"—I began to describe Braddock's emotional and physical history through the way he lived in his body. Luckily, the men were impressed enough by my perceptions to bring forth new vol-unteers, always with the usual barrage of commentary. Whenever I said that I hoped we would be past this level of homophobia by now, they simply waved me off.

"We're going to have a test today," I announce. They perk up; challenges appeal to them. "You're going to read my body," I brace myself for what will come next. Bedlam breaks out; a torrent of comments and jokes fill the room. "The test will be," I continue after the hooting and hollering settle down, "for you to identify on what side of my body I've injured myself." As I undress they snipe at me: "What're you doing after class, big boy?"

I'm standing in front of six men, their notebooks and pens ready. "I broke a bone in my foot when I was running track," I begin; "what foot?" They study my feet and then make a note. "When I was fourteen I fractured my knee, what knee?" All eyes focus on my knees. They scribble something in their books. We continue in this manner until we've reached my head. "When I was thirteen a small metal sliver imbedded in my eye and I had to wear a patch for ten days. What eye?"

I'm standing in front of them almost nude, six pairs of eyes looking intently into mine. This is unheard of; it's rare enough to have genuine eye contact with one of them, not to mention half a team at once. A rare moment for all of us. Suddenly I'm overcome by an uncontrollable mischief: I turn sideways, raise my eyebrows, limply put my hand on my hip, and say in a lilting voice, "Wanna get lucky, soldier?"

There is a moment of stunned silence; then Wilson slips partway off his chair groaning; Drucker pounds his fist, "Shit, I knew it. Damn you. You got us!" Now everyone is laughing hard, real hard. We've been suddenly relieved of some horrible, unspoken, unbearable weight. There's a flood of warmth through the room, like a palpable sunlight. When order returns we again look at one another. This time they're not studying me; they're seeing me, the person behind the eyes.

October 14

I'm sitting in the living room of our house with an icepack taped to my swollen right ankle. Shaba the dog is lying next to Anne, and my old and

dear friend Soto Hoffman sprawls across the couch. Jack comes in occasionally to glance at the video we're watching, *The Outlaw Josey Wales;*
Joel, whom we rarely see in the TV room as he is doing prep for the
biofeedback lab, spending time with Michelle, or simply meditating,
pokes his head in and inquires about my ankle.

Soto, whom I have known since we were sixteen, is with us for three
days as a visiting martial arts instructor. He's teaching classes in Capoeira,
a Brazilian martial art, and escrima, a Filipino stick-fighting art. Our
intention behind introducing these arts is twofold: one, to initiate the
men into the values of other cultures; and two, to demonstrate that a
fundamental principle of awareness lies at the heart of every martial art.

Capoeira arrived in Brazil in the sixteenth century when Portuguese
colonists imported African slaves to the New World. It's a passionate and
beautiful art that weaves fighting, music, dance, prayer, and ritual into
an urgent strategy by which a people learned to struggle, celebrate, survive, and live together.

Escrima has its ancestral home in the Philippines where the cultural
influences of Spanish, Moslem, and indigenous people blended into its
unique and effective fighting style. Unlike aikido, which is based on the
fighting arts of the samurai, a ruling class, escrima and Capoeira share
similar roots of an oppressed and revolutionary peasant class. Master
Ueshiba wrote that aikido "is not for correcting others; it's for correcting your own mind." Mestre Bimba and Mestre Pastinha, two famous
Masters of Capoeira, captured the paradox at the heart of their tradition
by stating only that, "Capoeira is treachery," and "Capoeira is everything
the mouth can eat." While the words of Ueshiba portray an elite's class
interest in self-mastery, the idiom of the Capoeira mestres reflects the
survival instincts of the street fighter. Yet under the surfaces of these arts
lies the connecting thread of a panoramic awareness emerging from a
universal center.

Yesterday during the *roda,* the circle in which Capoeiristas fight according to the tempo of the *berimbau,* the one-stringed instrument that sets the mood, speed, and ferocity of the play, I twisted my ankle eluding one of Soto's kicks. It immediately swelled and though I tried to hobble unobtrusively off to the side the medics saw my condition and immediately came over. Once again I'm the leading man in the tiresome rerun—"Compete Until You're Injured."

Sitting together in the living room, half-watching the flickering figures on the TV screen, we talk of this competitive urge and the other theme that martial artists usually find themselves addressing: conflict and the resolution of conflict. Dodging a self-serving emphasis on technical superiority and tempting equations like "faster is better," we return over and over to the underlying principles on which all martial arts are based. What keeps surfacing for us, in many different guises, is the question of violence. Specifically, when, if ever, is violence appropriate?

Perhaps because it's a Western movie, it occurs to me that much of our cultural response to violence is reflected in, and perhaps educated by, this genre. The traditional "Lone Ranger" Western makes a clear distinction between the good guys and the bad guys. The bad guys are unshaven, loud, and have bad manners. The good guys shave, pat children on the head, and tip their hats to women. It's a simple world of black and white. The genre also spells out what violence is: it's the sheriff and the bank robber shooting it out at the O.K. Corral; it's the rancher and the horse thief trading punches in the Main Street saloon; it's the calvary fighting the Indians.

In many ways this structure of good vs. bad also provides us with the *raison d'être* for justifying our violence: In the early Western of his name, Shane, played by a clean-cut Alan Ladd, orders a bottle of sarsaparilla at the town saloon. The bad guy at the other end of the bar begins to insult him. Shane keeps his cool. The bad guy gives Shane more mouth, throws a shot of whiskey on his trim-fitting good-guy shirt, makes comments about his manhood, and finally boots him out of the saloon. Shane's jaw tells us that he's nearing an edge, but with quiet dignity he leaves the saloon.

The bad guy celebrates his victory with a "Har! Har!" and more whiskey. When Shane returns his empty bottle (he doesn't litter and he's not afraid to come back in) the insults resume. When the bad guy sneers that Shane can't "drink with the men," the macho green light (to kick ass) finally goes on. Shane sends him reeling across the room with a beautiful right cross.

With little variation this pattern of idealization repeats itself through countless movies and novels, until we finally accept it as the culture's officially approved reason to commit violence. It runs like this: This good guy refuses to react to the taunts, provocations, insults, and physical abuses of the bad guy. Because he *contains* his urge for reprisal he establishes his moral superiority to his adversary. Finally the bad guy goes too far and commits an atrocity that demands—and we could even say morally demands—that the good guy finally retaliate with violence. An eye-for-an-eye transcends justifiability and becomes the moral imperative. At this point *not* to deliver the right cross, *not* to invade, *not* to drop the Bomb, becomes morally reprehensible. Appropriate, justifiable violence is the myth of a schizophrenic society that perpetrates violence while it legally and philosophically condemns it.

The Western ethos also teaches us that the good guy never initiates violence, he never provokes his rival. But . . . if the bad guy goes too far pushing our hero over the line, the license to strike back is morally approved. What is that line? Is violence the only acceptable response when it is crossed? The line, of course, is the holy measure of right and wrong. But at best it's a quirky line of shifting moods and arbitrary alliances. If twenty years of working with people has taught me anything, it's the incredible urge everyone has to be right. And whatever we consider right—there we draw that line.

In a Baptist church, for example, it's right for a man to remove his hat; in a mosque it's right for a Moslem to wear his hat. When I worked with the Crips, a Los Angeles urban black gang, I discovered the hard way that it was wrong to start a sentence with a B, as that was the first letter of the name of their rival gang, the Bloods. It was, of course, quite admirable to start sentences with a C. Fistfights, as well as wars, have been started over less.

The boyhood notion of "having a chip on your shoulder" as a dare to fight is the obvious metaphor for appropriate violence because of its pure arbitrariness. We can place that dare wherever we choose, but as a people we are so enamored of violence that we allow over ten thousand people a year to be executed by guns. While we have a formal constitutionalized peace, someone is injured by a handgun every two and a half minutes; on the average, one child under fourteen is killed by a handgun every day. We have put a nuclear chip on our national shoulder to let the world know where our line is. Unless we come to terms with our patterns of violence, it may be the last line.

A year and a half ago I returned home to find a car full of boisterous teenagers celebrating high-school graduation on the driveway up to my house. When I asked them to pick up their litter, some of which was broken bottles, they laughed saying the bottles didn't belong to them. I took a deep breath and pointed out that the bottles in their hands were the same ones that were broken in the driveway. A rough, angry voice from somewhere in the back seat growled, "Go fuck yourself; we're not bothering you." I took another deep breath. I told them I didn't want any trouble. They could stay, but I was concerned about my children hurting themselves on the glass, and I didn't want anybody puncturing a tire. Someone popped open a beer and burped. Everyone laughed. I might as well have been one of the trees.

I was working hard to keep my voice even, but inside I was shaking with anger. How was I going to work myself out of this situation? Finally a single voice in the back came forth, "I'll help you pick up the bottles."

'Great!' I thought to myself. "I'll help you pick them up," I quickly replied. I was relieved by the hope for a peaceful solution. I opened the door of the driver's seat to let out whoever it was that wanted to help. When I turned my back somebody shot out of the back seat, grabbed my arm, and spun me around. A bolt of adrenaline surged through me and without a moment's hesitation I backhanded him in the face. I was suddenly released from all restraints. I'd been assaulted physically, it was now my right to unleash the fury I felt from the beginning. As the driver came toward me I pushed his grab aside and pinned him by the throat against the car. The two girls were shrieking bloody murder, two other boy-men were standing on the other side of the car paralyzed. The kid I hit was stumbling around holding his face. I was in full-bloom righteous indignation by this point. Having given myself total permission to set justice in order I turned to settle matters with the kid under my grip. What I saw stopped me in horror. He looked at me in total and absolute fear. His eyes were glazed in terror; his body shook violently. A searing pain spread through my chest and heart. I suddenly lost my stomach for revenge.

I released the kid and cursed them out loud for getting me into this mess. I started picking up the beer bottles on my own. They piled back into the car and tires squealing, sped up the driveway. My arms full of empty Schlitz I started walking to the trash cans. Waiting for me, tire iron in hand, was the kid who I hit in the face. He was shaking with anger and the tire iron trembled in his hand. I stopped, took the *hanmi* position and said evenly, "You don't want to do that." He stood before me livid with rage. His friends stood behind him, expectant. My eyes never left him. Finally, he turned, called me an asshole, jumped in the car and drove off. Standing calmly like that was my best technique of the day.

Later when I recounted this story to friends, they all heartily agreed that my actions were appropriate. "Who really knows what they might have done if you hadn't acted so forcefully," said one woman friend. I noted that she couldn't bring herself to use the word "violently." "They were breaking the law. You were within your legal rights," an older friend told me. "Hey, man," a black-belt karate friend commented, "he grabbed you, he started it. You did the right thing." "Maybe it taught them an important lesson, maybe now they'll think twice about what they do," someone else offered.

Supposedly I had every right to do what I had done, but why didn't I feel the euphoria that one does when revenge is acted out in the movies? It was because I was the cause of the pain and fear in that kid's eyes. I found nothing redeeming about inflicting pain, regardless of how judicial. The same friends who rallied with positive responses to the incident completely dismissed this perspective. One friend said I was being too "thin-skinned," something Sergeant Rader often accused me of.

Seeing that boy's terror as I held his throat made me understand what Nietzsche meant when he wrote in *The Wanderer and His Shadow*, "Rather perish than hate and fear, and twice rather perish than make oneself hated and feared."

The revenge myth of the good guy at the O.K. Corral is not unique to the Western, or the Special Forces soldier, or the plethora of cop programs that dominate TV. Bernhard Goetz, who was lionized and enthusiastically supported by the New York public for shooting four would-be muggers in a New York subway, is a frank testimony that we don't live in a moral universe separate from Rambo, or Charles Bronson in *Death Wish*, or the Ayatollah Khomeini. The only difference seems to be where we draw the line, or when we decide to place the chip on our shoulder— not if we have the actual right to act violently.

All this consideration about violence and morality naturally brings to mind anonymous inspirational statements by great spiritual leaders to "Turn the other cheek" or "Relate to the part of your enemy that knows what's best" or "Shake hands and go have a beer." But these are easier said than done. The scene with the drunk teenagers clearly exposes my limitations. Nevertheless, I think there's always the possibility of a conscious choice. It comes from paying attention. What we need to pay attention to is that moment when the yellow light for murderous *intent* is about to change to the green light of murderous *action.* If we can awaken ourselves from our habitual preoccupations, there's the possibility of bathing in our own fire instead of rushing into battle. Such a bath may actually be more cleansing, and even sensuous, than a fight.

We also need to discover an ethic that's not based on right or wrong, or a shifting ethical line, but is more in spirit of what Barbara Tuchman perhaps intended when she asked in *The March of Folly:* "Why do we invest all our skills and resources in a contest for armed superiority, which can never be attained for long enough to make it worth having, rather than in an effort to find a *modus vivendi* with our antagonist—that is to say, a way of living, not dying?"

Pay attention. Stay awake. Be aware. That which is so simple is possibly the only thing we can do that will save our world.

October 17

George Leonard, my longtime friend and partner at Tamalpais Aikido, has been with us for the past three days. In the tradition of the samurai of Japan and the Renaissance man of Europe, George embodies a tapestry of experience that ranges from warrior, to artist, to social commentator, to teacher. He's the author of six acclaimed books on social and individual change; for seventeen years he was a senior editor at *Look* magazine; presently he serves as a contributing editor to *Esquire* magazine. He's a gifted clarinet and piano player and has written and composed a fully staged musical. George served as a combat pilot in the southwest Pacific in World War II and as an air intelligence officer in the Korean war. He began practicing aikido when he was forty-seven, a time when most athletes have retired, and then continued to earn his black belt when he was fifty-two. He is presently a teacher and *Sandan,* third-degree black belt.

In many ways George is also the connecting link among everyone in the project. Jack attended George's energy awareness training program at Esalen Institute. Chris Majer, the president and co-founder of Sports-Mind, was strongly influenced by *The Transformation, The Silent Pulse,* and *The Ultimate Athlete,* George's seminal works on human potential. When SportsMind was offered the Special Forces contract, Chris and Joel naturally sought George's counsel for matters of curriculum and teaching faculty. George immediately thought of Jack as the perfect team leader and me as the aikido teacher.

While George was here he taught all the aikido classes. Janowski taped my ankle and I trained with the rest of the soldiers. I found ways to compensate for my ankle on the aikido mat; as long as my weight didn't shift too far back and to the right, I was fine. It was a welcome change to be a student as it put me into a slightly different relationship with the men in aikido. Not having the responsibility of teaching, I was able to work longer and more intensely with different individuals.

In his brief stay George became the tribal elder. His reception by the men was perhaps best summed up in a comment by Dudley after class: "I was amazed the way he moved on the mat," he said. "When I first saw him, he was just this old guy with white hair. I mean he didn't look bad or out of shape or nuthin', but I never expected he could move so gracefully. Hell, he's twenty years older than me and I can't move half as well as him." For these men, unswerving, as we have seen, in their vigilance for pretense, George's ability to walk his talk on the mat, a domain where every action is magnified, gave credibility to his talks.

The contact the men had with George gave them a clearer sense of who we were. We became more real in their eyes. We weren't simply these guys from the West Coast trying to stuff strange and exotic teachings down their throats. For the first time they saw us as part of a larger community of people who are authentically committed to awareness work, much as they are to their own practice. George also sowed the theme of warriorhood throughout his classes, talks, and informal discussions. We had initiated such discussions before but were met generally with reluctance. When in his first meeting with the men George acknowledged them as "the warrior class of the modern military," I found myself anticipating the usual scoffing and looks of disdain that normally follow any remarks they may perceive as idealizing, any talk of themselves as being anything other than men committed to doing the best job they can. But this didn't occur.

"We could tell he wasn't just trying to jerk us off," Meredith told me later. "He meant what he was saying and we respect him enough to hear what he had to say."

"How many of you feel that Rambo represents the Special Forces soldier?" George asks in his first class. There is laughing and head shaking. Martin solemnly raises his hand, but the pucker at the corners of his mouth tell us that he's again being the prankster.

"How many of you enjoyed the movie?" George asks again.

Almost everyone raises their hands. "I liked the action," someone says.

"I took my nephew and then I told him the difference between the movie version and the real version," another man adds.

"If I don't see Rambo carry his ruck I'm not gonna go to any more of his movies."

"Yeah, where does he get his supplies and ammo? We carry it on our back, not Hollywood style."

When George asks how they would define the ideal warrior, their responses reflect the imperishable code throughout time—loyalty, intensity, compassion, service, calmness under fire, patience, strength of will. Jack adds, "The warrior is also aware of his limitations. It's not that the warrior doesn't have any holes, it's that he's aware of his holes."

The two virtues consistently at the top of the list are self-mastery and service. "We're always practicing to be better," Galt says laconically. "We may never have to use what we do but that's not to say we can't keep improving ourselves."

"It's not only improving our skills," Janowski adds, "it's improving ourselves, being the master of ourselves."

"We also need to differentiate between self-mastery and rigidity or over-controlling," I say.

"Control follows awareness," Oreson smiles impishly, feeding back to us the biocybernetic axiom we always present to them.

"It seems to me," George says, "the warrior virtue of service, and especially the service of protecting others, could also be a justification for your job." He pauses and surveys the room. "Does this mean service can justify a violent way of life?"

"I don't think we're necessarily violent men," James snaps. "We need to be comfortable with violence because it's part of our job, but we don't crave it. Part of this is believing in something greater than yourself. We're willing to put our life on the line, for example, to protect our country."

Dunham tells us how he reenlisted after leaving the service: "I was driving to work one morning on the expressway and I heard on my car radio about the Marines getting killed in Beirut. I remember seeing the rising sun, real red in my rear-view mirror. When I got to my exit, I just kept driving, and I went and signed up for another tour. I was making $30,000 as an electrician, and I could have made more. But I didn't want the money. I wanted to serve."

"My father, grandfather, great-grandfather, and all my uncles were in the service," Shell says, "and it just seemed natural that I to go in too. My father was in World War II, but not all of my relatives were in war and none of them made it a career. From a very young age I was taught that to join the service was just that, a place to serve. It wasn't about making money or making a name or being a man or going to war or any of that kind of shit. It was just a way to be of service."

"What kind of service?" I ask.

He looks at me quizzically, as if the question is too obvious to answer, "To protect others . . . and our country."

"And our rights!" Dunham jumps in. He's heated up; his fervor brightens his face to the color of his hair. There's a wide-open sincerity about this man that's both contagious and admirable. "We protect our right to sit here and talk like this. We protect the rights of those intellectual long-hair hippies in Berkeley or wherever, even here in Harvard Square, who talk down the country and badmouth us. Our job is to serve our country by protecting these freedoms. Maybe our mission will be to put our lives on the line someday, maybe not. But in the meantime, we're here to serve and protect those rights." This could be flag-waving, but from him it is a genuine realization of service.

"You know that big earthquake they had down in Mexico?" he continues. "They could've used us!" He shouts like it's as obvious as butter on toast and he wants everyone in the next state to know about it. "We could've helped. We just want to be part of the action. It doesn't have to be war; we just want to put our skills to use somewhere."

There's something exciting and infectious about this idea and others pick up on the possibilities. In a matter of minutes a half-serious operation has been roughed out: Depending on the geographical location and the extent of a disaster, a single Special Forces A-Team, or a unit as big as a company, could be parachuted into the area. The men would immediately set up a communications and logistics system, provide medical services, security against looters and rabid animals, and develop an operational plan for organizing the different aspects of the rescue effort.

"We're used to working twenty-hour days," Dudley throws in. "We could do this easily."

"How about a joint effort?" I offer. "Or even competition with, say,

the Soviet Union in responding to an international disaster?" Some eyes
light up with interest, their competitive edge piqued; others scowl, still
unsure about cooperating with the "enemy."

The excitement here is about doing something, about putting their
training and skills to use, about challenges and overcoming obstacles; in
the moment it clearly doesn't seem to be wed to the experience of war.
The quandary we circle around is whether or not the warrior has a place
outside of war and the military?

Mattelli, combat veteran, and in my opinion a warrior of high caliber, summons up an ancient initiation ritual when he says, "We're all
acolyte warriors until we've been tested in combat." So, despite my own
search for a larger definition of the warrior, I'm forced to acknowledge
the singular baptism of war itself.

There is a brief scene in the movie *Rebel Without A Cause* that exemplifies this need for initiation. When James Dean is about to play "chicken,"
his rival, Buzz, turns to him and says, "You know I like you."

Dean replies, "Then why are we doing this?"

Buzz shrugs and says, "We have to do something."

Yes, we have to do something. The question is, how can we do it without a myth of destruction?

What is it in war that we seek? In the great works of philosophy and
literature, both East and West (Plato's *Republic,* the *Bhagavad-Gita*), the
warrior class serves a noble and necessary position in the overall well-
being of society. But closer reading also shows us that the intrinsic virtues
of the warrior—commitment, service, courage, loyalty, comradeship—
are not his sole property, but belong to the entire human family. The
warrior class thus becomes more than a caste or a gender or location
for pieties, but a piece of the human heart that hungers for a passionate and wholehearted life. This urgent calling of nature longs to be tested,
seeks to be challenged beyond itself. The warrior within us beseeches
Mars, the god of War, to deliver us to that crucial battlefield that will

redeem us into the terrifying immediacy of the moment. We want to face our Goliath so we may be reminded that the warrior David is still alive, in us. We pray to the War Gods to guide us to the walls of Jericho so we may dare the steadfastness and strength of our trumpet call. We aspire to be defeated in battle by powers so much greater than ourself, that the defeat itself will have made us larger than when we arrived. We long for the encounter that will ultimately empower us with dignity and honor.

But the warrior cannot control the course of the universe, the progress of civilization, or the inventions of non-warriors that have transformed the battlefield from human to machine dimensions. Because we have blurred the distinction between the sacred treasure of the warrior's calling and the super technology of nuclear war, it's no longer possible to redeem our heritage by literally going to war. Doughboy managers, steelhead technicians, power-mouth bureaucrats, cyborgs, androids, and technocrats flip switches and punch keyboards that will begin and end a so-called war—and a civilization, and a planet—within minutes and hours. This is clinical relief for our urge to fight without the martial contest of struggling with our inner demons. Rambo *did* express some of the warrior's dismay at this co-opting of the battlefield when he shot up the computers at the end of *First Blood: Part Two.*

Backed into this nuclear corner, we perhaps cling to one remaining hope that we can call on the sympathetic magic of the warrior gods to cure us of our infirmity: Burn the brush to stop the forest fire. The malady is the remedy. Is it not dangerous to invoke this warrior energy while we're in such a precarious position, where one slip, one miscalculation could fry a million generations into the future?

But hasn't it also been the systematic repression of our warrior urges that has placed us in this danger? And isn't it risk that we want to expose ourselves to? Or is it to have risk expose what is truly inside of us? Be not mistaken: the longing is there and it's loving and terrible and beautiful and tragic. We must step lightly but courageously. We must take it easy, but we must take it.

"After my second tour in Vietnam," Jack tells us, "I realized it was not in the cards for me to die a quick and glorious death. I was going to live. So what was I going to do about that? How was I going to face and deal with living? That was stage two in the warrior game. I was going to live, and I wanted to live as a warrior. So I figured I better start planning to live a good life."

Then how are we going to deal with life? Own a BMW, drink the right wines, win a packaged vacation for two? I know Jack well enough to understand the degree to which he means something entirely different from that. Most of all, we need to wake up. Instead of taking the easy route for prescribing how-to-do-it formulas we must look inside ourselves and define our own personal battlefields. The gods of the spirit resent the obeisance to technology and they will eventually reclaim their portion of our lives. If we believe in spirit, let's petition those gods for guidance, and let's be sure to include Mars as well as Eros.

In *The Outlaw Josey Wales* Clint Eastwood, playing Wales, threateningly approaches the encampment of Ten Bears, the Comanche chief. Surrounded by young warriors, Ten Bears strides forth to meet him. He is impressed by the rebel who will not make peace with the bluecoats, and he offers Wales safe passage. Wales refuses it. "I reckon not," Eastwood says, for he is the last breakwater protecting many others.

"Then you will die," answers Ten Bears.

"I came here, to die with you," Wales responds. "Or live with you. Dying ain't so hard for men like you and me. It's living that's hard . . . when all you've ever cared about has been butchered or raped. Governments don't live together; people live together. With governments you don't always get a fair word or a fair fight. Well, I've come here to give you either one, or get either one from you. I came here like this so that you know my word of death is true—and that my word of life is then true. The sign of the Comanche, that will be on our lodge. . . . That is my word of life."

"And your word of death?" asks Ten Bears.

"It's here in my pistols. And there in your rifles. I'm here for either one . . . I ain't promisin' you nothin' extra. I'm just giving you life, and you're giving me life. And I'm saying that men can live together without butchering one another."

After considering this, Ten Bears gives his thoughtful response: "It's sad governments are chiefed by the double tongues. There's iron in your words of death for all Comanche to see. And so there is iron in your words of life. No signed paper can hold the iron. It must come from men. The word of Ten Bears carries this same iron of life and death. It is good that warriors such as we meet in the struggle of life. Or death." He slashes his hand with a knife and declares, "It *shall be life!*" Wales follows suit. They press their bleeding hands together.

Maritime Operations

October 19

The cold is unexpected and my fingers fumble awkwardly with the pen and paper. I'm sitting next to the door hatch, facing forward, on the starboard side of a Blackhawk helicopter. Chief Kirby is on my left, Sergeant Shell sits directly across from me, and the helicopter crew chief, in his insulated flight jumpsuit, gloves, and electronically wired helmet, sits next to him. Like the pilot and co-pilot, whom I momentarily glimpsed as I took my seat, the crew chief looks the part of the post-apocalyptic sci-fi android. Directly behind me is the huge fuel bladder that Rader made sure that I knew "is one of the problems with these aircraft . . . that oversized, underprotected fuel bladder will blow like a torch if it goes down. I heard" he snickered, "that one just went down last week at Fort Bragg." Leave it to Rader to find the weak link. I'm getting used to his sarcasm, but this doesn't do anything to ease my flying anxiety.

We're following the coastline north and at one thousand meters the marine dampness penetrates to the marrow. A pale blue cast begins to appear around my fingernails and my jaw is rattling. Across from me Shell sits calmly looking at a spot somewhere to the left of my ear. When I glance at Kirby he smiles back wryly. They're both dressed like me in fatigue jackets, trousers, and boots and they must be feeling the cold too, but they show no sign. The flight crew chief rubs his gloved hands up and down his shoulders and studies each of us separately. We must seem a bit loco to him, dressed as we are, but not seeming to be affected by the weather. When I look back at Shell he's staring directly at me this time. His eyes tell me that he *is* cold, but the game is not to let this flyboy know. It's the S.F. honor game: part macho, part pride, part meditation.

Beneath us the New England countryside unrolls like a Persian court rug. Lakes of navy blue, cream-colored cornfields, maple reds, sycamore and poplar yellows, blue-green spruce; fields plowed a rich sienna weave a colorful land tapestry next to a gray and sober Atlantic. The shadow of our warbird glides darkly across the fat land, dissecting small towns and their white steepled churches, perfect streets, and serious two-story houses. This is what these men serve: this calm, this abundance, this xenophobia. Looking down on this idyllic scene I wonder why someone would want to leave this security to go to some distant jungle to fight a war of little significance. Yet it's towns and communities like these, throughout America, whose war memorials are crowded with the names of their men. Glenn Gray considers this paradox in *The Warriors:* "We do not know whether a peaceful society can be made attractive enough to wean men away from the appeals of battle. Today we're seeking to make war so horrible that men will be frightened away from it. But this is hardly likely to be more fruitful in the future than it has been in the past. More productive will certainly be our efforts to eliminate the social, economic, and political injustices that are always the immediate occasion of hostilities. Even then, we shall be confronted with the spiritual emptiness and inner hunger that impel many men toward combat. Our society has not begun to wrestle with this problem of how to provide fulfillment to human life, to which war is so often an illusory path."

How do we fulfill our spiritual yearnings in a society that places materialism as its highest good? What makes life so dreary that men cheered in the streets when World War I was declared? Perhaps the men in these small towns are really marching away from boredom and lack of meaning, and not so much toward war. During his visit George mused that "it may not be that war is so often vivid, but that peace is so often drab.

The end of war may require the creation of a peace that is not only just, but vivid."

How, then, does the warrior provide himself and his community with spiritual fulfillment without taking the "illusory path" of war? On one side of my mind I can hear Jack saying, "Being a warrior doesn't mean winning or even succeeding. But it does mean putting your life on the line. It means risking and failing and risking again, as long as you live." On the other side I can hear Joel, "The real challenge is the inner journey. To go inside ourselves and find out who we really are is one of our greatest challenges." These are two aspects of the warrior ideal, a life of action and a life of the spirit, but if they are presented as either/or propositions each becomes dogma. At forty-one years old I risk more, and grow more, by challenging myself on emotional and spiritual levels than I do by putting my life on the line. At the same time I find it artificial to separate the life of my body from the life of my spirit. The challenges I meet and overcome spiritually will give integrity to my actions in the world; and the challenges I present myself with physically will strengthen my spirit.

The warrior ideal that I envision is a state at which the individual is connected to an inner core of spiritual experience, while at the same time actively engaged in the world. In Hindu literature the metaphor is that of the lotus, whose roots reach deep into the richness of the earth to feed and produce an exquisite flower. The martial arts, especially aikido, speak to this ancient yearning. In his book *Sources of Japanese Tradition* Tsunoda Ryusaku clearly describes the ethic of the Samurai:

Outwardly, he stands in physical readiness for any call to service, and inwardly, he strives to fulfill the Way. Within his heart he keeps to the ways of peace, but without, he keeps his weapons ready for use.

Training in the martial arts can provide the challenge of self-mastery in mind, body, and spirit while teaching something very practical—how to protect yourself and others in a hostile situation. Yet there is another side reflected in karate teacher Thomas White's tale about entering his first dojo in Okinawa while serving in the Army in 1963:

"For what reason do you come?" the Master asked him.

"I have come to learn the art of self-defense," he replied.

"And which self do you wish to defend?" he responded.

The crew chief eyes me curiously as I scribble furiously in my notebook. I'm part of this cadre of elite soldiers, but at the same time I'm not one of them. I wear their uniform, but I have no rank on my lapel. Like them I sit quietly, apparently unperturbed by the cold, yet I don't wear the green beret or have their flash symbol on my shoulder. I feel them as my brothers, yet we come from a different tribe. If I needed help I know I could count on them, and if they called on me I would come unhesitatingly to their aid; yet there's no fanfare about loyalty.

There is a shared affection for impermanence and the invigoration of life, but we don't philosophize about it.

The crew chief shivers and rubs his hands together. Across from me, so close that our knees almost touch, Shell sits straight and relaxed, his breath deep in his belly. His wide forehead and steady gaze indicate the depth of his equanimity, not just for his circle of friends but for the entire human community. His eyes are alive and seeing, but I know he's concentrating on something inside of himself. I feel proud of these men and proud that I'm somehow part of them and proud that we're sitting here still and relaxed despite the fact that it's so cold our breath clouds in front of our face. Perhaps, at least for now, it's fulfillment enough for the warrior to find combat with the cold and to perfect a state of inner control without controlling others.

October 20

It's night and I've cleared away a small corner of our crowded camp table to write. As the darkness closes in on my single light it draws the thick forest with it. Overhead in the cloud cover a lopsided, three-quarter silver moon floats in a cream-of-wheat sky. I'm hunched against a stubborn breeze that miraculously finds its way from the shore, about two miles due east, to our campsite. We're on the windward side of a small island off the northeast shelf of the continent, where winter begins early and prevails over six months. All around me I can feel the landscape hardening into a stiff, cold callous.

I'm fatigued from two ocean swims today, but if I close my eyes and feel deep inside myself there's an aliveness, a trembling that hovers somewhere between dread and pleasure. I'm drawn to this feeling, especially the promise of power, and at the same time I fear its pull. I wish to hold it and make it my own; but it alarms me so I keep a respectful distance, close enough to allow its shadow to touch me, yet far enough away to keep my perspective. The harsh beauty of the landscape and our intimate relationship with the ocean stirs me; yet the physical demands of the swims and the unceasing cold erodes my confidence.

Although today's swims were designed to be introductory in nature I was shocked to find that I'm already close to my limit. I'm concerned, knowing that the schedule is quickly to work us up to swims of three to six kilometers a day, plus boat work, plus casting out of a Coast Guard cutter at twenty knots. Today I was consistently last and I had that sinking beginner's feeling that I was holding up my swimming buddy Sheffield. At one point Dunham shot by me like a dolphin, talking effortlessly while I struggled to keep a straight line with my injured ankle. Everyone else seemed to be breezing while I had trouble even putting my dry suit on. As it turned out my suit had a hole too small to be detected, but large enough to soak my wool sweater, socks, and sweatpants I wear as undergarments.

After being in the ocean for an hour and a half I was almost completely soaked and chilled.

Up from our campsite there's laughter and hooting from 260's area. There's a card game in Farley and Martin's roomy stand-up tent; Larry Burback's raucous laughter cuts through the night. Larry arrived with George Leonard and he'll be with us until the end of these operations. An exercise physiologist and world-ranked triathlete, he's teaching classes in nutrition, endurance training, mental attitude, and his specialty—a high-voltage zest for life. The minute I laid eyes on him I recognized a friend and brother. His broad-faced grin and prankster eyes reflect the ironies of being a bareback bronco rider, policeman, commercial fisherman in the Bering Sea, skydiver, international rugby player, and restaurateur. More than Jack, Joel, or myself, or any of the guest presenters, Larry is most like these men in his audacity, Go-For-It mentality, and willingness to get down and dirty with them. While he takes nothing seriously, life is sacred to him. He offers something that no one else has: he makes the men laugh at themselves.

Yesterday while we were waiting for the helicopters Larry pulled a "classic Burback." Someone had told a joke about sucking cock when Farley said to the small group, "So how much would it take for you to give somebody a blow job? One hundred thousand dollars? Two hundred thousand?"

"No way!" most of the men shouted. "Much Much Much more than that."

With an absolutely serious face Larry says, "Are you kidding? One hundred thousand dollars? Hell yes, I'd do it for that!" Some of the men make protesting sounds, as if they're throwing up or gagging.

"Okay, Burback, you can start right here." Drucker acts like he's going to unzip his pants. Without missing a beat Larry squats down to hip level and starts this funny kind of squat walk toward Drucker pointing his finger inside his mouth.

"Put it right there Drucker. One hundred thousand dollars? No problem! Put it right there and it'll be the last time you're ever connected to it!" Drucker gets this horrified look on his face. He begins back-pedaling across the tarmac with Larry chasing after him with his squat walk, jabbing his finger toward his open mouth.

It looked like the childhood game where one kid is the monster and he scares everyone else. I was bent over with laughter. For a moment we were all very close, in an awkward, shy way. Inside each of us is this fourteen-year-old boy who loves to play with the guys and at the same time is terrified of the closeness.

To the south an owl hoots through the dark forest. The clouds break open and the moon colors everything chalk white. Cheering breaks out up at 260's camp. The light in Jack's one-man tent makes it look like a Disney glow-worm. The wind turns a colder, more bitter edge and I dream of a long, hot shower I once took with a lady friend.

October 22

Except to sleep I spend all my time outside. We roll out of our tents at six A.M. and drink hot tea or miso soup in the dark before the morning run. I hobble around on my ankle and afterwards Janowski tapes it while we shiver around the breakfast fire. He works steadily and confidently, his fingers gently probing the tissues.

"It's getting better," he says, "but you have to do what's the hardest thing for all of us. Rest." At night I dream of being at sea on the *U.S.S. Shangri-La*, an aircraft carrier my father once served on. I wake once in the early morning to the sound of a loud noise outside the tent. Raccoon? Weasel? Bear? Jack snoring. Hoping for a clear day I think I see the north star through the tent flap.

Dark banks of clouds pile into the coast while we enter the water in the rain. This morning the Atlantic is the majesty and tragedy of Rachmaninoff. The color of the water has no name; it's a green yellow gray and suspiciously calm. One hundred meters off the coast we swim into a dense fog. Through the whiteness I can hear the sounds of men's voices coming from rubber zodiac support boats. Because of the pain in my ankle my kick is lopsided and if I don't pay attention I start to swim in circles. Besides, I'm swimming with my right hand out of the water. I misplaced my rubberized glove, and since we swim on our backs and propel ourselves with a flutter kick I convince myself I can do it without the glove.

After I circle the swim marker at one thousand meters and turn toward shore, the sea unexpectedly begins to pick up. I momentarily lose Drucker, my swim buddy. The zodiac mates us up again, but as the swells and rain increase we again lose contact. I have the feeling that he and the zodiac are close, but the rain and fog from above, and the swelling mounds of water from below, form a thick, impenetrable blanket of wet and cold. At the top of one wave peak I think I see the black oily shape of the zodiac, but when I slide into the trough I lose sight of it. I can barely see twenty feet in any direction, whitecaps are beginning to wash over me. I'm suddenly alone and directionless, a quarter of a mile off the coast in rising seas.

I wrestle with the panic. I fight the water and I struggle frantically with the urge to escape, to swim away as fast as possible. But to where? I steady myself. Breathe in. Breathe out. Below me the ocean feels old and vast. I let go and feel comforted and held in its great sway. Strangely, I'm no longer afraid. I'm suddenly one with the waves, with the endless grays and lavenders, and I'm left with a quiet deep-boned ecstasy. The ocean is all mine. Dreamily I rise and fall with the swells, synchronizing my breath with their motion. Overhead a shearwater breaks out of the fog and glides a dozen feet above me, cocking his head to peer at me with a curious, compassionate eye. Oddly, I'm reminded of a surfing friend in Hawaii who, twelve years ago, went out one morning and never returned, his wife looking out to sea as it grew dark. It's a curiously comforting thought. I imagine his wise eyes and gentle way guiding me to shore.

In the distance I can hear the waves breaking and I lazily move in their direction. When I finally climb out of the crashing surf my hand looks faraway; a blank, numb claw. Am I very alive or very numb? I'm hollow and without thought in this beauty and vividness.

Almost everyone else is out of their dry suit when I stumble up the beach. Jack gives me one of his silent, unremitting, "Are you okay?" looks. Captain Thorne frowns and shakes his head.

"Yo! Johnny Weismuller!" Larry laughs.

October 23

Sometime during the night the rain stops and I awaken to a hard cold sky. Collars go up and black watchcaps go down against whimsical bitter gusts from the northeast. Beside a stand of conifers an unrecognizable brown hawk stiffens itself against the wind. Yesterday's episode in the water has left me in a state of grace; everything has that crystalline, etched look. I even find myself less irritated and more forgiving of my troublesome ankle.

I teach a daily mid-morning *jo* class in a swampy clearing to the west of our campsite. Seen from a small rise the vista of men working studiously in pairs with their *jos* looks like the pioneer version of a Spartan training camp. When they choose to be, these men are learning sponges; when they resist they're as responsive as a slab of ice. They've quickly learned the thirty-one *jo kata* and are now working on the more intricate *kumi tachi*, or partner moves. A few of them are quite adept at the first two sets. I have Galt and Farley demonstrate in front of the group. They perform the moves accurately and forcefully. Their Japanese oak staffs flash in the thin metallic light as they parry, block, and thrust. I move through the set with each of them. When Galt presses me I feel that odd pride a teacher experiences when being challenged by a gifted student. When I acknowledge his improvement and skill he looks away, shifting his chewing tobacco to the other side of his mouth.

After lunch Rader presents a class on ocean navigation in preparation for tomorrow's zodiac boat-navigation course. Like horses we block the wind with our backs, holding the maps down with rocks and hands. Stunned by Rader's brilliance I'm reminded of his potential as a teacher. He could easily be working in the private sector earning close to six figures. When I told him it was a well-presented class he looked down at me and shrugged his shoulders. As I walk away he calls after, "Were you able to stay with me?" This is his way of keeping the appropriate distance: If I get too close he moves back; if I move away he calls me back.

"For most of it," I reply stiffly, tired of his emotional push/pull.

Walking back to our campsite I see Oreson peering into the branches of a large fir, standing absolutely still, holding his *jo* in the striking position.

"What are you doing?" I ask. He remains silent, faithful to his position; a camouflage samurai frozen out of place and time.

Braddock, who is also watching, whispers, "He's after that squirrel. He almost got him. He's good; you ought to see him in action." Just at that moment Oreson strikes at a rust-colored squirrel that clambers safely up the tree.

He turns to me and smiles. "You know," he says, holding up the *jo*, "this stuff you're teaching us works pretty good. I'll get him pretty soon."

"I'm not teaching you *jo* so you can kill with it," I say angrily. He looks at me with that crazy blank smile, one eye aimed at the sky, the other drifting around our feet. He's still holding the *jo*, six foot three inches of solid muscle. I'm not afraid, but I'm fully aware of what he could do if he wanted.

"It's normal to hunt," he says. "That's what humans were born to do, to hunt. If we were still hunting there probably wouldn't be so many wars.

Wars mostly started with agricultural societies, not with hunters. If I kill that squirrel I'll eat it and I'll give some to you." He throws his arms up in frustration. "What's wrong with that?"

He walks away shaking his head. I wonder if he experiences the same feelings of contradiction that I do. He knows I have a vegetarian background and an interest in the sacred warrior; I know that he likes to hunt and has an urge to kill. Yet we like each other. If I was in a life or death situation he's one of the first people I would want on my side. Unsolicited he has often come to my assistance and I know he keeps a caretaker's eye on me. While he has the sacred warrior's desire to serve he also embodies the destructive power of the god of war. Through him, as in most of these men, I see these two sides in myself.

It is in the mythological marriage of Ares and Aphrodite that Harmonia is born, suggesting a balance point between the two great passions of Love and War. Harmonia is the dream of world temperance; and the dream of each individual in balance with himself. Is it possible? Despite our history of war and strife, somewhere in the restorative powers of imagination this archetype persists. Since human beings first began to dream, they conceived this possibility of love and destruction in a working harmonia, or balance. But because the Greeks valued rationality so highly, the instinctive, vigorous, and passionate Ares was subsumed in the shadow of Zeus. Do we then need to bring love (Aphrodite) to our Ares shadow in order to temper his violent outbursts? Translated to this moment, can I appreciate and recognize Oreson's love of the kill? Will loving our Ares shadow free the dancer, Ares' first training before he became a warrior? In Charles Boer's translation of the Homeric *Hymn to Ares* we have a clue that the emotions we so fear in Ares may paradoxically be the emotions that heal our destructive powers:

Hear me
helper of mankind,

beam down from up there
your gentle light
on our lives
and your martial power
so that I can shake off
cruel cowardice
from my head
and diminish that deceptive rush
of my spirit, and restrain
that shrill voice in my heart
that provokes me
to enter the chilling din of battle.
You, happy God
give me courage
to linger in the safe laws of peace
and thus escape from battles with enemies
and the fate of violent death.

As I watch Oreson disappear into the forest with his *jo* I feel a warmth and kinship with this young giant. With his hands ready for combat and his heart ready to serve he brings to life the gods of action, destruction, and loyalty.

October 24

I'm sitting in the back seat of our rented car. We've nicknamed it "The Dryer" because it's the only place that is dry; it's also stuffed with our rumpled clothes. The heat of the day has collected inside, making it womb-like in its comfort and warmth. A perfect place to write in my journal.

Our zodiac operation almost ended in disaster today. We launched in high seas and after we completed our first checkpoint the weather grew increasingly worse. The wind picked up and in a matter of minutes we were being pushed around by waves over six feet high. Unexpectedly, a mini-rouge wave of almost ten feet broke over us, nearly swamping the boat. Another wave immediately lifted one of the rubber pontoons. Tipping precariously to one side Parker and I hurled ourselves at the uplifted side to prevent us from capsizing. We were being tossed around like a matchstick, completely out of control. When I looked back to see who was at the helm I felt as though I had been kicked in the stomach. There was no one there. Seeing that empty spot made me want to throw up. Galt, who had been there, wasn't even on the boat. Martin saw this at the same time that I did and he immediately took the helmsman's seat, working on the dead motor. The boat was half-filled with water and slowly sinking. Everyone was furiously bailing while calling out Galt's name. One minute we would be balanced on the crest of a huge wave and in the next we would be plummeting down into a gray-green trough. Without the motor we had absolutely no control and were in continuous danger of capsizing.

Plunging down one wave, we suddenly catch a glimpse of Galt riding up the other side. We're working furiously to stay afloat, but he seems oddly relaxed. We seesaw like this for a few moments—us going down, him rising up; us rising up, him going down—while he steadily closes the distance between us. When he gets close enough he begins to shout directions. It's as if *he's* going to save *us*. As Martin starts the motor, we begin to maneuver carefully toward him. Positioning ourselves to pick him up we're unexpectedly lifted by another gigantic wave and hurled straight toward him. Almost in unison everyone has the same horrifying thought, "The engine! Turn off the engine!" We shoot past Galt, engine off, at the mercy of the raging sea. Those of us in the boat are like the three stooges while Galt is the Buddha, floating unperturbed, concentrated, seemingly at one with the water.

I laugh. I simply can't help myself. Perhaps I'm laughing out of fear or to relieve the tension. It seems absurd to be laughing and at the same time there's something absurd about what's happening. I think I should be concerned, but I'm actually having a good time, even though I know we could all be punished severely. As a friend of mine said, "The sea is perfectly equaniminous. It'll take anyone."

We realize we have to cut the motor so as not to injure Galt, but it has to be at the last minute each time to maintain steerage. We make five unsuccessful passes until someone picks up an oar; on the sixth pass Galt grabs it and we haul him aboard. While everyone is slapping him on the back and asking him how he is, he simply shrugs and shifts his chewing tobacco to the other side of his mouth.

We bail ourselves out and continue on to the next checkpoint. The seas worsen. It's beginning to rain in buckets. I'm no longer laughing. Water is coming in faster than we can bail it out. The engine conks out and is getting harder to start up again. It's getting dark and I find myself thinking about friends who have drowned at sea. When the decision is made to head home, I'm at first relieved, but then I realize that the mounting surf has taken away our beach landing site. I feel that deep bone-chilling fear that comes from the center of existence. I practice: Center. Ground. Extend *ki*. The thought enters my mind that with my surfing experience I could dive out and body-surf in. That's an unrealistic bolt of reaction. I center again. Fear arises. I center again, and again.

In the dark Farley shouts above the storm that he thinks he sees an opening in the surf. No reason to trust that, but we simply seize it and find our way in, the only injury being to the camera that Farley was carrying. Larry and some of the men from 560 meet us and help drag the zodiac to high ground. The other zodiac, the one with Jack aboard, is still not back.

Dunham says, "See, Richard, you should have been with us, 560, the scuba team. We run on time." Some of the others from 560 join in, "Yeah, right on." My irritation at 560's constant arrogance seeps through my fatigue and I wave them away, although I suspect they're right. Being with 260, The Dirty Dozen, is always full of surprises, some of them fun and some of them, like today, reckless.

An hour later, around ten P.M. the other zodiac makes it through the cascading surf. They also had engine trouble and took refuge from the storm on an outer island. Mattelli cut his hand quite badly while trying to cut a bailing bucket from an old plastic Clorox bottle. Karter, the medic on board, bandaged him with his T-shirt until he could be stitched up.

We were in a life or death situation today and everyone handled themselves well. Farley's and Martin's leadership capabilities shone through and Galt's level-headedness under pressure was exemplary. I know that if I said this to the men they would shrug and shift their chewing tobacco to the other side. It's the Lone Ranger mentality, "Don't thank me, ma'am; it's just my job. Hi Ho, Silver and away!" But behind this "aw shucks" attitude is a deep shyness of people and an unexamined but trenchant aversion to any kind of razzle-dazzle. Searching their faces I see the anti-hero, which is the phobic hero, but there are no martyrs or actors.

October 25

Visually, it could be a spring day. A Mediterranean blue sky with large cumulus cloud fortresses floating lazily overhead. Slabs of thick, golden light dazzling a calm sea. Plovers and gulls glide down the coast. But in real time the cold bite in the air and the dying leaves on the trees signal the coming of winter.

Our slick pontoon boat with a wooden floor bounces over the water's surface toward our second compass point at five thousand meters. There are seven of us in the boat, all dressed in seal-black dry suits. With hoods pulled tightly over our heads we're intimidating, like a cadre of ninjas, speeding toward a clandestine rendezvous. But in truth we're a bunch of boys on a day outing. We take turns lying on our bellies at the bow of the boat, hanging onto the bow rope, bouncing all over. We stand in the middle of the boat trying to keep our balance, first in the aikido *hanmi* stance, and then on one foot, as the zodiac lunges from wave to wave. We take turns at the compass and helm. Larry and I howl with laughter as Jack sits stoically while bucketfuls of seawater from the bow wake are heaved into his face. Just as I'm thinking this is a picnic (compared to yesterday) the motor stops.

Mattelli, wounded leader, immediately sets to work on the engine despite his bandaged hand. It starts! We cheer. A quarter of a mile later it stops again. He gets it started again, but after puttering fitfully for a few minutes it dies again. This time for good. Now, there's a lot of swearing.

"The goddamn Army!"

"The goddamn worn-out equipment they give us!"

"The goddamn mechanic whose neck I'm going to break if we ever get back!"

"Goddamn right we'll get back, even if we have to fucking swim."

"You couldn't swim your way out of a fucking bathtub."

I look up and all there is to see are water, sky, and horizon. The stark beauty is only enhanced by the loneliness.

"It looks like the goddamn 'Victory at Sea' TV program to me," somebody says. Mattelli has the engine hood off. He's traced the problem to a loose connection in the fuel line on which he's ingenuously trying to rig something together with a piece of wire. After repeated attempts with no success our nervous chatter is replaced by the sound of the wind and the waves lapping against the zodiac. It'll be getting dark soon. I wonder how far our small paddles can take us.

Seemingly out of nowhere the sound of a large engine pierces the horizon and approaches us, growing louder. We see a lobsterboat, and it sees us. As it slowly maneuvers toward us I can make out the name *Wind Song* neatly lettered on its side. Strangely, I think of a single covered wagon coming over the prairie. The skipper, and only person aboard, is a red-cheeked man in his mid-thirties, wearing rubber hip boots, thick suspenders, and a heavy wool sweater. He deftly nudges the *Wind Song* next to us and silently throws a line which we tie to the bow of the zodiac. We all climb aboard except Reardon who stays with our boat as it's pulled to shore. Still without a word, the skipper turns the *Wind Song* northwest and hits the throttle.

In our black suits we are a bunch of seals standing up on two legs gawking into lobster bins. Our host, seemingly oblivious to us, looks straight along an invisible trail over the sea. Mattelli tells him we need to phone to the mainland and he nods without taking his eyes off his course. Land comes into view. Soon we've ducked into a small inlet that widens into a medium-sized harbor filled with fishing boats. We tie up at a dock crowded with men unloading their lobster traps; the skipper gestures toward a small building with a sign that reads, **Little Cranberry Island Lobster Cooperative.**

Mattelli makes his call and we're told a Coast Guard cutter will pick us up. Fortunately, somebody has brought money; not having eaten since early morning we wolf down donuts and coffee. The children of the fishermen stare at us incredulously, while the wives side-eye us suspiciously.

I go to the edge of the pier and watch as the sun sets in a splash of crimson and red; to the east a half moon begins its lunar course in a darkening sky. Gulls, terns, and plovers crisscross in silhouette. Balanced between night and day, light and dark, the ebb and flood of tides, I'm suddenly released. In this still point between worlds all thinking, preconceptions, and opinions dissolve. The extremes of the day, from childlike ecstasy to deep foreboding, appear as momentary shadows against this profound stillness. The tears that unexpectedly wash my face are instantly dried by the night wind, and I'm laughing uncontrollably, until my tears and my laughter become a deep guttural sobbing. Half-sane, half-mad, I experience something like the dissolution of past and future into a pearly radiance of emptiness. As Democritus wrote on the other side of Western civilization, "Nothing exists but atoms and the void."

October 26

The white hull of the Coast Guard cutter looms ahead of us. There's an uncomfortable sinking feeling in my stomach. In a few moments we will board the cutter and begin the first of our casting exercises. Ever since this Maritime Operations ('Mar Ops' in Armyese) appeared on the schedule this casting drill has held the most fascination and apprehension to me. The ocean swimming would be an ordeal in endurance and stamina, and the simple boating turned out to be chancy enough, but right from the beginning, I was clear that casting would provide the real thrills and chills. Naturally, the soldiers built on the underlying apprehension by their constant goading, best characterized by Drucker's "Aikido and meditation may work well in the dojo, but when you're casting out of a helicopter or cutter at twenty knots we'll see how well it works."

We'll board the cutter and jump out of it three separate times, at ten, fifteen, and twenty knots. The height from the deck to the water is approximately twelve feet. On the last cast we will swim three kilometers to shore. As we climb aboard, Karter laughs and says, "Okay sensei, be centered now." We're instructed to form two single lines on either side of the boat and then walk toward the castmaster as each man casts off. When we reach the castmaster we're to turn around with our backs to the bow and wait for his signal. When we surface from the water we're to hold up a fist to signal that we're okay and a zodiac will come by to pick us up. The timing is crucial. There's no room for hesitation.

As the cutter moves into position Meredith says, "Make sure you're grounded, sensei; if you hit the wrong way you can sure ring your bell."

"Yeah, I knew a guy who was knocked out once. By the time they got him aboard he had swallowed a couple gallons of water." Braddock says this straight-faced. It's true that I'm afraid, although there's nothing specific that I fear. I've never been very good or relaxed at dealing with heights or speed, so the exercise unquestionably represents a challenge. The men, in their instinctive way, sense this and they relish putting me under even more pressure. They want to see if I can walk my talk.

"Are you afraid, sensei?" Karter yells over the roar of the engine so everyone can hear (including the Coast Guard personnel). At "Are you afraid?" an episode between my son and me instantly comes to mind. We were building a tree fort. After putting the wooden steps into place I climbed to a notch in the tree some thirty-five-feet off the ground. Although I had no real problem climbing up I felt a definite anxiety and had to concentrate on the task. Then D.J. climbed halfway up, stopped frozen in fear, and said, "I'm afraid. I can't do it." A rush of fear shot through me. I collected myself as best as I could, "It's okay," I said as calmly as possible, "you can do it."

"But I'm afraid," he replied. "I don't think I can do it."

My anxiety increased with his fear. 'I'm the father here, the responsible adult,' I told myself. 'I better get myself together.' I took a deep breath, glued a mask of confidence on my face, and said as calmly as I could, "D.J., you can do it. Just take one step at a time. You saw how I did it."

He hesitated, looked directly into my eyes and said, "Are you afraid?"

"No, I'm not afraid," I shot back, wanting to appear in control.

Without a trace of judgment and in perfect candor he replied, "You look afraid."

In that moment I felt a tremendous relief. The weight of the mask that I'd been carrying had been lifted. I felt free to be exactly where I was—in fear.

"You're right," I said, "I'm afraid, just like you." He grinned up at me, I extended my hand down to him and he climbed the rest of the way to the top. Openly sharing our fears as we sat in the notch of the tree banished our demons and brought us closer together. Admitting and owning my fear had made a space for us to relate on a more genuine—and considering the situation—safer level.

I looked at Karter, as my son had looked at me, "Yes, I'm afraid." I felt the sweeping sense of relief that comes when "what is" is acknowledged. Karter looked at me and nodded. The other men watched in silence. The roar of the engines increased and the cutter lurched ahead. Moving down the line toward the castmaster I felt bolts of electricity surging through me. When the man in front of me cast off a huge rush of breath filled my chest. Suddenly it's NOW. The castmaster points to me and I'm in flight, suspended for a moment over the blue Atlantic, great white clouds overhead, a distant roaring in my ears. There is a feeling of impact, like a small explosion all around me, and then a deep forgiving quiet. I pop to the surface like a cork and shove my fist into the air. I'm exhilarated and full of the feeling of success. The zodiac picks me up and hands are slapping me on the back. I feel as though I've just taken one more step to becoming who I am.

The final cast at twenty knots is considerably faster, and though I experience the same dread and excitement as before, I'm also filled with a gleeful anticipation. Now that I'm friendly with my fear, the faster speeds present the possibility of staying awake in the challenge, and growing from it, not just simply surviving. I hit the water leaning too far back and it does ring my bell. When I bob to the surface I'm disoriented and the large high-speed wake washes me under again. I do swallow some seawater. I find Braddock, my swim buddy, and still coughing we begin our three-kilometer swim to shore. The ocean underneath is a vast womb of support, the sky overhead a bowl of blue eternity. For the first time since we have been here I swim without urgency, and a deep sense of contentment.

October 27

The hard skull of ice is an opaque text across the landscape. I read: change, transitoriness, impermanence. The gun-metal sky presses down into the retreating earth; the cold has no center, only an unforgiving presence. The seagulls remain earthbound; standing quietly in ambiguous groups, even their raucous nature receding before the blanket of winter. In small, sloppy arrowheads duck and geese stragglers strain their way south along the coast. The passage from fall to winter is the most labored of the seasonal changes; even those animals that instinctively respond to its coming—squirrels, bears, ducks, humans—resist to the end. To do what we're doing now seems so ludicrous that even as I carefully maneuver over the icy rocks to the water I'm telling myself, 'This is happening: There is ice on the ground and you are entering in the ocean for a swim.' The others are on either side of me, grim-faced and silent; some have already slipped into the dark water.

Two kilometers out, two kilometers back. I'm astonished how quickly my exposed face adjusts to the cold; is this mind control or stupidity? I can't feel my nose. Despite a layer of polypropylene, a double pair of wool socks, sweat suit, wool sweater, and watch cap, I can feel the cold pressing against the almost half-inch protective layer of rubber dry suit. Swimming on my back each outbreath condenses into an oval cloud over my head. On the return trip I amuse myself by identifying over nine shades of gray in the clouds and air, from almost lavender to almost charcoal. On the shore we peel off our wet outer black skin and run the two miles back to camp in silence.

When I return I find the skin of a rust-colored squirrel under the ground flap of my tent. He's been placed face down with his back legs and tail showing, giving the impression that he's trying to slither under the tent. I'm revulsed and stung by it. Oreson soon appears offering me fire-cooked squirrel meat on a skewer. I'm prepared for outrage when he hands it to me with care and a shy haiku, "I just cooked it. It's good. I hope you like it." I was right. This is personal, but in a different way than I thought. There is nothing vicious in his actions, but rather a sacramental offering: "Take, eat, this is the flesh of our Lord and Savior Jesus Christ who gave His body and blood . . ."

"Did you kill it with your *jo?*" I ask.

"Yes." He replies simply and walks away.

I go into the forest with the burnt skewer and sit on the spongy humus. Nearby are the droppings of a small animal and next to that a decaying log that is already part soil. I remind myself that if it weren't for change, death, and the passing away of things, there would be no beginnings, emergence, and renewal. The part of me that has been a vegetarian for most of my adult life bows before the moment. I chew the tough stringy meat into a flat paste. I roll it in my hands, turning in the log soil, animal droppings, and yellow-green humus until it crumbles into thick, dark grains. "Take, eat; this is the body and blood of the Universe that gave us minds and hearts to be sacrificed for Love and Compassion."

Integrity

November 1

After being back at Fort Davis for only two days the Maritime Operations already seem in the distant past; the encampment is a lifetime ago. We could easily take a week to debrief these two sections of the program, but the schedule is tight and we roll ahead. In a few days Mike Blondell will be with us to present a week seminar in psychological values, then we'll begin the Brain Wave Training.

In the Trojan Warrior Project, aikido is the thread that connects us from day to day, from activity to activity. Yesterday I posted the dates for an aikido test. The men appreciate trials and challenges and in anticipation of the test there's a mounting tension.

"I don't know if I'm ready for this test," Thayer says. He looks perplexed, like a fourteen-year-old boy getting ready for his first kiss.

"It'll all work out. Just relax," Jackson says, going into his rap about taking things easy. "Why get excited about anything? Hell, ah try not to let anything bother me. No need to get uptight." He struts out of the dressing room, straightening his *gi*.

Glances are exchanged. There are forced coughs, someone snickers in the corner. "Yeah, right, take it from Sarge. He's about as relaxed as a two by four," someone pipes up.

"If that's Sarge relaxed, I'd hate to see him uptight," Martin adds.

"Maybe he oughta teach some stress reduction classes for the rec center," Drucker laughs.

The mood passes quickly as we bow in for the class, but what just went down was important. I hope Jackson picks up on it. He thinks of himself as being a good old boy from the south who takes everything in stride and "Since I've seen most all of it, nothin' much upsets me anymore." He's well liked, respected as a soldier, but what he says about himself and how he is on the aikido mat are clearly two different realities. Later Wilson remarked, "In a way I'm relieved to see how tense and rigid he is in aikido, because it's what I've always felt from him."

When someone is trying to hit you on the head your personal philosophy, or how you imagine yourself to be, doesn't matter much. What does matter is how you manage the attack without you or your attacker being hurt. On the training mat no one is interested in your ideas about how relaxed you think you are, but they are interested if you are relaxed in your movements. Are you moving with the flow of energy? Can you stay balanced while under pressure? Are you in tune with your partner? These are difficult tasks. They require sensitivity, inner strength, and a willingness to drop one's position of being right. The attitude for these challenges is clearly expressed in the words of the founder, Master Ueshiba, when he said, "The opponent is within . . . it (aikido) is not for correcting others; it is for correcting your own mind." This ethic of responsibility teaches us that harmony (and everything else for that matter) first starts with one's self; the resolution of conflict begins by first resolving it within one's self.

When the feelings of fear, aggression, survival, and power eventually surface in training we understand that they are ours to deal with and not reasons to excuse ourselves or blame an external "opponent." In this way aikido is an applied philosophy through which we can move beyond conceptualization to actually train our minds and bodies in the principles of peaceful reconciliation. We can, in other words, practice what we preach. Aikido teaches that true power is the result of flexibility, harmony, and relaxation; that violence never resolves conflict; and at a fundamental level all human beings belong to one family.

November 6

Mike Blondell moves from one end of the classroom to the other like a huge battleship cutting through rough seas. Even though the tension in the room is completely focused on him, he remains composed and unrelenting. He's a round man, over two hundred and twenty pounds, some of it hanging unceremoniously over his belt. Jack has objections to him teaching because of his weight, arguing that it doesn't model what we're trying to convey and will be just one more thing for the men to use as resistance. While this point is well taken I like Blondell; his heart easily outweighs his belly. Despite his size he carries himself with the dignity and grace that behooves a former Navy SEAL combat veteran. Besides, he's excellent at what he does, which is to ask people to look more deeply and honestly at the emotional issues in their lives. For these soldiers this has been at least as confrontational as the encampment, and in many cases, has made them more vulnerable.

Mike writes **Integrity** on a large pad of paper in front of the classroom and taps it for emphasis. "What does this mean to you?" he asks softly. Predictably, the first wave of responses are their habituated reflex toward resistance.

"Are you sure you spelled that right?" someone throws out from the corner of the room.

"Hell," Dudley drawls from the front row, "if we had that we wouldn't be in S.F." Scattered laughter.

Mike smiles and his entire face lights up, "Anybody ready to go deeper?" Different interpretations are put forth. Mike acknowledges each one, sometimes asking for a clarification or an example of what is meant. "Can we all agree," he finally asks, "that integrity is consistency in thought, word, and action?" When everyone acknowledges agreement he says, "Then let's look at where in our lives we're out of integrity."

For the past week thirty of us, soldiers and trainers alike, have participated in this seminar emphasizing psychological and emotional values. The seminar addresses the concepts of commitment, honesty, accountability, participation, expression, integrity, and, in general, how they're integrated in one's life. It has been painfully clear that this material should have been presented in the first or second week of the training, as a ground upon which everything else could be built. It could have meant, for example, that when we talked about commitment we all would agree on what it meant; in this case: *whatever it takes*. Translated into the encampment situation it would have meant that when the smokers committed themselves to quit they would have done whatever it took.

Early in the training Mike evoked ire by telling the men that they were avoiding important emotional issues with their machismo and bravado. He went on to say that if they didn't deal with these issues there was no way they would reach their full potential. They booed, hissed, and yelled, until finally Dunham, red-faced with clenched fists, stormed from the back of the room. I was sure that he was going to take a poke at Mike and I was fully prepared to intervene. As he angrily crashed to the front Mike calmly took a step toward him, quietly facing his charge. It was the ideal illustration of the power of the aikido *hanmi* stance—he was neither on the offense nor on the defense, he was simply being present. The rest of us sat in silence, riveted to our seats. Dunham stopped in a fury about two paces in front of Mike and began yelling in his face. Mike simply and profoundly just stood there, neither retracting nor fighting back. It was one of the best aikido-in-daily-life techniques I have ever witnessed. In a few moments Dunham quieted down and after looking at Mike in silence for a few minutes, muttered something under his breath and returned to his seat.

"That is a perfect example of integrity," Mike said easily. "What he was feeling on the inside was what he expressed on the outside. What he presented to us is what was true to him on the inside. Consistency in thought, word, and action."

What made this training most risky for these men was the experience of openly sharing their emotional lives—their beliefs, fears, and hopes. Of course, it's not that these men don't share and communicate with one another, but it was entirely new for them to do so in a structure that continually asked them to go deeper. In the very beginning when Mike informed them that they would be sharing their feelings, attitudes, and beliefs both with partners and the group, Farley stood up and immediately opposed the idea. In a movingly open and honest way he described how he was raised to be a soldier and taught by his father that men never shared and that "even now the word share makes me want to throw up." He continued for about ten minutes sharing deeply with us the reasons that he wouldn't share.

As each man expressed himself, feelings of camaraderie filled the room. It wasn't always easy or warm, but it was honest. Even those few that continued to resist were moved by those who chose emotionally to put themselves in harm's way. It was an event that, in part, fulfilled William James' call for a moral equivalent to war. Although physical life and death were not at issue, an emotional life and death were certainly at hand. For many of these men it was as frightening as facing hostile fire. Jumping out of a plane, no matter how many times it's done will involve a risk, but in this week there were much greater risks taken while standing in front of their friends and teammates. I saw again that sharing our humanity makes it possible to lift ourselves to higher ground. Opening ourselves emotionally, we can go beyond ourselves in the same way that an act of heroism or sacrifice in a physically dangerous situation can bring forth something deeper inside of us, something that we didn't know was there.

One exercise is to sit across from a partner, look in his eyes and ask,

"What is important to you?" After the person answers, the same question is asked again and again until hidden meanings and values begin to surface. Dunham is my partner and from the beginning he's uncomfortable looking into my eyes and sitting so close to me.

"What's important to you?" I ask.

He clears his throat, swallows hard and looks up. "Richard," he begins uncomfortably, "you're important to me. You're a teacher to me and I'm getting a lot from you . . . in aikido and other places." He pauses, gathering himself. "But," he looks down fidgeting, "when you wear those pink T-shirts, well . . . it just drives me crazy! I don't like it!" He hesitates for a moment. Making a fist in a show of fellowship he beams, "But you're also very manly and I like that! It's just that . . . well . . . I don't understand how both can be there."

November 8

After researching a variety of neurofeedback systems, Joel and Michelle commissioned Dr. Jim Hardt to develop and adapt his multichannel neurofeedback system for our unique training scenario. In preparation for nearly a month of intensive brain wave biofeedback training with the men, Joel and Michelle invited Jim to join us on base to install the system and help to fine-tune it after its installation. Jack, myself, Captain Thorne, and Anne Bartley all get an opportunity to be "guinea pigs" on the shakeout cruise of this extraordinary inner technology.

Following our shakeout cruise with the system, Joel and Michelle and I will begin the next wave of training, where after morning P.T. I will teach half of the men in the dojo while Joel and Michelle will run the other half of the team in intensive neurofeedback training in the lab. In the afternoons we will switch groups. The men who had been focused on learning the inner moves necessary to optimize the working of their brains and minds will come on the mat to practice integrating those inner *ki*-full moves with the intensity, complexity, and velocity of hand-to-hand combat training. This fine blend of inner and outer training will comprise a month of intensive sixteen-hour training days for the three of us, while providing an unparalleled opportunity for profoundly integrative training for the men.

The first time I meet Jim Hardt I think, 'Oh, no!' Medical psychologist, developer of brain synchrony training, and errant genius, Hardt is five-feet-six-inches tall, weighs one hundred and thirty pounds, wears round-rimmed glasses and a white lab coat with *Dr. Jim Hardt* monogrammed above the left breast pocket. He's with us to lead the men through the elaborate brain synchrony training. With his effeminate nature and forehead perpetually raised in wonderment he looks like the Mr. Peepers of Science. 'These guys will eat him alive.'

I pull Jack and Joel aside: "This will be a bloodbath. It'll be taking the sacrificial lamb to the wolves. We have to think of something else."

"I understand your concern," Jack answers, "but there's no way we can turn back."

"He's really the best in the world at this work. I've seen him handle difficult situations like this before. He does very well, actually surprisingly well," Joel adds.

They take Hardt into the classroom for his introductory talk. I go to our office to make a quick call. When I return I stop for a moment outside to prepare myself for catastrophe. But what I see when I enter is, standing in front of the men with his lab coat on, Hardt looking every bit the part of Harvey Milktoast. He's explaining the goals of the Brain Wave Training. The room is absolutely still, all eyes glued on him. In soft melodious tones, his delicate hands fluttering in front of him like two doves, he explains the intricacies of brain wave activity and how it can be measured and controlled. The men hang on every word. When he asks for questions, there's a prolonged silence. Once the questions and answers start he easily translates the complex workings of the nervous system into laymen's terms. Mostly the men want to know if it will make them Supermen. He answers, "Our potential is unlimited and we need to cultivate it."

Rambo would have agreed. Even he acknowledged, "I think the best weapon is the mind of man."

Filing out of the room I join a small group, "So, what do you think?"

"Sounds great to me."

"I think most of what we need is mind control anyway."

"It seems like an opportunity."

"Much better than the encampment."

"Explain something to me," I ask, "I thought for sure that you would have a reaction to Hardt, but you didn't."

Shrugs.

"Well, he's not exactly your kind of guy," I continue, "but instead of pouncing on him you're eating out of his hand. What gives?"

"He made perfect sense." Gibb answers. "It's something you can measure and quantify. There's a logic about it. You can tell if you're making progress or not. One of the troubles with meditation is that you don't know if you're on the right track or not." The others nod in agreement.

"Hardt?" Drucker picks up, "You're right, he's not our kind of man, but you call tell he's a master at what he does. You have the feeling that he's personally experienced what he's talking about. He has integrity."

Integrity. Authenticity. Self-Mastery. These three qualities continue to find their way to the head of the modern warrior's list. I myself had been mistaken to judge Hardt by his physical demeanor, and mistaken again to assume that the men would do the same. Warriors come in all shapes and sizes. Just as some of the most grounded people I know don't have legs, being a warrior doesn't depend on a physical or social stature, but rather what kind of inner life is lived.

Some of these issues recurred with subsequent visitors. When my colleague from Lomi School, Randy Cherner, arrived to do a week of bodywork he was quite nervous initially in addressing them. Much to my surprise no one confronted him or tried to put him under more pressure. When I asked about this later Farley said, "Yeah, of course we saw he was nervous, but he didn't try to hide it or be something he wasn't. He was simply who he was; that's all any of us can really be. He was real."

The counterpoint to this was an accomplished karate teacher who spent a few days with us as a guest instructor. At first impression this man fit the superficial profile of the warrior. He was big, well-conditioned, teaching an aggressive, fighting style of martial art. He was quick and effective at dispatching an opponent. I initially thought the men would respond to his kick-ass style. Yet when I asked them what they thought of him they shrugged him off, "Yeah, he was good at what he does but . . . well, he seemed to be on some kind of ego trip. He was more interested in showing how good he was than really teaching anything. I don't think I really learned anything from him. If you do this program again I'd skip him next time around."

We must revision the warrior beyond our preconceived notions of gender, physical size, strength, or earning honor through combat. The battlefield of the warrior must expand beyond the literal interpretation of war and destruction to include every moment of our lives. In order to live authentically with integrity we must have a certain kind of courage. Chögyam Trungpa Rinpoche spoke this very clearly when he said, "The key to warriorship . . . is not being afraid of who you are. Ultimately, that is the definition of bravery: not being afraid of yourself." When we're no longer afraid of being who we are we act from integrity and authenticity.

November 10

Darkness comes early now. It's dark when the men arrive at the biofeedback lab in the morning and by the time they leave in the late afternoon the failing light is soon gone. I remember reading somewhere the Eskimos' belief that when the days are dark our spirits must shine brighter. The seven hours the men sit in the windowless cells of the brain-synchrony lab become the forge for transforming the dark grit of their will and stubbornness into the dignity and compassion of spirit.

The training has made the biofeedback lab a modern day monastery. It also looks like a barracks-style hair salon. While one man sits, another combs his hair back, cleans the skull with an antiseptic solution, and then glues the electrodes in place. The kind of small talk that is a balm for too many early mornings leaves a frivolous buzz in the room. Hardt is at home in Joel and Michelle's dojo; floating about in his white lab coat chatting amiably, answering questions, combing out someone's hair, his hands ceaselessly moving, he conducts a symphony only he can hear. Seeing the men fuss over each other like this I'm full of glee and spontaneous laughter. They snarl back, but they don't understand how funny they really look and, besides, I'm having too much fun to hide myself. When I say, "You're kinda cute, soldier; where do you get your nails done?" they respond with a chorus of boos and hisses.

Inside the brain wave center they sit in absolute darkness with the electrodes from their skulls wired to a central computer. Through headphones they can hear the musical tones of their brain waves; in front of them is a digital read-out system that flashes their progress numerically. The training is designed so that they learn how consciously to induce the Alpha brain wave, which runs between eight and thirteen cycles per second and is characteristic of a relaxed yet alert, high-energy state. Disengaged from the usual chatter of the mind, the Alpha state is conducive to accelerated learning and creative problem solving. Over-efforting, with accompanying muscle tension, moves us out of the multi-dimensional Alpha state into a more linear, less open Beta state. When this happens the biofeedback monitors automatically signal the loss. The men gradually learn how they move out of Alpha and how they can move back into it. At the end of each session they spend approximately twenty minutes to a half an hour synchronizing with a partner. The tones of two people harmonizing their brain waves, or states of consciousness, sounds like a Latino street celebration. After the session, Hardt, with Joel and Michelle, debriefs them on their progress and answers questions.

While Michelle's contributions to the biofeedback program are considerable, they are in large part transparent to me, as she is often working in the lab with Joel and not present for the day-to-day interactions that Jack, Joel, and I have with the men during other parts of the training. I'm not present for her interactions with the soldiers when she is in the lab, but it's clear that her presence is significant and she's highly effective in this domain.

Some, like Shell and Martin, pick it up quickly and run up extraordinary scores. Others, significantly the Vietnam veterans, have a much more difficult time. Combat veterans seen not only to have anesthetized their capacity for Alpha in order to cope with the stress of battle, but to continue to defend against openness and relaxation as unmanageable, and perhaps too vulnerable a state. It occurs to me that this training would be an excellent way to work with post-traumatic stress syndrome so common among veterans. They would be able to relearn their Alpha capabilities in a safe, supportive environment.

After the lab the men walk up the company street to the dojo. They're uncharacteristically quiet as they dress and begin warming up on the mat. When I turn to bow in to them to begin class they are seated more deeply in themselves than I can ever remember; they are simply, yet wholeheartedly, just sitting there, no frills, no slouching—just plain sitting. This is what Zen calls the extraordinary uniqueness of the ordinary, the radiance of what is. There is a tenderness about them that has nothing to do with an emotional gushiness or a soft-minded timidity; it is rather a big-hearted openness. Chögyam Trungpa says that ". . . for the warrior this experience of sad and tender heart is what gives birth to fearlessness."

In this state of grace there's an inner connectedness about them that shows up as a fluidity and power in movement. In aikido class both Rader and Dunham demonstrate *jiyu-waza* (free movement) with a commanding yet relaxed presence. Yet they are bewildered that their effectiveness comes without the usual effort and struggle. When I acknowledge this qualitative leap in performance Dunham says, "It seems so easy, it's hard to believe that I'm really doing anything."

"The Alpha state is also the *aiki* of aikido," I suggest. "It's a state where relaxation and presence equal power." To their rational minds this doesn't make sense, but they experience its truth in their movements.

"I don't know . . . it's just so different." Gibb shakes his head. "I can tell my aikido is better, but I feel so damn vulnerable."

No one says anything for a long while; only the sound of the wind beating against the windowpanes can be heard. There's a quality of presence in their relaxation that makes it seem we're doing something, even though we're doing nothing. I'm perfectly content to remain like this, silent, allowing the glow of the moment to shine through us. As quiet as we are there's a lion's roar inside my head. In this fragile transparency there's both terror and vigor. We look at each other with fresh eyes. I'm not afraid of what they might see in me, nor am I afraid to look deep within them. For a moment we're one mind, one body, one heart.

Out of this deep, quiet pool Rader moves toward me, his fist raised for a *shomen* strike. I step to the side, merge with his movement, and lead his attack into a forward roll. Continuing his attacks we move together in a spontaneous *jiyu-waza*. After a few moments we effortlessly trade roles. I attack him; he becomes *nage*, I'm his *uke*. His technique is powerful and directed to my center, yet his usual abrasiveness and hard edges are gone. It's the openness of his movements, not his physical size and strength, that makes him potent. Wordlessly we stop, as if we're reading each other's minds. We then bow deeply to each other. I turn to the men and bow, as if to say to them collectively, "Now you do that."

A few weeks ago when I walked into the space where Randy Cherner was doing bodywork I had a momentary fantasy of seeing one end of the room piled high with the armor released from his work. I imagined well-forged breastplates, layered shoulder pads, neck braces, shields, face masks, leg tubes, swords, and lances lying in a silvery, cluttered heap. I further saw that each piece of armor was also an attitude, a way the men positioned themselves mentally and emotionally, as well as bodily, to the world. The vision made me smile because I knew the power of this bodywork and of Randy's touch. But the joy that spawned the smile came from knowing that the discarding of this dense and heavy armor would expose their hearts. And it was today that I saw this heart: a tender heart, iron strong with dignity, fearlessly inviting the world in. Randy's bodywork, the flexibility and stretching exercises, the encampment, Mike Blondell, the daily aikido training, the brain synchrony training, all have become the alchemical elements that fired the seed of warrior fearlessness.

I ask: Is there a place for this warrior in the very heart of our military, within the ranks of the Special Forces? How do we live in the paradox of feeling and compassion in an institution that demands homogeneity and abstraction? Is it possible to live at the heart of this contradiction? Gibb is right when he says, "It's so damn vulnerable to be this open." Yet the real question may be: Can we afford *not* to give this warrior his place? Standing on the precipice of our own survival or extinction we're in desperate need of a warrior who draw his power from an expanded awareness rather than a stance of fear and aggression. The Fourteenth Dalai Lama, the spiritual leader of the Tibetan people, exposed this situation very clearly, "Perhaps now that the Western sciences have reached down into the atom and out into the cosmos finally to realize the extreme vulnerability of all life, it's becoming credible, even obvious, that the Inner Science is of supreme importance. Certainly physics designed the bombs, biology the germ warfare, chemistry the nerve gas and so on, but it will be the unhealthy emotions of individuals that will trigger these horrors. These emotions can only be controlled, reshaped, and rechanneled, by technologies developed from successful Inner Science."

November 11

Earlier this evening my friend Catherine and I met Janowski and his lady friend at a nearby French restaurant. Janowski looked handsome in a double-breasted suit; his years of living in Europe had elegantly seeded his manners. His friend arrived from out of state to visit him and it was clear that he took pleasure in her companionship. I found myself intrigued being with Janowski outside of our usual roles. He is an easy person to hang out with, a man with whom I could have a long-term friendship. Because he doesn't carry the weight of machismo that burdens most men he's comfortable with his sensitivity. Although we talked some about the project the conversation ran from world affairs to the best time to plant snow peas to the possibility of him participating in the three-month bodymind training I teach at the Lomi School.

In many ways Janowski successfully rides the seesaw paradox of the sacred warrior. As a senior medic he's a rare combination of modern technical knowledge and the earthbound intuition of the shaman. At his heart he's a healer, yet he can also dismantle, reassemble, and accurately fire most automatic weapons made in the world today. Working in an institution that demands a harsh loyalty he's found a way to be free-thinking.

Toward the end of the evening I ask him if he ever felt regretful at never having gone to war. "I really have no desire to go to war," he answers laconically; "I'm content serving my country during peacetime." Lighting a cigarette he continues, "I think that well-trained Special Forces units should act as deterrents to war." He hesitates for a moment, toying with his cigarette in the ashtray. "But . . . there's always the question in my mind of how I would respond under the pressure of someone trying to kill me. It's not that I need it to feel like I'm a man, but in many ways it represents the ultimate test."

"Or you killing someone?" I ask.

"Well, of course that's in there," he replies, "but it's much less important than the idea of knowing that there's someone out there who wants to get me, and how I would deal with that."

"That sounds like war to me," I say. We jokingly lament the end of the good old days when you could go one-on-one with an opponent, as David did with Goliath.

In this brief exchange I again hear the need and call for the rites of initiation. What is it as men that we seek to be initiated into? In what fraternity do we wish to be admitted and recognized as full-fledged members? To deny that we need these initiatory rites is to turn away from a call as primal as the moment we risked standing on two legs.

Janowski's distinction between being in harm's way and killing someone is an important one. His initiation myth is not centered on taking a life, but rather on the need to test himself under fire. This seemingly primitive urge to test ourselves under pressure is more than a macho reflex, it's our need to enact the hero's journey. It is, as I have discussed many times before, a yearning for an initiation that will build and challenge the spirit of our inner hero.

It has now become painfully clear that the technology of nuclear war completely outstrips warrior virtues in military importance. Those who believe that conventional war is still an arena in which one can build and test their heroism and moral character need to read Richard A. Gabriel's stunning *No More Heroes: Madness and Psychiatry in War*. Gabriel writes, "Both the Soviet and the American military have developed conventional weapons that make those used in World War II pale by comparison. The explosive capacity of most modern weapons exceeds that of World War II weapons by at least five times. Rates of fire have increased by almost ten times. Accuracy has increased by twenty times and the ability to detect enemy targets has increased several hundred percent. On top of all this has been the introduction of weapons systems undreamed of in 1945. The overall result is that the ability of modern armies to deliver a combat punch has increased by at least six hundred percent since the end of World War II. Military technology has reached a point where conventional weapons have unconventional effects. In both conventional war and nuclear war, combatants can no longer be reasonably expected to survive."

John Keegan, the famous British military analyst, has further pointed out that many modern conventional weapons are at least as powerful, if not more destructive, than nuclear weapons. It's widely known, for example, that the F-4 Phantom fighter plane has more destructive power than a low-yield nuclear cruise missile. Gabriel goes on to point out that, "Confronting the real consequences of conventional war drives men mad in droves. War has reached the point where most human beings can no longer remain sane long enough to produce any military outcome except collective death and insanity."

In order to keep men sane in the horror of war both the American and Soviet military are hard at work developing a chemical that will block out the individual's experience of fear. Such a chemical will allow a soldier to remain effective in a combat situation longer because, while he would "know" he was in a dangerous situation, he would no longer "feel" fear. This "chemical soldier," in other words, would not respond normally to the anxiety and fear that combat stimulates. The drug would chemically create symptoms and behavior that we have traditionally defined as "mentally ill." The chemical soldier will become what is psychiatrically termed an "aggressive sociopath." We will be asking our soldiers to become crazy in order for them to behave "normally" in combat!

Gabriel concludes that, "For the chemical soldier military virtues will have no meaning and no function. Qualities such as courage, bravery, endurance, and sacrifice have meaning only in human terms. They indicate conditions in which men triumph over normal fear. Heroes are those who can endure and control fear beyond the limits expected of normally sane men. Brave men are those who conquer fear. Sacrifice for one's comrades can only have meaning when one fears death and accepts it because it will prevent others from dying or will permit an idea to live. If fear is eliminated from the soldier through chemical means, there will be nothing over which he can triumph. The standards of normal men will be eroded and will disappear. Men will be dehumanized and will no longer die for anything that is meaningful in truly human terms. They will just die. The military virtues—courage, heroism, endurance, bravery, and sacrifice—will be replaced in war by probability tables that measure the technical efficiency of 'human' performance. And the standard of performance will be the body count."

Our reliance on war to fulfill certain needs reflects the spiritual poverty of our society as much as anything else. But the immediate problem in front of us, and one which may hopefully be our salvation, is that nuclear weapons, along with the advances in conventional war, have eliminated war as the field in which these warrior virtues may be experienced. We no longer have the luxury of literally invoking Mars, and his host of warrior gods, to fulfill our need for transcendence. The hunter warrior who protected his clan from danger and demonstrated his bravery in tribal wars lived in a different world from today's modern soldier. Where a single spear might have once brought down a single enemy, a finger on a single button may now eliminate millions.

November 12

Ben Drucker is an in-your-face sort of guy; a one-man S.W.A.T. team. He stands like a gunslinger—hips thrust forward, arms cocked to his side, a gaze that could nail a door shut. Raised by an abusive uncle after his father died, he left home the day he graduated from high school. He taunts Army regulations by consistently pressing the limits in sideburn and hair length. A newly born first child is softening him with the power of love.

Drucker has been disdainful of aikido from the beginning, repeatedly questioning if it "really works." 'Prove to me that *ki* is more powerful than my youth and physical strength' says the contemptuous look in his eyes. His numerous attempts to provoke me into a confrontation are often staged in the presence of others: "Aikido would never hold up to a good boxer or wrestler! It's totally irrelevant to me professionally and personally." Drucker is half a foot taller than me, weighs almost forty pounds more, and is twenty years younger. When I don't respond to his provocations he looks down at me in anger and helplessness.

This afternoon, his most recent gauntlet tossed at the end of a particularly trying session, I finally reach my limit. "Okay, Ben, let's see if it works," I blurt out. As the words leave my mouth a bolt of adrenaline surges through me; it's too late to take it back. When I first decided to be part of this project, almost six months ago, I wondered if this crossroads would ever come—another of those moments I both longed for and feared.

"What do you mean?" He looks surprised.

"You want to know if this stuff works, so let's find out," I say, taking off my *hakama*.

The truth is we both want to know. I want to know if the subtlety of this art outweighs his youth and aggressive strength; he wants to know because he longs for something greater than his petty theatre of one-upmanship. For me, Drucker is the response to the question that has occupied my mind from the moment I was asked to work with these men: What happens when they challenge me? Would they beat me up? Would I injure one of them? Or worst of all, would I lose my temper and betray everything I'm teaching? Is the power of aikido—a power based in harmony and reconciliation—sufficiently part of me to defuse the aggression of this man? I'm as afraid in my uncertainty as he is in his desire, but we are both too uncomfortable to admit it. From our deepest shadows we have requested this song; now we are going to dance it.

In the growing darkness we quietly circle. Drucker's eyes narrow into thin slits. Faster than a thought, a powerful jab explodes toward my face. Panic. The danger light in my mind blinks furiously. Here is a young lion flexing for the kill. My thoughts accelerate through every strategy from swinging a tire iron to walking away from the whole thing. But as his blows become faster and stronger something begins to shift inside me. My breath deepens and settles into my belly, my legs fill with authority, the fierce pounding in my heart spreads evenly through my entire body. As I relax I begin to see certain openings; I detect how he signals his punches, I see how too much of him cares about my responses. There is even enough space to marvel at his strength and deftness. But the perception of this as a street corner game shifts instantly when the raw power of one of his jabs glances off my shoulder, reminding me of his intensity. Without thinking I slip the next punch, step in, and grip his throat. As he stumbles back I tighten my grip deeper into his larynx. It's painful only if he resists, so he quickly becomes still. We're eyeball to eyeball for a very long moment . . . then I release my hold and walk into the dressing room. That's all. What has happened has taken less than a minute, but I can hardly remember any of it. An enormous electric charge is streaming through me. We dress in silence. We leave the dojo without saying a word to each other.

I don't expect that this episode will dissolve the tension between Drucker and myself into a pals-for-life ending, but there was an initiation that led to a transformation. I suspect that our respect and understanding for each other has taken an immense step forward. Hopefully he will become more open to the lessons that aikido has to offer; I know that I'm more willing to consider his needs, which I also see as being in part my own.

I know that we're both now more sure that "it works," but for me that has nothing to do with winning or losing. I knew that if I had reacted badly and tried to stand toe-to-toe against Drucker he would have probably punched my lights out. If I had turned away from the confrontation, rapport would have deteriorated and mutiny spread to the other men. What "worked" was the discipline of harmony—the aikido principles of blending, centering, and *ki*.

The passage of initiation came when we looked into each other's eyes. At that moment everything that stood between us fell away; even though I held his throat in my hand there was no competition, aggression, or question of winning or losing. It could just have easily been my throat in his grip, but it would have taken us to the same crossroads. It was a choice of life or death: and through the pre-verbal language of *ki* we chose life. Every initiation, whether it plummets us into our deepest shadows or catapults us to the heights of joy, is finally reduced to this choice, of life or death. To choose life is to affirm our existence. To choose death is to continue the cycle of violence.

One of the most powerful versions of this tale was passed on to me by Robert Rheault, a West Point graduate, Special Forces commander, combat veteran, and retired Army colonel who now leads programs for Outward Bound. In the mid-sixties Rheault commanded a Special Forces unit whose job was to intercept North Vietnamese cadre as they made their way south along the Ho Chi Minh trail. He prefaced his story by explaining that because the Special Forces soldier is in the field for weeks on end, without the luxury of being resupplied, it's not uncommon for their packs to weigh over one hundred pounds. Because of this, he said, before every operation he would pack and repack his rucksack countless times to save space and eliminate excess weight. To our amusement he said he even went as far as cutting the handle off his toothbrush. Unless you've carried one of those monster packs through the bush for a couple of days this seems like a ridiculous detail; otherwise, it makes perfect sense.

After chuckling about his little idiosyncrasy, Rheault continued to relate how on one of those missions along the Ho Chi Minh trail he and his troops ambushed and captured a North Vietnamese infantry unit. After securing his prisoners he spent the afternoon routinely searching their equipment for any useful intelligence material.

Rheault said rather matter-of-factly how he found the same items in each pack—"a sock full of rice, a family photo, a change of clothes, a small bar of soap, a handwritten poem, and . . . " At this point Robert relaxed his West Point bearing, sat back in his chair and a broad smile covered his face. ". . . and this time a toothbrush with the handle cut off!" He laughed at his memory and then became more serious, "I called the man over and asked him if this was his pack. He said it was and I thought long and hard about what I was about to do. I walked him into the jungle, without his weapons and just enough food to last him a day . . . and let him go. I didn't think releasing this one soldier would make a difference in the outcome of the war and I prayed that he wouldn't return to kill an American soldier. But to tell you the truth," he said evenly and with great earnestness, "discovering that funny little sawed-off toothbrush in his pack made me realize that I had more in common with that man than with ninety percent of the American soldiers that were in-country at the time. I felt a deep personal empathy for who he was and what his experience was like and I just couldn't bear to see him put in prison."

While we imagine our initiations have to be marked by adventure and danger, they are often the most ordinary events that happen when no one is looking. If we open our vision, let go of our preconceptions about how we should be, I imagine we could see such possibilities of initiation in every moment. And as for Bob Rheault, these moments ultimately ask us to choose between life and creation or stagnation and death.

In Search of the Warrior Spirit

November 13

When the men first saw Bira Almeida I detected the disappointment in their eyes. I had described Bira, my Capoeira teacher and the two-time heavyweight Capoeira champion of Brazil, as one of the greatest fighters I have ever known. Perhaps they had envisioned a backlit Hollywood version of a martial arts master. When I added that he was also a master musician, who played in and directed his own samba band, had learned English in six weeks, was a friend and colleague of some of Brazil's best-known musicians and artists, and had walked arm-in-arm with the beautiful girls of Ipanema beach, perhaps they had hoped to see a muscular, brown-skinned Adonis who exuded menace and danger.

When Bira arrives at the dojo his full beard, unkempt curly hair, thick-lensed glasses, and perpetual smile make him look more like a backwoods river-rafting guide than a skilled martial artist. A few of the men mentally take a step back. Their looks of consternation say, 'There must be some mistake. Who is this man?' But Bira's warmth is irrepressible. "Hello, hello, how are you?" he says in a sensual Brazilian accent. He's shaking hands, moving easily among the men, his sunny disposition brightening up the dressing room. Suddenly everyone is smiling and picking one another up out of the corner of their eyes.

Out on the mat Bira at once begins to play the *berimbau,* the single-stringed instrument used in Capoeira. The eerie twang fills the large room. It's an old sound and there's both a dread and a joy in it. Bira begins to sing as he plays. His voice is rich, filled with vigor and feeling. His song tells a story of betrayal, revenge, and finally redemption. The rhythm and words tell each Capoeirista how to play in the *roda*, the circle in which two Capoeiristas test their martial skills. This particular rhythm is called *angola*; it calls for a measured, close-to-the-ground play that suggests a coiled reptile weaving through a dense, tangled underbrush.

Under Bira's direction we're in our own tight circle clapping in time to the music and singing the chorus to his lead. Wearing white pants and white T-shirts, instead of the formal Japanese *gi*, we look like Mediterranean novitiates in a pre-Christian pagan ritual. One by one we take our turns in the circle and "play" with Bira. His mischievous grin is hypnotic. The play is both challenging and playful. With each of us he momentarily demonstrates his explosive power and we reel back invigorated and respectful of his skill. He urges us to keep moving, to blend with his attacks, expand our field of awareness, and relax our stiff blocks and strikes.

The tempo increases, the clapping becomes a roar, our voices now fill the hall. "*Besouro antes de morrer Abriu a bôca e falou . . . ,*" Bira sings. "*Ai, ai, ai, Senhor São Bento Paraná e, Paraná e, Paraná . . . ,*" we follow as the chorus. T-shirts are thrown to the side, pools of sweat darken the mat. One by one we leave the circle blessed by the nearness of Bira's lethal kicks. In this primal ritual the fight is hidden in the dance; an ancient ecstasy is buried in a song of struggle. Our aggression is very real, but it's not contaminated with fear or malice. Blood and breath racing, we forget our terror of intimacy and join as a single body. The faces around me shine with the rapture of exertion. If the Apache Indian ceremonies are "the feet of birds treading a dance" to D.H. Lawrence, this is the charged exuberance of the panther. I have dreamed that we would share this primitive ritual of separation, grief, and return, and now that it's real I'm swept away by its power. The rising passion of our movements and voices is healing. I long for nothing more.

In his own book, *Capoeira: A Brazilian Art Form,* Bira described the power of the *berimbau* and its music:

I would leave the house, walking down the hill, with the *berimbau* sound still alive in my mind. Many times I would spend hours playing the *berimbau* alone, letting myself travel deep inside my soul, discovering different shapes of my spirit, my weakness, my strength, the consciousness of being alive and in tune with the universe. Carried by those magic moments, I would keep playing Capoeira through the dark of the night on the soft sand of Bahia's beaches. Soon I was not able to hear the *berimbau* anymore; I began to feel the sound everywhere, reflecting on the water, on the clouds, on the edge of the earth, resonating inside my body, vibrating in each portion of me. In those moments I felt the full dimension of the Capoeira music, the color of its sounds.

The *berimbau* can pacify the soul when played in melancholy solos; the rhythm is black and strong, a deep and powerful pulse that reaches the heart. It inundates mind, space, and time with the intensity of an ocean tide. The dense aura that emanates from the single musical bow slowly envelops you. Without your realizing it, the powerful magic of the *berimbau* has tamed your soul.

At times, the *berimbau* can put fire in your heart with the power of war horns, and bring your movements to fantastic speeds. In these moments, you have no fear. Your opponent can throw his or her attacks as fast as possible without finding anything. Only the empty space absorbs the deadly blows. It is as if the bodies lose their material consistency, no longer offering resistance. Attack and defense become one. Powerful strikes flash harmlessly. Following the *berimbau's* command you are protected.

Few people I have met embody the warrior ideal to the degree that Bira does. For instance, his description of his own developmental process is truly a map for the transition from fighter and foot-soldier to spiritual novitiate:

"In the first level, the student plays without knowing what is happening. He is lost in space. He sees nothing. Not only do the movements of his opponent seem to materialize by magic, but his own movements are beyond his control. I call this stage 'Playing in the Dark.'"

Following this, the new student gains a foothold in the techniques and flow of movement, this is called 'Playing in the Water.' Then there is a mastering of the form in which the Capoeirista demonstrates impeccable skill. . . .

"I reached this stage of 'Playing in the Light' many years ago, training so intensely that I would lose eight pounds each session. I was a fighting machine, challenging my own limits, other Capoeiristas, and martial artists of other styles."

This stage represents a shift from physical mastery to emotional control and the understanding of the philosophical elements of the art. It is a place where the inner art is developed.

"After four years 'Playing in the Light' I reached my limits and went into a depression. I had such good physical skills and such a strong attitude that I could not easily find challenging opponents. I had no motivation to train for so little possibility of physical and technical improvement. I felt stuck, as if I were facing a large stone wall. I could not see anything more in Capoeira for me. So I went to business school and decided to outfit myself in a suit. I graduated four years later, got married, moved to Sao Paulo, and worked in a big company."

After three years of not training, or even touching a *berimbau*, Bira awoke one morning unexpectedly transformed. He realized what he had been missing and was inspired to return to the *roda* and new challenges.

"I was then able to learn how to play in the fourth level which I call 'Playing with the Crystal Ball.' I didn't care anymore about my strengths, skills, speed, or any other physical aspect. I simply began trying to read the opponent's mind, and set myself in the right place at the right moment."

At this stage Bira understood that he must leave Brazil in order to continue his evolution. He felt America was the ideal setting to further develop the inner aspects of Capoeira. He deepened his study of all aspects of the tradition, seeking a universal expression for the art.

"Then I reached the last level which I call 'Playing with the Mind.' The opponent must do what your mind silently orders him to do. Such control has no other purpose than to help your opponent, even your enemy, to evolve and to reach a universal harmony through the Capoeira way. There is a rhythm to life and to the universe. In doing Capoeira, you can play to find it, to attune to it. As long as you are true to this rhythm, you cannot fight a false fight. The rhythm is joyful and gay; it is filled with life's imbalances, but it transforms them. It takes the unpredictability of the world and allows you to move on it."

Several years ago I participated in a formal discussion on the topics of nuclear war and the difference between the warrior and the militarist; our panel included not only Bira, but a practitioner of the Chinese martial art t'ai chi ch'uan and several other writers and anthropologists including the poet Gary Snyder. At one point in the discussion, Bira objected to the notion of any comparison between modern warfare and the true calling of the warrior: "Because of my background as a Capoeirista, I only can think in terms of a fight. A fight in the Capoeira context is an important process of self-understanding because when one confronts a serious opponent he's also confronting himself in a situation that uncovers his weaknesses and strength. I believe that the fight in this context is a step toward self-discovery, and consequently personal growth. This is an individual process that cannot be extended to a level of millions of people fighting with contemporary war artifacts, or to a massive extermination of human beings in a nuclear confrontation of nations.

"I think," he continued, "that a nuclear war is also a comfortable kind of war. The person who is pressing the buttons does not suffer the fear of actual fighting. Certainly there's fear of retaliation, but it's very different from the feelings that come during a personal confrontation. Think about the time when weapons were spears, swords, and clubs. You see your opponent running down a hill with a sword in hand. You can only rely on your own skill to defend the blows, or on your legs to flee.

"For the individual fight, the issue assumes a different perspective. At the moment you are fighting, your opponent becomes yourself. You confront your fears, your strength and weakness, your life itself. You do this without involving anybody besides your opponent and you. I have been involved in thousands of fights in my life, so I know what it is to feel this kind of thing inside. You know you must win. But to win means to win with yourself. But when you fight in a modern war, you have no dignity; you will be a samurai dying in the dirt and not wanting to."

November 14

It's late. Through the windows the moon breaks free of a phalanx of dark clouds. The wind hammers against the window, a chill creeps into the room. Upstairs a door opens and someone walks down the hall. It's probably Jack preparing for tomorrow's classes or Joel getting up from his evening meditation. Earlier tonight I had dinner with Rader and his family at their small duplex in the married enlisted man's quarters. My early childhood years of living on military bases have left an indelible print on my memory, and presumably on my character. Like the base houses I grew up in, Rader's home is simple, clean, and without pretension; its wealth is in the warmth of family life, not material possessions.

The evening evokes a dark and relentless grief. It's been just over a year since the break-up of my own family and it seems as if the healing has just begun. Being away from my children during this project has further intensified my guilt about them. While I long for family life I also feel completely inadequate about how to make it work. When I'm in this mood any philosophizing about warrior virtues seems completely frivolous. I cannot even maintain my own family.

Toward the end of the evening Rader tells me something that sticks in an odd way. The Brain Wave Training has invoked in him a vision of a cadre of Special Forces soldiers gathering intelligence through remote viewing and intercepting messages simply through the power of their minds. He suggests a scenario where a group of elite soldiers would go into a darkened room and collectively concentrate until they could project their consciousness any place in the world. He laughingly adds that it would beat the hell out of jumping from a plane with a full pack and then rucking cross-country to sit in a hide site for days and nights on end while monitoring troop movements, vulnerable to capture if discovered.

At first I was stimulated by the idea, a convenient and forward-thinking solution to the blood and guts of war. Extend his idea a few megahertz and it's easy to imagine that the entire drama of war could be acted out on the astral plane. No muss, no fuss. Maybe somebody would get their brains fried now and then, but that would only add the needed element of danger. Besides it wouldn't threaten the whole of civilization. It would deconstruct war into the imaginations of astral warriors. Everyone would sleep well in the knowledge that our Green Berets were out there somewhere in a Star Wars of the Mind fighting the enemies of democracy.

But the more I thought about this the more its real possibility was even more frightening than our present state of physical violence. Considering what we have just learned in the Brain Wave Training about the ability to train the mind, plus the incredible speed at which technology is progressing, some aspect of Rader's scenario may actually come to pass (the Soviets are already doing experiments in remote viewing). Scientists claim that we will be able to download human intelligence into a computerized robot in about fifty years. Even now there are robots fitted with artificial intelligence that can operate more quickly and efficiently than humans at certain tasks. But do we really want terrorist androids that can deliver nuclear backpacks? Or mind-waves destroying civilizations?

It may be clever, even brilliant technology, but at the same time it brings to mind the 1950s movie *Forbidden Planet* and its "creatures from the id." Both psychologists and spiritual teachers have warned us that the powers of the mind are ultimately not only greater but far more deadly than the powers of the body, even a "body" armed with weapons designed by the mind. The "creatures from the id" are, by definition, both primitive and unconscious; thus their hungers and jealousies are unrestrained and unpredictable. At least our present-day weapons of war are guarded by our conscious minds and trained intentions, however disingenuous, toward peace.

The parapsychologist Jule Eisenbud has observed that the ability to carry out combat with the mind may be an ancient vestigial capacity rather than a possible innovation. Perhaps (he suggests) predator and prey in the animal world carry out a psychic ritual of entrapment and submission at the same time that their bodies meet seemingly by chance on the "battlefield" of nature. He goes on to surmise that early societies tabooed psychic killing, simultaneously (and unintentionally) externalizing it as weapons. Voodoo and shamanism would be the relatively mild survivors of such profound materialization of our collective denial that we can kill with our minds alone. We overarm ourselves absurdly so that we do not have to take responsibility for our true potential—for the dangerous (and powerful) beings we are.

So is it better to regain our psychic weaponry and put the atomic jinni back in the bottle, or would we simply evoke even deadlier (in the sense of less controllable) weapons? Is this even a true psychic history of our species, or just a myth masking other truths? My own mind is finally confounded into silence and suddenly I realize these are not the real issues after all.

Yes, I find it personally satisfying that Rader is considering alternatives, but he ultimately misses the point. However seductive his scenario, it really only invents a new way to have war instead of unearthing war's root causes. We can all, according to our persuasion, instantly and righteously name a relevant "cause" worth fighting for—economics, nationality, geography, political ideology, race, religion, and their various camouflages and projections. But the lynchpin for any of these causes, which are not really causes at all but symptoms, is an old and weary theme that the speculation about psychic versus physical weaponry merely exploits: our worldview is based on an intricate web of oppositions that is essentially formulated as the division between flesh and spirit. This can also be understood in any of its permutations: mind/body; instinct/intelligence; heaven/earth; divine/profane; nature/civilization; animal/human; Dr. Jekyll/Mr. Hyde; primitive/modern; personal/global. While fundamentalist religion has declared the body sinful, and therefore evil, scientific rationalism, on the other hand, has colonized the body as a machine which can be understood through subjugation and quantification. No matter whether you are Christian, Jew, Muslim, or scientist, you are constantly being bombarded by this assumption of duality through our educational system, the media, and those invisible, but durable airwaves of the unconscious.

We oddly strive for a better world and to be better people by taking flight from our bodies. But isn't this first flight from the flesh also the first war? And if we carry this duality around in us aren't we always going to be at war, with ourselves, as well as others? Victorious on the battlefield during the day, we'll sit down to dinner with our loved ones at night and the war will be continuing inside of us. We need to ask, and by "ask" I mean experience, what it is in ourselves that we tolerate so little that we do everything we can to break away from it. Different psychospiritual traditions accentuate their own justifications for this flaw, all of them, unfortunately irremediable—the birth process itself, the cutting of the umbilical cord, separation from the mother, a lack of transmission of authority from the parent, discontinuity with the Divine. These may be facts of nature and psyche, but they create holes in us and imbue us with the regret of the original separation. When we first experience a hole or gap we're horrified, not only because of a sense of emptiness, but because of the immense yearning we have to fill it. While this yearning may be overwhelming, even out of control, it also represents the sincere urge we have to become whole. Our yearning to mend ourselves is experienced as an undifferentiated state of vulnerability; in our fear of this transparency of being we abandon our bodies. This initial division between body and spirit is then continuously projected outward into the world. There is self, and there is other. There are allies, and there are enemies. The broken world that we live in is a reflection of our broken souls.

When I say to these men that we must learn to live more fully in our bodies, they don't exactly know what I mean. They say that they want their bodies to perform better. They wish for a better body; a superhuman body that will help them surpass their previous limits; a body that is the dream of science, and their dream of manly perfection. I stop them from this line of thought. Not a performing body, I say, but a lived body, with feelings and emotions. The initiation we long for is one that will bless the union of our spirit and our flesh. When we live *in* our bodies we understand that it's more satisfying to *be* than to *have*. When we're embodied, love becomes more important than being right.

They become wary when I talk about feelings and emotions; they back off when I mention love. Of course, it's at first frightening to live in the body. When these men have their initial experience of embodiment it's usually accompanied by terror. To live in the body is to live truly in the condition of being human—what we know is that we're helpless and vulnerable. We're going to die. That frightens us. It also gives us choice. If we are someday going to die, we have a choice to live, to fully embody our destiny as human beings. But even though we're afraid, afraid of our yearning because it reminds us of our loss, we yearn deeply and constantly for wholeness. This yearning is experienced only when we're living in our somatic reality. It is painful, but arising from an awareness of it, a profound embodied awareness, is compassion, and with it the understanding that every human, regardless of sex, nationality, race, or degree of wealth or leisure, lives in this same condition of emptiness and yearning for a primary wholeness. We are one body.

We keep ourselves busy running from this painful recognition, but we're successful only in the lie. The author John Fowles says, "All our acts are partly devised to fill or to mark the emptiness we feel at the core." Perhaps our most destructive diversions are the fear and greed that lead to war. Maybe, we secretly convince ourselves, if we dominate somebody else we won't have to feel this pain; or maybe if we have, as Tracy Chapman sings, a "mountain of things" we will forget our oceanic need to fill the emptiness. In class I tell the men that everything is at stake here. What the warrior must explore is what he fears the most. The warrior must descend all the way into his body and soul and live in that gap where the world falls apart. To be with our desperation and need, instead of masking it with knowledge is an evolutionary choice. To live in uncertainty, but with aliveness and immediacy, demands the courage and durability of a warrior.

November 16

Last night I dreamt of a sword that cuts things together. In today's aikido class I spent the entire time emphasizing how to blend: Blend with your partner; blend with the attack; blend with what is; work with the situation and not against it. I slowly dissect the movement itself, describe what I'm doing, elevate its importance to the level of sainthood. Their questions are intelligent and tell me they're listening to what I'm saying. But then they practice and within a minute they're butting heads; there's not a blend to be seen within ten miles. Their urge to meet any incoming force head-on seems almost insurmountable. If you shout they outshout you. If you push they push back harder. If you disagree they take it as an attack and attack back. They instantly escalate anything that even remotely resembles a confrontation into a conflict. There's no middle ground; if you're not for me you must be against me—is their basic stance.

I'm irritated and I let it be known. But for some this simply becomes an invitation to act out even further, and the class edges toward mayhem. I know that I have to make more of a blend—a sword that cuts things *together,* I remind myself. Aikido is just plain difficult. The average time to earn a black belt training four to five times a week, is five years; the attrition rate in the average dojo is over ninety-seven percent; some techniques are called "the twenty-year throw" because they take twenty years to master; and it's not uncommon to find people who have been in the art for over fifty years who still consider themselves students. These men will not excel in aikido, much less master it, even after practicing nearly two hours a day for six months.

Sergeant Dunham motions me over. "I get it," he says, as though he just discovered the theory of relativity. "We're used to meeting each other head on, crashing into each other, but in aikido we're supposed to lead the other man, to work with him." His face is bright, alarmingly open. My heart swells. He continues to look at me in that frank, curious way of his, like a child waiting to be told, 'Yes that's the right answer.' I stop the class and tell everybody to stay where they are. I ask Dunham to tell the class his insight. He repeats what he told me. I ask him to demonstrate his insight. He blends with the force of his partner so well that the partner is hurled effortlessly across the room. He turns to me and says what

I have heard myself say and what I have heard many others say when their *aiki* is touched by luminosity and power, "That seemed too easy; it was almost as if I wasn't doing anything."

The notion that the only alternatives to conflict are fight or flight are imbedded in our culture, and our educational institutions have done little to challenge it. Traditional American military policy raises it to the level of a law of nature. The aikidoist, however, trains to respond to aggression by entering into the center of the attack, blending with its energy, and then guiding it into a neutralizing joint lock or throw. If the attacker can be seen as a metaphor for the many attacks of everyday life (conflict with a teammate, disagreeing with a superior officer, running late for an appointment, etc.), it's possible to translate this experience of blending into ordinary activity and interaction.

Despite my frustration today I can see that these men are beginning to experience the effortless and satisfying power inherent in blending. They're experiencing how working with the energy of a conflict, instead of fighting against it, can lead paradoxically to its resolution, how going with the force of an attack is a far more powerful response than attacking back. But as inspiring as they find this new experience, a nagging confusion continues to nip at their minds, "Yes," they tell me, "blending is effective and it *is* powerful, but it contradicts the rest of our training."

Once again we face the central dilemma: How can they identify with the retaliative mentality of the modern military if they begin to blend with conflictive situations instead of fighting against them? Isn't increased aggression (firepower) the only sanctioned strategy for winning a fight? If we blend with an aggressor won't that make us subordinate to them? I don't pretend that there are simple answers to these questions, or that aikido is an antidote for the habituated violence and aggression that infects our military and its policymakers. I do know that it is having an astonishing impact on these men, both in their bodies and in their way of thinking. As their rigid musculature responds to the emphasis on relaxation, they're becoming more flexible and are able to feel more, both from within themselves and from other people. Additionally, the emphasis on being centered makes them more aware when they're off center, and consequently more responsible for their own acts of aggression. More importantly they are experiencing an alternative way of dealing with conflict. They're recognizing, on the most fundamental level, that blending with a conflictive situation is usually the most efficient, graceful, and least damaging way to resolve it. This radical alternative is a language they use in their daily activities. Whether we're in the dojo, the classroom, on a military exercise, or having dinner in their homes I see the language and spirit of aikido subtly being revealed through their words and actions. They're sustaining and tolerating more feeling and more real power—a power that comes from within.

November 18

Brother David Steindl-Rast, a Benedictine monk, spent the last two and a half days with us. Unassuming in appearance, Brother David radiates a powerful and contagious inner calm. After recounting his military experience from being drafted into the German army as an Austrian teenager to being saved at the last minute from a firing squad, he was asked why he chose to be a monk. "A friend loaned me *The Rule of St. Benedict,*" he began in his Austro-German accent, "and when I read it I thought 'this is the form of life I had been looking for.' But where was there a monastery putting this into practice? St. Benedict lived fifteen hundred years ago. Someone suggested I should visit Mt. Saviour Monastery. Well, I said, I'll take whichever comes first, the right monastery or the right girl. After a few hours at Mt. Saviour I knew that this was it! That was in 1953, and I'm still a member of the community." He now spends over six months of each year in the monastery and the remaining time teaching and lecturing.

"I take the time to feel grateful for all that I have," he said. "And there's so much to be grateful for—what we're given to eat, loving friends, the health of our children." He laughed and added, "I could spend my entire day being grateful." He surprised the men by pointing out that there was a strong similarity between being a monk and being a soldier, at least in the areas of service, discipline, and dedication.

At one point he took an inventory of religious inclinations. Most of the hands were raised in the Christian category, with a smattering of agnostics and atheists. Johnson, indicating that he was an agnostic, and leading with his jaw, as usual, challenged, "What do you mean by God anyway? How do you know you're leading a spiritual life?"

Unfazed, Brother David defined spirituality as a sense of belonging or connectedness—with a person, with nature, with a community, with an inner feeling.

"Do you feel any of these things?" he asked Johnson.

Johnson's jaw softened. "I feel very connected to my newborn son and, of course, I have a deep bond with my teammates." The room grew quiet. "This feeling of being part of something," he continued, "increased tremendously with the birth of my child. It was one of the most fulfilling and powerful motivations in my life."

"Then," Brother David said simply, "from my point of view this is a spiritual life. In fact it sounds as if you have a wealth of spirituality in your life."

"Yeah, since you put it that way I guess I do feel there's spirituality in my life." He relaxed back, radiating a warm glow.

In closing, Brother David said that he saw that the lifestyle that these men had chosen was ultimately their way to relate to something greater than themselves. He went on to say that he considered this urge to go beyond oneself always a spiritual urge. "In your drive to go beyond yourself," he said softly, "I hope that you can see, as I do, that your profession can be a vehicle for worshipping that which is sacred. If you wish, your chosen profession can be an expression of your highest spiritual values." The room was quiet for a moment as we let his words sink in. Then as he began to leave a very moving thing happened. The men stood in a spontaneous gesture of respect and many of them went up to him and silently shook his hand. They recognized Brother David as a warrior of the heart.

November 19

First snow. A wide storm front rolls down from the northeast. The landscape drifts to sleep under white pastures. My struggle against the wind and cold has abruptly stopped. The change is so sudden that my emotions swing quixotically from reverence to mischievousness. Alternately I want to run headlong into the oceanic whiteness, then I want to sit quietly and listen to the sound of the earth returning back into itself.

My friend Catherine and I drive northwest to Barre to visit friends at the Insight Meditation Society, a Buddhist retreat center established in the early eighties. Joseph Goldstein and Sharon Salzberg, two of the founders of the center and longtime personal friends, are in the middle of conducting a three-month retreat, but they happily greet us at the door. The center is the classic large, rambling New England building; it was once a Christian seminary. The mood in the hall is solemn and darkly quiet, almost morose. It's such a radical change from the Army Post that I feel as if I'm sending a huge wake before me as I walk through the hushed hallways.

Joseph and I are cut from entirely different molds, but we have developed a mutual respect over ten years of friendship. He's tall and gawky. When we first get together he'll pat me on the head and ask in mock seriousness, "Why haven't you grown in the past year?" I chide him that he sits too much and maneuver him into an aikido joint lock. Despite his large frame he's elfin in spirit except when he talks about the Dharma—and then a clarity and luminosity transform him. His book *The Experience of Insight: A Natural Unfolding*, which is required reading for the soldiers, expresses the light touch and penetrating insight of his teaching. After graduating in philosophy from Columbia University he went to Thailand and India with the Peace Corps. There he was introduced to Buddhist meditation. Since that time he has dedicated his life to teaching and practicing meditation.

As always, our conversation eventually includes a discussion about warrior virtues in the contemplative and martial disciplines. While Joseph and I have our philosophical differences, we both view the archetype of the warrior as being essential for probing the deepest elements of mind and body. Courage and impeccability are warrior themes that often crop up in our ongoing conversations on this subject. Tonight Joseph adds "waiting" as another warrior virtue, waiting in terms of patience and stillness of mind.

"Waiting to me," Joseph says, "means not being driven to action by our desires."

I observe that waiting can too easily be interpreted as inaction or even hesitation. Joseph expands the concept into "stillness of mind, whatever the activity." For both of us this evokes the Chinese sage Chuang Tzu: "The non-action of the wise man is not inaction. It is not studied. It is not shaken by anything. The heart of the wise man is tranquil, it is the mirror of heaven and earth . . . Emptiness, stillness, tranquility . . . silence, non-action—this is the level of heaven and earth."

It seems to me that this notion of waiting is a subtle but crucial one for the modern warrior. After training for days, months, and years on end, he experiences a tremendous desire to test this training. "Does it work?" "How will I perform when I'm engaged outside the training hall?" History has shown us that at some point a well-trained standing army begins to tug at the bit, eventually finding itself in combat, even if it has to be a government coup or civil war. Perhaps this notion of waiting has an even more appropriate place in a peacetime army. Remember how during the time of extended peace in Japan's middle ages the samurai pursued meditation, poetry, and flower arranging along with their martial skills. There were outlets for their prodigious energy that didn't have to be channeled into war. In my mind I hear Dunham saying, "We just want to do something. We want to be put to use. It doesn't have to be war." So, why not create specially trained units that could respond to national and international emergencies? Or even launch programs where these men could go into drug- and crime-infested inner cities and work in intelligence and security, or creative rehabilitation.

The consequences of not being able to wait are well proven by the experience of the naval warship *U.S.S. Vincennes,* which shot down an Iranian passenger airline over the Persian Gulf, killing all two hundred and ninety people on board. Commander David Carlson, who was on the frigate *Sides,* twenty nautical miles away, commented that the *Vincennes* was known as the "Robo Cruiser" for its "consistently aggressive" stance. He surmised that the *Vincennes* crew "hankered for an opportunity to show their stuff." They were particularly anxious to try out their high-tech Aegis anti-aircraft system. The result of impatience, or lapse in attention, was an incredible amount of pain and grief that continues to radiate through the complex field of cause and effect.

As we drove home through the fields of snow I thought again of how Joseph and Brother David are worlds apart from the Special Forces soldiers . . . and yet, in many ways, utterly similar to them. While they respectively represent the polar Priest and the Warrior archetypes they possess many of the same qualities—courage, discipline, service, an urge for transcendence, and a quirkiness that puts them on the outskirts of the culture. Considering Joseph a warrior of the mind, Brother David a warrior of the heart, and the Special Forces soldier a warrior of the *hara,* or action, I found myself merging them into a Nietzschean vision together making up the whole man: Mind, Spirit, and Body.

November 24

Two days ago during Thanksgiving back in California an upsetting thing happened: I'm in line at the post office waiting to mail a package to the East Coast. A young mother steps up to the long counter with her two-year-old boy. He's cranky and fidgety, she tells him to quiet down as she rummages through her purse. He puts his hand in her purse and she tells him to stop. He looks curiously into the purse reaching for something inside. Turning abruptly she slaps him hard across the face. "I told you to stop!" she shrieks. The two people in front of me drop their heads, the clerk at the desk acts as if nothing had happened. Anger surges through me. The child grows red in the face. He begins to howl. The mother turns toward him raising her hand, threatening to strike. "Don't pull that on me," she hisses. The boy trembles and holds his sounds back in sucking gasps. I was outraged.

I wanted to pull her teeth out with my bare hands. I walked around the block twice until I was collected enough to drive my truck.

Reading an article about a bar in Dearborn, Michigan, now transforms the episode in my mind. In this establishment men are given black plastic miniature Uzi submachine guns. The miniature Uzis are built to shoot hard streams of water, not bullets. The evenings they hand out the water Uzis are called Rambo Wet-Panty Nights. On these particular nights women go on stage dressed in skimpy T-shirts and G-strings. Rock music blares out, men begin to shoot at the women's crotches. There's a lot of yelling and stamping. The bar's manager exhorts the men on, "Shoot those guns! If you guys were like this in Vietnam, we would have won the war!" The woman who does the best job getting shot at wins one hundred dollars.

The comments of shooters are certainly explicit: "I got her. She's hot; I know she likes it. She likes it, and she knows that I know she likes it"— that from a computer marketing specialist.

"You work hard all day, and this is a release. I worked twelve hours today, and this is a way to get some aggression out"—worker at a plastics manufacturing company.

"You don't get to do something like this every day . . . how many times do you get to shoot a girl in the pussy? This is great"—auto worker.

"This gives you a feeling of power and authority. The ultimate machismo. I'm aiming at her clitoris. She knows I'm shooting at her crotch and she knows it's me and she gets stimulation from it"—batch processor in a chemical plant.

"Maybe they don't like it at first, but when they get all wet they've got to like it. They've got to like it"—auto worker.

It's as though the boy in the post office will someday grow up and go to a bar like this and shoot Uzis at women's crotches and not know why. His wife will be angry at him for being out without her and she'll take her anger out on their son. This son will grow up and take it out on other women . . . where does the cycle of violence end?

Why do I see more of this loosely strewn throughout the world than I do among the soldiers themselves? Perhaps military parades, marches, swords, halberds, spear points, shouted commands, disciplined drills, pennants, emblems, patches, medals, ceremonies, gold braid, rank, sublimate the violence from literal confrontation into dramas of pomp and circumstance.

November 28

The sky is a deep cobalt blue. A splinter of setting sun catches the western edge of the roof. Opaque drops of melting snow slide to the roof peak, pause for a moment as if taking a quick survey of their destiny, and fall effortlessly to the ground. I remember sitting at this desk over three months ago entranced by the luxuriant green fields and the weight of a humid summer day, then later marveling at the coming of autumn and the kaleidoscope of color that layered the hardening earth. Now a carpet of virgin snow unravels from my window to the distant tree line. Most of the songbirds are gone and only ravens and dark, brooding raptors perch on the elm's bare branches.

I went to Supply today to check out gear for the winter operations we'll be taking to Utah. We expect sub-zero weather, and I needed a large pack plus part of a duffel bag's worth for this month-long operation. Special Forces issue is a couple of notches above regular Army and I was impressed by the quality of clothes and ski equipment. Having virtually no experience skiing I look forward to the training that I'll receive, most of it from Horst Abraham, a world-class instructor.

Winter operations are planned for the first week in January through the first week in February. During this time there will be no SportsMind classes; we will essentially be along as observers. The plan calls for the men to parachute into a military installation, spend most of a week acclimatizing and sharpening their mountaineering skills, then cross-country skiing over rugged terrain by night into a remote hide site. The next two weeks will be spent at the hide site observing any movements—trucks or ground troops—through the area. Our official job is to see if the work we have done with the men will have any effect on their performance. This particular winter operation is notorious for having produced a multitude of injuries in the past, from broken legs in skiing accidents, to frostbite, to debilitating flus and colds; we want to see if our work with healing, diet, concentration skills, and centering will improve things. Because they will be required to remain motionless for long hours, without much sleep, to observe and record precisely numbers of military trucks that will pass through their area unannounced, this is mainly a test of the meditation and concentration skills learned at the encampment and biofeedback lab. They also have to accomplish all this undetected as there will be "enemy" teams out trying to find them.

Our unofficial agenda will be to see if we can keep up with them and deal with the same pressures that they will be under. At this point it appears it will be Jack, Horst, and myself in the operation. While I look forward to this for its novelty and adventure, I also feel unprepared. I have virtually no experience in such extreme cold weather conditions; there's much I need to learn in the next few weeks.

December 1

It's a pristine day with a stiff breeze scattering maverick clouds to the southwest. The dark shadow of a large raptor, perhaps a turkey vulture, passes overhead sending a pair of brown sparrows off in a whirr. Five of us wait on a small knoll for Horst to instruct us; the lesson is downhill skiing with mountaineering equipment. I'm exhilarated being outside learning how to ski in such beautiful conditions.

While we're standing around, Rader skis up and unexpectedly plants his skis on top of mine. He pushes hard, and I fall awkwardly at the feet of the other men. If he's testing to see how I will react, I failed. It's frustrating to be caught off guard, but once I'm floundering in the snow I foolishly and unsuccessfully try to trip Rader with my ski poles. I'm flailing and twisting in my skis and poles, swearing at Rader and generally being a fool—with Dudley standing over me saying, "Well, well, Richard, what in heaven's name are you doing down there? Maybe you better think about getting yourself up before you try and get back at Rader."

I'm angry at Rader and ashamed of myself. I keep coming up with revenge fantasies toward him. I'll throw him extra hard in aikido class or freeze him out during a technique. Maybe I'll fail him in the next aikido test saying he doesn't have the right spirit. But the truth is that he caught me off guard and under pressure I blew it. Somewhere along the line I'm sure I'll appreciate this as a teaching, but at the moment I'm furious.

December 3

The weather has turned gray and cold; I'm increasingly taut with irritability. I meet an old acquaintance for lunch and he immediately launches into the same weary conversation about the ethics of teaching the Army. I've heard this so many times now that I almost go numb when it's brought up. He keeps trying to convince me of the danger of teaching spiritual disciplines outside of their original context. When I tell him I'm hardly a spiritual teacher he persists by saying, "Do you think that by teaching aikido or karate in the context of the military you'll be able to transcend the aggressive part of the arts?"

"I'm not trying to transcend anything," I reply, "in fact I think it would be a much saner society if everyone learned a self-defense art, which would include directly experiencing our aggression." His eyes darken and he looks at me disapprovingly.

"How would you feel," he continues, carefully accenting each word with his stiff finger jabbing toward my chest, "if one of those soldiers you're teaching used an aikido technique against a Sandinista militiaman?"

This seems so ludicrous that I look again to see if he's joking. He isn't.

"Well, how would that make you feel?" he says pompously, the finger jabbing closer and harder with each word.

I take his finger carefully but firmly and bend it back. With the other hand I tip the water glass so the water runs into his lap. "Gee, I might wet my pants."

Later I am struck by the similarity between Rader standing on my skis and pushing me over, and me twisting this man's finger. Teaching these men is looking into a mirror. The lessons are mine to learn.

December 5

Saotome Sensei will be visiting us in a week. I review dojo protocol and sharpen the training. I have some ego investment here; I want the men to look good when he arrives.

Today I taught *irimi nage* which literally translates, "entering throw." This is a powerful, lightning-quick move, the famous "twenty-year throw." I nod to my *uke,* positioned two or three paces away, and he quickly moves toward me, raising his right hand to strike my face. I simultaneously move toward him, raising my right hand to meet his, not as a block but a joining. From one perspective, our arms appear as crossed swords. At the last minute I angle off of his strike and bring my arm inside of his; as the momentum of his attack draws him forward, he clotheslines himself on my arm, his feet are upended and he falls at my feet. Less than a second has gone by.

I execute the move over and over, pointing out the small details, emphasizing the mood or character of the technique. The men are attentive, taking in as much as they can. The main principles of aikido—centering, blending, relaxation, entering, *ki* extension—are all present. I make an analogy between these principles and the members of an A-Team: all the parts need to work in unison with each other. When I mention that one can think of entering into the attack as a metaphor "the solution to the problem may be in the problem itself" some faces light up in recognition, while other faces distort in consternation. "It's confusing enough as it is, why do you have to throw that in?" they seem to say.

They bow to partners and begin practicing *irimi nage* for themselves. It's clear once again that they're trying "to conceptually understand" the movement without feeling it, which makes their movements rough and awkward. Like most of us, these soldiers have been schooled to develop their mental capabilities; their bodies, like a beast of burden, are to carry out the commands of their minds. Equating strength with big chests, massive biceps, and broad shoulders, they muscle their partners down like rodeo steer wrestlers. In truth their overly developed upper bodies make them top-heavy and much easier to throw off balance.

I stop the class. We go through exercises that help them transfer their base of power from their muscled chests and shoulders to their hips, what the Japanese call *hara,* or center. We have done these exercises many times before, but after years of identifying their masculinity with a thickly armored torso and shoulder girdle, it is difficult for them to trust the balance, power, and confidence that originates in the hips and *hara.* Whenever they become confused or impatient they abandon their centers and quickly return to their conditioned tendency of pushing and shoving with their upper bodies. Only after repeated failures with this top-heavy strategy do they become more open to the aikido principle of moving from *hara.* But this sequence must be repeated with each new move.

As the class progresses they begin to shift their identity away from their upper bodies and cognitive thinking to their *hara.* New potentials begin to appear. Their movement is more fluid and they begin to sense the direction of an attacker's force before the attack is initiated; their breathing is deeper and more rhythmic; relaxation becomes an ally of power and vitality. They realize that if they truly listen to their bodies, they'll receive valuable information about themselves, others, and the environment—information that is not available to the rational mind.

This unconventional wisdom was succinctly categorized by the company commander when he said, "It was the first time that I successfully learned a sequence of movements without trying to memorize them. I realized that through feeling the movements I could duplicate them later and that I could do this in any pattern of physical activity. In fact, I have introduced this method in my other interests to improve my performance, such as skeet shooting."

As the men have grown in their aikido training they see its overall usefulness. They comment that they move with their one-hundred-pound packs more effortlessly and without as much pain. Many of them have already noticed that their balance in skiing has increased from the previous year. Some have mentioned that understanding the principle of blending has even improved their relationship with officers. Overall it seems that the men exist in a more balanced and effortless manner, both on and off the mat. Then there are some who, like myself, simply fell in love with aikido and are already asking me where to train after the program ends.

December 7

We go to a nearby resort to practice downhill skiing. Wearing the same camouflage equipment we'll take to Winter Ops we're clearly part of the Army. While we're waiting in a crowded ski lift line a kid dressed in trendy ski clothes says insolently, "Hey, do you guys like war?"

"Do you like cancer?" Oreson says. There is scattered applause among the other skiers.

December 10

"*Musubi.*" Standing in front of the kneeling line of men, Mitsugi Saotome Sensei forms a triangle with his hands. His flat gaze, chestnut-colored face, and samurai bearing give him the appearance of a Mongolian chieftain. With the triangle held before him he strides forward. The movement is beautiful and deceptively powerful in its simplicity, like a salmon steadily cutting an edge upstream. His crisp *hakama* and immaculate white *gi* snap as he suddenly turns toward the line of men, "Not to fight," he says in his thick accent. "Join with your partner. *Musubi.* Tie into their *ki.*" His hands dissolve from the triangle and begin to weave together into a spiral pattern in front of him. "Do you understand what I mean?" He looks intently at the men. His flat gaze and broad impassive face unexpectedly light up into a wide toothy grin, his eyes sparkling mirthfully. "Good," he laughs. "Now you try it."

We train for a while and then he claps his hands, indicating that we should stop for further instruction. He takes a *bokken* off the rack and motions for me to take one. I move carefully toward him, my *bokken* extended in the on-guard position; I don't know what to expect so I'm alert for anything. He's holding his wooden sword to the side, seemingly open, his head and chest unprotected from an attack. I step closer, preparing to deliver a *shomen* strike to the top of his head; suddenly I feel as though I'm bumping into something, like an invisible inner tube that is extending out from his body. It's as if something has already engaged me, despite the physical distance between us; it is difficult to move toward him. Saotome remains absolutely still, as if he were watching a sunset instead of someone preparing to strike him with a sword. I circle to his left searching for an opening in the inner tube. He faces me as I turn and the unseen wall which I'm unable to penetrate follows me. I make an abrupt feint, as if I'm going to thrust the tip of my sword into his throat, but there's not even a ripple in his field. He is profoundly balanced. It's as if I'm facing a man who is not intimidated by the possibility of injury or death. Paradoxically, it seems that the more determined I become to strike, the more I feel it's me, not him, who is in danger. Then unexpectedly there's an opening in the invisible wall and I'm as much pulled into it as I'm consciously trying to enter into it. There's a flurry of movement as I slash downward and Saotome is suddenly standing next to me, a wide grin on his face with his sword tip pressing lightly against my throat.

We put the swords down. I attack vigorously and he demonstrates the same technique without weapons. He gracefully turns my energy into a circle and throws and subdues me with a pin. With each attack I feel as if my strike will reach him, but at the last minute he moves a razor's edge off the line and I have the feeling of being swept into an enormous vacuum, floating effortlessly as if I'm being supported by a universe of space, until I'm upended and fall to the ground. He turns to the men and says, "Learn to wait. Be still in yourself. You don't have to jump out after your partner." He mimics the way in which they struggle with their partner. "Wait and tie into your partner. Practice *musubi*."

After a day and a half of training with Saotome Sensei I seesaw between elation and a sinking feeling of despair. While I'm elated that Saotome Sensei, a true aikido master, is with us, I'm equally consumed by a sense of failure as certain aspects of the rigidity and stiffness of these men appear unchanged from the first week. Jack tells me later that I'm tired and inordinately hard on myself. He reminds me of the first month of training and really how far we have all come together. But most important—and what I only half want to hear, probably because it's most true—is that when my teachers come I become both the son to their father and the father to their son. I understand what Jack points out to me as a fundamental aspect of my neurosis—unfinished business with my own father.

I've noticed that starting with Brother David and now with Saotome Sensei there's been a change of attitude in the men's response to the guest instructors, and in many ways to us, the core teachers. In the past the men would sit quietly and attentively during a visiting instructor's initial session, with their bullshit detector turned on high. During the second session they would ask polite, but controversial questions. By the beginning of the third session their predator instinct prevailed and they went for the kill. They challenged, cajoled, disagreed, fought, and criticized wherever they felt a discrepancy. Sometimes they did this by making brilliant, scholarly arguments; at other times they would simply shout "Bullshit!" Then there would be the times that they would humorously mimic the style of the presenter. If the presenter responded with dignity and genuineness to the confrontation he would win the respect of the men. If he became defensive or evasive the men would either scornfully withdraw or escalate the confrontation. Then afterwards someone would always come up and say, "I hope you're not too thin-skinned. Don't take our attacks too seriously, we really don't mean anything by it."

They also pinpointed the idiosyncrasies of our team to perfection and took every opportunity to reflect them back to us. Sometimes it was lighthearted and fun but often it was brutally and painfully accurate. They see clearly, but the way they say what they see makes it difficult to hear. Their feedback, if you can call it that, has the effect of creating a distance, as if they want to define contact only within the parameters of conflict and polarization. This constantly elicits the feeling of being tested. After showing you the sensitivity of their perceptions they shield themselves by delivering it in such a way as to keep you at arm's length. They're afraid of closer contact, but at the same time they want to be seen for their sensitivity.

Over time I point out this approach/avoidance pattern to them by equating it to the concept of *maai* in aikido. *Maai* refers to the proper distance between you and your partner. If your partner is too close you move back; if he's too far away you move closer. These men are masters of *maai*. While this is one of their strengths, it's also a limitation when it's a habituated, knee-jerk reaction. At heart they are solitary; the lone cowboy riding the range, but they're also intimately connected in a tightly-knit group. They balance precariously between that required closeness and a primitive, almost claustrophobic urge to disappear into the wilds. It's actually to their credit that they tolerate spending so much time with other people. When some of these men finish their service I imagine them sailing alone out to sea or raising sheep on a remote farm.

It has been obvious that their level of resistance tends to escalate every time we come close to anything vulnerable. A first line of defense for them is that we're civilians and not one of "them." This was hardly worth bothering with initially except that it revealed a basic stance they had toward us: We were too far out of the mainstream and therefore we couldn't entirely be trusted. Even though we repeatedly told them that the material we were presenting wouldn't take anything away from their previously developed skills but would only add to them, each new class was still met by a spectrum of resistance that stretched from reticence, to noisy rowdiness, to self-righteous denial.

It was only when we provided exercises that gave them the opportunity to experience these new concepts were they able to accept what we were teaching. Many of them came to realize that in some previous setting they had already experienced what we were talking about, and the material turned out to be more familiar than they had pre-judged. When I initially introduced the notion of a bodily intuition, for example, they were predictably skeptical. But once we began exercises to investigate and train such an intuition most of them already had a previous experience to draw on. Yet even though we continually bring attention to the mechanical and repetitive pattern of their resistance, we always have to endure the lengthy challenge and resistance period of cat-calling, inattention, blank stares, and denial. Only during the encampment did we realize that the intensity of their resistance acted as a barometer to how close or far away we were from their vulnerability.

It became clear to us that the louder the defensiveness, the deeper the resistance, and the closer we were to something they were protecting. If loud volume was the fireworks to hide behind, then their seductiveness was the smokescreen. If the fireworks approach failed they would then resort to a strategy of charm and enticement to lead us away from what we were after. We learned that whenever they would become inordinately complimentary, agreeable, or congenial, it signaled that we were getting too close to their vulnerability. Their humming the theme from "The Twilight Zone" was a first level of resistance, but their acknowledgement that they were being obstinate and frequent apologies marked a second level, both of which cloaked a deeper fear.

Of course their real apprehension, which surfaced during the encampment, was hidden from us because it was in front of our nose, almost begging to be seen. What we know now is that it is vulnerability itself that frightens them. They're in a profession where vulnerability is seen as a weakness and it's disguised or weeded out as quickly as possible. Thus, they will fight off harbingers of change almost axiomatically.

When Saotome Sensei talks about tying into your partner's *ki*, it challenges the notion these men have around intimacy and aggression. Yet with both Saotome Sensei and Brother David there was a change in their reaction pattern. From the very beginning they were very respectful of Saotome, and he reflected sincerity back to them.

"I respect you for your chosen work and for your commitment and integrity. Your work makes you face death. It's essential for a man of *budo* to be serious in this way," he says with great formality. By telling them that he would teach them combat aikido, which he did, he paid them a very high compliment. After the first class when we were filing out of the dojo I overheard someone remark, "Now I know what it means to be a martial artist." The warriors had finally met.

December 15

When we leave the house in the morning it's dark and when we return in the evening it's dark. The cold weather forces us inside for morning P.T. We meet at the dojo to go through our usual routine of stretching, strength exercises, aerobic activity, and the ski exercises that Horst has introduced. Despite the cold I'm grateful when we go outside each day to practice Nordic skiing on the Post golf course.

We've just completed the last class in what we called Warrior Values. The men were assigned different reading material on the subject and were asked to review three articles, "Why Men Love War" by William Broyles, Jr.; "Naming the Cultural Forces That Push Us Toward War" by Charlene Spretnak; and "Mars, Arms, Rams, Wars: On the Love of War" by James Hillman.

The "warrior" has become a familiar concept and catchphrase in the fields of psychology, philosophy, literature, business, and in the movies. In urban cultural centers one can hardly find a bulletin board these days that doesn't include the word "warrior" to advertise some seminar or class. One can be a fighting warrior, a gentle warrior, a warrior athlete, a road warrior, a gay warrior, a Wall Street warrior, a woman warrior, a new warrior, an earth warrior, a warrior monk, an executive warrior, a dream warrior, or an ultimate warrior. Warriorship has great press, precisely because it suggests kicking ass in a moral and socially conscious way, though most people don't have a sense of what it entails.

In many ways interest in the warrior first reached the general public when an anthropology graduate student at U.C.L.A. published *The Teachings of Don Juan: A Yaqui Way of Knowledge.* In this book Carlos Castaneda movingly describes his initiation into a mystical body of knowledge by an Indian shaman he calls Don Juan. Early in his teachings Don Juan informs Castaneda that to become a man of knowledge one must be a warrior. Yet he does not define warrior in the classical sense of someone who goes to war. Throughout this book, and the five that followed over the next thirteen years, Castaneda clarified what it means to be a warrior. There is some question about whether Castaneda actually experienced Don Juan or made up his adventures, but there is little doubt that he redefined the warrior as an internal seeker playing in the complex outer world of nature rather than a Hollywood version of a Mongol general or Indian chief. Along the way his books became a seminal inspiration for a generation of Americans seeking spiritual insight through a life of impeccable action and wholehearted living. The appeal of Castaneda's books was instantaneous and since that time there has been a tremendous upswelling of interest in the notion of the warrior.

Previous to Castaneda's books the word "warrior" seemed to have very little airplay. There was little or no recognition of a person such as

Don Juan. Our positive warrior mythology was a composite of John Wayne, Charles Atlas, James Dean, and your favorite athlete: Though independent, strong-willed, and brave, these men were only involved in external gun, sword, and fist warriorship. They were bright, handsome, fit, and forever dangerous, constantly pushing some edge to the limit, but compared to Don Juan or even Saotome, they were plodding literalists who served only ethnic patriotism and would have been dazzled into paralysis by a spirit-being or jolt of true *ki*. O-Sensei spoke to the depth of warriorship when he said "True *budo* is to be one with the universe; that is, to be united with the Center of the universe."

Perhaps one of the trendsetters in a somewhat different lineage of promo was a sixteenth-century samurai named Miyamoto Musashi, whose work suddenly found a new generation of readers during the 1970s among those who admired the Japanese way of commerce. After defeating sixty opponents by the age of thirty, Musashi began to formulate his philosophy of "the Way of the Sword," influenced by Zen, Shinto, and Confucianism, into *A Book of Five Rings*. Although written by a sword master the text is, in the words of Musashi himself really, "a guide for men who want to learn strategy." No doubt the interest in the American business community stems from the fact that many Japanese industrialists and entrepreneurs use his book as a guide.

American seminars titled such things as "The Executive Warrior" which translate Japanese martial techniques into business stratagems are rapidly gaining popularity among major corporations. Books such as Tom Peter's *In Search of Excellence* and David Roger's *Fighting to Win* continue to promulgate this notion of the Japanese warrior in the boardroom, which is appealing on one level and clear delusion on another.

In their own hard-hitting, go-for-results way, the business warriors seek some sort of ancient morale and justification for their conduct and a path of self-development and service even while selling goods. Though strangely confirming the Marxist notion of business and capitalism as pure class warfare, they attempt to transcend class and personal gain by seeking an honor in their globalism and a humanity in their role of keeping the economic base of civilization afloat.

But there are many other paths of seeking warriorship. Men and women run through forests and canyons in camouflage clothing shooting at one another with paint-filled pellet pistols. For a fee, one can spend a day in the forest in mock combat defending a position, trying to capture prisoners, or kidnapping the "enemy's" sacred object. Some of these war games are so loosely organized that members of the same team meet for the first time on the day of the game. Other combat games have elaborately constructed buildings and organized teams that train and play together over extended periods of time. These events are gaining such popularity that there are national organizations with newsletters offering information concerning schedules, special events, and biographies of winning teams and individuals. So what do paint pellet games give that basketball or tennis do not? Most of the paint gun soldiers say the challenge lies in pursuing and being pursued, and surviving—a high-tech Capture the Flag. In this simulated combat environment, executives, machinists, artists, and housewives find a ritualistic physical-mental challenge that is missing in their everyday lives. Though they are hardly Green Berets, they too are seeking a ritual; these afternoon combatants with their harmless air pistols are making demands on themselves that wouldn't normally be available in front of the television set. They're choosing to participate rather than look on as a spectator; and to put themselves on the line rather than on the sofa.

A more significant embrace of the warrior archetype has been a part of the consciousness or human potential movement. Launched at Esalen Institute in the early 1960s, the *Zeitgeist* has affected such diverse fields as psychology, philosophy, education, medicine, sports, religion, the arts, physics, and anthropology. Its primary premise has been to explore and uncover those hidden reserves that are inherent in every human being. A cross-disciplinary, new-paradigm lifestyle was obvious fertile ground for the warrior ideal, so the "warrior" began to infiltrate into self-growth workshop descriptions in the late seventies and eventually appeared in such seminar titles as: The Warrior's Path, The Code of the Warrior, The Warrior Spirit, Warriors Without War, and The Sacred Warrior.

In the 1980s many New Age males felt they were becoming too soft, their feminine sides overdeveloped; the warrior archetype provided a sense of dignity and groundedness for their psychological work. The warrior quest was of particular interest to men who found themselves wondering about the nature of their manhood after spending years trying not to be rigid and uncommunicative figures like their fathers. After involvement with meditation, drugs, and sensitivity-training, these "feminized males" found themselves lacking presence and a certain boldness. They began to ask, "If I'm not going to be like my father, who *can* I model myself after?" The traditional warrior seemed to be an ideal way to explore sensitivity without losing their toughness and the archetypal male rituals. For many liberated women the warrior was a way to project their growing sense of strength without becoming *macha* or rigid. One could, in other words, be sensitive and aware without being a wimp; or strong and assertive without being controlling. Of course, just as mock warriorship has produced many phony businessmen who continue their avariciousness in a new guise, it has given false license to many repressed "wildmen" who have sold themselves on certain stereotyped machismo as the way of the gods in everyman (or everywoman for that matter). However, in the best of circumstances, it has replaced vacuousness, passivity, and moral neutrality with a sense of serving the planet, its threatened environment and peoples, and its old neglected gods.

In the late seventies the Tuscon Eco-Raiders, a radical environmental group that burned billboards and "decommissioned" bulldozers in the Southwest, became the inspiration for Greenpeace, a group dedicated to protecting the oceans and their denizens. In 1980 Earth First! gained national prominence when some of its members camped at the tops of redwoods to save them from being harvested by lumber conglomerates. Referring to themselves as the "earth's warriors" the individuals representing these organizations draw attention to the pollution of our natural environment by physically confronting the men and equipment that decimate our ecosystems.

Before retiring from his post-Vietnam war job at the Army War College, Lt. Colonel Jim Channon composed a fantasy training manual for "warrior monks" dedicated to world service. These "warrior monks" would be members of "The First Earth Battalion." The purpose of the outfit was captured in their central pledge: "My allegiance goes beyond duty, honor, and country . . . to PEOPLE and PLANET." Circulating thousands of his manual throughout the U.S. Army officer corps, Channon believes "there are enough dedicated soldiers who have committed themselves to higher principles that we could see the American Army pioneer the idea of global service."

Speaking from a different, but ultimately parallel perspective, James Fallows asserts in his book *The National Defense* that our military preparedness suffers because our Defense Department is not recognizing the importance of the warrior spirit. "The warrior's perspective," he says, "has counted for little, perhaps because there is less and less connection between the military culture and the most influential parts of the civilian world."

The warrior qualities of involvement and service also now appeal to many people in the general human growth movement who once might have rejected other aspects of warriorhood or adopted some shallow mythos of the cosmic shaman during the sixties and seventies. After years of self-study and work on their faults, many have felt that their path of introspection led them only to an isolated self-centeredness. The "Me" generation now seems to be more and more interested in service. The growth of organizations like Esalen's International Exchange Program and John Mark's Common Ground indicates an increasing "consciousness" involvement in political and social issues. Far from its Hollywood version as Roman soldiers and road warriors, the real spirit of the warrior has surfaced where men and women are seriously experimenting with new social forms and holistic ways of perceiving the world.

No doubt the bizarre and complete commercialization of the warrior archetype has taken place, as only it can in America, but that does not diminish its inherent worth. The interest in the warrior ideal is growing and has expressed itself in various forms over the past twenty years. Ultimately these forms reflect aspects of the culture more than they address the ancient issues of warriorhood itself; perhaps only subliminally do they answer the why of our present invocation of the warrior spirit. Yet this surge of interest does signal a growing need in our culture for a new way of being, a way that *embodies* the qualities of commitment, courage, compassion, and service while being rooted firmly in an awareness discipline. So, we need to continue to ask ourselves, "Who is this warrior and why are we so interested in him now?"

Emerging from the anxiety of the nuclear age is a new vigilance. The atomic bombing of Japan represented the birth of a novel and horrifying consciousness. At that moment a seed was planted defining our choice and responsibility for the future. When Einstein said that "With the splitting of the atom everything has changed, save for man's way of thinking" he threw a strike on a three-and-two count. In an awkward attempt at self-preservation we have backed ourselves into a corner that contains a riddle more profound than the Sphinx and would seem to have no escape. When Don Juan tells Carlos Castaneda that "I wanted to convince you that you must learn to make every act count, since you are going to be here for only a short while, in fact, too short for witnessing all the marvels of it," he hints at a glint of light, a possible way out of this dark corner. He speaks to that warrior in all of us whose impeccability is strengthened by the knowledge of his or her own death. To come to terms with our expanded technology we need to invoke our inner warrior: a person who can live warrior virtues without war; an individual who can claim primal aggressive instincts without hurting others; men and women who live with dignity and security without making others insecure and undignified.

Perhaps Rodney Collins foreshadowed the mystery at the heart of this in 1949: "When a new gift, a new possibility, is given to the earth, it is always presented in two ways—in unconscious form, and in conscious form. In the hydrogen bomb we recognize the unconscious form of a power hitherto unknown on earth. We await the demonstration of the same power in conscious form, that is, incarnate in living beings."

Shadow and Light

December 17

The slow winding down that has taken place as we move toward Christmas break shifted abruptly today when General Stevens' visit to the project was announced. Stevens is a two-star general and head of the Army's Special Operations Command. The news that he and his staff will be among us in three days has sent everybody scurrying. Big Daddy is coming to town, and regardless of anyone's opinion about the program, rank, or inspections, the heat is on.

Besides cleaning the offices, biofeedback lab, classrooms, and dojo there will also be extra attention to haircuts and uniforms. While the men predictably scoff about too much emphasis on protocol, it's obvious that Stevens' V.I.P. credentials are respected by everyone. The plan is to present mini-demonstrations of each phase of the program as the General is toured around the premises. I choose Braddock, Janowski, Galt, Fine, Rader, and Dunham to demonstrate the aikido section. They will execute both open-handed techniques and the first three sets of the *jo kumi tachi* (staff partner practice). As I work to prepare them, I'm secretly elated by how far they have come. I take on a firm, serious tone, correcting even the smallest detail, but inside I'm pleased by what I see. Not only are their techniques precise and strong, they also communicate the *aiki* spirit of a resilient, grounded strength. I can see that the last four months of practicing *aiki* movements plus the constant rolling and falling has wrought significant changes. I note the solemn countenance of Master

Ueshiba as he gazes down from the photo in front of the dojo and I imagine him nodding his head in approval.

December 20

A linen blue sky stretched over fields of bleach white snow makes me forget that it's winter. A shiny black raven barks at us as we navigate the icy street in front of the offices. Someone throws a snowball at him and he circles us once, twice, and then caws back as he heads a perfect compass west.

I'm waiting inside the classroom with Joel when General Stevens' aide, Sergeant-Major Wycolyski, comes in. In addition to honors for valor and courage while under fire, he is decorated across his chest with commendations that must cover at least three wars. "Good morning Sergeant-Major," Joel says.

"Beautiful day wouldn't you say Sergeant-Major?" I say.

"A beautiful day to kill communists!" he shouts back enthusiastically in a thick eastern European accent. "Only trouble is you can't find 'em when you want to." He shrugs his shoulders in mock hopelessness and gives us a big smile. Later I'm told that he aided the OSS as a member of the European underground resistance during World War II, immigrated to the U.S. after the war, and became a member of the Army's Special Forces. It seems that he lost most of his family to the Soviets at the end of the hostilities and it has made him a staunch anti-communist as well as a fierce combat soldier.

Out the window I can see General Stevens and Colonel Barnes, our Group Commander, sitting in the back seat of Stevens' staff car. His driver, a Spec 4, listlessly cleans the windows while the two men confer inside. They could as easily be two Mafia dons talking business, or family patriarchs on their way to a wedding. What do they talk about: Budgets, psychic warfare, whether or not to fund this program again? How do they feel about the planet that their grandchildren will inherit? Wycolyski side-eyes me, keeping an eye out for his boss maybe, or perhaps a little unsure of how my lavender SportsMind sweater fits into what he hears of me as a martial arts teacher.

When General Stevens suddenly enters the room Joel and I join everyone else snapping to attention. Looking straight ahead, his retinue trailing behind him like a camouflage gown, he murmurs, "Relax" out of the corner of his mouth. Colonel Flynn introduces everyone and we immediately pass to the dojo through the classroom door. The six men in their *gis* and *jo* interrupt their practice and come to attention. I give them the signal to begin the demonstration and while I explain to the General how aikido fits into the program, I notice, for the first time, what a big man he is—at least a head taller than I. He nods silently, asks what the *jo* is used for, and how the men are taking to this art. Even as I tell him that these men are doing well considering it's a difficult art to master, I look down and see Rader and his partner completely blowing one section of the *kumi tachi*. I can't believe what I'm seeing. Rader has accomplished the same move hundreds of times without a hitch and now it's as if he has amnesia. What's worse: Instead of just completing the movement (General Stevens would never know the difference) he fumbles around at the point of his mistake and then starts all over again. I'm overtaken by paranoia, thinking he's doing this on purpose to discredit aikido and the program. Our eyes meet and his look of exasperation actually relieves me.

Without warning Stevens turns to leave and everybody is caught momentarily in an awkward bottleneck at the door. It's a logjam of camouflage green, lavender, polished black leather, and the quick shuffling of feet. Jack saves the moment with the best aikido move of the day by opening a passage and Stevens passes through with everybody else filing behind him. At the last moment I look back and cuff Rader with a scowl; he shrugs.

In the lab Parker is explaining the biocybernetic axioms when Stevens interrupts him and point-blank asks, "Has this worked for you? Can you raise your temperature at will?" Parker stammers something incoherent and both Shell and Martin become very alert, thinking they may be next.

"Huh . . . yes sir, I can, pretty much sir," Parker finally concedes. 'Pretty much?!' I think. 'He *can* do it. I've seen him do it. Why doesn't he just say—Yes, sir?' Are they sabotaging the program or simply choking? Is everybody trying to cover his ass just because Big Daddy is in town? I remember this charade from being around my father and his fellow officers when the brass showed up: Men trying to find the center of gravity in a situation where the shit rolls quickly downhill and promotions are achieved by trudging diligently the other way, and everybody is ready to point fingers at the ass-kissers. Tricky navigation. Only Colonel Flynn, our Battalion Commander, seems relaxed.

"Could you do it right now?" Stevens asks Parker. This time Parker is unexpectedly clear and tells him that it takes a while to prepare one's mind, but he knows how to do it and he's getting better at it. Stevens nods and moves on.

Later we hear that Stevens was impressed by both the men and the program and this, of course, pleased Colonel Flynn and Colonel Barnes. When I see Rader I ask him what the foul-up was about, I'm disappointed with the way he sloughs me off. I guess I expect him to be as demanding of himself as he is with us.

As I watch Wycolyski walk away I wonder what horror he witnessed so many years ago that turned him and made him so ferociously one-pointed. Can his wounds ever be healed through killing? I wonder if he has days that are good for not killing communists? Will his vengeance ever be complete? As if shaken loose from the blue pastel sky, Shakespeare's ". . . Farewell, Othello's occupation gone" comes to mind and I wonder what Wycolyski will do when he must say farewell too.

December 27

Winter creates an odd polarity of sloth and stimulation in me. I flip-flop between wanting to camp out in the living room with a handful of video movies to running wildly through the mounting snow drifts. But the upcoming demands of Winter Ops inspire me to maintain my conditioning schedule.

A just-arrived Christmas card from the company commander shows a Minuteman standing sentry on a clear, cold winter night away from the comforting lights of home and family. The brief passage inside is a reminder that freedom and peace have a cost and it's because men and women are standing duty to defend these privileges, even on this most sacred of nights, that we're able to enjoy them. I put it up on my wall. On the facing page I write, "Peace inside makes peace outside."

January 7

The darkening sky matches my despair. I'm sitting up in bed with my left leg wrapped in ice. Even the slightest movement sends a stabbing pain into my groin and pelvis. I'm both angry in my helplessness and afraid of the relentless, searing pain that has become my constant companion. Behind all anger is fear; I'm afraid I have done irreparable damage to myself.

The day before we were scheduled to leave for Winter Ops I was training at Kanai Sensei's large dojo in Cambridge when my life took an unexpected one-hundred-and-eighty-degree turn. I was working with two other black belts and we were enjoying a fast, hard training when I felt a grabbing pain in the upper inside of my left leg. I carefully stepped off the mat to feel it out. I could tell something was off, but it didn't seem to be a major injury, or so I reassured myself, and being accustomed to training through injuries and pain I rejoined my partners. It was a fateful decision for which I now punish myself. A moment later, as I was being thrown, I suddenly felt as if someone had plunged a knife deep into my groin and then ripped downward. There was a frightful tearing that traveled down to my knee. I cried out in pain and instantly collapsed in a heap on the mat. I half-crawled, half-walked into the dressing room and lay down in a state of semi-shock. Bewildered by what had happened the teacher and one of my training partners tried to alleviate my pain, without success. I had severely torn a groin muscle in my left leg and it left me barely able to walk.

When I look back on it there was a small, but distinct voice that I chose to ignore: "Pay attention. Be careful. Something is not right here." Asking myself over and over why I didn't listen to this voice I keep returning to the same painful answer: I didn't want to be seen as a quitter. Because this makes absolutely no sense at any other level than that of my own bull-headed, macho ego I'm left feeling defeated and deeply humbled. This is the same ill-fated vanity that has brought injury to me throughout the program. Like a habitual spasm in the muscle of my psyche this rigid competitiveness is born out of a deep sense of insecurity. Somewhere in the cornerstone of my being is a missing link, a gap in my self-acceptance, that makes me feel I must continually prove myself. If I have learned nothing else in this project, I have learned that acting out of this impulse only brings pain. Besides, in this acting out I never address the deeper issues of inadequacy. The constant dull throb in my leg is a reminder of the deeper, more mature work that I have in front of me.

I rose with Jack and Horst to see them off, promising foolishly that I would stay in contact and join up with them in a week's time. I'm bitter about not being able to go and I sullenly confine myself to bed.

January 15

With my leg tightly bandaged I can now limp around, drive, and am no longer afraid that permanent damage is done. There is no sign of a hernia and my meditations have become exercises in healing the muscle tear. Joel and I drive into the Post together and begin the extensive statistical work that will go into our after-action report for the Army. Spending more time together we fill in blank spots between us; my appreciation for him deepens. He was raised almost solely by his mother and never participated in organized sports, military service, boys' clubs, or a college fraternity, so this tour with the Special Forces is in many ways a sudden and sobering initiation into the world of men. His carved angular face brightens when I remind him that despite how different he is from most of us he has earned the respect of all the men.

As we organize our facts and figures we're slowly coming to the realization of how much these men have changed, at least on paper. The figures from the biofeedback lab show quantitatively enormous increases in their ability to organize and use their attention. I'm finding similar figures in the physical conditioning section. In certain areas, flexibility for example, some of these men have increased by almost two hundred percent from where they started. I know that shifts like this in the body have tremendous affect on one's attitude and emotional range.

Joel tells me that when a committee member from the National Science Academy visited the project a few months ago he expressed amazement at the radical changes in the men's biofeedback scores. He had never seen such improvement within the military before and he didn't understand our success. "What he missed," Joel said, "was the synergistic approach to our work. Even though I pointed this out to him the concept seemed to totally evade him. I told him the success of the project was because of our emphasis on the interconnectedness of mind, body, and spirit. It was difficult for him to understand that our emphasis on the continuity of attention in all the activities, from P.T. to team communication to meditation to aikido to rucking, is what made the difference."

January 25

Joel received word that the wife of the battalion sergeant has almost completely reversed her Raynaud's Syndrome using our biofeedback equipment. Earlier in the program Colonel Flynn told Joel about her condition and asked if biofeedback could be of any help. Joel put Flynn through a mini-course on what to show her and then sent him home with books and equipment. Flynn showed her what to do and three months later, *voila!* God works in mysterious ways.

February 1

A distant ringing wakes me at dawn. The sky is a pale violet and the top crust of snow looks freshly lacquered. The phone is in the hall and I look out the window as I pick it up. The cold this morning is brittle and translucent; I'm not happy to be up at this harsh hour. The voice on the other end speaks with a heavy French Creole accent.

"Mr. Richard Heckler, please"

"Yes, go ahead please"

There is static and then I hear a voice struggling to find its way through the noise. It's my old Haitian friend Evelyn. For the past few days the front page of *The New York Times* has reported widespread violence and bloodshed in Haiti as Baby Doc Duvalier is being pried from power. She wants me to know that she is all right, but a mutual friend of ours has been shot. From what she can gather, our friend was driving home when a Ton Ton Macoute, the muscle for the Duvalier regime, fired on her in her car. Miraculously she was able to drive herself to help and is now recovering in the hospital. I realize now that what I thought was phone static is the sound of automatic weapons. She tells me that gunfire and mortars have gone on all night throughout Port-au-Prince.

"It's horrible." Her voice finally breaks and she begins to sob.

I express my helplessness by crouching tight-fisted and angry in the cold hallway. Outside a dusty brown dog pees a chartreuse stream on something only its nose can see. I want to help my friends but I'm helpless.

"The hate is horrible," she says, "It's unbelievable what they are doing." She tells me of passing a shouting crowd gathered around something burning. In the middle was a smoldering human torso with all the limbs hacked off. "They were stoning it and hitting it with sticks," she sobbed. "I don't understand it."

I tell her that she and her family should leave immediately. She tells me there are no flights and it's chancy by sea. She thinks that she and her family should stay; perhaps they can be of some help there. Static now squeezes Evelyn's voice against the sound of gunfire and our connection dims. We promise to stay in touch.

I'm furious in my helplessness. I want to be mad at somebody but I don't know who—our government for always seeming to be on the wrong side? Some faceless Ton Ton Macoute? Baby Doc? His father, Papa Doc? A recessive gene? There is a sickness among us and its battle line is the human soul. It is everywhere. It is now. Its dark shadow touches my life and I'm suddenly watchful of my loved ones sleeping quietly in the next room. How simple it now seems for our early ancestors to have stood outside their caves guarding against the fang and claw of predators. The evil that we must stand vigilant against is like a virus, starting from deep inside us, eating its way out until we're devoured by and become its madness.

Through the window I watch a gentle snow luff by the sleeping birch and disappear into the hard white crust. The bareness of my thoughts and the frozen stern landscape are harshly invasive. "Peace inside makes peace outside," I read. The battle is fought on my meditation cushion.

My tears are in sorrow for our condition and in gratitude for a way to combat this madness.

February 9

Everyone returning from Winter Ops looks exhausted. We take a few days off for recuperation and so the men can be with their families. I, of course, feel as though I've had a month off; I can't bear the thought of doing any more paperwork. Jack is full of stories and I'm envious of his adventures. Although Colonel Flynn broke his leg downhill skiing the reports of our two teams show that they exceeded everyone's expectations. Flynn confirmed this: "I've seen at least one-hundred-and-fifty teams come back from these kinds of exercises and they're always surly, cynical, and generally wiped out. These teams didn't look tired, sleepy, fatigued, or annoyed. They were spirited." The Battalion S-2 commented, "They recovered extremely quickly and gave the best briefings I've ever heard."

Even though our two teams drew the most difficult mission, having to travel further and stay longer than any of the other teams, we suffered no injuries or illness, while there were seventeen injuries to members of the other Battalion teams. Our teams successfully navigated approximately thirty kilometers of snow-covered mountainous terrain at altitudes between 7,500 and 8,500 feet with loads averaging ninety-five pounds. They remained in their hide sites undetected for ten days and completed as high a rate of accuracy in their reports as any team in the Battalion.

Compared to winter operations in previous years this exercise was particularly successful in terms of how the soldiers applied the work with us to an extremely arduous event. By all accounts they performed with a degree of body control not previously observed; and they did so without giving up any of their creative instincts for daring and aggressive action.

February 11

It's over. Things are moving fast, too fast for me. I want us to make a clean, clear ending, but as the men are preparing for their next assignments, we're packing things in boxes. Their way of handling the ending I know well. Growing up in the military you make friends, get assigned a new station, and then are gone. Oh, the care and feeling are there . . . but don't get too attached; you'll just have to leave.

I take an inventory of all the guest presenters and ask the men if they had to spend a year with one of the presenters which one would it be. The year might be spent in combat, at the Post, or even sharing family time: "Who would you choose as a fellow warrior? Who would you choose as a fellow team member?" The pros and cons of all the presenters were discussed and the majority unequivocally chose Brother David Stendl-Rast, the gentle-hearted Benedictine monk.

"Why?"

"Because he wouldn't lean on you."

"He had an internal strength."

"You could depend on him to carry his own weight."

"He was true to himself."

 I'm sad.

I feel so much loss.

I go into the dojo and for the last time take a *bokken* off the rack, bow into the photo of Master Ueshiba, and practice my sword cuts. Sweat forms on my forehead and then begins to drip off of me. The light pales and soon it's dark. My cuts are faster and more furious. I slash at both the demons and the angels of the last six months. I want to purify myself by slaying them all.

Oreson opens through the classroom door and walks down the side of the mat toward the dressing room. At first he doesn't see me and I continue my sword cuts. Startled, he stops. "What are you doing in the dark?" he asks apprehensively. Through the gloom I can barely make him out.

"You're the prince of darkness," I say. "I thought you liked the shadow."

"There's only a shadow if there's light," he replies.

Epilogue

February 12

I'm sitting at the back of the dojo while Harner and Rollins student-teach aikido to a team from another company. Supervised teaching is the last thing they do in the program. The same process is taking place in the biofeedback lab, in P.T., in nutrition and diet, meditation, communication skills, all within the framework of the mind-body-spirit synergy.

As I watch them demonstrate and talk about aikido it helps me understand what they have learned and how they integrated it. I hear my words in their words and I see that in many ways they're more effective in teaching their own kind than I was. Closer to the minds and hearts of the Special Forces soldier they know how to "enter into and blend with" the soldier's point of view. Watching them share their insights I feel proud as a teacher, because of what they have learned. But I'm even more proud that they have made it their own.

I see these soldiers, and myself, as the inheritors of a very old and honorable warrior tradition. In a moment of inspiration I picture, like ghosts in the collective mind, the legions of Japanese Samurai passing their heritage of self-mastery to those who would become the teachers of Master Ueshiba; and Master Ueshiba, witness to the horrors of atomic war, transmitting a yet deeper wisdom to a generation who would eventually become my teachers; then my colleagues and myself, emerging from a culture made vulnerable by lies, hopeful that by a growing consciousness we can express new definitions of warriorhood to our students. Before me now, I see these soldiers passing their knowledge to another generation. In this vision I see how each generation, according to the individual and cultural needs of the time, have added their particular flavor to the art. I also see that, within this changing mosaic, the timeless and inspirational essence of aikido has remained alive. In this vision I'm at the cutting edge of a historical moment that spans some seven hundred years. But the edge itself are these soldiers who are now practicing the aikido principles of harmony and universal understanding.

For those who haven't experienced the aikido principles or who fail to see the person inside the military uniform this is a frightening vision. They forewarn that soldiers will use these principles for destructive purposes. I think otherwise. I believe that bringing aikido to the military is a step toward a more sane and more compassionate America.

Harner addresses the men in front of him as he spins gracefully out of the way of Rollins' strike and guides him into a tight spiral to the ground. "You're all used to clashing with each other and butting heads," he says in his commanding voice. "There's another way. It will take you a while to get used to it, but it's easier. Blend with the attack. You don't have to fight back to accomplish your goals." He smiles at them, but I know it's for me.

March 25

Joel, Jack, and I meet at my house in California to begin work on the after-action report. In addition to analyzing the stacks of quantitative data in the brain wave, biofeedback, psychometric, cholesterol/body fat, blood chemistry, cybex, and physical training sections, we also sort through ours, and the soldiers', subjective evaluations of the "gut check," Winter Operations, Maritime Operations, and aikido.

Three months later an eight-hundred-page tome, which included all the appendices and raw test data, was completed. This was condensed into a bound two-hundred-and-forty-five page after-action report that was delivered to General Stevens, (at the Special Operations Command); Colonel Flynn, our Battalion commander; Colonel Barnes, the Group commander; and selected personnel in the Department of the Army. There was a wide range in individual progress achieved, but on the average the soldiers' abilities across the program goals increased by seventy-five percent from the points where they started. The results of the objective testing and subjective evaluations indicate the following average individual change for each contractual goal:

Physical	**Average % of increase**
• to understand new concepts of fitness	95
• to understand effects of diet on performance	150
• to be able to control pain (promote healing)	55
• to fine-tune body performance	85

Psychological	
• to better manage stress and shock	85
• to increase mental abilities	100
• to coordinate mind, body, and emotions	65
• to solidify key values (e.g. accountability)	70

Team Cohesion	
• to strengthen team	50
• to strengthen leadership skills	40

Mission Specific	
• to enhance abilities to:	
remain alert and motionless	70
control temperature in extremities	40
extend sensory awareness	80
rest and rapidly recuperate	100
• to manage energy output (gain endurance)	90

Company Commander Thorne made one of the most astute observations when he wrote, "This training is designed to produce changes in lifestyle rather than impart knowledge for future use. In this regard it differs completely from most formal schooling our personnel have attended. Our greatest challenge in the future will be to find ways to prevent the closing of our soldiers' minds."

The Trojan Warrior Project, at least on paper, was an obvious success. General Stevens and the Special Operations Command were pleased and gave the go-ahead for another program. We recommended, with Special Operations approval, that the next training focus on developing soldier instructors for future programs. A new Group commanding officer, replacing Colonel Barnes, announced that funds were unavailable for another project. The grapevine reported he said he had an Army to run and didn't want to hear about meditation, martial arts, or brain waves. The program was put on the back burner.

Colonel Flynn was appointed to the Army's prestigious War College; Captain Thorne was transferred overseas; Teams 260 and 560 were reorganized as many of its members were reassigned to duty stations and military schools elsewhere. We continue to receive letters from a number of the men requesting information on meditation and stress reduction, inquiring where they can study aikido, and telling us how the project has continued to enrich their lives.

When the after-action report was completed Joel went into a one-year silent meditation retreat with his teacher. Jack became Director of Development for SportsMind and was instrumental in acquiring the contract to train managers and executives at AT&T in communication skills and mind-body awareness. I bought a small ranch in the coastal foothills north of San Francisco where I teach aikido and hold trainings in the themes presented in this book.

Three years after the program ended Jack, Larry Burback, and I held a similar, but briefer training for a small group of Navy SEALs.

Was the Trojan Warrior Project a success?

A third of the soldiers would clearly say no; stating that the time would have been better spent training at their military specialties. Others consider it a major triumph, positively affecting their lives and Army careers. Perhaps it was a success, as some say, just because we were asked to do it.

The questions and contradictions that I faced at the onset of the program only intensified as time went on. My search for answers to a personal dilemma and a global crisis simply led to more questions, which in turn became, like a Zen *koan,* an unanswerable paradox. While there were no handy answers to my quest, it turned out that what I taught these soldiers were the lessons I was still learning. I realized once more that aikido and meditation are disciplines that inspire lifelong learning and self-development. And though I fell from these paths, they also caught me, becoming the ground from which I could find a foothold to stand again. The program was a success because it asked us to acknowledge the wisdom and power of compassion.

As for the warrior? I remember an evening Jack and I were sitting by dark waters. Drawing inspiration from a glittering night sky, he mused: "Believing you can be perfect is the fatal imperfection. Believing you're invulnerable is the ultimate vulnerability. Being a warrior doesn't mean winning or even succeeding. It means risking and failing and risking again, as long as you live."

 I gratefully acknowledge the following authors for their insights and efforts.

Almeida, Bira, *Capoeira: A Brazilian Art Form,* North Atlantic Books, Berkeley, CA, 1982.

Beaumont, Roger, *Military Elite,* Bobbs-Merrill, New York, 1974.

Broyles, William, Jr. "Why Men Love War," *Esquire Magazine,* November, 1984.

Caputo, Phil, *A Rumor of War,* Ballantine Books, New York, 1977.

Chagnon, Napoleon, *Yanomano: The Fierce People,* Holt, Rinehart & Winston, New York, 1977.

Clausewitz, Carl Von, *On War,* Penguin, New York, 1968.

Cunliffe, Marcus, *Arms and Men: A Study of American Military History,* New York, 1956.

Dyer, Gwynne, *War,* Crown Publishers, New York, 1985.

Egendorf, Arthur, *Healing from the War,* Houghton Mifflin Company, Boston, 1985.

Eisenbud, Jule, M.D., *Parapsychology and the Unconscious,* North Atlantic Books, Berkeley, CA, 1983.

Fallows, James, *The National Defense,* Random House, New York, 1981.

Gabriel, Richard A., *No More Heroes: Madness and Psychiatry in War,* Hill and Wang, New York, 1987.

Gerzon, Mark, *A Choice of Heroes,* Houghton Mifflin Company, Boston, 1982.

Gilbey, John F., *The Way of a Warrior,* North Atlantic Books, Berkeley, CA, 1982.

Gray, Glenn J., *The Warriors,* Harper Colophon Books, New York, 1959.

Grossinger, Richard, and Hough, Lindy, editors, *Nuclear Strategy and the Code of the Warrior,* North Atlantic Books, Berkeley, CA, 1984.

Grossinger, Richard, *The Night Sky,* J.P. Tarcher, Los Angeles, 1988.

Harris, Marvin, *Cows, Pigs, Wars, and Witches,* Vintage Books, New York, 1978.

Hart, Gary, with Lind, William S., *America Can Win: The Case for Military Reform,* Adler & Adler, Maryland, 1986.

Holmes, Richard, *Acts of War,* The Free Press, New York, 1985.

Homer, *The Odyssey,* trans. R. Fitzgerald, Doubleday Anchor, Garden City, NY, 1961.

Homer, *Homeric Hymn to Ares*, trans. Charles Boer, Spring Publications, Dallas, 1970.

Keegan, John, *The Face of Battle*, Penguin, New York, 1976.

Kovic, Ron, *Born on the Fourth of July*, Simon and Schuster, New York, 1971.

Leonard, George, *The Silent Pulse*, E.P. Dutton, New York, 1978.

Meggit, M.J., *Desert People*, University of Chicago Press, Chicago, 1960.

Musashi, Miyamoto, *A Book of Five Rings*, trans. Victor Harris, Overlook Press, Woodstock, NY, 1974.

Nietzsche, Friederich, *The Portable Nietzsche*, trans. Walter Kaufmann, Viking Press, New York, 1968.

Nitobe, Inazo, *Bushido: The Soul of Japan*, Charles E. Tuttle, Tokyo, 1969.

Rappaport, Roy A., *Ecology, Meaning, and Religion*, North Atlantic Books, Berkeley, CA, 1979.

Simpson III, Charles M., *Inside the Green Berets: The First Thirty Years*, Presidio, Novato, CA, 1983.

Sun Tzu, *The Art of War*, trans. Samuel B. Griffith, Oxford University Press, London, 1963.

Trungpa, Chögyam, *Shambhala: The Sacred Path*, Shambhala Publications, Boulder, 1984.

Tsunetomo, Yamamoto, *The Book of the Samurai*, trans. William Scott Wilson, Harper and Row, New York, 1979.

Tsunoda, Ryusaku, De Barry, Theodore, and Donald Keene, compilation, *Sources of Japanese Tradition*, Columbia University Press, New York, 1958.

Tuchman, Barbara, *The March of Folly: From Troy to Vietnam*, Knopf, New York, 1984.

Turnbull, S.R., *The Samurai: A Military History*, MacMillan Publishing Company, New York, 1977.

Walker, Edward E., *The Emergent Native Americans*, Little Brown and Company, Boston, 1972.

White, Thomas M., *Three Golden Pearls on a String*, North Atlantic Books, Berkeley, CA, 1987.

Five Years Later

Summary 1990

I'm sitting with my back to the barn looking toward the eucalyptus grove one hundred yards away. Under my feet the sere ground stretches like a stiff hide to these massive trees. High above a single red-tailed hawk spirals slowly earthward. In his measured descent he looks black against the white summer sky; his head occasionally angles inward, peering into the center of his narrowing spire. There is nothing distinctive about his flight, but as he moves to settle into an outside limb a fierce *scree scree* breaks the silence and another adult male, wings drawn inward, hurls downward from a higher branch, slicing toward the intruder.

They engage, roll into each other, unfurl, cartwheel, and then break apart, only to resume their impeccably-matched aerial dance. At first I assume this is adaptive play: two red-tailed hawks, perhaps brothers of the same nest, in mock combat, honing and testing their prowess. But after a few minutes I know this is the real thing, a challenge for territorial rights. They continue without either one gaining or losing advantage, twisting and swerving in attack and parry, their piercing cries building in intensity until even Belle, our lethargic Dingo-stock dog, stands with ears cocked to their spirited drama.

I see beauty and it fills me with the kind of passion a match between two martial arts masters would. I take no sides. In their maneuvering there is only grace and abandon, an elegant and paradoxical union between two predators. I am keenly aware that to judge what I see and indulge in questions of right and wrong is a particular human luxury. What would it be like, I wonder, to act with immediacy and directness, without the burden of a rational conscience? The thought leaves me with a twinge of guilt.

Suddenly, one red-tailed hawk veers off; the other lifts itself onto a dead branch, folds its wings, and stares implacably toward the distant hills. When the hawk glides to the right of the barn I squint to see if he is hurt or disappointed. Has he lost his territory or failed to conquer another's? But there is no expression, only the downward-cast eye looking for prey.

In my lap the front page of today's newspaper shows another version of the spectacle that has just unfolded in front of me. In the grainy, slightly blurred photo Iraqi tanks advance through a main street of Kuwait City. Iraq claims that Kuwait has always been within Iraq's territorial borders and they're simply liberating the Kuwaiti people and reclaiming the land for its proper owners. This is one of the oldest justifications for war: claiming territory and the wealth that goes along with it—in this case, oil. Religion is one of the other primary calls to battle, and in this case they're conveniently tied together. A holy war to reclaim land that is rightfully Iraq's. This is historically a bad mix—fighting for land with God on your side—and I take a deep breath, thinking of the explosive temperament in that entire area.

For the past week I have been reading reports on the inside pages of *The New York Times* about Iraqi troop build-ups on the Kuwaiti border. Perhaps if Kuwait and its allies had taken a stronger position sooner, or as we say in aikido, been in *hanmi* with the proper *maiai* (correct stance and spatial relationship to your opponent), the situation might have never proceeded this far. But that's all conjecture, and who knows, maybe somebody wanted this war to happen. But mostly I think of the men in the Trojan Warrior Project, and their families, and how this must radically affect their lives.

My thoughts roll back to a year ago. Walking through an East African wilderness area I encountered a more subtle, yet equally destructive kind of territorial invasion. Ten of my closest men friends and I hiked with a Masai chieftain and his two *morani*, young warrior novitiates, through their tribal lands. Seeing our journey as a bio-reconnaissance patrol for the First Earth Battalion, we walked the plateaus and valleys of the Masai highlands and then descended into a remote river valley in the Rungwa wilderness area to be guided by a local game warden. Calling ourselves the Motherhood of Man, we came as quiet witnesses to the power of the wild and the preservation of wilderness. It was also an inward journey. Our desire was to become still, listen to the pulse of Africa, and open to new horizons within ourselves.

The effortless stride of the lithe Masai warriors takes us ten to twelve miles a day, and I'm sure they could easily go twice that. Their dignity and simplicity add a straightforward perspective to warriorship. Dressed only in thin cloths draped around their waists and shoulders, leather sandals on their feet, and carrying a spear and broadsword, they become part of the landscape, leaving little trace of where they have walked or slept. "REI would go broke out here," one of my companions jokes after the first day out. The Masais' quiet presence grounds the joy of our camaraderie with the sweeping turns of the Mzombe River, the majesty of the baobab tree, and the night cough of the leopard.

Chief Coye, the Masai chieftain, has recently been released from a half-year prison sentence for his political work defending his tribal homeland. The socialist government of Tanzania is forcing the Masai people into smaller and smaller sections of land in an attempt to limit their tribal customs. By restricting where they can drive their cattle, the government is forcing them to give up their semi-nomadic way of life. "When the people are put into the metal government buildings," Coye tells us, "they become sick. The government is trying to impose a way of life on us that is foreign. Now they tell us we can no longer carry our spears and swords into the towns and that we must wear western clothes. They say they're doing these things to help us, but it will only destroy our ways. They don't really try to understand what we need or what's important to us. They're only doing it for themselves. They want our traditional grazing lands so they can build more villages and towns." Chief Coye spoke without bitterness, but the sadness in his eyes mirrored his voice.

I, too, am sad, not only because the government's action is crude and stupid, but because it may be too late to do anything about it. Coye wants his people to be educated without losing their traditional ways. The government sees the Masai as a nuisance, a backwards, primitive people who are keeping Tanzania from joining the twentieth century. The traditional Masai care little for Tanzania as a nation-state with its invisible borders between countries. They read the landscape as a text: the rivers, hills, and craters are a language that transmits the myths of their people, animals, and gods to each generation. Acknowledging that these warriors may be the last of a dying tribe, I strive to receive their particular knowledge. But I am left frustrated and awkward over my self-conscious attempts to make contact. I'm aware of a buried rage that I don't let myself entirely feel over these people losing a battle being fought with bureaucratic paper-shuffling and a language not their own. Their hearts and minds are being invaded, their wise and unique culture robbed of its soul.

Too polite to stare directly at us, as we do with them, they still observe us with a childlike curiosity. They want absolutely nothing from us, although they seem mildly interested in our Walkmans, the buckles on the packs, our folding knives. Sitting quietly at dusk the morani prod and laugh at each other, like young men everywhere. They take great pleasure in each other's company and seem enchanted by their own voices and the stories they trade. Kashu, the tallest of the three, finds me staring at him and for a moment he looks directly back, as if waiting for me to say what's on my mind. Then a brilliant smile flashes across his dark face and he proudly throws his head back. These three are strikingly handsome, although one notices their bearing first.

*They do not wear shirts with collars, have a classroom education, or report
to a job as the Tanzanian government might wish. They have instead humor,
leisure time, dignity, a commitment to a place and community, and an unrelenting generosity. When I think that this culture may be gone by the time my
children are adults I feel a great emptiness.*

Another red-tailed hawk, perhaps the same one, arcs toward the eucalyptus grove when a defiant *scree, scree!* from the upper branches tilts
him into a wide berth around the trees. I look down at the newspaper
again. The tanks in the photo resemble dark, menacing beetles infesting
a manicured garden. Looking closer I see that one of the Iraqi tank crew
is holding up the V-sign for victory, and I recall a calligraphy of O-Sensei's, *Masaka Agatsu*—"True victory is the victory over the self."

Fall 1990

An unseasonable front pushes iron-dark clouds in from the Pacific. After
almost five years of drought this creates an expectant buzz in every conversation. A boisterous gang of crows swirls around the gum trees and
Belle, her tawny hair caught in the fading light, runs to the commotion.
Their oily black wings match the shade of the darkening sky and their
raucous, playful humor helps me understand why many Native American
legends place humans as descendants of the crow or raven. A number of
birds have already shown up on their southern migratory routes and the
usual summer/spring residents, many of them raptors, are off to warmer
weather. On the human side of things we are inventing our own migratory route, calling it Operation Desert Shield. A mind-boggling exodus of
men and equipment are transported daily to the Persian Gulf.

Earlier in the day an aikido student who had formerly distinguished
himself in the Army Rangers phoned. "I'm being activated and was asked
to qualify for the Special Forces. I'm calling you," he said, "to ask if you
think it's possible to be a true warrior, in the *aiki* way, like you talk about

in your book, while fighting in this war?" As he spoke I could see out the window that the unexpected weather had excited the horses and they were racing at breakneck speed in the front pasture. In their powerful surges I imagined the horse soldiers of Genghis Khan or the warrior braves of the Plains Indians riding furiously to war, and the first battles by horseback thousands of years ago in Mesopotamia, now choked with mechanized armor. I groped for some kind of response. What could I tell him?

"Sir," he interrupted my silence, "I'm not asking if you think I should reenlist or not. I just want your opinion because it's important for me to live my life true. I'm not afraid to die and I want to serve my country, but if I go back in I want to do it as a warrior." I pressed my palm against the cold window, leaving an imprint of my hand. It sounded as if he were already living his life as a warrior. "Yes, I think you can accomplish your goal wearing the Green Beret." In a brief squall the horses romped and played like teenagers in a touch football game. Do they feel their martial roots, I wondered? Are they fulfilling their warrior heritage running the hills of California, far from the sound of cannons and the cutting edge of swords?

Turning to my notes from Africa I am reminded of how an older culture, the Masai, initiate their young men into a warrior tradition.

African dawns are long leisurely affairs. The darkness is first broken by a milky white hue, then a delicate salmon color tinges the east, slowly deepening to a near crimson until, finally, a lurid rouge signals the rising of the huge scarlet sun. All the while the sky fills with birds, the larger raptors and storks above everyone.

In this clear, cool morning we leave Coye's village, cross a small saddle and continue along the ridge line, always south by southwest. On a distant slope a steady eastern wind fans a fire up the ridge. This may be either nature's spontaneous combustion or purposefully set, since fires are often used to burn off the top layer of vegetation for new growth or to flush game.

It's a controversial issue, yet many game wardens, as well as the isolated vil-lagers, continue the practice, claiming the flora and fauna now count on it. Because burning is so commonplace, the animals have also become accus-tomed to it; consequently you cannot be sure to frighten off a predator with fire. The hundreds of eyes reflected in the beams of our flashlights each night, at the edge of our campsites, attest to their fearlessness. Jim Channon, founder of the First Earth Battalion, remarks, "This is what I did most of the time in Vietnam, hiked with a pack on my back over burned-out areas."

At the top of a small rise a single Masai elder sits under a stately camel thorn tree, sharpening his sword on a piece of granite. "It looks like you've come a long way," he says without emphasis. He touches the young mora-nis' head and spits on them, the Masai blessing, and exchanges local news with Coye. We take this as an opportunity to rest and spread ourselves under the sparse shade. At a break in the conversation I ask Coye about the train-ing of the warriors; he translates to the elder and they collaborate on the answers. "Whenever there is work requiring strength or courage," Coye begins, "people will ask, 'Are there no warriors around today?'" He lingers on this statement, giving it portent, and I take it as the essence of the Masai warrior. He goes on to say that the government has outlawed killing lions as an initiatory rite into warriorhood, as well as banned forays into neigh-boring territory to rustle cattle or fight territorial disputes. "But if a lion or leopard takes from our herd or kills one of our people, the warriors will hunt him down. It's also true that if someone tries to steal our cattle, then we will go to war. But it's good there are no more wars," they say solemnly, "we need to unite to fight other battles now."

Warrior training begins around age fifteen with circumcision, which is seen as a mental as well as physical ordeal. They believe that the warrior novitiate able to endure the pain of the operation unflinchingly will be able to survive the challenges of life. Once healed, the young man enters into the warrior stage of life; he grows his hair long, covers his body in a red ocher, and is given a long spear as well as new clothes, necklaces, and earrings. As a generation of warriors these men enjoy a close camaraderie, spending most of their time together tending cattle, exploring territory, building thorn fences, fending off intruders, hunting and sharing everything, including girl-friends. Besides their service to the community they participate in feasting camps where they go in retreat to eat large amounts of meat, train in the use of the spear, sword, bow and arrow, and compete in races, wrestling, and jumping dances. Around age thirty-five this generation of warriors is pushed into elderhood by the upcoming generation. It's with great sadness that the warrior's long, plaited hair is cut and his head scraped bald in preparation for the responsibilities of eldership. As the warrior evolves into the stage of elder he is told, "Drop your weapons and master the art of the tongue and wisdom of mind."

Observing Coye and his fellow Masai in the dry heat I'm struck by how he, in the very moment, embodies the elder ideal. He does not seem preoccupied with anything, yet he notices everything, sitting poised and steadfast as Mt. Meru in the distance, and at the same time attentive and light as the cinnamon-breasted bunting that balances in the brittle combretum behind him. Although he is known for his great skill with the spear and sword Coye modestly refuses to posture with his weapons or demonstrate his prowess. Yet when I demonstrate how the blend works in aikido he remarks keenly, "This would be especially useful in politics." When someone leaves a water bottle behind, he takes notice, and he also knows to whom it belongs. Retrieving it with great care he solemnly returns it to its owner, in the way of people whose every act in life is a small ceremony. In the excited appreciation that follows, his mood remains unchanged except, perhaps, for slight perplexity at the commotion over something that simply needed to be done. It's the same when he takes the rucksack of a struggling, dehydrated member of our group. Not setting himself apart because he is a chief, Coye simply responds to what is required, and he walks away ignoring the pseudo-macho protests. When he is offered food he eats carefully, but thanks are not in order, nor does it occur to him to repay his giver with even a look or smile. At times he seems invisible, without purpose. When he rises from his haunches, spear and sword handled deftly, I recognize a coiled power within him.

Walking away from the group, Coye shades his eyes from the unrelenting sun and looks west toward the four-billion-year-old Precambrian hills, the old bones of the world poking through the leathery hide of Africa. He places one foot on the leg of the other and balances lightly against his spear in the relaxed stance of the Masai warrior. Time suddenly has no weight and I'm seized by an inexplicable longing, like a child crying out for his mother who he fears will never return. It seems almost a dream, that this scene exists within the chaos of the late twentieth century. There is the feeling of being strangely disembodied, suspended between a distant past and an inevitable future. Sobered by this hard, clean glimpse into the moment, I'm left with a poignancy for a disappearing way of life, and also refreshed by a knowing that the long heritage of the warrior is not confined to a place or season. It is to be here, now, present to the unfolding wisdom of just this.

Winter 1991

The day after the United States began its aerial attacks on Baghdad I wake from a troubled sleep just after daybreak to hike a neighboring rancher's ridge a few miles away. In town a bitter wind stiffens the ubiquitous yellow ribbons and American flags into patriotic erections. Stopping for gas and coffee I notice one of our town's homeless gesturing from an empty street corner. Violently hammering his fist at a vacant field he shouts repeatedly, "I don't give a fuck what you say, I'll do what I want. Just fuck you."

I'm intrigued by the vague sense of pleasure his outrage gives me. Is he my projection of unexpressed anger at the war? Or an oracle speaking for spiteful nature gods who are dishing out a fifth winter of drought in California? I finally conclude he's merely reflecting the collective neurosis of the world's so-called leaders. Passing in front of him I see dried blood has matted his hair and stained his temple. "Fuck you! I'll do what I want," he shouts, looking right through me.

Me too, I think, so I walk the ridge north to south for an hour until I find shelter from the wind against a granite outcropping. Washing down figs and almonds with the heavily sugared coffee from my thermos, I sight a pair of golden eagles across the valley. I glass them for ten minutes, making notes about their gender difference until they disappear into an old stand of black oak. Warming my hands around the coffee cup, I look up to see that the darker and larger female has mysteriously returned, circling fifty feet above me. Another oracle, I think, but for what I don't know. It does occur to me, however, to be grateful that it's a raptor overhead and not a F-16 strafing me with five-hundred-pound bombs. Being able to do what I want, I head home to watch the bombing of Baghdad on TV.

It's a confusing time. As the news ratings soar, "smart" bombs, Tomahawk missiles, and Patriot battery teams become overnight superstars; people all around me are being called to duty, including a local fifty-three-year-old ophthalmologist and a couple of grandmothers; liberals go from candlelight peace vigils to give blood for soldiers; women demand the right to be sent into combat; a local Marine becomes a conscientious objector; the anti-war movement includes pro-warrior sentiments. The ethical green light for war is flashing, and those who had previously taken a political beating about military spending are now gloating. It's difficult to reconcile the revulsion I feel at the death toll mounting in Baghdad with the excitement I experience from seeing footage of bombs the size of Volkswagens leveling bridges and airstrips. I feel like I'm watching the Superbowl and my team is winning; except real people, mostly civilians, women and children, are suffering and dying. At night at the dojo we end every aikido class sending healing *ki* to *all* the people in the Persian Gulf.

While the world is being transfixed by one of history's most recurring spectacles, I am being transformed by another: the birth of a baby daughter. At forty-six I'm a father once again. Watching my wife go through labor I thought that if a young man was given a choice to go through labor or go to war he would probably choose war. She struggled tirelessly in hard labor for over fourteen hours, but in the end her narrow pelvis made a natural birth impossible. Watching her Caesarian section I looked deep into my wife's body, and in that mass of quivering tissue and scarlet blood life emerged. While she recovered I gazed deep into my child's eyes. In that innocence and vulnerability was the wisdom and strength of God, but I had to wonder what kind of world we were bringing her into. I was born during World War II, Tiphani born in the middle of Vietnam, and now Paloma delivered during the Persian Gulf War. America is right on schedule, giving birth to a war every fifteen years. My world is filled with the joyous gift of life and the haunting specter of apocalypse.

I know that many of the men I worked with in the Trojan Warrior Project are over there. Those that I had been corresponding with have suddenly quit writing or calling. Psychically they have removed any vestiges of themselves. I can no longer feel them—who they are or where they have gone. Upped and vanished into the unpublicized world of the Special Operations soldier. My connection to them naturally brings me into a more personal relationship to the war. When I examine my feeling of missing out on something by not being over there, I see it is directly linked to my relationship with these men.

I imagine my Masai companions following their cattle through ancestral lands, wondering if they hear these distant drums of war.

Apricot dawn rises over the ledge of the world. Sweet tea, dark bread, and oranges are shared around the small fire. This is the fourth day of the Mzombe river trek and I feel unexpectedly strong today. A sudden increase in game has brought a new vividness to our journey. Yesterday we sighted a pair of greater kudu drifting ghostlike toward the river. Crouching behind thickets and termite mounds we kept downwind, carefully stalking them while a Verreaux eagle owl watched vigilantly from a river acacia. Their prints led into a dry wash that eventually circled back to the small bluff where we first sighted them, but they were mysteriously gone. It was as though they had vanished into their own tracks. I'm reminded of the stories by Hemingway and Ruark about the magic of the kudu. Bending over the spoor, Dave Peterson, our guide, comments, "The more you try to find them, the less you see of them. It's the kind of animal you have to be receptive to. You have to let them find you."

Today we follow a narrow game trail north by northeast, the river always to our right. The sun becomes a single crimson eye rising over the baked landscape. Hornbills, kingfishers, white-crowned shrikes, starlings, and hoopoes fly invisible paths in the flat white sky. A troop of baboons shrieks hysterically at us from the far bank. The large males form a loose perimeter while the babies cling precariously to the slate-colored backs of retreating mothers. A bull hippopotamus, a half-submerged boulder with eyes and ears, watches our ragged line move through the thorny bush.

There are sixteen of us: Dave Peterson, a cross between Tarzan, Crocodile Dundee, and Aldo Leopold, heads the line with his powerful .458 large-bore rifle. The Motherhood of Man, the name for our group of ten men, follows; next are our three porters, their dark, coffee-colored skin shining under the weight of heavy loads; then comes Charley, Dorobo chef and camp jokester. Carrying a double-barreled shotgun, Kashmiri, the veteran warden for this section of the Rungwa wilderness, brings up the rear. His sad eyes and furrowed brow reflect the responsibility of protecting the wilderness from poachers the past seventeen years.

The river broadens and the sandy bank plunges steeply to the water. Other than day-old prints and soccer-size dung balls, we see no sign of elephant. "They're skittish," Dave whispers, "real savvy. Lots of them have been killed and they don't trust man." He speaks matter-of-factly, like a scientist giving a report, but underneath it I hear his pain over the greed and insen-

sitivity that has so radically reduced the elephant population of Africa. For a moment we stand silently around the large print, both in reverence and sadness, as though it were a marker at the grave of a beloved friend. From a nearby baobab tree a honey guide bird pulls us out of our private thoughts; his excited call is an invitation to follow him to a nearby beehive and the prized honey within.

It's past mid-morning and the sun's heat reflects tenaciously off the ground into our faces. We stop for a short break to snack on biscuits and oranges, refill our canteens, and wet our bandannas and hats in the slow-moving river. Jack Cirie quickly strings his hammock between a thorny acacia and a spreading tamarind; Jim Channon climbs the thick trunk and lounges in the gnarled limbs; the rest of us spread out under its generous shade, relaxing against our backpacks. One hundred meters downstream two male impalas step out of a small ravine and carefully pick their way to the river. As they dip their heads to drink, the sun reflecting on the water gives the impression they are watering from a thick, gold light. Suddenly I am overpowered by the Eden-like view that is in front of me. The mind is silent, there are no intrusive thoughts. The shrill call of the cicada becomes the hum of the Universe. The balance between simplicity and diversity in this wild, idyllic spot stuns me into silence. The impalas catch our scent, raise their slender necks, and bound gracefully out of sight. The mood is broken, but a deep reservoir of contentment has been opened inside me. This richness is the intimacy of experience; a wealth that comes not from the accumulation of things, but rather from an appreciation of what is.

Evenings under the Southern Cross we shared meals of dried wildebeest, maize, and dark bread. Talking late into the night we all agreed that more than ever, this was the time for the warrior, civilian, and military to focus his attention on the environment. "The allegiance of the First Earth Battalion as I always envisioned it," Channon said, "goes beyond duty, honor, and country to people and planet. Warrior monks are guardians of the good, guardians of humanity, nature, and planet. Right now there are warrior monks in the United States Army who are already teaching soft tactics, and the modern Citizen Samurai in day-to-day existence is engaged in moral combat to reorganize and focus personal life to its highest good." Grinning at his own seriousness he laughed, his playful eyes shining, "Yeah, and what fun we can have doing it!"

We decide to walk another hour and a half before breaking for the midday meal. Reading the map and compass I am third in line after Channon and Tom Lutes, my college rugby teammate. The river straightens after a short dogleg and opens into large pools and small rock islands. A narrow beach appears to our right and I am delighted to see another hippo. 'How fortunate,' I think, 'more animals.' In the next instant everything is transformed into a fluid, slow-motion dance, the events happening in a single moment, released from time. To my left Dave expands and brightens, as if his energy body had suddenly tripled in size. He backpedals, like a quarterback stepping back for a pass, and I am caught up in his movement. To my right, perhaps fifteen meters away, four lions crouch drinking at the river's edge. Their heads turn as one and they reflexively lower themselves, powerful shoulder muscles tightening to spring. The young male darts off to the right, the other three cross in front of us. The large lioness unexpectedly turns toward us and growls, as if she is suddenly reconsidering why she is running. A surge of adrenaline crests inside me, somewhere faraway I hear Dave chambering a round in the rifle. I am not afraid, I am not anything. I am the present. Everything is vivid and still, absolutely bright with aliveness. The she-lion turns and disappears into the bush. There are more growls, sounding as if they are an inch inside my skull. Time snaps back into place, a thousand silver fish winnow up and down my body. I adjust myself to the tremendous current that runs between my legs and the earth. The faces around me, my black and white brothers, are flushed with excitement. Just as we begin to settle down the hippo feints powerfully in our direction, sending a wake to the shore, and we collectively jump. He looks bemused and we laugh nervously. This frag-ile camaraderie between predator and prey is psychic and primeval. Above, a dark raptor dips his hunting arc over us and the distant, Precambrian hills are still with equanimity.

The renewal we felt from this episode is not the posturing that comes from surviving a potentially dangerous outdoor "adventure." It is much deeper than that. It's the knowledge that there *is* wilderness in the world, a place untouched by civilization and human tampering. The experience of wilderness is the recognition that it also resides within us, it is part of our spiritual legacy. With this knowledge we also bear a greater respon-sibility: to destroy our wilderness is to destroy ourselves. To preserve the wild is to honor the values that our ancestors formed over millions of years on these plains and rivers and forests. Just as stumbling across a pride of lions gives new meaning to the notions of impeccability, account-ability, and consequences, we must find the trail within ourselves that returns us to the mysterious beauty of the unturned stone.

Reconnoitering

A few weeks after completion of the Trojan Warrior Project in 1985, Teams 560 and 260 participated in Operation Flintlock with NATO troops in western Europe. This was a military exercise that required the men to parachute into the northern part of Europe and then move hun-dreds of miles south, by whatever means possible, without being detected by "enemy" soldiers, or civilians, who might turn them in. Through the grapevine we heard that Team 260 performed exceptionally well, receiv-ing the highest marks. We wanted to think that the Project had some-thing to do with their performance, but we had no way of knowing, and the soldiers, of course, were not about to give out that kind of credit.

After Operation Flintlock the teams broke up. Most of the men were posted to other assignments. A few stayed in contact with us. Janowski called, asking for reminders about the meditation practice, saying that a friend of a friend was having emotional problems and he thought visualization might help her. Mattelli, soon to be promoted to sergeant-major, was transferred to a language school and inquired about aikido schools in the area. Martin wrote that he had been transferred and was using the techniques from the Trojan Warrior Project in his personal life. Captain Thorne was transferred to Europe. Drucker wrote a cryptic note indicating he might leave the Army but was still looking for a good warrior. Braddock, returning from a family vacation, mentioned that the program made it easier for him to express his love to his parents. Reardon sent a postcard showing a girl in a bikini, wondering if it would be possible to visit if he ever came to the west coast.

Farley, reassigned to a duty station in the Midwest, went to enroll in a local gym when he heard a familiar thumping sound coming from an adjacent room. Looking in, he saw an aikido class in progress. He told the instructor he had done some aikido before and asked if it would be possible to take the class. "What's your affiliation?" the teacher asked Farley. Not sure what he was asking for, Farley said he trained with a teacher named Strozzi-Heckler who taught through the Army. "Your name didn't mean much to this guy," Farley said, "what should I tell him? Affiliation with what?" Like everything else, aikido has its politics, so I told him what tradition and teachers I was connected with, but mostly I encouraged him to sidestep the bureaucracy and tell the instructor whatever he needed to know, as the training itself was the most important thing.

On a business trip to Boston I stopped to train at the local aikido dojo and was surprised to see Galt. In our delight we spontaneously moved toward each other, arms outstretched. "Strozzi!" he said warmly, his face bright and open. About six feet away he looked like he suddenly remembered something, slowed down and held out his hand, formal-like, maybe even a little stiff. We were glad to see each other, but he was with a friend and didn't have time for coffee. He told me the teams had broken up and only he, Braddock, and Reardon were left on 260. He looked the best I had ever seen him, something lighter about him, more contactable; I remember thinking that maybe he had fallen in love.

After that, except for a sporadic call or postcard, we slowly fell out of contact with most of the men.

The ground war in the Gulf was mercifully short. Then America burst into a spasm of muscular patriotism. Old-fashioned parades welcomed home the troops, and a mood of confidence visited many living rooms and bars across the country. But most of all we were victorious without much cost. More men between the ages of twenty and thirty-five were killed at home with guns than during the one-hundred-hour ground war in the Gulf. Overall, there were almost as many non-combat deaths, one hundred and eight, as there were combat deaths, one hundred and twenty-four. All POWs were immediately returned, and there was none of the anguish that accompanies MIAs. Ironically, one of the major problems of the ground war was what to do with the enormous number of surrendering Iraqis. America was relieved, and fortunate, that the Mother of all Battles was only a postscript to the air war.

The relief I felt over the quick end of the conflict was soon replaced by a growing horror over the massive ecological damage. My mind reeled at the idea of five hundred oil wells burning out of control, at sixty gallons of oil per minute being flushed into the Persian Gulf. Then there was the problem of the thousands of Kurdish and Shiite refugees fleeing Iraqi reprisals. American soldiers had to look on helplessly while hospitals and refugee camps were shelled. This all sounded like work for the First Earth Battalion.

I went through a number of channels, unsuccessfully, to locate the men from Trojan Warrior. I was concerned about them and felt compelled to know if they were alive and well. Then one day a few weeks after the war had ended I received a call. "Hey," the voice said, "my legs aren't so thin and stick-like." It was Reardon and he had just finished reading this book. He had left the Army and returned to school, although he remained active in the Special Forces reserve. He was working for a construction firm to support himself and had been promoted to a supervisory position. "It was difficult getting back into civilian life," he said, "it seemed that no one had the integrity I was used to on an A-Team. Now I'm getting used to it and it's okay, but it was hard for almost two years." When I asked him what he thought of the project five years later, he immediately responded, "I've never been the same since. The program made me think more about my life as a whole. I'm much more aware." Later he wrote in a letter, "Although I do not actually sit (meditate) as you do, I use the mental relaxing techniques you taught us almost daily. Particularly when I was a crew foreman, I kept my cool countless times in situations where three years before I would have lost it.

"As far as the physical fitness curriculum from the course goes, I use all of the techniques the Trojan Warrior cadre taught us. And for what it's worth, I'm in better physical condition now than when the program started. The same goes for the nutrition classes; my diet is eighty percent to twenty percent carbos to fat ratio. By the way, I ran the Boston Marathon last week in 3:15. Piece of cake, pal.

"Perhaps most importantly, my idea of a warrior has changed from that of a combat-tested soldier type to a more universal definition of a supremely dedicated and proficient individual in his or her discipline. I am finally learning that there are warriors outside as well as inside the military. My contempt for many civilians is slowly waning, Strozzi. This letter only scratches the surface of what I'd like to tell you, but time is short, so it will have to do. Congratulations on your new wife and baby, Richard, and say hello to Jack or anybody else you might see." Months later I wrote a letter of recommendation for his application to Harvard Business School.

I then received a call from Jim Oreson. Without any social amenities he started right in, as if we had been in an ongoing conversation for the past five years. "A friend of mine down here in the outfit I'm in just read the book, and he does some kind of martial art, you know, an asskicker sort, and he wanted your address to write you some kind of letter saying, 'Dear Sir, I respect what you do and do you know anyone down here who teaches aikido as you put forth in your book and so on,' some kind of nonsense like that, so I said, 'Hell, you don't have to go through all that bullshit, let me call 'em so that's what this is about. So how in the hell are you anyway?" In his drawl he went on to tell me that he, Galt, and Braddock had been promoted to an elite section of Special Operations and were assigned stateside during the war as a precaution against Iraqi terrorism. When I queried him about his reflections on Trojan Warrior, he replied that he didn't think it had any operational benefit. "But it set everybody thinking in a certain way about the importance of the ideas of mastery and integrity, about being an individual who wasn't motivated or affected by politics. It wasn't any of the techniques that were so important, but what was behind them. What was important was what was driving those techniques. One of the problems of the program was there was too much pressure to produce something, to come up with some kind of results. That got in the way, it's politics again."

When I asked him if he thought the program was valuable enough to do again, he recounted an amusing anecdote. "Hey, there's guys down here that claim to have gone through Trojan Warrior. Braddock, Galt, and me were standing around with a bunch of guys bullshittin' and this fella starts to claim that he was part of the Trojan Warrior Project and tellin' us what he learned and so on and so forth. I said, 'Well, that's interestin' because I know for a fact two individuals, plus myself, standing right here who were in that program, and not one of us seem to recall you.'" We laughed that maybe that was the true sign of it being a success—people claiming to be in it who weren't. Most likely, however, the work filtered down to others through those who later taught at various Army schools.

Oreson gave me Braddock's number, and I surprised him with a call at home a few days later. He had married his hometown sweetheart and told me he liked his new duty assignment. "I feel real fortunate working where I am and with the people I work with." Responding to my questions about the project he replied, "I'm five times more perceptive now. But one of the problems with Trojan Warrior was the age factor. The people should have been older; it's hard to accept and learn that kind of material when you're too young. Anyway, you'd be interested in knowing that we do visualizations as part of our training here. The best part of it is that they present it like it's nothing special, just another part of our training that will help us become better soldiers. In Trojan Warrior I think things were built up too much and it made our expectations too high."

The Army sent Captain Parker to graduate school, and when I spoke to him he was teaching French at West Point. "The Trojan Warrior Project becomes more and more important to me as time goes on. It has given me more peace of mind, and the accountability training was the most important." Asked it he would elaborate, he said he wanted to think about it and would write me a letter. Soon after he wrote, "It would not be exaggerating to say my 'philosophy' of life has completely changed (since Trojan Warrior). I feel more aware of what is behind my actions (as well as those of others). An example is my facial expression. Remember when you told me I often had a cynical smirk on my face? I am often aware of this now and quickly remove the expression. The removal is not what is important to me. What is important is the greater knowledge of myself which leads to the removal—the awareness of the smirk, the acknowledgement of a need to show cynicism, and the implications of that need. This type of awareness has permeated to just about everything I do, and leaves me much more accountable than in the past.

"I am constantly surprised at how my relations with others are changing. I feel much less combative. I am not interested in 'proving' anything, and it seems in not 'proving' anything, I end up 'proving' much more anyway. When you make yourself accountable you become less combative. This strength also lets me be more honest with others—especially in my disagreement with them. I feel much more assured of why I disagree and don't hold it against them—I just simply disagree. This has caused some problems for me in the Army (especially upon my return to the 'real' Army at West Point). Now I can see how frustrated you guys were in teaching us.

"You may want to know some objective results I've had from the program, although I don't hold these as very important. I ran the Paris Marathon three minutes faster than any marathon I ran prior to Trojan Warrior. I don't think I would have improved my time if it were not for the mental techniques learned in Trojan Warrior.

"My diet is totally different. I rarely eat meat but don't miss it. It is amazing how good eating makes all physical activity easier. I guess one of the many gripes we had during Trojan Warrior was the focus placed on techniques of exercise. We complained that learning techniques of running, swimming, etc., would make us better at those particular skills but not improve ourselves as 'warriors.' I now disagree. Learning the techniques creates an awareness of what goes on in your body to achieve a certain task. This awareness and subsequent control has many applications in all aspects of life."

Three months later Parker wrote that after ten years he was leaving the Army and taking a job in banking. "As you can probably guess," he wrote, "I have a bad tendency to look down at those in executive positions in the civilian world, and thus far my experiences only reinforce this. Their narrow vision of what is important does not encourage me. Once again, thanks for your advice—your viewpoints were different and appreciated."

In a brief phone conversation with James I learned that he had been in the Persian Gulf for over six months as an advisor to a Kuwaiti Brigade. "It was interesting," he said cryptically, "but I don't know if I would want to do it again."

"You mean you disliked being in the heat and desert?" I said.

"No," he replied, "I liked the desert. All the space gave me room to think. Being out in the middle of that big open space with just the sound of my tent flapping in the wind . . . well, sometimes it was just beautiful." He had read this book and wanted me to know that his faith in Christianity had deepened. He had five years to retirement and was looking ahead to what he might do.

Martin and I began a communication that spanned three continents. Soon after this book was published he wrote from Europe, "I would like to thank you for your generous comments in your book. The Trojan Warrior Project added a great deal of impetus to my recovery from my addictions, and from Post-Traumatic Stress Syndrome. I have been in meaningful recovery since early March 1987. Necessarily, but painfully, it was darkest before the dawn. Personally, I think your assessment of our resistance, especially during the 'Encampment,' was right on target. I wish to apologize for my childish behavior and lack of consideration for you back then. I had yet to let go of my own demons, and I envied you. Most of my personal growth has occurred over the past eighteen months.

"I was involved fairly actively in service work for the year or so before I left the States. I used to spend an hour or so each week with the detox cases at Wamack Army Hospital, and did some work as a volunteer at the county detox center. This kind of thing did a whole lot to keep me going forward."

From a Kurdish refugee camp he wrote, "Thanks for your card. Got in with the afternoon stage. My company stood down today. We are now in a tent-city base here. All of the services plus the Brits, French, Canadians, Dutch, and Italian have people here. The operation at my camp complex was superb, the credit for which I give to our company commander, Major H. I saw Colonel Flynn, by the way; he is a full colonel now. Spoke to him a couple of times. I shared responsibility with one other guy for about three thousand or so Kurds, including a company of Pesh Marga (guerrillas). There were upwards of seventy-five thousand refugees in our camp complex, which was just across the border from Yekmal, Iraq. There were sixty-three of us S.F. supermen. Most of the Kurds asked for pictures of George Bush.

"About Trojan Warrior . . . during the last several months I have encountered, time and again, the unwillingness of the majority of my co-workers, and about all of my superiors, to know themselves and to live in reality. 'Pretending not to know,' I think, may well be a crucial factor in military sociology. [During the Trojan Warrior Project we had a sign in the classroom that said, "What are you pretending not to know?" which we pointed to when we felt there was denial or irresponsibility present.] The greatest vulnerability is to deny one's own shortcomings to the degree that one is entirely blind to them. This denial is almost universal in Special Forces. At this stage of my life, especially having experienced four and a half years of real growth in recovery, I am nearly exasperated by the immaturity and dysfunction that hits me in the face like a bucket of gravel, every day."

A week after the last letter from Martin there was a message from Rader on my machine. "Hey, this is a voice from the past. I'd like to hear from you." He was stationed at a language school a couple of hours away, and we set a day when he could come up to the ranch with his family. He hadn't read the book, so I sent him a copy. A short time later he called and said the book was generating thoughts and feelings that he would write down and either bring up or send later. As he spoke about his thoughts it was clear that he was at odds with a number of my points and still had mixed feelings about the Project itself. As his visit grew closer, a vague feeling of dread accompanied the eagerness I felt at seeing him.

I feared this would be a Trojan Warrior mini-confrontation, with us battling over the same issues we did five years ago. I also knew I wanted something from him. From our phone conversation I thought he missed a primary point in the book—the need for men to reexamine the initiatory process and how we can redefine ourselves as men. I wanted him to acknowledge this. It was clear to me that he also felt misunderstood and misinterpreted. We both wanted the same thing: to be seen and acknowledged for our feelings and efforts.

The day Rader and his family arrived my misgivings quickly evaporated. Though I felt awkward, in the way men can be with each other, I was delighted to see him. We had lunch together, my wife took his daughter for a horseback ride, I did aikido with his son, he held my new daughter and practiced Filipino martial stick work with my son. He showed me his photographic artwork and we goofily clicked pictures of each other. There was the feeling of being part of a larger tribe; a genuine warmth flowed between us.

Walking on the land, we spoke of our visions of the next evolution of the Trojan Warrior Project. I told him of my plans of having an extended warrior training on the ranch that would include aikido/martial arts, meditation, healing arts, community building, and working with the land. He shared how he imagined former Special Forces soldiers working with communities in developing countries or poor rural areas in the United States to improve their way of life through the soldiers' skills in medicine, agriculture, communications, and engineering. One of the last things he said as he drove away was, "What do you say we run an advanced course at your place next summer? Aikido, meditation, discussion . . . hell, we could lay out the groundwork for the First Earth Battalion for 1999."

A few days later he sent a twenty-page response to this book, a thorough analysis that was classic Rader—bright, cutting, thoughtful, and generous in its opinions and directness. Many of his points were enlightening and others seemed like he simply needed to give his side of the story. He added a postscript that said, "All contents private thoughts not for publication without expressed written consent, okay?" I was sorry for that because so much of his material would have added greatly to this additional chapter.

He did consent, however, for me to reprint this section: "Was the Trojan Warrior Project a success? I was one of the one-third who said in the evaluations that 'From an Army skills point of view' the time would have been better spent; but does that mean the program was not a success? No! The things we learned and experienced will be with us always. They are still put to use and will multiply into the future and touch the lives of more and more soldiers. How much, we will have to wait and see, but certainly it will. If, however, the success of the program is based on whether SportsMind got another contract or not, that cheapens the beauty of what was taught and contradicts again the values behind what was being taught. If that is to be the only measure of success then perhaps it is good that we 'failed.'"

After being posted to a new team he wrote, "It's hard to educate some young stud who says 'I run faster than you, so why should I listen?' Empathy with the boys from SportsMind! I have determined that my quest is not to be found on some distant battlefield, but rather wherever I am. My battles are fought within the organization, to return the application of common sense to how we do business. The first steps were taken five years ago on Team 560 and are being continued here today. I am excited by the possibilities that await both me and my detachment. In that I will find my sense of accomplishment."

The other soldiers: Janowski is a senior NCO in the ROTC program at a large midwestern university; Sheffield is now a warrant officer on active duty; Dunham was in the Gulf War and is a team sergeant; Thayer is a team sergeant back at Fort Davis; Johnson left the military and is in the building trade somewhere in the south; Dudley, Harner, and Kirby retired; Flynn was promoted to the head of Special Operations in Europe and was kept busy during the Gulf War; Harwood is now a company commander, served in the Gulf, and is remembered with high regard by Rader. Shell was chosen as the Army's Special Forces representative to the British SAS, an extremely high honor. The rumor is that during a reconnaissance mission in the Gulf War, Drucker, along with his three-man team, was discovered by a young Iraqi girl in a hide site. Choosing not to kill her and save themselves from discovery, they ended up battling a company-sized Iraqi unit until they were rescued by helicopter. When I heard this I immediately thought of James' question at the encampment when he posed his moral dilemma of what he would do if discovered by a civilian during the course of his duty.

There has been renewed interest in the Army, as well as the Air Force and Navy Special Operations, along with various police departments, about designing and implementing another project. This, naturally, has made me think about what I would do differently a second time around. To begin with, I would define the context of the training differently, emphasizing on accountability, responsibility, commitment, and communication at the very beginning. This would set a standard of relating that could be carried through the rest of the program; it would create the basis for a working language. I would also follow this up with weekly sessions to keep the emotional space clear and to support these new communication and relationship skills. I would make meditation a daily practice along with aikido. I would limit the number of guest instructors and focus on the material at hand. While physical fitness would be taught, there would be less emphasis on testing and results and more responsibility placed on the individual for his own level of fitness. I would develop more dialogue on visioning the new warrior and more open communication with the participants about the program of instruction. In the Trojan Warrior we were too secretive and kept too much distance. This would help reduce the Us and Them dynamic. Novelist and poet Jim

Harrison made a clarifying observation on this when he commented that the too-sudden elimination of meat and cigarettes at the encampment "set up a situation where people felt compelled to be dishonest . . . too idealistic in the effort. Often that is the problem of the American Zen community, too—which turns it into a form of the Episcopalian, where there is an obsession with self-control." Surprises, trials, and tribulations would be part of a revised program, but not in a way that would alienate the participants. Yes, I think it would be important to have women participants and teachers.

As to the question of the mission of the modern military warrior? Unequivocally the answer is the environment. Gary Zukav, physicist, former Special Forces officer, and author of *The Dancing Wu Li Masters*, wrote an article titled, "The New Mission of the Military: The Military and the Environment" where he states, "National security has become synonymous with the protection of life on the Earth. The only strategy for the military that has a future is the strategy of protecting all life on our planet. The ability of the military collective to clothe, feed, train, deploy, and command groups of people is unmatched. It is the only organization, potential or actual, that has the capacity to address environmental problems on the scale that they exist."

The logistical genius of the military in the Gulf War clearly demonstrates the capability of our Armed Forces to make a major contribution to the preservation of the planet. Administrative skills that maintain combat missions could be transformed to support projects that help restore the environment. Transportation units could deploy troops to areas in need of protection or restoration. Intelligence systems could monitor environmental abuse and problem areas. Naval vessels could patrol the seas for pollution; the Air Force could evaluate weather conditions. The Army Corps of Engineers could initiate projects that would be environmentally constructive. At the same time the military could maintain a high level of combat readiness. Over ten years ago, Jimmy Carter said that working to protect the environment is the moral equivalent of war. The time has now arrived where protecting life on the planet is the mission that best serves the military.

Fifteen Years Later

THE MARINE MARTIAL ART

June 16, 2000

The sere and rugged hills of southern California roll out in front of me like the furrowed skin of a sleeping animal. In the far distance the light gauze of summer fog lingers over the ocean. A red-tail hawk wheels in the thermal winds high above. I'm sitting on a bench in the front of the Senior NCO staff room. Behind me I can hear the raucous laughter of the Marines. It's the spirit of camaraderie that's in the air; the charged feeling that comes from going through something difficult . . . as a team.

Earlier in the day we completed the graduation ceremonies for the Marine Warrior Project, a six-week rigorous program that is the prototype for the new Marine Corps Martial Art. I've come outside for a moment to take a break from the festivities, and to reflect on the possibilities and significance of what we've just accomplished. With this part of the project complete I can feel the fatigue deep within me begin to rise to the surface. As the team leader for the project I feel as if I can let go of some of the responsibility I carried over the past several months, and it's tempting to slide into a dreamy oblivion.

One of the Marines breaks my reverie as he wanders out and introduces me to his wife. It's an awkward moment and there's a bit of shuffling going on as we make small talk and attempt a feeble joke. We've spent over fifteen hours a day together for more than six weeks and as we re-enter the larger world after our cocoon of intensive training we're trying to find new ground. A deep and intimate bond has been created between us and we're now looking for an appropriate way to say thank you and good-bye. It's the old saw of men trying to express their love and care for each other in a respectful way. Judging from the moment it doesn't seem like I've mastered it yet.

Suddenly the voice of Larry Burback rises above the rest, followed by a loud shout and laughter. Larry taught with me in the Trojan Warrior Program and in a subsequent program with the Navy SEALs. He has been a competitive athlete all his life, including college football, international rugby, the rodeo circuit, and innumerable marathons and triathlons. He continues to compete in triathlons, having completed sixty-five, including sixteen Iron Man triathlons and twenty marathons. He's a master in the subject of practical physical fitness, incorporating nutrition, flexibility, strength building, and endurance training for peak performance in the physical, mental, and spiritual realms.

Larry and I were older than all of these Marines' parents, and as the men got to know and trust us, the age difference sparked a number of funny interchanges. Once when we were stretching after a particularly arduous run, one of them straight-faced asked, "Dr. Strozzi-Heckler, do you and Larry buy your Geritol by the case?" Admiring Larry's shoes, another asked if it took all his social security check to buy them. And once after a taxing combative drill they looked at me and remarked, "That Viagra must really work." When I trained with them in the martial practices a number of young Marines would say in all seriousness, "Are you sure you will be OK with this, Dr. Strozzi-Heckler?" And then be surprised when I could give out a thumping ... as well as take one. Larry could outperform all of the Marines in the abdominal work and outrun many of them. While we had many laughs around this they maintained their respect as Marines, and I believe that we were able to model for them the possibility of staying fit and active as one gets older.

When the Marine and his wife go back inside I begin to relax in the summer warmth. Mesmerized by the red-tail hawk circling lazily overhead, I return to a hot summer afternoon eight years previous, in 1992, which was the beginning of the Marine Warrior Project and subsequently the Marine Martial Art. I was repairing a horse fence when I was called in to answer a phone call. "I think it's someone from the Pentagon," my wife said quizzically. I had been consulting for the military the past eight years, so it wasn't unusual for me to receive a call from one of the services; but it was unusual to hear from the Pentagon. Taking the mobile phone I moved to the window so I could keep an eye on the horses and the unfinished fence while the voice on the other end introduced himself as John Petersen, founder and CEO of the Arlington Institute, a Washington think tank. John was also a former Navy pilot and apparently on the short list for the appointment to the next Secretary of the Navy.

Secretary of the Navy?! For a kid from the Navy projects this was like the Vatican calling a Catholic.

I immediately formed an image of a man in conservative blue suit sitting behind a dark mahogany desk with the American flag on one side and the Navy flag on the other. The image was incongruous with my present condition of dusty boots, sweat-stained shirt, and the smell of horse manure. I felt exhilarated. The Secretary of the Navy! In the next frame of my mental picture I saw myself next to the man in the conservative blue suit with the two flags on either side of us. There was a steady feeling of inflation. The world held great promise. What did he want from me? Outside the horses didn't seem to notice that the corral boards weren't nailed on.

John had read *In Search of the Warrior Spirit,* and he was intrigued by how the practices and technology we used might be introduced into the other services. The possibility of working at the highest levels of the Pentagon to create a program that would introduce traditional warrior values into the Armed Forces was a long-held dream of mine. In my mental picture I was now shaking hands with the man in the blue suit.

At this point in the conversation my youngest daughter, Paloma, came in and headed in my direction. She was two and already accustomed to the full run of the ranch. I half-turned away from her to signal that I was unavailable, but she remained undaunted and tracked me down as I moved through the kitchen, phone to my ear. Her pace was deliberate and considered, almost ceremonial. In my peripheral vision I could see that both of her hands were raised to shoulder level, palms up, as if she were a supplicant making an offering. Out the window the horses were nosing around the unfinished fence. At the same time I was becoming more and more swept away by the idea that I was conferring with the possible next Secretary of the Navy. A background conversation about being a person of great consequence was taking shape in the recesses of my mind. I was gaining momentum imagining a future in which I would be involved in something significant and weighty.

Finally Paloma cornered me and held her imperial position until I turned toward her. I looked down. A perfectly shaped turd was cupped in her hands. She stood very still, formal, in an altogether serious manner, as if we were joined in some sacred ritual and it was clear that I was the benefactor of her gift. She remained completely composed while I picked it up and then she turned and slowly walked off. Not a word passed between us. Without thinking I bowed slightly as if to complete our bizarre transaction. My world suddenly fragmented and then reformed. My feet were now firmly planted on the ground and I could see everything in vivid detail. All my lofty aspirations were suddenly absorbed by the bleached white sky out the window. Somewhere in the distance I could hear a voice coming through the phone. I looked at the phone in one hand and the turd in the other. It was as if an ironic god intent on schooling me in my own folly was mocking me. Years later, after this initial conversation developed into the Marine Warrior Project, the Marine Martial Art, and the Leadership Dojo—offers that initiated large institutional change in the military and business—this incident became a compass bearing for staying grounded in the face of ambition, power, and responsibility. From then on it was referred to as TOT, Teachings of the Turd.

A few months later John visited the Ranch and we continued our dialogue about learning, human potential, and the changing role of the military. John is an astute observer of future trends, and as an exceptional out-of-the-box thinker he oriented our conversations around the themes of science, technology, and the untapped human potential. In our discussions the idea that reappeared over and over was how the accelerated advancements in technology had begun to erode the role of traditional warrior virtues in the military, and the culture at large. This ranged from fundamental human values such as honesty, integrity, selflessness, commitment, service, and accountability, to developing mind/body skills that enhanced awareness, perception, and performance. We didn't have a particular destination in mind in these conversations, but they held an implicit promise that at some future time we would find a venue to give them form.

John ultimately withdrew his name from the selection process for the Secretary of the Navy, concluding that he could accomplish more through the Arlington Institute than the Government. Toward the end of 1994 he approached me about helping design and deliver a project for the Marine Corps entitled *Vision 21*. The purpose of *Vision 21* was to provide a forum for the Marine Corps senior leadership to explore the trends that would affect the role of the Marine Corps in the 21st century. In the spring of 1995, with General Krulak recently nominated as the next Commandant of the Marine Corps, a select group of political scientists, physicists, technologists, defense consultants, ecologists, and futurists gathered at Camp Pendleton in southern California for *Vision 21*. The speakers provoked fresh thinking among the Generals with their recent research on subjects that ranged from energy, environment, trends in consciousness, training, the battleground of the future, and new ideas in physics.

During my presentation I outlined the history, philosophical background, methodology, and results of the Trojan Warrior Project. I presented statistical and subjective evidence that demonstrated how the emerging mind/body/spirit technologies we taught to the Army Special Forces produced significant and impressive increases in their physical fitness, mental focus, values enhancement, and team cohesion. Through slides, graphs, and anecdotal material I charted the dramatic improvement in their ability to fulfill their mission. As I reviewed the data I was reminded what an extraordinary training the Trojan Warrior Project had been. It had deeply affected the personal and professional lives of all the soldiers involved, and it had opened a new wave of thinking about training in the military establishment. The Navy SEALs and the Air Force Pararescue Jumpers had requested similar projects, and it became evident that we could duplicate our success in the other services.

But when I looked out on my audience I was quickly sobered by the sea of blank, stony faces staring back at me. A bunch of square-jawed, steely-eyed, buzz-cut Marines taking everything in without a clue to what they were thinking. There was no note taking, no nodding of the head, no change in expression whatsoever that would indicate what they were thinking, either good or bad. The uncomfortable thought scurried across my mind that this had been a terrible mistake. It was a colossal oversight to think that the Marine Corps would be interested in anything as experimental as the emerging mind/body/spirit technologies. I prepared myself to be politely, but curtly, shown the door. Concluding my talk I took a deep breath, bracing myself for what was to come, and asked if there were any questions.

To my shock a thicket of hands immediately punched into the air and the room filled with an excited buzz. Each question reflected a penetrating interest in how a program like this might be relevant to the concerns of the Marine Corps mission, ethos, and culture. The intensity of the discussion was so high that we went beyond the allotted time and were finally asked to clear the room. Even then a number of the Generals grabbed me in the hall, firing questions and debating whether a training of this type could be implemented into their specific units.

This was an unexpected but welcome surprise. What was more astounding, though, was how often they returned the conversation to the subject of spirit. Over the years I've learned to be circumspect about how I approach the topic of spirituality in institutions. There are many interpretations on the subject, and on more than one occasion I've encountered fundamentalists who manage to unproductively dominate the conversation. But it was clear that for these men this was an essential matter that was not to be overlooked. They insisted, no, demanded, that training the spirit be first on the agenda. The concern for spirit, ethics, and morality was more in the foreground here than in any of the other institutions in which I had worked—by a landslide. What did it tell me? The senior leaders of one of the oldest institutions in America were deeply and sincerely committed to the ethical, moral, and spiritual development of the young men and women in the Marine Corps, and by extension the United States. This didn't surprise me because I had reason to believe otherwise, but because the majority of their counterparts in the business world— Chairmen, CEOs, Senior Vice-Presidents—came nowhere close to this level of commitment to their people. This was an entirely different perspective, one that exposed the humane core of these men. Soft, no, caring, very much so. This was a perspective that would greatly challenge the liberal establishment's view of the Marine Corps. I left the meeting hall with an extraordinary appreciation for those whose watch includes not only national security but also the ethical and moral development of the youth of America.

General Richard Hearney, the newly appointed Assistant Commandant of the Marine Corps, invited me to have lunch at his table. General Hearney is a tall, athletic figure whose bearing exemplifies everything you would think of in a leader. He's ramrod-straight, a fascinating story-teller, a discriminating listener, and someone who takes a genuine interest in others. From the very beginning of our lunch he spoke passionately about the importance of emphasizing values in the training of a Marine. For the first time in their history the Marine Corps were receiving second-generation and sometimes third-generation recruits who were raised in single-parent homes. They were entering the Marine Corps without the strong ethical and moral foundation that usually starts at home. This was showing up as an increase in thefts, fights, disciplinary problems, and rapes. He told me how a young Marine explained that if someone left his or her locker open, he wouldn't consider it stealing to take the wallet. When asked why, he replied as if it were common sense, "If it wasn't locked up the person must not have wanted it. So how could it be stealing?"

In addition, the military was now training recruits with more diverse racial, religious, social, and ethnic backgrounds than ever before, and the senior leadership was keenly aware that it was critical to re-tool aspects of their training process. General Hearney acknowledged the importance of integrating technology into the Corps but he considered it a grave mistake to make it more important than teaching core values. He was acquainted with *In Search of the Warrior Spirit* and he was curious if something like this could be designed for the Marines.

At one point during our conversation he collared a very large man walking by and introduced me to Major General Jim Jones. Over six feet five inches tall and two hundred and thirty pounds, General Jones' soft-spoken demeanor and relaxed style contrasts with the seriousness of his focus and the strength of his mind. He was soon to be appointed Military Advisor to Secretary of Defense Cohen—a unique appointment for a Marine and one that spoke to the respect that Secretary Cohen had for him. General Jones told me that he had a special interest in the martial arts aspect of my presentation. Thirty years ago when he was a Platoon Commander in Vietnam, the South Korean Marines' practice of the martial art tae kwon do made an impression on him. He observed that their martial arts regime positively affected their discipline, fierceness, and motivation. The Koreans also seemed to intimidate his own Marines, and the Vietcong were reluctant to engage in the ROK's area of operations. Years later, in 1986 at Camp Pendleton when he was a Battalion Commander, Jones enlisted a retired Gunnery Sergeant to teach martial arts to his Battalion, with startling results. Alcohol and drug abuse decreased, incidents of domestic violence went down, unauthorized absences fell, bar and street brawls declined, morale rose, and overall performance increased. His Marines would practice their techniques during their spare time instead of going to the base club or hanging out in the barracks. At that time he pledged that in future commands he would do whatever he could to have a martial arts curriculum available to his Marines.

I spoke to them about a way of learning the martial arts in which one could train fighting and self-defense skills while at the same time embodying character values that could be used on base, deployment, or at home. This is an age-old concept grounded in classical martial arts training and one that is relevant to what they are now facing. I suggested that certain martial principles, like being centered, for example, while fundamental for success in a physical confrontation are just as pertinent in every aspect of life. At one point I offered to show them instead of just talking about it, and without hesitation we all three stood up in the dining room and did some of the centering and extension practices we do in aikido. It was a strange scene—us doing aikido exercises in the middle of lunch—but quickly other officers approached and wanted to try it out for themselves.

This penchant for jumping in with both feet is a hallmark of the Corps and one that I clearly remember during my time as a Marine. It's also an image they dearly love and will reinforce at every opportunity. As a teacher it is a trait that I wholly appreciated, in that every Marine we taught gave 105%. Uncertainty and hesitation are not trademarks of the Marine Corps. "First to Fight" is more than a marketing slogan, it's a way of life that says: Get Involved. Learn. Contribute. Be of Help.

In the camaraderie of the moment I began to feel that tipsy, intoxicated feeling that appears when the synergy of minds hits a new octave. Teaching martial arts, as both a fighting system and value system, to the Marine Corps—what could be more fulfilling than that? In this nebulous expansion of being I remembered the Teaching of the Turd and a smile came over my face along with a bit of perspective. The men and women in this room were like parents looking after their children's welfare. They are devoted to the well being of the entire Marine Corps family, and I felt like I could help them with that. Looking out over the room of senior officers, confident in themselves and itching to midwife their institution into the next century, I had no way of knowing that I was building relationships that would extend far into the future. Unbeknownst to me, six years later I would recognize this as the genesis of the Marine Martial Art, which ultimately would be institutionalized throughout the entire Marine Corps.

At the conclusion of the *Vision 21* symposium General Jones shook my hand and asked me to stay in touch, adding (which now seems a bit ironic) "Perhaps we can put something together in the future." Over the next five years I met with General Jones, General Hearney, and other senior officers at the Pentagon and the Marine Corps Headquarters on numerous occasions. We did a smaller project at the Infantry Officer Corps and The Basic School. I arranged for General Jones to speak at a conference for the senior executives at Capital One, and General Hearney spoke at a leadership seminar at the Strozzi Institute. I also began implementing the practices of the Leadership Dojo in large corporations in the U.S., Latin America, Europe, and Canada as well as in successful start-ups and smaller companies.

In January of 2000 General Jones, who was then Commandant, invited me to a meeting in Albany, Georgia, with his senior officers to discuss a program for the Marine Corps that would be the prototype for what is now the Marine Martial Art. At the end of the meeting General Jones declared that he wanted to have a prototype designed and delivered by the end of summer. Accustomed to the lengthy bureaucratic process of government contracting, my first thought was "This year?" Indeed, he wanted it completed, including an after-action report, to present at the General Officers Symposium that fall. He was serious so I hastily began forming a team. At the same time I began extensive conversations with the Commandant and his senior officers to dig deeper into what we wanted to produce with this initiative. In these discussions it quickly became apparent that the idea of creating a Marine Martial Art was driven by two primary factors: preparing the Marine to be combat-effective in a changing geo-political environment, and enhancing character values on deployment and at home.

Our conversations revealed that the character of contemporary warfare is changing, and a fundamental shift in thinking is necessary for the Marine Corps and the U.S. to act powerfully in this new world. In the age of Operations Other Than War (OOTW), traditional "phase-line" thinking simply does not apply anymore. Non-combatant Evacuation Operations (NEO) and humanitarian aid place U.S. Marines directly in harm's way with aggressive populations. The traditional markers of combatants such as uniforms, a well-defined enemy, and ordered units are often absent, giving the man on the ground operational vertigo. The individual Marine has to operate with unreasonable Rules of Engagement (ROE), in situations set by political agendas and viewed by the judgmental eye of the world media. Business as usual is clearly not good enough. The Marine Martial Art had to be designed with these circumstances in mind. The question was how can the Marine successfully complete his mission *and* exemplify traditional warrior virtues?

This changing landscape of war, in addition to domestic pressures that challenge the moral conduct of the Armed Forces, has created a demand for a higher standard of character and leadership within the Marine Corps. Issues of values and right action on the battlefield, as well as at home, are of paramount concern to the future success of the Corps and its promise to the nation. These changes are exacerbated by a tight recruiting market and the fact that the type and quality of incoming recruit have changed radically over the past decade. In the nineties the promise of high-paying jobs, the accumulation of wealth, and a booming economy lured many young people away from national service. Most of the services are not meeting their recruiting numbers, and they have lowered their standards for induction. In addition, many of the new recruits lack the discipline, morals, and ethics that are the hallmark of strong family values. Include the increased diversity of race, creed, and color of the new recruits and you have a complex challenge in educating the new Marine. The incentive for the creation of the Marine Warrior Project resulted from the question of how to train the 21st-century Marine to be physically and morally prepared for a combat environment that increasingly calls for non-lethal force, *and* to be an exemplar of ethical conduct at home and abroad. Simply put, Commandant Jones commissioned the Marine Warrior Project to determine the feasibility of a martial arts program that would improve the combat capabilities of the Marine Rifleman, as well as developing character values and team cohesion. It was the invocation of the classical warrior ideal: outwardly ready for decisive action and inwardly peaceful and resolute.

We began this innovative and historical experiment on May 15, 2000, at Camp Pendleton with members of the 1st Combat Engineer Battalion from Camp San Mateo. Forty-two Marines began the program and forty graduated. A Navy Corpsman was also part of the project. One Marine was removed from the program because of drug use, and the other Marine failed the standards for graduation. Twenty-one Military

Occupational Specialties (MOS) were represented. The average age of the Marines was twenty-two years, ranging from nineteen years old to twenty-eight. Marines from different units were brought together to test how quickly unit cohesion would develop, and in order to test improvement across a wide spectrum, Marines of varying levels of performance were included.

On day one of the program we defined the Marine Warrior as the individual Marine who defends, protects, and sustains the values of his family, community, Marine Corps, and the Constitution of the United States of America. In order to do this he or she must be physically fit, mentally disciplined, and must live according to ethical, moral, and spiritual values, as well as embody the combative skills to defend these values. Thus, the program integrated courses of study in physical fitness, combatives, and warrior (character) values.

The unique, holistic aspect of the program, and its overwhelming success, came from the way we established linkages among the various program elements, then produced practices that manifested these connections on a daily basis. This methodology is significantly different from a checklist approach in which a subject is taught, checked off as completed, and then everyone moves on to the next subject to be checked off. In this checklist approach subject matter is addressed, but it's quarantined to its own area. It's the separate smokestack analogy, which doesn't consider the importance of connecting the different areas of our life, or embodying the learning so it is operational. For example, in our methodology when we taught the warrior value of accountability, it didn't begin and end with a lecture and definition of terms. First the Marines would read a brief paper on accountability during the evening. The next day we would have a short lecture, and then they would break into small teams to discuss their ideas on the subject. (This small group structure added a surprise value in that it gave each Marine the opportunity to speak in front of a group. This helped many of them build the leadership skill of standing and talking in front of a group, something which many of them had never done and would be required to do as they advanced through the ranks.) The character value of accountability was then experientially engaged at the beginning of the day during Physical Training (P.T.) at 0530 (5:30 A.M.) when each Marine committed to take personal responsibility for his physical fitness. This theme became operational in that they saw they were responsible for their body weight, body fat, endurance, strength, flexibility, and agility. From there we moved to breakfast and linked how they were accountable for what they ate and how that affected health and performance. During combatives, accountability became a living concept in regard to how, where, why, and with whom one trains to be combat-ready. This included accountability for the appropriate use of force if necessary, whether in a NEO operation or in a bar on Saturday night. Similarly, accountability became part of the element of team cohesion. We produced the practices and sensibility that are necessary for the Marine to be accountable for the mission of his platoon, for the success of his family, and for his and his teammates' career advancement. As the program unfolded, the element of accountability continued to resurface and blend with the other warrior values to become a coherent whole. It lived as an on-going conversation, sensibility, and practice. In this way the warrior character values lived not only in the realm of intellectual understanding, but as consistent, skillful action in the world. Accountability and the other character traits became embodied values in word and action for the Marine on base, at home, on liberty, and when he is deployed.

Warrior Values include:

- Awareness
- Attention
- Choice
- Centering
- Accountability

- Honor
- Courage
- Commitment
- Integrity
- Honesty
- Trust
- Dignity
- *Hamni* (Taking a Stand)
- Respect
- Blending
- Compassion
- *Zanshin* (On-going Awareness)
- *Irimi* (Entering)
- Extension
- *Musubi* (Connecting)
- Relaxation

At the center of the Marine Warrior Program is the Combatives Section. Combative skills and the confidence to use them are a necessity for the modern Marine. Combatives must be part of his force options, not simply something to do if his rifle malfunctions or if he runs out of ammunition. Combative skills give him the ability to make composed decisions and access the correct option along the force continuum. However, this confidence doesn't come from learning a hodgepodge of martial moves. It comes from disciplined, realistic, and intelligent training that results in an embodied skill that can be used in an appropriate way at the appropriate time.

To understand what distinguishes the Marine Warrior Combative Section, it's helpful to look at how unit commanders have customarily viewed combatives, which is either as a way to develop aggressiveness or as a "last-ditch" option in the event that the primary weapon could not be used. These attitudes developed from conventional phase-line warfare thinking, which influenced the choice of techniques and doctrine. Leaders believed—correctly for the time—that if it came to hand-to-hand combat things had gone horribly wrong, so that such training was either an annual motivational exercise or, at best, a casual afterthought. In the case of Operations Other Than War (OOTW), however, this orientation is no longer useful. Even more important is that martial art practices are taught that produce both calmness and a capacity for effective action, which the trained individual can take into every aspect of his or her life.

The methodology of this program is notably different, however, from what is followed in traditional martial arts programs, which introduce numerous techniques in a short period of time. These techniques are linking moves that are complex and extremely difficult to employ in a combat situation. The complexity of these moves also requires a partner who is cooperative and exerts minimal resistance. In addition, these techniques are rarely practiced at full speed and full power. While one may learn qualities of movement, increased coordination and balance, connecting to a partner, and dynamic relaxation, the techniques are unlikely to be effective in a combat situation. This is because it requires much more time to embody moves this complex. Moreover, without training at full speed and full power one cannot experience the full effectiveness of a technique. This, in turn, makes the individual less confident in his capacity to make full use of his training.

In order to ensure that the Marine learned both a martial skill and the ethical principles of traditional dojo training in a short period of time, the methodology of the Marine Warrior Combatives Section integrated three elements: **Technique + Principles + Values = Competence.**

Techniques: The techniques were simple, easy to learn, and highly effective. The basic platform techniques were knee strikes, elbow strikes, and neck wrestling. These techniques were repeated over and over in every class. They were included in the warm-up and the *kata* (practice form), and practiced at full speed and full power on pads. Dress ranged from T-shirts and trousers to packs, helmets, with M-16s, and with opponents constantly changing their attack and intent. The daily repetition of these moves made them an embodied part of the Marine's capacity to fight and defend himself. On this foundation are taught techniques for joint and restraining locks, choke holds, blocking moves, and throws.

Principles: To effectively employ these techniques the *aiki* principles of correct body placement, dynamic relaxation, extension, balance, centering, reading your opponent, entering, fluidity of movement, blending, and power are folded into the training.

Warrior Values: Warrior values training consist of the discipline of spirit within a combatives context. The warrior values section was the foundation on which the other elements of the program were built. It was realized early on that teaching combat skills without an ethical and spiritual foundation ran the risk of producing bullies, mercenaries, and mindless violence. At the same time it was made clear that to understand the warrior values only intellectually, without grounding in combat skills, would be useless when combative action was called for. At one point the Commandant told me that the values section had to be the core of the program. He clearly stated that building an ethical, moral, and spiritual character was essential to the success of the program. If it relied only on learning martial arts moves we would have failed. It recalled the words of Napoleon when he said that the physical is to the spiritual as one is to five.

The warrior values taught the Marines to differentiate between, and to respond properly to, perceived and real threats. It made the options of walking away, defusing, neutralizing, defending, and lethal force an embodied response instead of a reaction based in fear, machismo, or emotionality. The integration of the values aspect provided the Marines with an ethical basis for their decision-making in the use of force. This is particularly useful when our military is closely watched and held accountable by the world media. It trains the Marine to be able to think and speak coherently about why he took the actions he did.

Skills and Competence: The result of the three preceding elements produced a proven and effective combative skill that can be used in various environments against diverse opponents. It is the appropriate use of force at the appropriate time. This is radically different from training that requires that "one technique fit all." It taught the Marines how to move fluidly between many different situations and opponents. We thoroughly debunked the idea of the photo-shoot martial art paradigm, which leads one to believe that "If someone does this you do that." Our program taught the Marines to move appropriately in relation to the situation.

As the program progressed, the number of reports by Marines *choosing* to walk away from fights in the barracks and in weekend liberty significantly increased. They either saw that they were in the wrong, admitted so, and acted accountably, or else, confident that they could handle the situation, they decided it was unnecessary to injure the person and risk being involved with judicial consequences. In addition, those with reputations for engaging in physical confrontations had no incidents during the program at all. Those individuals reported that it just didn't seem as important to fight anymore. This anecdotal material supports the conclusion that the Marines acquired new choices for how to deal with potentially violent situations. What is important is that their decisions were based on an increased confidence in their martial ability and an increased self-esteem. Their psychological evaluations and remarkable improvement in their combatives test validate this.

In addition, we produced team cohesion from widely diverse elements in a very short period of time, with Marines from different units. Within a week the command staff, as well as the individual Marines, remarked how quickly they formed into a working team. Many of them observed that even in this short period of time they actually became a more cohesive team than the unit they came from.

Pre- and post-tests were administered in Combatives, Physical Fitness, Swim Qualifications, Psychological Evaluations, Body Fat, and Attention Testing. Following is a summary of the test results:

WARRIOR VALUES (Psychological Evaluations)
- Significant increase in self-worth and self-esteem.
- Significant increase in self-satisfaction.
- Significant increase in sense of well-being.
- Significant increase in positive affect (e.g. enthusiasm).
- Significant increase in honesty in self-examination.

ATTENTION TRAINING
- Overall ability to concentrate and stay focused during distractions improved by 33%.
- 35% of the participants improved their ability to concentrate and stay focused during distractions.

COMBATIVES
- 98% of the participants increased their scores to 100%.
- 38 out of 39 participants responded combat-effective during the Military Operations in Urban Terrain (MOUT) test.

PHYSICAL FITNESS
- 97.5% of the individuals increased their PFT scores.
- 74% of the individuals increased their # of pull-ups.
- 46% of the individuals increased their # of sit-ups.

- 87% of the individuals increased their run time.
- 69% of the individuals reduced their body weight.
- 87% of the individuals reduced their % of body fat.

Body wt	Body fat	PFT	Pull-ups	Sit-ups	3-mile run
% Group change					
−1.28%	−17.48%	+12.12%	20.21%	7.21%	−5.33%
Total group change					
−92 lbs.	−134.5%	+1045	+96	+260	−48:32
Greatest ind. change					
−11 lbs.	−10.4%	+87	+8	+30	−06:02
Average change					
−2.3 lbs.	−3.4%	+25.3	+2.5	+6.7	−01:09

 Following is a selection of written comments from the Marines at the completion of the program (the names have been changed):

The benefits to me personally are that I have gotten insight into me and I know I have more confidence. I find both the values and combatives valuable to a Marine. The values because they teach a person to be more accountable and aware. The combatives are important because they teach a Marine a skill and give him the confidence to use it.

—Sgt. Hull

The course allowed me to more clearly recognize the purpose and definition of a modern-day warrior. The combatives have given me more confidence in my physical abilities as a warrior. The course required that

I give 105% every day. This allowed me to see where my edges are and how to work with them.

—Lt. Davidson

I think this would be an outstanding course for Marines because I think this course gives Marines the confidence and awareness they need for everyday ops.

—Cpl. Fergen

It has helped me to be more in control of my emotions, particularly anger, and to see the world in a different light. I am aware of choices that I didn't know I had and it has helped me build my self-esteem. The course has made me a better team player, which is a quality I've always lacked.

—HM3 Ballard

Beyond a doubt this course has value to the Corps. It teaches how to evaluate yourself to make you a better leader, teaches how to build and sustain teamwork, and to maintain health and good eating habits, and improved combative skills enormously.

—Cpl. Bair

I think the accountability trait is what will be the most beneficial because it already has begun to change my whole attitude. I will stop being a victim and start taking control of my life. I think that Marines bitching about how they got screwed by the Corps would stop because they will be accountable for themselves and the Corps.

—LCpl. Perez

It shows Marines that they have choices every day. I also feel that the course does a great job of emphasizing accountability. Both taking accountability for one's life and one's actions. The combatives are very practical and fundamental. I also think the centering practice is useful to the Marines in that it can help them in their day-to-day lives and potentially in combat.

—Lt. Attal

I feel as a Marine the benefits of this course were:

1. The combatives. They will help during the three-block war.
2. The attention training to help focus on specific tasks.
3. The centering training to help clear your head.

I feel that the combatives and centering are key. This course has not only changed me as a Marine but as a husband and father.

—SSgt Zanick

This course has given me tools to accomplish the goals that I set for myself and built upon my commitment to the Corps. My ability to defend myself especially in areas that are politically sensitive and where using military weapons may set off an incident are vastly improved. Also my self-confidence has risen considerably.

—LCpl. Barn

I think that it helps me as a Marine because the reason that I joined was to be challenged and warrior spirit definitely does that and there's a lot of Marines who join for that same reason and this program is a very good challenge.

—LCpl. Nave

Now I can control my temper, emotions, and feelings, this will help me in all ways of life. It builds self-esteem and how to defend yourself. These are all things a Marine needs to be a good Marine. This course was outstanding. Every Marine should go through this course. If the Marine Corps doesn't put this program into effect it will be a mistake.

—Cpl. Billings

This training, if implemented into the Marine Corps, could open up a whole new aspect of what it means to be a Marine, thus increasing performance in daily tasks as well as overall morale.

—Cpl. Stone

The benefits are better leadership, better fitness. I learned more options, opened my awareness to what I can do. It helps people to see what is pissing them off or making them happy. People better understand what to do.

—PFC Clifford

It taught us a good, better way of fighting than line training and helped me relax.

—PFC Casey

The quantitative test results, subjective material, and personal anecdotes all point to a Marine who is now more physically fit, transformed in his ability to defend himself, and has an increased ability to choose his actions on a foundation of ethical and moral considerations. The Marine Warrior Project is a prototype program that demonstrated the possibility of producing an individual who embodies ethical, moral, and spiritual values, and has the capacity to defend, protect, and sustain these values in word and action—an example, truly, of what it might mean to be a warrior in the 21st century.

As of the publication of this edition (2003), the core of the Marine Warrior Project has been expanded into the Marine Corps Martial Art. Every new recruit goes through the Marine Martial Art program, as do the candidates at the Officer Candidate School and The Basic School for officers. Every Marine has the opportunity to train throughout his career in this art and, if he or she commits to it, to advance to a sixth-degree black belt. Whenever a Marine passes a test, a small colored strip designating his rank is attached to his web belt. This means that along with the recognition and pride in what they have accomplished, the Marines at barracks or deployed can identify other Marines with whom they can train. I have continued on as a consultant to refine the program and help it become institutionalized within the Corps. The Marines have received the program enthusiastically, and the Commandant has recently assigned the second director for the Marine Martial Art.

An added treat was that my oldest son Django was at Marine Combat Training (MCT) when I was teaching at Camp Pendleton. I spent part of a morning with him and his Commanding Officer on the rifle range, and he visited the program when he graduated from MCT. He makes three generations of Naval Service in our family.

During the time we spent at Camp Pendleton I had the honor of developing a friendship with Sergeant Major Royce Coffee that continues to this day. At the time Sergeant Major Coffee was the Sergeant Major of the 1st Marine Division, where he was and continues to be an enthusiastic supporter of the program. (He is now Sergeant Major of the Marine Forces Pacific, the second highest enlisted Marine in the Corps.) He has served in the Marine Corps for over thirty-five years, and his honors and awards are too numerous to mention here, but suffice to say that when he is in his dress blues his chest is crowded with ribbons and medals. Among his many duties he was First Sergeant in a Reconnaissance Battalion and served combat tours in Somalia and Desert Storm. As a lifelong martial artist, Sergeant Major Coffee has earned black belts in tae kwon do (4th degree), aikido (2nd degree), kobudo (2nd degree), hapkido (1st degree), and senior rankings in both Escrima and Hindiandi gung fu. With this background one expects the classical campaign poster Marine who is a cigar-chomping, hard-drinking, bad-mouthed leatherneck. Sergeant Major Coffee is a vegetarian, doesn't drink, smoke, or have a single tattoo, and "friggin" is the most extreme profanity I've heard exit his mouth. Yet, if you were in a bad situation in a dark alley, you would most definitely want him on your side.

As the program became institutionalized in the Marine Corps, Sergeant Major Coffee has been a consistent sounding board on how to best implement the design. In addition, he and I presented an aikido demonstration for the 1st Marine Division, and he has assisted me at the Strozzi Institute's School of Embodied Leadership Course. (The School of Embodied Leadership Course takes the best elements of the Trojan Warrior Project, the Marine Warrior Project, and the work with the Navy SEALs and offers a 5½-day intensive leadership course for leaders in business, government, education, non-profits, military, and health.)

As Sergeant Major Coffee travels the globe from Korea to Bahrain in his job with the Marine Forces Pacific he consistently relays news about the results of the Marine Martial Art in the fleet. For instance, when Marines are in cramped quarters aboard ship in close proximity with Sailors, it is historically a highly combustible environment. Fights and brawls occur more often than anyone would like. With Marine Martial Art Instructors placed on the ships so the Marines can train regularly, the incidents of fights between Marines and Marines, and Marines and Sailors, has been dramatically reduced. Furthermore, Sailors watching the Marines train are asking in a mood of camaraderie if they can participate. In a distant outpost in Afghanistan, Sergeant Major Coffee came across a small detachment of Marines who were training every day and said it was a primary factor in keeping their morale up in very difficult conditions. On a weekly basis reports come across my desk indicating that where units are training regularly there is a significant reduction in alcohol and drug abuse, domestic violence, police incidents, and overall blotter occurrences like unauthorized absences, lateness, fighting, and poor morale. There has also been positive press in *USA Today,* CNN, *The Washington Post,* and *The Wall Street Journal.* (In the October 9, 2000, issue of *The Wall Street Journal* I was surprised to find myself on the cover with the lead story about the "New Marine Martial Art.")

In July 2002 the Commandant sponsored the World-Wide Commandants' Conference and hosted thirty-three Marine Commandants from different countries. As part of their visit they observed a demonstration of the Marine Martial Art. At their final evening they gathered with their wives in their full dress uniforms at the Commandant's house at the Marine Corps Headquarters in Washington, D.C., for a reception and parade. I asked a number of them what their reactions were to the martial arts demonstration. To a man they were impressed with the energy, discipline, rigor, and scope of the art.

What they couldn't see within the excitement of the martial moves was the deep work being done with the character, ethical, and moral values of each individual Marine. It is clear that every Marine who goes through this training will come out a better person for it. This program will positively affect the way they handle themselves in all situations. When they eventually return to civilian life, after four years or thirty-five on active duty, they will unequivocally enrich the fabric of our society. The credit for this unique and creative innovation belongs to the vision and determination of General Jim Jones, the 32nd Commandant of the United States Marine Corps. It has been an honor in helping bring his dream into reality.

As the Commandants and their wives began to file slowly from the garden to the evening parade, I asked the Commandant if he was satisfied with the demonstration. He smiled broadly, straightened himself a bit before he spoke, and replied, "They were outstanding! Everybody was impressed. Thank you for your part in this." As the light waned and dusk gathered around us I recalled how this art had begun so many years before as an idea in one man's mind. As we shook hands I thought of the words of the fifteenth-century philosopher and poet Sir Francis Bacon, who said, "I know not why but martial men are given to love."

October, 2001

A local magazine asked if I would comment on the events of 11 September 2001. What follows is my response.

The events of September 11 have irrevocably changed our lives and placed us in a time of personal and national trial. There has been much said about this incident, some of it very wise and some of it horseshit. Every day we hear from another pundit rushing to the Internet announcing their particular angle. Public commentators infantilize us with their pseudo-therapeutic bromides of grief management, confidence-building, and emotional healing. Yes, let's restore ourselves in communities, but let's not be absurd together, and let's not have others treat us as if we're stupid. Because of the daily congestion of electronic and printed traffic on the subject I never considered I had anything worth adding to the pile. But because of my relationship with the Pentagon and Department of Defense over the past sixteen years I've had numerous requests to share my observations as well as my personal reflections. My thoughts are those of a private citizen not those of an expert or one whose opinion will necessarily make a deciding difference.

My interactions with the Pentagon have increased dramatically since 9/11. I have many friends posted there and I am naturally concerned about their well being. Thankfully, they are all safe. I have also been invited to be on a committee specifically formed by the events of 9/11. My impressions are that the military, as a whole, is urging restraint, well-considered plans, and intensified diplomatic, political, and economic measures, as well as the appropriate military interventions. The people I speak with are clear that this situation has no precedent to fall back on, and the battle lines are none like we've seen in the past. These are men and women who deeply care about not only the country, but about the lives of the Marines, Airmen, Seamen, and Soldiers who put their lives in harm's way.

In short, they are warning against an emotional reaction of going hot. And the final decisions, as always in a democracy, lie with our political leaders.

The situation we find ourselves in is analogous to the physicians of the Middle Ages who came to the conclusion that bleeding their patients to restore their health didn't really work. Their patients, however, insisted on the bleeding treatment and since the physicians didn't know what else to do, they continued to bleed them. We know a large-scale mechanized war will not work, but we're not really sure what will, so through the lens of CNN we see our aircraft carriers, armed to the teeth, steaming to the Persian Gulf. This placates and settles many minds, and upsets others. But those at the head of the table know that "restoring health and dignity" requires building alliances, maintaining friendships (instead of using people and then throwing them away), distinguishing between Islam and the terrorists, blocking their economic stream, learning from our past mistakes, and bringing the perpetrators to justice. These are the elements that I also endorse.

For years I've seen the military and intelligence communities raise flags about the very real possibility of an event like this occurring. For the most part they have been waved aside and we now live with the horrible aftermath of our complacency. Since 1993 we've had five major terrorist acts committed against us here and abroad. And after each one they said this is just the start. I sat in on a meeting years ago where an Army Special Forces Colonel described the exact scenario we just experienced at the World Trade Center. As passionate as he was he couldn't rally any support upstream for the resources and assets to follow through. What our tax dollars did pay for were political correctness programs ensuring that our recruits didn't have their self-esteem damaged during boot camp, and personnel monitors making sure that in the Southern Command the men "didn't show up" the women by running faster in the morning runs. Meanwhile 15% of our armed forces personnel are on food stamps because their paychecks don't cover food and rent. These are the same men and women who will spend this Thanksgiving and Christmas thousands of miles from their families in duty to this country.

We convinced ourselves that we were invulnerable, that the land of the brave was impenetrable. Soft and overfed, we now face an opponent who has demonstrated that his disenfranchisement has become his ultimate weapon. Remember that evil is impervious to a consciousness-raising chat and that courage is a morally neutral virtue. We are called upon, individually and as a people, to re-examine our lives and priorities. We must close ranks, watch each other's backs, and in doing so not back down from building a mature democracy.

We also find ourselves in a moment of great opportunity. This offers itself on two connected tracks: as a historical evolution and as a consciousness evolution. On the historical track it is important to confront the aggressors and deliver the appropriate consequences with the collaboration of the international community. On the consciousness track it is equally if not more important to recognize that violence will not necessarily end violence. History reflects this over and over. It's too much in our face to deny. To defend our way of life we need to decisively and effectively confront our enemies, but fighting for peace is like fucking for virginity.

Historical and consciousness evolution means redefining who we are as Americans and as people. We know what we're fighting against; we need to stand for what we're fighting for and to ask the deeper question of why. Terrorists want to bring down more than buildings, and it requires us to ask what we will fight and die for. My short list includes having my daughters be able to play basketball in shorts, accountable government, pulled pork sandwiches for my friends who want them, educational opportunities for all, evolutionary theory, free speech, the right to choose religious and spiritual practices, dancing, shaving, a multi-party political system. I was ashamed to be a human when I saw the attack and proud to be a human when I saw the firemen rushing up the stairwells while others were running down. This is the daily conundrum we live with as these two forces battle in our own bodies. Krishnamurti said it well, "War is but an expression of our everyday lives." We are the battle lines.

Instead of panicking or returning to "business as usual," commit to grounded compassion, pragmatic wisdom, and skillful action. Let awareness be your weapon. We are summoned to something great, so be vigilant not to reduce it to our smallness. These catastrophic events demand that we go to the deepest levels of a generous and courageous spirit. Many say the firefighters and police died for our freedom as they rushed to help others. I prefer to think that they died for the opportunity, as a nation, to cultivate wisdom.

Be there for those who have suffered more than we have. Step beyond yourself and be of use to someone. Be courage in uncertainty. Be love in chaos. Take it easy but take it. This is what I tell myself.

Twenty Years Later

Afghanistan
August 2004

🌓 We step off the C-17 into an endless blue sky and interminable heat. Immediately a phalanx of armed guards surrounds us. The NATO representative for Afghanistan and the commander of the International Security Assistance Forces (ISAF) in Afghanistan step forward and greet General Jones, the Supreme Allied Commander of Europe (SACEUR). The formalities are starched, quick, and in a blink our security detail hustles us to armored SUVs with tinted windows. The morning sun is a giant shield of bronze that penetrates everything with its relentless heat. The bone-dry slopes of the Hindu Kush look down impassively as they did when Alexander the Great's invasion of this country left behind centuries filled with war, tribal conflicts, foreign invaders, and more war. The last twenty-five years have been uninterrupted war, yet only a footnote in comparison to what these silent vigil-keepers have witnessed.

The Russians invaded in 1979 and left in 1989 at a price of 1.5 million Afghan lives, countless amputees, and a devastated infrastructure. The Mujaheddin, financed by China and the U.S. with billions of dollars' worth of arms and logistical support, fought the Russians and then turned on each other in a protracted civil war. Following this, a well-armed and organized Taliban fought and overthrew the fragile government. Over two decades of uninterrupted fighting left another scar of suffering and disruption on the ethnic and cultural history of Afghanistan.

Six weeks earlier I'm working on a project called the Mideast Aikido Project and Training Across Borders. Its mission is to bring together people from the Mediterranean basin, whose countries have been warring for decades, to train aikido together. I'm speaking with my co-director about the possibility of holding it on the island of Cyprus when my assistant pokes her head in the door. "They want you to go to Afghanistan," she says flatly. My mind does a quick somersault. The "they" is General Jim Jones, who, after completing his tour as the Commandant of the Marine Corps, was appointed SACEUR. Since we worked together on the Marine Corps Martial Arts Program (MCMAP), we've stayed in contact and he's considering initiating a similar project with the Afghan National Army (ANA). I'll be part of a select group that will consist of members of Business Executives for National Security, the European and American press, and the long tail of his military and civilian staff from NATO headquarters. I'll travel throughout the country speaking to Afghanis and ISAF personnel to determine the feasibility of a combatives program for the ANA. When I tell people where I'll be in August they look at me sideways. I get busy rearranging my schedule.

Before flying to Kabul our group is bused to NATO headquarters in Brussels to be briefed by an English Vice Air Marshall. He's round and bald and I wonder what he looks like fitted into the cockpit of a jet fighter. He delivers an informative and compelling narrative about how the problems of Afghanistan will soon become the problems of the world if we don't intervene. Aside from the obvious threats of Al Qaeda and the Taliban, he recites a sobering litany in which Afghanistan as a rogue state would become a well-traveled route for child slavery, child-sex trade, prostitution, arms transportation, illegal immigration, and the drug trade.

"These activities are already affecting the economies and infrastructure of Europe and they can easily spread to other continents. We haven't even seen the scale this can expand to." He spends more time on the opium problem than any of the other topics. This will become a theme that is repeated over and over on my trips here. When I ask him about this emphasis, he simply says, "It underlies everything."

He points to multiple solutions including economic, educational, social, legal, and military, with ample assistance from the international community. This briefing helps shape my thinking on the role of the ANA in stabilizing the country. Without a secure environment, there's no chance for autonomy or economic development for Afghanistan and the responsibility for security will eventually have to rest on the shoulders of the ANA. Aside from bringing the Army up to speed in terms of personnel, training, and equipment, there's also the possibility of it being the arena in which a combatives program becomes a way for helping unite the different factions and ethnic groups of the country.

On the overnight flight to Kabul, I sit next to General Jones and we talk about the possibilities of the program, who I should meet, where I should go, and what to look for. For this VIP crowd, the fuselage of this transport plane is cleared and fifteen rows of quasi-business seats are inserted. There's plenty of legroom and the seats tilt back; folding tables are set up with food and drinks and a festive mood sets in. This is a vast physical and psychic distance from how I've normally flown on military transports, which is strapped into hard plastic, straight-back seats, shoulder to shoulder with the soldier next to me. This I prefer.

Every ten minutes, one of General Jones's staff appears with a question to answer, a document to read, or a briefing on a breaking event. In addition, there's a steady queue of visitors who want time with him, with which he's unfailingly generous. He meets everyone with equal attention. I'm always struck by his bright, analytic mind combined with an expansive, open heart. We cover a wide range of topics including our sons being deployed to Iraq, the state of affairs in post-Taliban Afghanistan, aikido, how to position the combatives program for the ANA, Sufi poets, and

French red wines versus California reds. I'll stay with the VIP group at the beginning (they'll be in country for only a few days) and then I'll move throughout the country with a military escort. I'll contact as many American trainers as possible, observe the Afghan soldiers going through their exercises, and speak with Afghan leaders to pitch the idea of a combatives program.

Travel fatigue sets in and General Jones hands me a set of headphones that dull the roar of the huge engines, and as I go to the rear of the transport with a blanket to lie down, someone takes my seat and immediately engages him; the queue to speak to him never seems to get any shorter. He goes long and hard hours and his staff jokes about how everyone seems to get tired except him.

After an eighty-mile-an-hour ride dodging craters in the road, bicyclists, vendors, donkeys, pedestrians, and children playing soccer with tin cans, we arrive at ISAF Headquarters in Kabul. Lieutenant General Jean-Louis Py from France welcomes us and then turns it over to his chief of staff who outlines our stay and the protocols. Our group includes a couple of Under Secretaries of State, a retired four-star General, a former Secretary of the Navy, and an array of CEOs, presidents, and chairs of various boards with formidable credentials in the business community. They have extensive biographies following their names, which include categories like *Professional Background, Company Profile, Affiliations;* mine simply states: Dr. Richard Strozzi-Heckler, Marine Corps Martial Arts Program, United States Marine Corps. Reading from the itinerary the chief of staff says the name of each group and who's in it. I'm in a group of one under the title of "Other" and when he comes to my name he pauses, looks up at me, and simply says my name. I wonder if they think I'm CIA.

When I'm in Kabul I'm billeted at the Turkish Embassy guest quarters a few blocks from ISAF headquarters. I'm in room 117 and my bunker (if we're mortared or come under attack) is Bunker 1, Container 5. This is a large, three-sided concrete block, side by side with other large concrete blocks. The adult, war version of Legos, except gray and dense. In the bunker, it's like a sauna with all of us packed in with our body armor and helmets, but infinitely more attractive than standing in the open while mortars fall from the sky.

The Turkish Embassy covers about three acres in the center of Kabul. King Zahir Shah gave this site to Turkey early in the twentieth century after Afghanistan gained full independence from Britain. It has well-tended gardens, a small stable, a kennel inhabited by three German shepherds, and a newly built, cream-colored embassy—an oasis I gratefully return to when I'm in Kabul. The new embassy building stands out not only because it's a color other than brown, but because it's unmarked by bullet holes or bombing. In my time in country I never saw a building built before 2001 that didn't show some signs of war. Many were simply cavernous shells where a bombardment turned everything into a heap of rubble, with lines of pockmarks left on walls by the rounds from a Kalashnikov.

When I ask the staff if I could use the gardens in the morning to work out, they tell me not to start before 5:30 a.m. Responding to my quizzical look, they inform me that they let the German shepherds out at night to patrol the grounds and they aren't returned to the kennel until then. The next morning I slowly peek out my door and cautiously inch my way into the gardens. Peering around the corner of the guesthouse, I see someone in running shoes and shorts briskly walking toward me. This turns out to be Minister Hikmet Cetin, the Senior Civilian Representative for NATO, with whom I spoke the day before. He's a small, tidy man with an inquisitive intellect who is universally well regarded by all elements in the current military and political arenas. He's been in this position almost a year and he's positive about the changes he sees in the country since the U.S.-led coalition forces regained it from the Taliban.

We talk about the SACEUR's vision of a combatives/leadership program for the ANA and he asks how MCMAP has impacted the Marine

Corps. I relate a story that happened to me nine months prior. I was on a plane flying from Portland to San Francisco and I sat next to a young man and woman. The man was on his way to recruit training in San Diego and the woman was a Marine stationed at Camp Pendleton. We small-talked for a while; I told them I was a former Marine and my oldest son was currently in the Marines and we spoke about deployments to Iraq and Afghanistan. When I asked them why they had joined the Marine Corps, the young man said he had a favorite uncle who was a Marine and he recommended he enlist and added, "And, I'm really jazzed about the Marine Martial Arts!" This lit up the other Marine and she said it was the reason she joined also. "Our CO is into it and we practice as a company three times a week. I have my green belt," she said proudly. I then told them that I had assisted the Commandant in designing and implementing the program. There was a long silence as they looked down at their hands and then looked up again and said, "Yes sir," but their eyes said, "Old man, that's a bunch of B.S. How do you expect me to believe that?"

Minister Cetin, who's seven years older than I am, laughed appreciatively. "Ah youth!" he replied. He noted that if the Marine Martial Arts is this compelling to these young people, it says a lot for the power of it in building esprit, plus the added benefit of attracting them to join the Marine Corps. "I think this would be good for the ANA and the country," he beams in his characteristically positive way.

In the time I spent in country in 2004 and 2006, I consistently received this kind of positive response. The exceptions were those officers in the American military that trained the ANA. They thought it was a good idea, but were concerned about how to fit a program of this sort into the training regimen of the Army. Their mission was to create a standing army of 70,000 in less than two years and they felt the very real pressures of this task. To allocate additional time to train in a martial art raised the eyebrows of these soldiers and Marines. They were facing tremendous challenges in building a new military and police force from the ground up and, while they were supportive of the concept, they would shake their heads in exasperation thinking about how to find the time and space to put it into the curriculum.

One afternoon I visited with Marine Colonel Reggie Smith (all the names of the military have been changed in these chapters) at his office inside the U.S. Military Command. Colonel Smith is a genial, gregarious man who has a ready smile and his handshake swallowed mine. He's in charge of operations for training the ANA. As he led me into his office he studied me, which consisted of mostly looking down at me as he was easily a foot taller and weighed at least fifty pounds more. I've become accustomed to this kind of scrutiny from practitioners of the martial arts, especially in the military. It's like going through a scanner at the airport, subtle yet very thorough.

Colonel Smith immediately spoke of his friendship and respect for Colonel George Bristol. (This is his true name and I give it here because Colonel Bristol is now retired and it's important to fully credit him for his invaluable efforts in designing, creating, and assuring sustainability for MCMAP.) Colonel Bristol is a lifelong, highly skilled martial artist with advanced ranks in a number of arts and whose skills have been tested in competitions, street fights, and hand-to-hand combat in war zones and covert operations. During the initial phases of MCMAP as Colonel Bristol and his team trained a company of Marines, my team trained a platoon. While we had a slightly different approach we agreed to disagree and would often violently agree. He's an honest, direct, modest man who would sometimes begin his conversations with, "I know you don't think much of me Dr. Strozzi-Heckler ... but," and then he would launch into the conversation. This always perplexed me as I have a great deal of respect for him. In short, Colonel Bristol is a primary force in the success of MCMAP and whenever I run into someone who knows him, like Colonel Smith, they inevitably speak of him with respect and admiration.

As Colonel Smith spoke about his positive regard for MCMAP and

Colonel Bristol, he began to rub his shoulder, "I tore a rotator cuff practicing one of the moves with George. He had me in a pin and I thought I could muscle my way out of it because of my size, but he just held steady and the shoulder gave. He felt bad about it, but I actually did it to myself by struggling against him. He's a good man and a good Marine."

"Sounds like the Marine thing to do, never quit," I chided.

He laughed, "It's OK for you to say that since you're a former Marine. I had it operated on and it's almost 100% now. Pretty soon I'm going to get back on the mat and earn my next belt."

We turned the conversation toward a combatives program for the ANA and what it would mean for Afghanistan. I told him that I thought that a martial arts component of the ANA training regime would further the goals of national security as well as build a corruption-free Army that could reflect the traditional standards of the Afghan people. The ethical and moral standards embodied by the ANA, I suggested, will be critical in building trust of the Afghan government by its population. Furthermore, a Martial Arts Program will advance the identity of the ANA as a unifying symbol of the nation of Afghanistan.

My position was that the Afghan National Army Martial Arts Program (ANAMAP) would create:

- An effective non-lethal combat skill for all soldiers (for crowd control, prison riots, prisoner restraint, hand-to-hand combat),
- A platform from which Afghan instructors would teach and reinforce time-honored Afghan values,
- Increased discipline,
- Increased confidence,
- Increased morale and unit pride,
- Increased physical fitness, and
- Increased commitment to the mission of the ANA.

I told Colonel Smith that, judging from my visits to the ANA's training sites, the American soldiers who trained the Afghanis thought a combatives program like this would be a valuable addition to what they were already doing. They would all inevitably add that wrestling was a national pastime and how in their free time the Afghan soldiers would wrestle with each other, indicating it would be a good fit. When I observed the Afghanis in their training, from small-unit tactics, close-order drills, mortar teams, and marksmanship to learning the elements of firing rocket-propelled grenades, they were attentive and respectful of their American teachers. Because literacy in the Afghan Army is less than thirty percent (an accurate reflection of the general population of the country), all teaching has to be oral; there's no relying on papers or written documents. This slows the teaching down, but it seems to focus the students since there's nothing they can review later. I also noticed that when they had free time they would begin to wrestle with each other in a stylized way and practice big roundhouse kicks. This is similar to young men throughout the world; give them some unstructured time and they'll begin sparring with each other, all in a good mood and at the same time testing themselves. In other words, it's a no-brainer. Martial arts, plus testosterone, plus discipline and a good dose of values as part of the training and you have a sure winner.

Colonel Smith folded his tree-trunk arms over his chest and leaned back in his chair. Knowing the value of MCMAP and understanding how a combatives program of this scope could be beneficial to the ANA, he easily agreed with me. As the person in charge of keeping the ANA training schedule on track, however, he was in a quandary.

"Yes sir, I understand your point and I'm of the same mind as you, but where in the hell am I going to put it in?" His staff shifted in their seats and we all looked at each other.

I told him I didn't know but suggested we take a look at the program of instruction as it now stood and I was sure we could invent something together. Colonel Smith stared at me. The muscles in his jaws rippled like waves in the sea.

We both knew that it wasn't his decision if this program were to happen or not and that it would be somebody up the food chain who would give it a green light if it were going to become a reality. I couldn't tell if he welcomed the challenge or was hoping that by the time this had traction he would be finished with his tour. All the American personnel in charge of training the Army or Police reflected the same dilemma—there was clearly value in the proposition, but where to fit it in the training schedule? When I suggested it become part of their physical training time, they gnashed their teeth and made groaning sounds. They all thought it was a terrific idea, but the training curriculum was so full it made them delirious to think about it.

As I left Colonel Smith's office, I thought back to the Trojan Warrior Project over twenty years ago when the cost of traditional warrior values being crowded out by technology, mass marketing, and an impersonal bureaucracy was at the forefront of our conversations. As I turned to shake Smith's hand I saw in him the personification of the dynamic between the values of the warrior—selfless service, integrity, courage, honor, commitment—and the grinding forces of history. It was as if I had returned to where I started a generation ago and for a moment I felt without bearings. His grip brought me back to the moment and I remembered that through the struggle of the complexity and paradoxes of our lives, we discover the values we choose to live by.

I sit up on one elbow and peer into the darkness. A dog barks in the distance. A truck downshifts and growls off into the night. I'm dreaming of bobbing in huge waves in an endless sea when the sound of Kalashnikov gunfire wakes me. I sit up and listen into the thick heat. The chatter of the Kalashnikov and return fire from an M-16 breaks the silence again. A running gun battle is moving down range. There is movement around the compound and I hear the sound of disembodied voices crackling through hand held radios. In my grogginess, I'm reminded that this is a theater of war and I locate my body armor and remember the location of my bunker. My watch says 2:30 and it must be around 95 degrees. I reach for my water bottle and empty it in one drink. I'm fully awake now and write in my journal and then meditate. I can't tell if I'm exhausted or on full throttle, but when I close my eyes I'm instantly asleep until I jerk awake sweating with the sun full in my room.

Colonel Mark McKenzie, one of my escorts, meets me in the compound with Lieutenant Dofer, and our driver, Specialist Merkle. We'll head west in a two-vehicle convoy in the direction of Bamiyan to a joint American-Canadian base. Bamiyan was the home of the colossal statues of the two-hundred-foot-tall Buddhas that were dynamited and destroyed by the Taliban. At one time Afghanistan was the meeting place of Buddhism and the culture of Alexander's Greece, and an artistic style known as Gandharan distinctively influenced the portrayal of the Buddha. Over two hundred feet tall and at an altitude of eight thousand feet, these Buddhas had stood for over fourteen hundred years marking what was once the frontier of the Buddhist world. The loss of these great statues is a tragedy beyond knowing and the Taliban wreaked their destruction in the face of protests from all quarters. An international team is now doing what it can to safeguard and document what is left.

Colonel McKenzie is a career Marine who wears a green t-shirt when he's off duty that reads, "I Bleed Green." His stocky, well-muscled frame and cauliflower ear reflect his time as a champion college wrestler at Virginia Military Institute and University of Washington. Even though ISAF discourages running in Kabul because of the high fecal- matter count in the air, he runs for his PT. He tells me his next posting will be Iraq where he'll be a Battalion Commander and if he had his say about it, he would be there now. He's definitely a hard charger with a sharp intellect and a broad curiosity about many subjects, among them Afghan history and their language Dari, which is similar to Farsi or Persian. We have long conversations about the Martial Arts Program and like everyone he fully endorses it with, "And they really have a packed schedule as it is."

Dofer is an Army Lieutenant who went to Officer Candidate School after serving as a Sergeant. He is an able soldier. He's engaged in investment properties in the Midwest and he's always eager to share his investment strategies. Specialist Merkle is from New Jersey and he enlisted in the Army to get out of trouble with the law. When I ask him about what kind of trouble, he changes the subject. He tells me he's getting his college degree online and that ultimately he wants to be a policeman. I remark that there's something ironic about him becoming a policeman after his brush with the law and he immediately falls back into his blank expression. He reveals that American literature is one of the subjects he's studying and when I express an interest he replies, "We're reading short stories now and I just don't get it. All of a sudden they just end!" and he throws up his hands in exasperation. When I ask him what he thinks a good ending would be, he looks at me suspiciously. The conversation turns to the Martial Arts Program for the Afghanis and he says, "Hell yeah sir, I'd love to do that. I did Tae Kwon Do for a while and there's a couple of heads I'd love to bust."

We receive the usual convoy briefing: route, alternate routes, who does what in case we're attacked, radio channels, codes. I put on my flak jacket, pick up the MP-5 weapon I was offered, and head toward the vehicles when an Afghani with a white beard and wearing a long *shalwar kemis* shirt, baggy trousers, a Chitrali cap, and a brown *patu* blanket under his arm stops in front of Colonel McKenzie with his right hand to his chest and says, "*Salaam aleikum. Chetor hastid? Jan-e-shoma jur ast? Khub hastid? Sahat-e-shoma kub ast? Be khair hastid? Jur hastid? Khane kheirat ast? Zinde bashe.*" Which in Dari means, Peace be with you. How are you? Is your soul healthy? Are you well? Are you healthy? Are you fine? Is your family flourishing? Or, "Hello." It's a standard greeting and with two natives speakers it sounds like a call-and-response chant.

Colonel Mc Kenzie replies slowly in Dari and the old man smiles. His face looks like a dried-up riverbed. His steady, dark eyes shine like onyx under his thick gray eyebrows. He introduces himself as Seyyed Umar, emphasizing the title *Seyyed*, meaning descendant of the Prophet Muhammed. He easily looks like he could be in his late seventies but is probably more like fifty—about the average life span in Afghanistan, which has the highest childhood mortality rate in the world. Speaking with Seyyed Umar reminded me of the great esoteric spiritual traditions that come from this part of the world, Sufism being one of them. Gurdjieff, the Russian mystic, reputedly studied with the spiritual masters throughout central Asia, including Afghanistan, and brought back their teachings to the West. Perhaps this old man is one of the inheritors of this tradition, or a Taliban sympathizer, or a terrorist, or a simple farmer.

I say, "*Dast ba dar, Del ba yar,*" which translates "Hands in your work, your Heart with God" in Farsi. He looks at me curiously and then his face opens into a wide toothless grin. "*Salaam aleikum, besar khub,*" he replies. This is a quote from a poem by Jelaluddin Rumi, a thirteenth-century Persian poet and mystic whose followers founded the whirling dervishes. Three decades ago I had a fellowship to study Farsi and was fortunate enough to have a professor who pointed me to the great Persian mystics and poets, and I've kept my hand in it ever since. Because Dari is similar enough to Farsi, I could make myself somewhat understandable and I could catch the drift of simple conversations.

There are members of the U.S. military, like Colonel McKenzie, who have made personal efforts to learn the language and customs of Afghanistan. And like Colonel McKenzie, they make sincere efforts to communicate with the people in their own language. It's a simple act, but it has a profound effect. In a country that has endured centuries of foreign invaders, they are naturally suspicious and cynical. Afghanistan has a rural population who simply want to get on with their lives; when they encounter foreign troops, their questions begin: "How long will you be here?" "Will you fix my road?" "Will you help me dig a well?" They're accustomed to dynasties and nations invading, fighting, and then departing. After a while they start to blend together. An example: A senior military officer was flying by helicopter when he received small arms fire from the ground. Looking down he saw a goatherd shooting at the helicopter. The officer told the pilot to land and he got out with his security team surrounding him and asked this goatherd why he was shooting at him. "Because in the nineteen-eighties you killed my family and it's now my responsibility to kill you," he answered. Incredulous, the officer explained to him that was the Russians, and we're Americans.

"What's that?" the goatherd asked.

There have been so many different invaders and colonialists traipsing through Afghanistan over the centuries, to say nothing of the last three decades, that they begin to meld into a single, impersonal face. Inside of this ongoing invasion of competing interests, it's extraordinarily powerful when someone like Colonel McKenzie makes an attempt to speak their language and is genuinely interested in who they are and in their customs and history. Our troops are woefully unprepared to the do this. They're usually given a one-page cheat sheet of common terms without any instructions in how or why to implement them. It would be a powerful experience for American servicemen and servicewomen to have a fuller experience and an appreciation of a different culture and its language; and it would only increase their military effectiveness. "Know your enemy," Sun Tzu said in the *The Art of War*.

As our small convoy leaves the city, I can see the hills that house Emperor Babur's tomb. His grave lies below a dark mountain on a wide terrace. Beside it are the splintered stumps of two large plane trees, which may be the very same trees Babur describes planting in his journal when he was nearly forty years old. Babur was the first Emperor of Mughal India. He was born in 1483 as the prince of an isolated kingdom in a destitute part of Uzbekistan. Before he reached his twenties he had lost all his land, but by the time he was twenty-two he and his loyal followers conquered Kabul. The same year he visited Herat, the most civilized city in the Islamic world at that time. Soon after he pushed east to conquer Delhi and found the Moghul dynasty.

He was a direct descendant of Genghis Khan and when he died, he was the ruler of one of the largest and wealthiest empires in the known world. The tomb and adjoining mosque of this once all-powerful ruler are now derelict: crumbling plaster, rotting floors, walls disfigured from bullet and mortar shells. Surely a testimony of impermanence that invokes the question of what are we really fighting for. "The earth in all its bounty and beauty" is my prayer.

Suddenly, I'm jarred out of my reverie by Colonel McKenzie shouting, "Don't let him block you! Go around him! Go around." I look ahead and there's a large, dilapidated truck slowly turning in front of us. In an instant a scene plays out in my mind of this truck blocking our forward progress, an unseen truck blocking us from behind, and suddenly we're in the middle of a ferocious gun battle. We're heading straight for the side of the truck at seventy miles an hour. I brace myself for the impact. We're on a narrow, pitted, two-lane dirt road with vendor's stalls, people, and donkey-drawn carts lining both sides of the road a few feet away from our vehicle. They become a blur of brown, and somewhere in the background is the incessant sound of the horn as Merkle bears down on the accelerator and begins to curve to the right to go around the now-stopped truck. I think I hear people screaming, but it may be me or all of us collectively inside the SUV. I see snatches of startled faces outside the window and hear the bump of us hitting something and through the rearview mirror I see a wooden and cloth stall collapsing.

Suddenly we're past the truck and everything is quiet, no horn and no voices, only the sound of the tires bumping over the ubiquitous holes in the road. I look back and see Afghanis angrily waving their fists and mouthing blasphemies I cannot hear. McKenzie asks if we hit anyone.

"Good job," I say to Merkle. He stares straight ahead, his mouth a tight line. He navigates the crowded streets and potholes at high speed. I can now feel my pulse pounding from my gut to the top of my head, and my mind begins to fill with chatter after being so quiet and so still, so nothing, during the last fifteen seconds of a lifetime. No one says anything for a long time.

In Afghanistan, as well as in Iraq, if you hit someone or do significant property damage with your vehicle you never stop. Never. To stop means risking your life: a sniper's bullet, a mortar, a rocket-propelled grenade, an IED, or an angry, anti-Western crowd armed with clubs and knives. This is not to say there wouldn't be sympathetic Afghanis who in the Islamic custom would unhesitatingly take you into their homes. But what you're trained to do is throw out a damage-claim form that one could fill out and demand compensation. Just after I left the country, an Army truck hit and killed a pedestrian and was attacked by an angry mob. It was only with the help of support troops that they made it back to their base without causing a major international incident.

The soldiers, Marines, airman, and sailors I've met here are sincere and believe in the mission. While there's a possibility to start a combat-ives/leadership program to strengthen the ANA and the country, the majority of the Afghan soldiers I spoke to were rural villagers (Afghanistan is ninety percent rural agriculture), and had never traveled thirty kilometers from their homes. They were illiterate, lived without electricity, and knew very little of the outside world. Differences between groups were deep, long standing, and elusive. Some had suffered under the Taliban, some had prospered under them, and most had unhesitatingly subjugated other ethnic groups to violence and abuse. One clan chieftain I met disagreed with the Taliban only on the issue of furniture; he wanted to sit in a chair, they required him sit on the floor. This seemed insignificant, but sufficient for him to give intelligence to the coalition forces. Fiber optics, gender tolerance, a democratic civil process, and urban design were foreign ideas and hard to sell; yet a martial arts program seemed to ignite everyone's interest. Is this the media influence with black market Bruce Lee and Steven Segal DVDs, or a deep-seated response in all humans for self-mastery and the traditional, time-honored virtues of the warrior? My intuition still signals a green light and I'm moving with a full commitment with General Jones's backing to make it happen.

Throwing a claim form out a window after hitting someone with your car seemed a great moral distance from building friendships and a combatives/leadership program. Over 500 years ago Emperor Babur passed through here with his medieval version of rampage all the way to India. As I deliberate over the repetitive nature of history, our interpreter points out a house that Osama bin Laden's third wife lived in. A cottage industry, I think, guided tours to houses of famous people in Kabul, just like in Beverly Hills . . . almost.

This year is the twenty-year anniversary of the Trojan Warrior Project, which the reader will remember this book is based upon. During this time I've kept in contact with many of the participants, and Larry Burback and I have speculated about a twenty-year reunion. James Braddock lost a leg in Somalia (see the book and movie *Blackhawk Down*), he retired as a Sergeant Major and now works for a company that makes prosthesis; I wrote a recommendation for Matt Reardon to attend graduate school and he's now a successful CEO with four children; he was called up for the Gulf War and finished a successful deployment to Iraq healthy and sound. He's visited me in California and we speak once a year; I heard that Jim Oreson joined the Secret Service after completing his enlistment; Gil Galt earned the Medal of Honor posthumously in Somalia; Phil Dunham served in the first Gulf War and it was reported that he assaulted an officer who he felt was without integrity and after the incident was discharged from the Army; Victor Mattelli disappeared into the ether with rumors that he joined the French Foreign Legion; Larry Janowski finished out his career as the head of a ROTC unit at the University of Nebraska; Tom James retired as a Sergeant Major and lives in the Washington, DC/Northern Virginia area; Bruce Radar has his own consulting company and he's visited when he's out in the Bay Area for business; I spoke with Larry Farley and pointed him to a contracting job that took him to the Middle East; I heard Steve Parker has a restaurant in Los Angeles; I spoke to Dan Johnson and he has his own landscaping business in Georgia; Ken Getty retired as a full Colonel and works inside the beltway for the government; Captain Thorne is now a flag officer.

The rest I've not seen or heard from, except Ray Martin. Ray and I have kept in continuous contact thanks to his efforts. Every two or three months, he consistently e-mails succinct messages of his mood and whereabouts. For example: "This place is filled with yuppies who I can handle except for the spoiled brats at the school. Don't know how much longer I can stay where I am. My health has come back strong. How's the family?" I was a reference for his admission to graduate school, where he earned an advanced degree, and he also joined AA and beat his alcohol addiction, which had gone untreated for years. After a stint teaching at a private school, Ray decided it was not the life for him and he joined a private security contracting firm and works in the Middle East and Afghanistan. He was stationed in Kabul while I was on this trip and we made plans to get together.

We met outside the entrance of the ISAF headquarters in Kabul. He didn't have the clearance to come inside the wire so we talked under a single halogen bulb with a .50 caliber machine gunner looking down at us from a guard tower. He was vintage Martin—quick-witted, ironic, sarcastic, chain smoking, and constantly looking over his shoulder. He arrived in the customary SUV with two bodyguards who worked for him and could have been his sons. They stepped out of the vehicle and without a word fanned out into a perimeter with their automatic weapons. I was so happy to see him that I bypassed his outstretched hand and gave him a big bear hug. A moment of pleasure showed through his awkwardness though he checked the reactions of his security detail. Martin has lived in a decidedly male culture his entire life that still looks suspiciously at men sharing a moment of non-sexual, genuine affection. Seemingly from this moment of self-consciousness he apologized that he was bit overweight and still smoked, ". . . though it's been years since I've had a drink." He immediately launched into his political opinions, which ranged from "How are the idiots that got us into Iraq going to get us out?" to his new boss being so incompetent that he has to monitor him closely or he'll "get a bunch of people killed." When I asked him how he liked it here, he replied that he had met someone interesting from the State Department at the U.S. Embassy.

As we catch up on our lives and the people from the Trojan Warrior Project, the two security men slowly come out of the dark and join us around the edges. There's a mood of camaraderie and pride between Ray and me at having been at the beginning of a bold and innovative experiment that continues to have a positive effect to this day on both the military and civilian population. I believe the men felt this and at one point one of them said he had read the book and found it interesting. When I asked him what "interesting" meant he replied that the methods used, however simple, had such a positive effect on the soldiers' performance.

"Yeah, it wasn't so interesting doing Larry's (Larry Burback) PT program." Ray snorted. And then he went into a quick litany about the positive changes that happened for everyone, even those who resisted the entire time. It was a classic Ray Martin move, cynicism quickly followed by the affirmative. Ray's IQ is pushing 200 but his EQ is just getting off the ground. He's bright and very intuitive, but a history of defenses guard against a deeper closeness. I've come to appreciate and respect Ray and it's very fulfilling to finally see him after all these years of electronic correspondence. There's not much I wouldn't do for him.

I'm soaking in the irony of our meeting in Kabul after twenty years when I'm suddenly struck by the image of two elders speaking over a campfire and the younger members crowding in to hear what they're saying. It's a new moon and outside the pool of light from the overhead bulb it's dark, and there's danger out there. We're all leaning in together and for a moment no one speaks and there's only the buzz of the cicadas.

"Gotta go." Rays says abruptly, throws his cigarette into the dirt, and gives me a short, but heartfelt hug. "Watch your six," he adds.

"*Vi Cit Tecum,*" I say. The motto of the Trojan Warrior Project: May the Force Be with You.

His bodyguards look at me quizzically.

"He'll explain," I say.

Colonel McKenzie and Captain Freeman invite me to a dinner their interpreters (they're called terps in Militarese) are having for them at their house. It turns out that Captain Freeman and I met in the late eighties when he was in a program designed for selected enlisted personnel to become officers at the Marine Corps Recruit Depot in San Diego, California. I helped start an aikido dojo on base for these officer candidates with Bob Burns, a former Marine. Freeman was part of the program. He had trained with me at that time and when Colonel McKenzie introduced us he remembered our meeting. He told me he was now training in MCMAP when he could, but his deployment schedule made it difficult to continue in aikido. When I asked him what stayed with him about his aikido training, he replied, "This idea of using the attacker's energy to disarm him is very interesting, and effective too. The blending practices are powerful, but difficult to pull off, but when you do, it works, it's practical." He reflected momentarily on what he just said, and looking at McKenzie, chuckled and said, "It's also useful to have an M-16 if things get nasty."

He was refreshingly unperfumed in his directness as Marines tend to be, but I read a subtext behind what he said that was not unfamiliar to me. When Freeman spoke positively about blending, I sensed a moment of self-consciousness pass over him. Perhaps being in front of McKenzie that made him concerned about appearing too "soft"; perhaps he felt he might have been sending me the wrong message. In other words he felt he had to annotate what he said about the power of blending in case he might appear outside the norm. This brings to mind that qualifying something of value to maintain one's status is a fundamental way to limit innovation and transformation. This ego fortification is pervasive and it plays in every domain: military, business, education, health, politics, family, etc. What is being defended is not only the ego or perceived identity, but a worldview. When this worldview is challenged, the self feels challenged. If the change is extreme enough the self often experiences itself as dying, so it fights for its survival. Fighting for an old, outdated structure constricts curiosity and openness, fundamental principles for building relationships and discovering new solutions to old problems.

While curiosity and openness are not historically supported in military education, they are now more critical than ever as we move into a new phase of war fighting. We have seen the end of large-scale set battles and are now fighting an adversary that doesn't represent a nation state or a set geographical location, but operates in a 360-degree battlefield. A curiosity and openness about the underlying influences of this conflict are basic to understanding how to resolve the conflict before triggers are pulled and innocent people are killed. In my recent work with Special Forces in counterinsurgency, it has become increasingly clear that building and sustaining relationships with diverse ethnic and religious groups is essential for our success. Besides, I believe that from a somatic point of view this notion of blending builds a deep listening in the conversational space—a listening necessary for talking to those who live in religions, cultures, and languages different than our own. A tribal chieftain in the mountains here told me that when coalition forces visit him (or anyone for that matter), what he primarily listens to is their "air." By this he meant their energy, mood, and presence, even more than their content. It's this kind of listening that we need to build in our military, especially civil affairs units that meet with foreign nationals to help them rebuild their communities and relationships with the West.

McKenzie and Freeman dress in civilian clothes but wear flak jackets and carry sidearms. They look like civilians, but not really, especially since the high and tight Marine haircuts give them away. We drive through crowded narrow streets to endless blocks of Soviet-era-gray cement apartment houses. We could be in parts of the Bronx except bullet holes and mortar shells scar every building. At seven in the evening the heat is still oppressive but has little effect on the energy of the innumerable children playing in the littered lots. When they see us they all rush over and McKenzie and Freeman hand out candy and try out their Dari to the delight of the children. Many of these kids are missing arms or legs and I notice one who is blind, his face covered with jagged scars. A sad reminder of the costs of modern warfare: children as victims and more non-combatants killed than combatants. Handing out candy and speaking my clumsy Farsi seem an insignificant gesture to these children growing up without a childhood. Hamid, one of the terps, appears and shoos the children away and leads us up three flights of stairs in a crumbling apartment building. The stairwells are dark, and the smell of urine and fried food fills the halls.

Hamid bangs on a door and Hoshin, another terp, welcomes us warmly into an entirely different reality. A new, red Bokhara rug covers the entire floor; another stunning rug hangs from one of the walls, bright handmade pillows and cushions line the sides of the room, and there's a forty-inch flat screen TV mounted on the wall. Leaning against the walls are three AK47s and a single RPG; the smell of cooking food and incense fills the apartment. The other terps emerge, five in all, and there is a festive mood as they greet us. The customary tea, pistachios, almonds, and raisins are brought out and they insist, to our objections, that they show us a DVD. It's their way of demonstrating the highest form of hospitality even though we object and have no interest. "We have American movies!" they shout and wave off our protests.

There's an obvious respect and warm-heartedness that the terps have towards McKenzie and Freeman and their conversations are far ranging, including social life, families, politics, as well as professional interactions. They're interested in what I'm doing and I demonstrate an aikido blending movement with one of them and it brings murmurs of curiosity and laughter as they excitedly speak to each other in Dari. They fully support a program of this sort being brought to the Army and volunteer to interpret for it. I once had a terp who dressed like Don Johnson in *Miami Vice* and he began every sentence with motherfucker, dawg, or yo bitch—the MTV School of Interpreters. Apparently he had learned English mainly by watching TV, and while he was enterprising and did a good job, he had no idea what he was saying and it was very difficult explaining it to him. These men are well educated and a number of them have spent time in the U.S. Their translations are precise and they use us to continue their education by asking the exact meaning of words and idioms.

A large plate of lamb, goat, rice, and vegetables is brought in and we sit on the rug and eat with our right hand only. At the end of the meal they bring out a pitcher of water and pour it over our hands and we wash and dry them. Weathered, handmade stringed instruments, drums, and a tambourine are brought out and they spontaneously begin to sing an ancient love song between a village boy and girl. I'm told the song is over five hundred years old, and their voices and musical accompaniment transport me to a different time and place. I'm reveling in being witness to an old, deeply wrought culture when I notice that all the Afghani's heads are turned toward the TV as they sing and play the instruments. Captain Freeman's mouth is open in shock and when I turn around to see what they're looking at, Sharon Stone is doing Michael Douglas in the movie *Basic Instinct*. McKenzie, Freeman, and I look at each other incredulously while the others continue their performance still watching the movie. They have no pretense about what they're doing or awareness of the paradox we are living in at the moment. They make comments in Dari and then laugh between their refrains.

I feel suspended between intersecting worlds but cannot make sense of how to navigate through them. When we try to explain that this is not our way of life but a Hollywood version, one of them says, "Yes, but she has such pretty legs" and then something in Dari at which they all howl with laughter and shake their heads approvingly. I look at the screen, yes, she does have nice legs, but I don't want to think about this now. In the moment, I see how we are all becoming trapped in this web we call globalization. We tell them how much we respect their rituals and in some ways are even envious of the depth of their traditions. I say how these traditions and rituals are important for me to know in order to successfully design a program for their Army. Furthermore, I tell them that watching American DVDs is not interesting to me. They nod and light up another cigarette. The images on the screen are more mundane now, a conversation taking place in an office, and they turn away and resume singing and playing.

When we leave, the children charge us like we're magnets, their hands outstretched. "Candy, cigarettes," they shout. Colonel McKenzie tells a boy with one arm he shouldn't smoke, it isn't good for him. The heat is thick and dominating, but it doesn't seem to affect them. As I put candy in the hands of these children I wonder if someday they'll be learning martial arts as a traditional warrior value. I wonder if they think that we live like the lives portrayed in the black market DVDs sold in the markets. I wonder deeply about how to cross the cultural divide in instigating such a program for the ANA.

The C-17 I'm traveling on back to Europe stops at the U.S. base in Uzbekistan to pick up more passengers and it's discovered that we need to replace a part so I take a helicopter into the desert with a small Special Forces contingent. We put down, the helo leaves, and they rig up some electronic equipment. The heat is unrelenting and condemning; the moment I drink water, it feels as if it's instantly being pulled out of my body. This is a desolate piece of land and from the helo we didn't see any sign of life for miles. There's no shade and we huddle under a makeshift tent made of camouflage nylon. A brief sandstorm comes in and we hunker down and as it clears we see a figure walking out of the haze. They tell the person to halt and get on the radio to see if there's been any report of people in the area. Negative. As the sand begins to settle, we see it's a female. She's not wearing a *burka*, the head-to-feet blue covering traditional to Afghani women, but a scarf over her head and in front of her face. They ask her to open her shawl to show she's not carrying any explosives and I'm acutely aware that we're in her neighborhood. Yes, unlike our neighborhoods at home, but it's her turf and she's comfortable in it and knows her way around. She could be a Taliban spy setting up an ambush. She says she's looking for a lost goat and asks if we have any water.

She's called in and told to move slowly; weapons are pointed in her direction and the men form a perimeter in which they look in all directions. When she enters our circle the soldiers look through her meager possessions; she's given a bottle of water and then walks abruptly up to me, takes a lined piece of paper out of a cloth bag, and puts it in front of my face.

"What do these words mean?" she demands in broken English.

There are two lines of words printed in pencil in a child-like hand, ten words in a line. "Indignant," "savory," "tension," and "verdant" are some of the words. How do you describe *verdant* in this environment? She looks at me intently as I attempt to describe the meaning of the words; if I look at her too long, she drops her gaze and brings her scarf up. Her face is a bronze shield with the high cheekbones and dark, slanted eyes of a Genghis Khan, her emerald green eyes from Alexander the Great.

"How would you use that in a sentence?" she asks occasionally. She's serious about learning and the initial amusement of the soldiers drops away. They pipe in when I stall or when they think there's a better description than mine.

"What languages do you speak?" I ask.

"Uzbek, Russian, and some Pashtun."

"Why do you want to learn English?"

"I want to go to school in America," she says, her eyes dark, fierce.

"Where do you want to go to school?"

"U.C. Santa Cruz."

I look at the soldier next to me and our eyes say, "Holy Shit!" How do I explain this back home? I look around; rock, sand, brown hills shimmer in the menacing heat. Overhead the sky is a cerulean dome marked with a distant vapor trail. For a brief moment I wonder if I'm on Candid Camera. I tell her that I know where Santa Cruz is and that my brother-in-law went there and at one time I lived in the San Lorenzo Valley near Santa Cruz and that it's in California where I live, blah blah blah. I notice that her eyes have glazed over and none of this has any meaning for her at all.

"What do you want to study?"

"Interior design."

"Interior design," I say to myself, glancing at the soldier. He's looking at the ground, expressionless. I look out over the khaki-colored hills. Ninety percent of the houses in the country are made of mud with dirt floors. Shale, dirt, scree spread across the empty, hard pan.

The Uzbek Martha Stewart? I want to laugh out loud, not because I doubt her, but because it's so surreal, and I can imagine it.

As she leaves, we watch her become smaller and smaller and finally a speck swallowed up by the gloaming. In her bag were her English words, some new ones I wrote down, two water bottles we gave her, an MRE (MREs are Meals Ready to Eat, standard fare for U.S. military; her meal was pasta Bolognese), but no goat. I gave her my card and told her to call me when she's in Santa Cruz. I have no doubt she'll be there someday if the commitment I saw in her eyes means anything.

A close encounter with globalization. Who knows how she got these ideas; the Internet, a U.S. serviceperson, magazines thrown away at bases? But it does point to a flow of information that cannot be underestimated in its scope and power. Information operations, or strategic communication as it is referred to in the military, is birthing a brand new warrior. This military warrior shapes public opinion and builds relationships with civilian populations in order to gain trust and acceptance. They may not be extraordinarily physically fit or sharpshooters, but their role is becoming increasingly important. Their battlefield is both virtual and face-to-face contact with those of different cultures and belief systems. Their weapons are computers instead of rifles and they need to be disciplined mentally, emotionally, and culturally. Brainpower and sophisticated technical skills are the requirements of their trade. This is the new face of winning hearts and minds.

When our Uzbek friend approached out of the sandstorm, these soldiers had to make a split-second decision. More than any other time since Vietnam, the military needs quick thinking, highly disciplined, emotionally mature soldiers. Combat zones are more gray than black-and-white. Inside of hostile territory, they must synthesize more information than any American fighters before them, integrating tactical awareness, cultural sensibilities, and an appreciation for the strategic implications of their actions. In addition, a TV camera could be placed in front of them at a moment's notice and they'll be asked to account for their actions in front of millions of people worldwide.

A combatives/leadership program for the ANA is important tactically and strategically; more significant, however, is training *our* military to develop long-term sustainable relationships, build trust with those from different cultures and belief systems, and be able to distinguish between enemy and friend—whether to shake hands or pull the trigger. It's possible to integrate this new vital skill into training regimens, but first our policymakers need to see this as a real need if America is to fulfill her moral and spiritual mission in the twenty-first century.

Landing in Europe I'm met by a NATO escort and taken to a remote military airbase outside Brussels to debrief General Jones on my trip. He had just returned from a trip to Poland and was about to fly off again, his jet standing ready on the tarmac. Despite his saturated schedule and the amount of responsibility he holds, I'm again struck by how present he is and how his level of vitality remains high. His staff included a number of those who were on the Afghanistan trip and we had a brief but warm reunion. There is the glue factor of camaraderie that is formed when traveling together in foreign and dangerous environments. They were genuinely interested in how the program progressed and they wanted to know when it would begin. It has a way to go I told them, but I was struck by their interest, especially since their plates were so filled with NATO business, and I asked them quite frankly what they thought of it and why it had stuck with them. They deferred to General Jones's enthusiasm, but when I pressed further they said they were intrigued by the notions of "combining the martial with the moral," that "leadership can be trained through the martial arts," and "it can be a powerful element of unifying the country." While learning through the body seems elementary to me, I see how novel it appears to others. I'm also heartened by how this notion of the moral and spiritual domains being intimately linked to the physical body has captured the imagination of this group.

I reported to General Jones the overall positive reception I had to a combatives program from the American side as well as the Afghans, from boots on the ground to senior officers. I told him that after meeting a number of Marines in Afghanistan who had advanced ranks in MCMAP, I thought they could form the core of the teacher cadre. His report was positive as well and he said he would get me in touch with someone at Central Command who could help ferry this forward.

Soon both of our sons would be going to Iraq and as we shook hands, with the verdant fields of Belgium around us, we did so not only professionally and as friends, but as fathers who will keep the fires burning at home while our sons serve overseas.

Nicosia, Cyprus
MidEast Aikido Project
Spring 2005

This large room was once the library of the Hotel Ledra in Nicosia, Cyprus. With me are thirty delegates from fifteen countries, primarily from the Middle East and the Mediterranean Basin. The majority of these individuals represent delegations from Israel, Palestine, Iraq, Jordan, Bosnia, Serbia, Greece, Turkey, and northern and southern Cyprus. It's hot and the overhead fan does little to circulate the air in the stuffy, overcrowded room. The Hotel Ledra was once a watering hole for Richard Burton and Elizabeth Taylor and I imagine them having a gin and tonic in this room. At that time the Ledra was a destination site for the chic and elite, but now it's like an old dowager, in disrepair but with traces of a long-ago elegance appearing through the cracked wallpaper. It now houses a battalion of United Nations security forces and will become a meeting place for our seminar. The Ledra is in the buffer zone one hundred meters off the green line that separates northern and southern Cyprus; rolls of concertina wire surround it, men with guns sit behind sandbags, and its bullet-damaged walls attest to the decades-old conflict it has witnessed, and continues to witness.

In spring of 2004, almost a year ago to the day, Don Levine who is the Peter B. Ritzma Professor of Sociology at the University of Chicago and the head of the University of Chicago Aikido Club, and I sat down and cooked up the idea of the MidEast Aikido Project. Don is also the President of Aiki Extensions, of which I'm a founding member, an organization that is dedicated to bringing the principles of aikido to areas such as education, business, government, military, youth outreach, conflict resolution, health, leadership, and so forth. Our idea was that through Aiki Extensions we would gather people together from the Middle East who are historical enemies to practice aikido. In this way we could put to the test the merits of aikido in resolving conflict, building long-term sustainable relationships, and developing an instrument of second-track diplomacy in these war-torn countries. Where would be a better place to host this than the island of Cyprus, the only divided country in Europe? When I look back to this first meeting, I laugh at how naïve and innocent we were. We joke that if we knew what we were getting into we wouldn't have started, but I think this is the case in most situations in which something new and innovative is being created.

The four-day aikido seminar, which we've called Training Across Borders, will begin in a few hours and this group is gathered for an orientation for the following days. Don and I will welcome the group, center them on the purpose of this historic seminar, and then turn it over to Philip Emminger, our third partner, who was instrumental operationally in putting all of this together, a daunting task. Despite endless setbacks, Phil successfully pulled it off.

As we move into logistics, a Palestinian man I will call Hamid (these names will again be changed to protect their identities and safety) says in a heavily accented voice, "I have something to say." He looks across the room at the Israeli delegation, straightens himself and speaks slowly, "I was raised to hate you. You've killed many of my people and for this I'm angry." No one moves, people begin to study the corners of the room and stare at their laps. The only sound is the whirring of the overhead fan; someone clears his throat.

In many ways this was the moment we were hoping for; it just came two days earlier than we thought. Because of the tension between these different groups we publicized this only as an aikido seminar, simply a martial arts training. This was true in that the quality of instruction would certainly elevate and inform their level of practice; and we didn't want to advertise it as something else because we didn't want to draw attention from radical elements. But our other agenda was to open up conversations and practices among the participants that could lead to greater understanding and good will among them. To do this we knew there would be a certain level of confrontation and this would be a good thing as it would surface the underlying issues and we could process it through aikido principles and training on the mat. Well, here it was and it felt like all the air had been suddenly squeezed out of the room.

Hamid continued, "I'm not going to say that we will be friends at the end of this seminar or that I will like you, but I do know that we have to do something different."

Silence.

"I'm sorry this happened to you," an Israeli says, "It's the same for me."

Silence.

"Then maybe we're more alike than we think. Two bald guys talking." The Israeli smiles, slowly rubbing his hand over the dark skin on the top of his head. Hamid passes his hand over his head and they begin to laugh, slowly at first, and then full throated, together, as if they were one voice. Everyone in the room smiles and laughs and lets their breathe out.

Beginning that evening and the following three days, the Training Across Borders seminar in Nicosia, Cyprus, was an unqualified success. There were one hundred participants from fifteen countries training together under four ranking aikido *senseis* (teachers); workshops on aiki-influenced areas such as leadership, communications, trauma healing, youth outreach, and education were well received; colorful buffets aside the UN headquarters in the buffer zone, a hilarious talent show, and dancing all spawned spontaneous discussions in which a greater degree of intimacy and understanding prevailed. This was the very first aikido experience for some of the participants and others had been practicing for over ten years. It took the members of the Iraq contingent almost three days to get to Cyprus even though it's less than an hours flight. We had arranged visas for them, but they were turned away at various borders and detained at holding stations, crisscrossing the country on unpredictable and violent roads to finally get into Jordan where they could fly out. This was the similar to the experience of the individual representing the Turkish contingent, who was only a forty-five minute flight away. It took him two days to arrive because of political checkpoints. I mention this to point to the wholehearted commitment required for many of these participants to simply arrive without harm.

It enabled the first-ever meeting of leaders of the aikido communities of North and South Cyprus, countries still separated by barbed wire, UN guards, and incendiary posters. A life-changing experience, many said. Before the seminar began, many confessed to growing up with hatred for one another and being fearful about physical contact with their "enemies"; three days later, they had learned to joke and dance together and, yes, befriend one another. In an e-mail after the event one participant asked the name of the "environmental biologist who was with us at the dinner in Larnaca" because "he might be able to help me with a project I'm doing." A few days later the biologist responded and replied with what pretty much summarizes what had occurred during the seminar, "I'm the biologist you asked about. When we first meet I was your enemy, then I was your training partner, now I am an offer for you. We've come a long ways in three and half days. I like being an offer to you most of all."

A precedent-setting event, for sure. In its wake Israeli and Palestinian participants have initiated four new Salaam-Shalom Dojos and are pursuing an ambitious long-term program to expand such activities. Others have organized a Pen-pals Across Borders program, in which letters and drawings circulate among young aikidoists from Brazil, Iraq, Israel, Jordan, Palestine, and Turkey. A Brazilian participant plans an event dedicated to the Arab and Jewish communities of Brazil, where children from his *favela* outreach project will demonstrate aikido and show photos and videos from the seminar. Another participant has organized a summer camp in Zurich, where Arab and Israeli aikidoka, "in the spirit of the Training Across Borders seminar," will join participants from nearby areas. Aiki Extensions helped fund mats for two new dojos in Iraq. An Ethiopian participant, with the assistance of Aiki Extensions and in response to the civil strife in his country, started a Peace Dojo in partnership with the Ethiopian Institute for Peace Studies. Filmmaker Heath Curdts created an extraordinary DVD, *Training Across Borders, Cyprus 2005*. As I write this plans are underway for another major Training Across Borders seminar somewhere in the Middle East.

My learning is the ongoing confirmation of the power of somatic practices in building grounded compassion, skillful action, and pragmatic wisdom with individuals and groups. Aikido is certainly one of these practices if it done with an open heart and a commitment to bringing people together, instead of alienating them. As the founder, Morihei Ueshiba, said, "Budo is a Way to bring people together and heal the world."

Afghanistan
Late Winter 2006

I'm standing on the marble veranda of the Afghan Ministry of Defense complex with my chief security escort Colonel Bill Hilden. In front of us, a group of Afghani soldiers scurry about sweeping and laying down a long red runner from the curb, across the walkway, and up the steps into the three-story building. Another group rehearses the pomp and circumstance for a visiting dignitary. The usual camouflage uniforms supplied by the American military are replaced by the Afghani traditional dress uniform of green wool, polished leather belts, and a peaked colorful cap that looks like the headdress of an exotic bird. For the ceremony they drill with the old bolt-action Springfields instead of the ubiquitous

M-16A1. Officers strut around barking orders and straightening the uniforms of the honor guard. Some of the soldiers are earnest and crisp in their movements and others saunter about holding hands. Colonel Hilden catches my eye with his weary "I've seen it all" look, which I'm sure he has. A career Army officer, Hilden retired after almost thirty years and then returned to service after 9/11. He's a sober-faced man who takes his responsibilities seriously; in this case that would be me, and he lacks the charm of small talk. This will be his last deployment and he'll retire again. "Don't know what I'll do, maybe follow my wife around for a while."

I chat with a senior French officer and he asks, "What is your mission for NATO?" I tell him about my visits to the newly built training base for Afghan recruits, the National Military Academy of Afghanistan (NMAA), which is their West Point, and being on patrol with the Afghans and observing their live-fire exercises. I tell him that all the senior Afghan military officers and policymakers I speak with respond enthusiastically. One General even asked, "Can you begin tomorrow?"

"They're very happy we're here. The first time they've had peace in twenty-five years, but it's very delicate. Now we have to help them save themselves. Maybe your martial arts program can be a part of that," the French officer comments.

General Jones arrives in a large convoy of SUVs and reviews the troops; there's a lot of saluting, handshaking, cheek kissing, presenting arms, and his ubiquitous security detail stands out in their vests, dark sunglasses, ear transmitters, and customized weapons. They instantly form a tight perimeter. The head of General Jones's security, Dave, has been with him for years; he's a jovial, bearded man with an expansive personality who could easily be mistaken for a river-rafting guide. He sees me the same time General Jones does and they wave me over. I slip into the entourage as they move into the building and we walk on exquisite Afghan rugs to the second floor.

General Jones is here to meet with General Abdul Rahim Wardak, the

Minister of Defense. We met with Vice President First Deputy Ahmad Zia Massoud at the Presidential Palace and the day before, with the National Security Advisor Dr. Salmai Rassoul and Minister of Interior Zarar Ahmad Moqbil. During the Russian occupation, the current officials of President Karzai's government either lived in Pakistan, entering the country surreptitiously over the years to fight the Russians, or they stayed continuously in the country for the last twenty-five years fighting with an intractable determination. Their faces are carved with commitment and a deep tiredness, or is it resignation, or sadness? They have lost much: family, friends, property, limbs, dignity, and they're starting all over again. There has been a great cost; nonetheless their resolve is palpable.

Our briefings these past few days include sobering figures about modern-day Afghanistan: forty-four years is the average lifespan; it has the highest infant mortality rate in the world; fifty-three percent live in poverty; ninety-two percent of the world's opium, the raw ingredient of heroin, comes from Afghanistan, a multi-billion dollar business, very little of which stays in the country and is reported to fund the Taliban insurgency; there are over 50,000 war widows; four out of five women cannot read or write; Afghan needle users increased in number tenfold in the last year and a half, increasing the threat of an AIDS epidemic, which would overwhelm the health care system and collapse the social infrastructure.

Suicide bombings and IED attacks were rare in Afghanistan, but have now become common. This year, 2006, there will be five thousand people killed, including a hundred and ninety-one foreign troops and at least a thousand civilians. By contrast, half that number were killed in 2005. As the conflict increases, incidents involving the killing of Afghan civilians by American troops, though unintentional, have increased, causing growing discontent. Billions of dollars committed by the U.S. in 2005 toward an "eight pillars" plan including building the justice department, eradicating the poppy crop, and funding alternative developments programs have little to show for their efforts thus far.

Despite this the Afghans are quick to note that the Taliban had been defeated before; there have been free elections with over seventy percent of the people voting; a President and government have been elected; schools have re-opened; the Army and the police are being trained; NATO is helping secure the country. They are not dreamers and they know how much work needs to be done to make their country independent, but they consistently take the high ground. There are also visible signs of this change since my visit in 2004; the roadways are now crowded with people and vehicles hauling goods and the marketplaces are full and bustling. There is a vibrancy in the air that didn't exist then.

Yet there are some nagging thoughts that don't go away. What disturbed me the most was when a BBC reporter asked about the threat of suicide bombers and she was dismissed with, "It's not in the Afghan character." When I brought up Arab infiltrators, the same answer, "We don't do that in Afghanistan." It seems to me that this generic 'we' doesn't compute to the number of insurgents who have historically streamed through the porous borders to fight. Obviously they'll bring their unique points of view, which translate into ways of terrorizing the population, Iraq case in point.

The other piece was how intractable the government was about alternatives to the heroin situation other than spraying the poppy fields. Suggestions such as letting the pharmaceutical companies take them over or subsidized farming were summarily waved off. The standard government line: "We don't want any poppies at all. Destroying all of them is the answer." Considering the history of poppy farming, this seemed highly unlikely, especially since crop production is increasing every year despite eradication efforts. A businessman in our group argued long and hard about subsidy programs like those for American farmers, and he was stonewalled without an ounce of curiosity or openness to something new.

All this made me again consider the priority of a combatives/leadership program for the Army with all these other issues crowding the country's agenda. Would it be more valuable to work on health care, raising the poverty line, education for women? Yet I return to the importance of placing values in the foreground, which a combatives/leadership program would do. Not American or Western values, but the values of Afghanistan. What we run into, however, is the wide spectrum of ethnic groups, tribal factions, and cultures that comprise this country. Is it possible to have a one-size-fits-all values aspect of the program? This will require me to be somewhat of a scholar of Afghanistan, ancient and modern. These questions are not easily reconciled and at the moment it feels important to take a bite-sized chunk and work it to completion, something which seems entirely possible. Clearly this is an experiment and I believe we have to kill the sacred cows of the past and expand our thinking in new directions.

We enter a large rectangular room and General Jones signals for me to sit close to him. We're seated at a large walnut table over twenty feet long that dominates the entire room. There aren't enough chairs for our party and some stand behind the chairs and crowd against the wall. It occurs to me that this table must have been constructed, piece-by-piece, inside this room as there is no way it could have possibly been brought through the single door. One RPG through the window would certainly take out a significant amount of Afghanistan's military leadership. On the wall is a single poster exclaiming the adventure of Afghanistan with a photograph of the gigantic Buddhas of Bamiyan. These massive Buddhas, cut into the sandstone 1,400 years ago, now lie in brown rubble on the valley floor compliments of the Taliban. The Adventure of Afghanistan: there's an understatement.

Minister Wardak enters and sits directly across from General Jones with his entourage sitting on either side of him lining the table. He's a large man with silver hair who's comfortable with himself and his role. His English is impeccable and he seems as familiar in boardrooms as on the battlefields where he's been the last three decades. His staff are solemn men in suits without ties who never take their eyes from their notebooks in which they write furiously. The customary tea, raisins, almonds, biscuit cookies, and pistachios are brought in and the pleasantries begin. General Jones and the Under Secretary of State for the region reiterate America's commitment to Afghanistan in aid and military assistance. Minister Wardak listens slowly, turning a pencil over and over in his thick fingers. He thanks them for all that the U.S. has done and he recites the progress made and ends with "Much more is needed." They all nod. The giant Buddhas in the poster look down on us, imposing, regal. I think of the brown rubble and the vermiculate patterns they make like a map of the world becoming. Something that cannot be put back, but leaving the question of whether something can be made right. The Koranic standards of retribution and revenge, eye for eye, tooth for tooth, passed on through the centuries are fed upon in this very room. Yet the land is more ancient than man, and in the deep valleys the mystery of time and continuity glimmers.

"General Wardak, I'd like to introduce a colleague of mine, Dr. Richard Strozzi-Heckler. Richard helped me with the Martial Arts Program for the Marine Corps." I snap back from my thoughts and General Jones nods to me. General Wardak turns his massive head my direction and begins to slowly turn the pencil in his hand.

"Richard, take a few moments and tell General Wardak about the combatives program for the ANA." Heads swivel in my direction, the pens of General Wardak's staff momentarily pause.

Center. Breathe. Extend.

I tell General Wardak I see how things have changed since I was here eighteen months ago and this is a cause for hope. I tell him about the positive response from the troops and commanding officers of the ANA about a combatives program and that while it would certainly teach unarmed combat and the range of force from negotiation, to submission, to lethal force it could be a platform to teach leadership values based in Afghan traditions. Moreover it could assist in softening the lines between tribes and ethnicities and in doing so could be the crown jewel in uniting the country. I outline how the program would look and who and what it would involve.

General Wardak looks at me and then to General Jones. He stops turning the pencil and lightly taps the lead end into his notebook. The solemn men to his left and right continue to write even in the silence and all heads now turn to the General when he clears his throat.

"I have to say that I entirely believe in this mind-body thing."

Did I hear that right? Did he say "this mind-body thing"? Is he kidding? Remember I never once mentioned "mind-body" nor any of its derivatives like holistic, physical, mental, emotional alignment, heart, mind and body, mind/body/spirit, or wholeness. For a moment the only sound are the pens and pencils of the scribes briskly recording who knows what. What is the word in Dari for mind-body, I wonder.

"Yes, this is a good idea and we should do it. I wish I had that now for the prison riots. If I send in the Army someone will get shot and killed and I don't want that. That would be bad for everything now, bad for everyone. If they were trained in a martial art they could calm everyone down without anybody getting hurt; you know, maybe a broken arm or knocked out or some cuts, but that's okay. But, nothing big. That would be bad for the country now." (At the time there was a prison riot on the outskirts of Kabul, reportedly started by an American. The rumor was that this American was the prison kingpin and he had objected to a change in the uniforms for the prisoners and had called for a riot. Later I heard that he was in on drug charges and ran his thriving business with a cell phone.)

General Wardak said he would put me touch with someone in his cabinet and that he very much wanted to pursue this.

"If it's good for your Marine Corps, it could be good for us." He stood and shook General Jones's hand.

"That's promising," I said to General Jones on the way out.

"Good job, we'll see what we have to do. I have a couple of ideas."

On the flight out of the country I was invited to sit in the flight deck of the C-17 with the pilot, co-pilot, and navigator. As we began taxiing out the runway we were told to hold. Apparently there was a gunfight in progress at the end of the runway where someone had been setting up a mortar attack, or something, since war zones are filled with an endless stream of rumors. Finally we take off and it's glorious; the orange light reflecting off the snowcapped mountains, the Kabul river a khaki-colored thread of silt and snowmelt sliding away, and in the deep valleys beneath us thin lines of green marking a stream or river and a small village. Just as we clear the mountains, a loud, incessant beeping goes off in the cockpit and everyone kicks into a higher gear, touching computer screens, pushing buttons, and turning their heads both directions looking out the windows as if they were pulling out into traffic with their minivan. There's an increase in radio traffic, which I can hear because I have headphones on but I can't understand all the acronyms. Nobody is frantic, but they are paying attention in a totally different way, different by a magnitude of ten. There is real concern in our tiny space.

"What's up?" I ask the navigator.

"We're getting signaled that there's an incoming missile."

My life didn't flash before my eyes, but I thought, "And they're looking out the windows? A missile is coming and they're looking out the windows! This is the twenty-first century, we have the technological advantage, and we're looking out the windows?!" So I begin to look out the windows to be of help. I didn't know what that help would look like, but it's what the experts were doing.

No one on the ground or in the air reports any sign of a ground-to-air missile in the area and everyone begins to settle down and the beeping sound ends, which I had forgotten about and remembered only when it was off. I asked what it was that activated the warning light and the pilot said the instruments are so sensitive that even light reflecting off the snow could set it off.

"Happened to me all the time in Bosnia. Light would reflect off the lakes and radar would pick it up." The captain shrugs.

As I settle back into my chair, it occurs to me that this event reflects our involvement in Afghanistan, and Iraq. We arrive with a long train of personnel, equipment, and technology that can quickly be rendered useless by something as mundane, or poetic, as a shard of light reflecting off a mountain snowfield. I wonder if what we're doing here is the best possible strategy, with the best possible tools. Afghanis live in poverty, sickness, and unemployment, with an increasing addict population without a health care system to inform and treat them. It's also clear that without a secure environment no foundation for nationhood can come to pass. The Taliban is waiting in the wings and they're preparing to do their bad things again if the opportunity presents itself. I think of Colonel Paul Vann, referring to Vietnam, who said the best way to fight that war was with a knife. Already our bombing runs are killing innocent civilians and firefights kill women and children who are caught, or used, in the line of fire. Yes, security is needed, but wouldn't longer deployments by our troops that don't endanger career opportunities help develop the long-term relationships necessary for building strong partnerships with this new government and the other coalition partners.

In my proposal for the ANA Combatives program, I'm writing in a "train the trainers" element so it's in their hands as soon as possible, and it highlights the leadership development aspect so these men have a choice around the use of force and how they can help unify the country. I've organized a number of Marines in country who are now conducting informal combative beta projects with the Afghanis, who, I'm told, greet them with great enthusiasm.

The Hindu Kush stretches out like a great white blanket in front of us, tranquil, pristine, and comforting in its endless reach while the static of disembodied voices from miles away reaches through to the headphones. A reminder that a strategy of hearts and minds must include not a disembodied, technological communication, but real-time, face-to-face, heart-to-heart connections that are engaged over time.

On my return I get busy putting together a proposal for Central Command who will fund and oversee the program. On this last trip General Eikenberry, the commanding general of American troops in Afghanistan and Central Asia, gave his recommendation to the program and connected me with a contract officer. I began to gather a team and put together a timeline and supplies needed. I sent off a proposal with a program of instruction that not only taught the martial requirements but, in many ways more important, taught mind-body principles and core values. Excitement began to mount. In early January of 2007, we received a notice from the contracting office that there would be an "open house" in Kabul conducting a tour of the location and facilities of the training area. I had already visited this proposed training site but it did signal that some of the large players in the contracting/security business in Afghanistan and Iraq, like KBR and Blackwater, were poised to throw their bids into the arena, even though they had no history or specialization in this kind of program. Nonetheless, with the recommendation of Generals Jones and Eikenberry plus my background and experience, I assumed we would be on the short list.

On February 13, 2007 we received the following message from the contracting officer.

Dear Sir/Ma'am,

Please be advised you are receiving this email as representative of your firm who submitted a proposal under XXXXXX-XX-X-XXXX. After evaluation of all proposals submitted, the Government did not find any offer or proposal to meet the technical objectives entirely. In addition, the prices proposed were not found to be fair and reasonable. As a result this solicitation is hereby cancelled and there will be no contract awarded. If you have questions please feel free contact me. The U.S. Government and Government of Afghanistan appreciate your interest in this project and looks forward to receipt of proposals on future projects.

My impression and the one that has been verified by different sources is that this translates that someone higher up decided to completely eliminate the concept because of closer scrutiny of budget matters, because of mishandled funds in Iraq, and the concern of a mounting Taliban offensive. Instead of taking the longer view and building a strong core for the ANA, someone decided to hose it away. I know for a fact that we met the technical objectives since I was instrumental in putting those objectives in place and that our bid was significantly lower than the bids that the large contracting companies put together.

I let General Jones know of the news and though he's retiring he took the high ground and said he would do what he could to keep it alive. The outstanding team I had assembled were as disappointed as I was, and while I don't think they entirely close this chapter, recent incidents in the Middle East turn the government's attention to other areas.

Pacific Area Special Operations Command on Counterinsurgency
April 2006

In the spring of 1992, Fred Krawchuk, Captain United States Army, appeared at my door and asked if I was the person who wrote *In Search of the Warrior Spirit*. Fred stayed with my family and me for a week, training in aikido, doing ranch work, and engaging in long conversations about the future of the warrior ethos in the military and public life. Fred is a West Point graduate, a Green Beret who has led soldiers in the infantry, special operations, and information operations in the U.S., Europe, Asia, and Latin America. He has a Master's degree from Harvard in International Relations, was an Army Olmsted Scholar in Spain and the Army Senior Fellow with the State Department. He's also a martial artist and has a meditation practice. Over the last fifteen years Fred and I have maintained our relationship and he's now the military and global security advisor for Strozzi Institute, as well as a personal friend.

Fred is now a Lieutenant Colonel stationed at Camp Smith, Hawaii, with Special Operations Command Pacific (SOCPAC). Recently he's initiated a program on counterinsurgency that, among other things, includes conferences on counterterrorism and counterinsurgency, sponsored by the Pacific Area Special Operations Command (PASOC) in Hawaii. In addition he's hosted counterinsurgency conferences in San Antonio, Texas, and one in Monterey, California, in partnership with the Naval Post-Graduate School and Sandia Institute. Over the past two years he's asked me to help with the design of these programs and to present to the entire group as well as facilitate the small-group discussions. The PASOC conference gathered military from over twenty nations in the Pacific Rim and Southeast Asia, as well as the U.S. military, State Department, CIA, FBI, NGOs, and AID. These conferences are groundbreaking in that they gather a diversity of nations and presenters that have never come together before, as well as build stronger communication among the different elements that need to coordinate around issues of counterinsurgency and counterterrorism. Partnering with Fred and SOCPAC has opened an entirely new direction for my work with the military and Special Operations.

Over the years Fred and I have engaged in an ongoing conversation that revolves around a central organizing question: what is the role, training, and sensibility required of the warrior of the twenty-first century? The nature of conflict has radically changed in the last twenty years as a fluid 360-degree battlefield has replaced traditional battlelines. In this environment the enemy is no longer marked by a uniform, signifying patches, or even large-unit cohesion. He melds into the population as a civilian when necessary and transforms into a combatant as the opportunity arises. There are more nuances of gray than clear black and white lines in this scenario. The U.S. Defense establishment is comfortable in cold war thinking, which is counterproductive to what is occurring with this elusive foe. This is a war that will not be won by bullets and bombs. Tactical military success will mean nothing without winning the hearts and minds of the citizens of the Muslim world.

Counterinsurgency (COIN) is fundamentally different from traditional warfare. COIN is a confrontation of ideologies, religion, and sociopolitical movements. To engage successfully in this confrontation, it's necessary to learn and understand the ideologies, worldviews, socioeconomics, and the historical and cultural landscape of a people. Disciplines such as cultural anthropology, psychology, somatics, religious studies, and the perennial philosophies and scholars from a wide range of disciplines can help us understand the human factors that join people together or make them adversaries. Moreover it's necessary for a wide range of stakeholders to effectively coordinate in COIN. The State department, AID, military, FBI, and intelligence community, as well as a host of NGOs, need to stay in close contact to share information and collectively coordinate their efforts. These groups historically compete with each other and there is much work to be done to have interagency cooperation.

General Edward Lansdale, arguably the godfather of modern counterinsurgency, said that effective counterinsurgency was thirty percent pulling triggers and seventy percent digging wells, improving sanitation, providing medical assistance, teaching military tactics for self-defense, providing educational materials; in short, helping improve the standard of living of people, which includes teaching them how to do it for themselves. When President Kennedy inaugurated the Green Berets, this was very much his vision: a highly trained soldier, a Special Forces individual, who was trained in combat operations of all kinds and at the same time had the breadth and depth to be able to assist, educate, and care for others. Truly, this is the warrior ideal. Because of accelerated advances in technology and the drift of the current administration, this balance has been reversed, that is, seventy percent shooting, thirty percent helping others. What is becoming more and more apparent is that this doesn't work. The soldiers on the ground call it "whack a mole," taken from the county fairs where after you shoot the 'mole' at an amusement booth, another immediately pops up. We will not win this conflict through body counts; it will not be won with weapons, but by winning hearts and minds. It's time to embrace General Lansdale's equation of a warrior ethos that can defend those who cannot defend themselves and by helping them improve their quality of life. This is not just a sentimental idea, but one that is proven to work in the insurgency environment.

Al Santoli, a decorated Vietnam veteran and Pulitzer Prize nominee for his highly regarded book on Vietnam, *Everything We Had,* was an executive at the American Foreign Policy Council and is Founder and now Director of the Asia America Initiative. Being on the Board of Advisors for both of these organizations, I've been able to watch closely how his approach of building sustainable communities has produced off-the-chart results. For example, in Mindanao, Philippines, there was a growing Al Qaeda footprint at the time that Al and his organization began offering grassroots community work. He brought in medicine, computers, generators, and educational supplies and provided scholarships for women at a college in Manila without asking for anything in return. Over time the Al Qaeda influence dwindled to almost nothing and the head Imam of the region publicly declared that Al and his organization were "our friends." His message: hands off these people. They are truly helping us and are to be protected.

I asked Al what was the essence of what his organization does.

"Human kindness," he replied.

This is not wishful thinking, fantasy, or lack of realism, but a fundamental virtue on which long-term, sustainable relationships are built. I believe that virtues such as kindness, justice, and good will are in our national character. And like most things, if they don't get used they get lost.

The seduction of technology is one of the things that has tipped General Lansdale's 70/30 percentage towards violence and destruction and away from assisting people in becoming autonomous, self-reliant allies. Smart bombs, pilot-less drones, sophisticated listening devices, electronic reconnaissance, and modern weaponry are highly persuasive in having us think that we can overpower an enemy through state-of-the-art technology. As I've mentioned before and have reiterated over and over is that this approach is failing. I'm not endorsing that we eliminate the advancements in technology, but stating that we cannot stand on it alone in bringing peace to the world.

The idea that technology can solve all our problems is what the English soldier, poet, and philosopher Sir Francis Bacon called an "idol of the tribe." He was referring to a "truth" that is based on insufficient or inaccurate evidence. This "truth" will be self-reinforcing, defended, and celebrated by the organizational members, thus keeping it in place. Families, tribes, organizations, institutions, and nations are capable of applying great force of will based on certain principles, but it is only with great difficulty that we are able to deconstruct the principles we've created. The group will find it more acceptable to stagger from breakdown to breakdown than to ask the question: Is what we believe true, relevant, and coherent? Crumbling idols are always accompanied by resentment and resignation, but ultimately it's a good thing because it clears the space for more effective action and a more direct look at the root of the problems. If we don't let the idol tumble, we will exhaust ourselves with an effort that will most likely sustain the problem.

In the war on terrorism and insurgencies, we are blinded by the idol of technology.

We must put technology in its proper place and recognize it's not the answer to everything. What we've forgotten is the human element. It's the moral and pragmatic obligation of the government, military, and private sectors to vanquish the idol of technology and invest in building structures for justice, trust, and respect among people.

The position that I represent at these conferences is twofold and they are interconnected to the human element.

First is the importance of educating ourselves to the ideological, socioeconomic, political, cultural, and religious differences that create terrorists and insurgents. It's critical that we grasp the conditions that create their radical environment. If these issues are not understood and remedied, no amount of military intervention will produce victory. In fact we need to redefine what we mean by victory. It is increasingly obvious that killing people is not the remedy, but rather greater understanding and action into the root causes of this situation.

Second, we must place more attention and training on the human terrain of counterinsurgency. This will allow the Special Forces soldier, civil affairs units, strategic information officers, boots on the ground, State Department, AID, NGOs, etc. to create relationships with foreign nationals that are built on trust, respect, and sustainability. In addition, the emphasis on this kind of training will also be beneficial to bridging the gap between our own interagency rivalries. If all the concerned stakeholders do not work together, much of our resources will slip through our hands.

Those who think this is too "soft" need to be reminded of the recent research in neuroplasticity and brain imaging. A good three months before infants are walking, they are seeking a limbic resonance with those around them. Limbic resonance means they are looking for an emotional connection with others. In other words it is factory loaded in all humans to seek genuine, trusting connections with others. Research now shows that infants who do not get this connection have compromised immune systems as they age and often die for the lack of the connection.

Through the practices of somatics and a body-oriented psychology, it's possible to learn to make this kind of connection that creates a deep listening to others, fosters genuine trust, encourages respect and dignity in the treatment of others and the negotiation of conflict in a way that results in a win-win outcome for all involved.

At the completion of the PASOC Conference, a Filipino Seal Commander stopped me in the hall and asked if he could speak to me.

"I want to thank you," he began. "Last year on patrol we were ambushed and during the fight we were in close quarters with the enemy and the U.S. Marine advisor was able to take down one of the enemy who was about to shoot one of my men and subdue him. After questioning him, we gathered valuable information that saved lives."

I still wasn't sure why he was thanking me and I asked him.

"It was because of the Martial Arts Program you started for your Marines that he was able to do this. This is a very good thing and I want to thank you for it and someday I hope to study this program myself."

While I was very touched by this story, I don't tell it because of any self-importance attributed to me. The credit for MCMAP truly goes to General Jim Jones the visionary and Colonel Bristol and his staff who put in the genius and hard work to make it practical and institutionally viable. I tell this story because it illustrates a theme that has been central throughout this book and my life. That is, when people engaging engage in shared somatic practices, it's possible to open new avenues of communication and connection that would not previously be possible. It's a simple idea but a powerful one. After felling our idols we can ask ourselves: What are the practices necessary to build a peace that is sustainable and self-generating?

Working together, the warriors of strength and heart can make a better world.

ABOUT THE AUTHOR

Richard Strozzi-Heckler is President of Strozzi Institute, The Center for Leadership and Mastery. He has a sixth-degree black belt in aikido and a doctorate in psychology. An All-American in Track and Field at San Diego State University, he won the 100-meter dash at the pre-Olympic meet and Central American Games in Mexico City in 1967. He is founding member of the Lomi School, Tamalpais Aikido, and Two Rock Aikido dojos in northern California.

Dr. Strozzi-Heckler has taught the principles of embodied leadership and mastery to business, government, military, non-profits, health care, and education for the last thirty years. He has consulted with the American military for over eighteen years, and his recent work with the Marine Corps was featured on the cover of *The Wall Street Journal* in October 2000. He is the author of *The Anatomy of Change,* which shows how learning and mastery occur through the body; the editor of *Aikido and the New Warrior,* a collection of essays by practitioners of aikido, and *Holding the Center,* which highlights how place, community, and an embodied identity produce meaning and purpose; he is also the editor of *Being Human at Work: Bringing Somatic Intelligence into Your Professional Life,* a collection from the Strozzi Institute about the importance of bringing the totality of ourselves—mind, body, and spirit—to work.

If you are interested in the programs at Strozzi Institute or the work of Richard Strozzi-Heckler you can contact us at:

mastery@strozziinstitute.com

ABOUT STROZZI INSTITUTE

Strozzi Institute is the premier training institute for Embodied Leadership. We offer public and private programs for corporations, small businesses, and individuals interested in developing teams, a leadership presence, and effectiveness.

For thirty years, Strozzi Institute has pioneered a distinctive somatic methodology that develops leaders who execute on commitments and are aligned with their highest purpose. Our somatic methodology incorporates psychology, perennial philosophies, linguistics, and martial arts. This results in the most critical component of leadership: self-mastery.

Strozzi Institute's clients include Fortune 100 teams and executives, entrepreneurs, non-profit leaders, political leaders, Olympic and professional athletes, educators, the Army Special Forces, Navy SEALs, and the Marine Corps.

Strozzi Institute also offers a world-renowned somatic coaching certification program.

For more information on any of our programs call 707-778-6505 or visit our website at www.strozziinstitute.com.